The Official Ubuntu Book

The Official Ubuntu Book

Benjamin Mako Hill and Jono Bacon
Corey Burger
Jonathan Jesse
Ivan Krstić

PRENTICE
HALL

Upper Saddle River, NJ • Boston • Indianapolis • San Francisco
New York • Toronto • Montreal • London • Munich • Paris • Madrid
Capetown • Sydney • Tokyo • Singapore • Mexico City

Many of the designations used by manufacturers and sellers to distinguish their products are claimed as trademarks. Where those designations appear in this book, and the publisher was aware of a trademark claim, the designations have been printed with initial capital letters or in all capitals.

The authors and publisher have taken care in the preparation of this book, but make no expressed or implied warranty of any kind and assume no responsibility for errors or omissions. No liability is assumed for incidental or consequential damages in connection with or arising out of the use of the information or programs contained herein.

The publisher offers excellent discounts on this book when ordered in quantity for bulk purchases or special sales, which may include electronic versions and/or custom covers and content particular to your business, training goals, marketing focus, and branding interests. For more information, please contact:

U.S. Corporate and Government Sales
(800) 382-3419
corpsales@pearsontechgroup.com

For sales outside the United States, please contact:

International Sales
International@pearson.com

 This Book Is Safari Enabled
The Safari® Enabled icon on the cover of your favorite technology book means the book is available through Safari Bookshelf. When you buy this book, you get free access to the online edition for 45 days.

Safari Bookshelf is an electronic reference library that lets you easily search thousands of technical books, find code samples, download chapters, and access technical information whenever and wherever you need it.

To gain 45-day Safari Enabled access to this book:
• Go to http://www.prenhallprofessional.com/safarienabled
• Complete the brief registration form
• Enter the coupon code NVHP-RKRH-RVE2-KEHR-5E93

If you have difficulty registering on Safari Bookshelf or accessing the online edition, please e-mail customer-service@safaribooksonline.com.

Visit us on the Web: www.prenhallprofessional.com

Library of Congress Cataloging-in-Publication Data

The official Ubuntu book / Benjamin Mako Hill ... [et al.].
    p. cm.
  Includes bibliographical references and index.
  ISBN 0-13-243594-2 (pbk. : alk. paper)   1. Ubuntu (Electronic resource)
2. Operating systems (Computers) I. Hill, Benjamin Mako, 1980–
QA76.76.O63O34348 2006
005.4'3—dc22
                                                        2006016172

ISBN 0-13-243594-2
Text printed in the United States on recycled paper at Courier Stoughton.
First printing, August 2006

This book is dedicated to the Ubuntu Community. Without your tireless hard work and commitment none of this would be possible.

Contents

Foreword   **xix**

Preface   **xxv**

Acknowledgments   **xxvii**

About the Authors   **xxix**

Introduction   **xxxi**

About This Book	xxxi
The Scope of the Book	xxxii
The Menu	xxxii

Chapter 1   **Introducing Ubuntu**   **1**

A Wild Ride	2
Free Software, Open Source, and GNU/Linux	3
Free Software and GNU	3
Linux	5
Open Source	5
A Brief History of Ubuntu	7
Mark Shuttleworth	7
The Warthogs	8
What Does Ubuntu Mean?	10
Creating Canonical	11
What Is Ubuntu?	12
What Is a Distribution?	12
An Ecosystem of Distributions	14
The Debian Project and the Free Software Universe	15
The Ubuntu Community	16
Ubuntu Promises and Goals	18
Conduct Goals and Code of Conduct	20
Technical Goals	21
Bug #1	23

Canonical and the Ubuntu Foundation   24
    Canonical Ltd.   24
    Canonical's Service and Support   25
    Bazaar and Launchpad   26
    The Ubuntu Foundation   27
Ubuntu Subprojects, Derivatives, and Spin offs   28
Summary   30

Chapter 2   Installing Ubuntu   31

Choosing Your Ubuntu Version   32
    Other Ubuntu Distributions   33
    Is It Still Ubuntu?   33
Getting Ubuntu   34
    Burning a CD   34
Installing from the Desktop CD   36
    Language   37
    Configure Your Keyboard   38
    Location   38
    Identification   39
    Disk Space   41
    Finishing Up   44
Installing Using the Alternate Install CD   45
    Choosing Your Spot in the World   46
    Networking   47
    Creating Partitions   48
    Configuring a User   51
    Finishing Up   52
Post-Installation   52
    Configuring the Login Screen   52
    Setting Up Printers   53
Summary   54

Chapter 3   Using Ubuntu on the Desktop   55

Taking Your Desktop for a Ride   57
    Starting Applications and Finding Things   58
    Find Your Files and Folders   60
    Configure Your System   61
    Shortcut Icons   61
    Applets   61
    The Notification Area   62
    The Clock   63
    The Taskbar   63

Shutting Your Computer Down and Logging Out   64
Using Your Applications   65
 Browsing the Web with Firefox   66
 Creating Documents with OpenOffice.org   69
 Managing Your E-Mail and Calendars with Evolution   71
 Create Graphics with the GIMP   75
 Communicate with Gaim   81
 Cutting-Edge Voice Over IP with Ekiga   83
 Exploring the Ubuntu Landscape   90
The Ubuntu File Chooser and Bookmarks   99
Ubuntu in Your Language   100
Customizing Ubuntu's Look and Feel   101
 Changing the Background   101
 Changing the Theme   101
 Configuring a Screensaver   102
Managing Your Files   103
 How Linux Stores and Organizes Files   103
 Selecting, Copying, and Moving Files/Folders   107
 Using the Sidebar   108
 Using Emblems   108
Ubuntu and Multimedia   109
 Installing Codecs   109
 Listening to Audio Files   110
 Playing and Ripping CDs   112
 Watching Videos   114
Summary   115

Chapter 4 Advanced Usage and Managing Ubuntu 117

Adding and Removing Programs and Packages   118
 Installing and Using Add Applications   118
 Terminology   121
 Installing Using Synaptic   121
Keeping Your Computer Updated   125
 Installing Updates   126
 Learning about What Was Updated   126
 Using Synaptic to Check for Updates   127
Moving to the Next Ubuntu Release   128
 Doing the Actual Upgrade   129
Using and Abusing Devices and Media   129
 Using USB Key Rings   130
 Burning CDs   131
 Using Floppy Disks   132
 Using Digital Cameras   132

Configuring a Printer in Ubuntu   132
    Making It Easier with Gnome CUPS Manager   133
    Note about Using Gnome   134
    Gathering Information   134
    Launching the Wizard   135
    Remote Printing   136
    Mission Accomplished!   137
    The Printers Window   138
Graphically Access Remote Files   139
The Terminal   141
    Crash Course in the Terminal   141
Working with Windows   145
    Running Applications   145
    Using Windows Files on Another Partition   146
Summary   147

Chapter 5   The Ubuntu Server   149

What Is Ubuntu Server?   150
Installing Ubuntu Server   152
    A Couple of Installer Tricks   153
    Partitioning Your Ubuntu Server   153
    The Story of RAID   154
    Setting Up RAID   156
    The Story of the Logical Volume Manager   158
    Setting Up LVM   160
    You're Done—Now Watch Out for Root!   162
Ubuntu Package Management   162
    The Ubuntu Archive   162
    APT Sources and Repositories   163
    dpkg   165
    Installing a Package Manually   165
    apt-get and apt-cache   166
    Running a Distribution Upgrade   169
    aptitude   172
    Tips and Tricks   172
Ubuntu Server Security   173
    User Account Administration   174
    Filesystem Security   175
    System Resource Limits   176
    System Log Files   177

	A Sprinkling of Network Security	178
	Final Words on Security	179
	Summary	180
Chapter 6	**Support and Typical Problems**	**183**
	Your System	184
	Ubuntu Won't Start!	185
	The Ubuntu Logo Appears Corrupted or Just Looks Odd While Booting	186
	When I Start My Computer I Get Text Instead of a Graphical Interface	186
	I Tried to Use a Word or PowerPoint Document, and the Fonts Are All Wrong	188
	How Do I Install a Package?	189
	I Want to Install an Application That Is Not in Synaptic	190
	Nautilus Is Painfully Slow—How Can I Make It Run Faster?	191
	Add TrueType Fonts to Your Desktop Quickly	191
	How Can I Test That an ISO File Works?	192
	I Downloaded an Autopackage But I Don't Know How to Run It	193
	How Do I Compile an Application?	194
	I Can't See the Hidden Dot Files and Folders in the File Manager	195
	How Do I Restore Something I Deleted in the File Manager?	195
	The Desktop Has Hung—What Do I Do?	196
	My Screen Resolution Is Wrong	196
	How Can I Automatically Login without Having to Enter My Login Details?	197
	I Tried to Upgrade My System, but I Get an Error	197
	I Am Running Out of Disk Space—How Do I Free Up Some Space?	197
	I Deleted Something in the File Manager, but I Don't See the Extra Disk Space	199
	Another Version of Ubuntu is Out—How Do I Upgrade to It?	199
	Applications	199
	When I Click the Close Window Icon, My Program Doesn't Go Away	200

The Upgrade Notification Bubble Keeps
    Appearing, and I Want It to Stop   200
Extending Nautilus with Scripts   200
I Went to a Web Site in Firefox, and the
    Macromedia Flash Plug-in Is Missing   201
Java Is Not Installed on My System   202
I Have Heard Desktop Search is Cool—How
    Do I Install It?   202
My E-Mail Doesn't Work in Evolution   203

Multimedia   204
I Downloaded a Particular Media File,
    and It Won't Play   205
My DVD Won't Play   205
DVD Playback is Jittery and Jumpy   205
When I Start Some Applications, Ubuntu
    Says I Don't Have Access to /dev/dsp   206
My Microphone Doesn't Work   206
How Do I Change the Visual Theme?   207
How Do I Find and Install New Desktop
    Themes and Backgrounds?   208
How Do I Turn My Ubuntu Computer
    into a MythTV Box?   209

Networking   210
I Can't Access My LAN   211
Nameserver Problems   212
How Do I Use ssh (Secure SHell) for
    Transferring Files across a Network?   212
How Do I Use a Graphical Application
    Remotely with ssh (Secure SHell)?   213
My Wireless Card Is Not Working   213
I Need to Use WPA or I Use WPA-PSK
    on My Wireless Access Point   215

Hardware   216
Ubuntu Has Not Detected My Old Sound Card   216
My Cardbus Adapter Is Not Being Recognized   219
I Plug in My USB Stick and Nothing Happens   219
I Copied Some Files to/from My USB Stick, but
    When I Access It Later the Files Are Not There   220
My CD-ROM/DVD Is Not Working   221
My CD-ROM/DVD Drive Won't Eject   221
I Bought a Device, but It Doesn't Work in Ubuntu   221
My Computer Says It Is Out of Memory   222

How Can I Copy Photos from My Mobile
Phone to My Ubuntu Computer with Bluetooth?   222
I Can Read My USB Storage Device, but I Can't
Write to It   222
Filesystem Fun   223
How Do I Format a Disk?   224
The Keys on My Keyboard Spit Out the
Wrong Letters/Symbols   225
My Serial Mouse Is Not Working   226
My Mouse Scroll Wheel Does Not Work   226
My Remote Control Doesn't Work   226
How Do I Find Out Which Hardware Works
in Ubuntu before I Purchase It?   227
System Administration   227
How Do I Schedule Things to Happen?   228
How Can I Copy a File from One Computer
to Another?   230
I Know an Application Is Available in Ubuntu
but Synaptic Can't Find It   231
I Am Running Ubuntu on an Older Computer,
and I Would Like a Faster Desktop   231
I Have Reinstalled Windows, and Now
Ubuntu Won't Start!   232
How Do I Fix My Disk after a Power Failure?   234
Ubuntu Takes Up Too Much Disk Space
on My Old Computer   235
My Computer is Running Quite Slowly—How
Can I Find Out What is Going On?   236
How Can I Find Out the Different Options
for Commands?   236
How Do I Get My Root Account Back?   236
I Forgot My System Password—What Can I Do?   237
How Do I Access My Windows Partitions?   238
Ubuntu Is Slow on My AMD K7 Computer   239
How Do I Add Users?   239
Other   240
Running Another OS In Ubuntu   240
It Was Suggested I File a Bug Report,
but I Don't Know How   241
How Can I Monitor the Weather?   243
How Do I Make Ubuntu Bread?   243

How Can I Prevent the Pain I am Getting
in My Fingers When I Type?   246
Summary   246

Chapter 7   Using Kubuntu   249

Introduction to Kubuntu   250
History of KDE   250
History of Kubuntu   251
Navigating in Kubuntu   252
Shutting Your Computer Down and Logging Out   254
Installing Kubuntu   255
Where to Find Kubuntu   255
Can I Switch to Kubuntu If I Have Ubuntu
Installed Already?   256
Guided Installation   256
Installing from the Live CD   256
Using Sudo   259
Customizing Kubuntu   259
Customizing the Desktop   260
Get Hot New Stuff   262
Customizing Applets and the Kicker   262
Customizing the K menu   263
Systems Administration   264
Installing New Packages   265
Managing Repositories   268
Installing a Package   269
Upgrading Kubuntu   273
How to Keep the System Up-to-Date   273
System Settings   273
Managing Files with Kubuntu   279
Introduction to Konqueror   279
Finding Files and Folders   281
Ripping Audio CDs   281
Accessing Windows Partitions   282
Accessing USB Drives   283
Managing Music   284
Common Applications   287
OpenOffice.org   287
Web Browsing   288
Using Firefox for Browsing the Web   290
Burning CDs—Audio and Data   290
KaudioCreator   292

Instant Messaging	293
Kontact	294
Krita	297
Watching Movies and Playing CDs	299
Internet Relay Chat	301
Kiosk Mode	302
Exploring the Kubuntu Landscape	304
Tips and Tricks	307
Finding Help and Giving Back to the Community	308
Finding Help	308
Accessing KDE Help Manuals	309
Giving Back to the Community	310
Summary	310

Chapter 8   The Ubuntu Community   311

Venues	313
Mailing Lists	313
Ubuntu Mailing Lists	314
Internet Relay Chat (IRC)	318
IRC Channel List	318
Web Forums	322
Wikis	324
The Fridge	326
Conferences and Sprints	328
Planet	330
Teams, Processes, and Community Governance	331
Teams	332
Local Community (LoCo) Teams	332
MOTU	333
Community Council	334
Technical Board	335
SABDFL	337
Ubunteros and Ubuntu Members	337
Getting Involved	338
Advocacy	338
Support	339
Ideas and Feedback	339
Documentation	339
Artwork	340
Translation and Localization	340
Quality Assurance and Bugs	340
Programming and Packaging	341
Summary	341

Chapter 9	Ubuntu-Related Projects	343
	Partner Projects	344
	Kubuntu	344
	Edubuntu	345
	Derived Distributions	346
	Guadalinex	348
	Xubuntu	348
	Nexenta	349
	nUbuntu	349
	Ufficio Zero	350
	The Open CD	350
	Baltix	350
	ImpiLinux	350
	The Launchpad	351
	Soyuz	352
	Rosetta	353
	Malone	354
	Other Functionality	355
	Bazaar	356
	Summary	356
Appendix A	Welcome to the Command Line	357
	Starting Up the Terminal	357
	Moving around the Filesystem	357
	Manipulating Files and Folders	359
	System Information Commands	360
	Searching and Editing Text Files	361
	Dealing with Users and Groups	362
	Getting Help on the Command Line	363
	Searching for Man Files	363
	Using Wildcards	364
	Executing Multiple Commands	364
	Run Sequentially	364
	Passing Output	365
	Moving on to More Advanced Uses of the Command Line	365
	Books and Web Sites	365
Appendix B	Ubuntu Foundation Documents	367
	Code of Conduct	367
	Introduction	367

Ubuntu Code of Conduct   368
    Mailing Lists and Web Forums   369
Ubuntu Philosophy   370
    Free and Open Source Software   370
    Free Software   370
    Open Source   371
Components   372
    "Main" Component   372
    "Restricted" Component   373
    "Universe" Component   374
    "Multiverse" Component   374
License Policy   374
    Ubuntu "Main" and "Restricted" Component
      License Policy   376
    Documentation, Firmware, and Drivers   377
    Software Installed by Default   378

Appendix C   Creative Commons Attribution-ShareAlike 2.0
Open Publication License   **379**
    Attribution-ShareAlike 2.0   379
    License   379

Appendix D   Ubuntu Equivalents to Windows Programs   **387**
On the Ubuntu Desktop   387
    Word Processing   387
    Spreadsheet   387
    Presentation   387
    Database   388
    Web Browser   388
    E-Mail   388
    Media Players   388
    Photo Editor   388
    Instant Messaging   389
    Voice Over IP   389
Additional Applications   389
    Office and Finance   389
    Drawing and Modeling   390
    Games and Edutainment   390

Index   **393**

Foreword

IT'S A SMALL CELEBRATION for me to write this foreword—almost exactly two years after the first meeting of a small group of free software professionals that turned into the Ubuntu project. A celebration because two years ago none of us would have predicted that our dream would spawn several million CDs, three or four million enthusiastic users, hundreds of commitments of support from companies large and small, a minor prime-time television reference, and now *The Official Ubuntu Book*.

The dream that brought us together can be simply expressed

> To build a world-class operating system for ordinary desktop computer users, that is genuinely free and freely available, that is immediately useful, and that represents the very best that the free software world can achieve today.

In setting out to build a platform for "ordinary desktop computer users" I had no idea that I would have the privilege of meeting and working with so many *extraordinary* desktop computer users. Some of those extraordinary individuals are the authors of this book, people who both understand the importance of the free software movement and who have the talent to have been real contributors to its success. Others make up the backbone of the Ubuntu community—the small but dedicated army of a few hundred people that works to produce a new release of Ubuntu every six months. They are at the heart of a network that reaches out through the global free software community—through the world of Debian, an extraordinary project in its own right and without which Ubuntu could not exist, and on out to the thousands of projects, large and small, that produce the code and documentation that we pull together and call *Ubuntu*.

While this huge extended community can often appear to be fractured and divided along infinitesimal ideological lines, we are all broadly in agreement about four key ideas, and it is those ideas that are central to the Ubuntu promise

- That our software should not come with a license fee. That we should be able to share our software, modify it, and then share our modifications, too.

- That this free software should be the best version available, including regular security updates, and not a tease for a better, commercial product.

- That full-scale, high-quality commercial support from local and global companies should be available for this free platform.

- That this software should be usable in as many languages as possible and usable by as many people as possible regardless of disability.

The seventeen of us who met in London two years ago come from a very wide variety of countries and backgrounds, but we all agreed that the goal of producing a platform that could live up to that promise was a worthy one, one that we would devote ourselves to wholeheartedly.

For several months we worked quietly. We wanted to come to the world not only with a manifesto but also with a clear demonstration of work done toward our goals, something that people could test and comment on. We had no name (though industry insiders called us the "Super-Secret Debian Startup"), and, as a result, we hosted most of our work at www.no-name-yet.com. We were looking for a name that could express the beauty of the free software community development process—collaboration, inter-dependence, sharing, standing gently on the shoulders of giants, and reaching for lofty goals. The only word which comes close to that, of which I'm aware, is the African word *ubuntu*. It is found in many forms in many different African languages. And so we adopted it as the name of our project.

We knew that our first release would have blemishes—warts—and gave it the codename "The Warty Warthog." We called ourselves the warthogs and coordinated our work on the #warthogs IRC channel. Today, for better or worse, that's turned into a tradition of codenames such as "Breezy Badger" and "Dapper Drake." As lighthearted as they sound, these codenames come to embody the spirit of our community as it works toward a particular release. This next one—Dapper—is exactly that: a man emerging from youth, professional, bold, confident, and energetic. This is our first release that is designed to meet the needs of large organizations as much as those of developers and engineers. In the same way, the Ubuntu community has moved from being something of a rebellion against the "Linux establishment" to a strong and professionally organized group.

What Makes Ubuntu so Popular?

First, this is the time for free software to come to the forefront, and Ubuntu is very much the beneficiary of the vast amount of work that has gone into building up a huge body of work in the GNU/Linux world. That work has been underway for nearly thirty years, in one form or another, but Ubuntu is one way in which it is suddenly becoming visible to the nonspecialist computer user. We are in the middle of a great overturning of the industry status quo. The last time that happened, in the mid-90s, was when the world suddenly found itself connected to itself—by the Internet. Every major company, especially those in the field of technology, had to examine itself and ask the question "How do we adapt to an Internet world?" Today, every major technology company has to ask itself the question "How do I adapt to a free software world?"

I would speculate and say that Ubuntu represents an idea whose time has come. We did not invent the free software movement—that honor goes to Richard Stallman and many others who had a vision far more profound at a time when it was hard to see how it could ever become reality. But Ubuntu has perhaps the honor of bringing that vision to a very wide audience in a form that we can all appreciate. I hope that the real visionaries—those who have led the way—will appreciate the decisions and the choices we make in bringing you this project. Some will take exception—I know Linus prefers KDE to GNOME, for example, so he's likely to be more of a fan of Kubuntu than Ubuntu. But in general, the ideas that others have had, the principles of the free software movement, are well expressed in Ubuntu.

Second, Ubuntu is a project on which *you* can have a real impact. It has the benefit of deep and reliable financial backing and a corporate team to give it muscle, but it is in every regard an open project, with participation at the highest levels by true volunteers. We work in a fishbowl—our meetings take place online, in a public forum. That can be tricky. Building an operating system is a fast-paced business full of compromise and tough decisions in the face of little information. There are disagreements and dirty laundry, and mistakes are made (I should know, some of them are mine. You should hear the one about the Warty Warthog desktop artwork). The transparency of our environment, however, means that we can count on having robust conversations about our options—all of them, even the ones the core team would never have dreamed up. It also means that mistakes are identified, discussed, and ultimately addressed faster than they would be if we lived and worked behind closed doors. You get a better platform as a result.

We work hard as a community to recognize the contributions of all sorts of individuals—advocates, artists, Web forum moderators, channel operators, community event organizers, writers, translators, people who file and triage bugs . . . whatever your particular interest or talent, we will find a way to integrate your contribution.

Perhaps most important is the way our approach to community differentiates Ubuntu from other free software projects with similar vision. We try to do all of this in a way that recognizes that disagreements are important but prevents those disagreements from creating deep divides in our community. Our code of conduct may not be perfect but it reminds each of us to remember the meaning of the word *ubuntu* —that each of us has our best impact *through* the relationships we maintain with one another. Finding common ground and maintaining healthy communication are more important for us as a community in the long run than a particular technical decision or the specific choice of words with which to translate "File" into Spanish. Our community governance structures—our Technical Board and Community Council—exist to ensure that debates don't become personal and that decisions can be made after all sides have been heard.

If you are a software professional or curious about Linux, this book and this platform are an excellent choice. You will learn about the world of Ubuntu and, indirectly, Debian and GNU/Linux. These are great foundations for working with the tools that I believe will come to define the standard, the everyday computing base upon which we build our homes and offices.

I once heard a proprietary software vendor say, "Linux is more expensive because skilled Linux professionals are more costly." This is true. It means, of course, that Linux skills are more valuable! It won't be true forever because the world of Linux is expanding so rapidly that sooner or later we will have to accept a position in the mainstream, and that takes off some of the "geek points" associated with being part of the future of technology. But right now, without a doubt, being ahead of the curve on Linux and on Ubuntu is the right place to be. If you're this far into the Foreword, you are clearly going to make it. ;-)

It's difficult for me to speculate on what the future might hold for the Ubuntu project. I know that I, along with many others, are loving the opportunity to be at the center of such an exciting initiative and are committed to seeing where it leads us over the coming years. I believe that it will become a pervasive part of our everyday computing environment, so I would like to help make sure that we don't make too many mistakes along the way! Please, come and join us in the fishbowl to help ensure we do a very, very good job.

—Mark Shuttleworth
Ubuntu Founder

Preface

WRITING A BOOK is a difficult process. When you decide to write a book about a particular subject, you collate your knowledge on a subject, present it in a clear and easy-to-read way, and organize your ideas and knowledge in a sensible order. This is difficult enough when the subject you are writing about stays largely the same for the writing period. It becomes even more complex when you are writing about a moving target.

When we began writing this book, the Dapper Drake release of Ubuntu, which has been released and is used on computers around the world, was not actually finished. With Dapper heavily in development, the idea to create *The Official Ubuntu Book* emerged. After a few months of authors meeting to flesh out an outline, writing began about three months before Dapper was complete.

This moving target made the writing process particularly interesting. As an example, as Jono was writing the chapter on Ubuntu installation, the new graphical Ubiquity installer had yet to be completed. Each day Jono would download the latest code and update the chapter accordingly. As Jono kept a close eye on Ubiquity's progress, he became more involved in its development and contributed bug reports and thoughts to Colin Watson, the primary developer behind Ubiquity.

This is particularly interesting as the development of this book largely mirrored the very ethos and semantics behind the development of Ubuntu itself. Ubuntu is an operating system that grows organically. The proposed feature set and development process within the Ubuntu community are created in a largely iterative way. Every day the distribution grows in slightly different areas, with members in each area working together to move Ubuntu forward. Within the book's development process, the content was also crafted, rewritten, adjusted, and allowed to mature in different ways—much like Ubuntu itself.

With such a different take on book development, it is important to stress that *The Official Ubuntu Book* is not a typical book at all. Traditional books are typically written about a specific subject by one or two authors, published, sold in bookshops, and *that's it*. But *The Official Ubuntu Book* is different.

First, although the majority of this book was written by the authors listed on the front cover, we also sought contributions directly from the Ubuntu community. Jono drafted an announcement seeking recipes. Jeff Waugh then posted the announcement on the Fridge, Ubuntu's news site (http://fridge.ubuntu.com/). Though Jono had completed half the chapter, he was keen to add diversity and open the chapter to contributions from the community.

More than one dozen contributors submitted recipes to Jono, which are included in Chapter 6. Other community members pitched in as well. James Stanger explained the basics of printing, and our excellent tech editor, Quim Gil, shared the Guadalinex success story. Jorge O. Castro helped describe Edubuntu, and Dennis Kaarsemaker wrote about using wireless. Matthew East joined the tech editors to offer valuable feedback on the entire book.

Ubuntu is by its very nature a community-driven, collaborative platform, and the development of this book has been inspired and driven by this process. This is why the book is available under the Creative Commons Attribution-ShareAlike license and why some chapters (Chapters 3, 4, and 7) are actually included with Dapper itself. With this in mind, we hope the content in the book continues to grow and evolve in new areas and bring more and more users over to Ubuntu. It is an exciting time to be a part of Open Source and an exciting time to be a part of Ubuntu.

Acknowledgments

SPECIAL THANKS to Mark Shuttleworth and Jane Silber for all their efforts to get this book out into the world for both new and veteran Ubuntu users. Thanks also to Victor Ferns, director of Canonical Ltd., for his attention to the project. Many people at Canonical provided immeasurable assistance in the production of this book.

We reached into the Ubuntu community for a top group of reviewers, each of whom greatly contributed to the strength of the manuscript, including Dennis Kaarsemaker, Matthew East, Jorge O. Casto, Quim Gil, Jonathan Riddell, and Dinko Korunic.

Other folks who helped shape the book in the beginning stages include Micah Anderson, Chris Negus, Peter C. Norton, and Scott Dier. Many thanks for those early insights.

We received a truly global response from the Ubuntu community when the call was put out on The Fridge for solutions to common problems. In less than a week we collected useful recipes from Alabama, Australia, California, England, Jamaica, Mauritius, Minnesota, the Netherlands, Paris, Quebec, and Sweden. Hearty thanks go to the following avid Ubuntu users for sharing their knowledge: David Bain, Alan Barnard, David Clayton, Manu Cornet, Scott Dier, Oskar Jönefors, Avinash Meetoo, Julien Rottenberg, Stephen Sandlin, David Symons, Paul van Genderen, and Andrew Zajac. James Stanger also pitched in with a very useful section on how to print from Ubuntu.

And finally we appreciate the efforts of the Prentice Hall team, including Debra Williams Cauley, Chris Zahn, Mark Taub, Noreen Regina, John Fuller, Elizabeth Ryan, Nancy Hendryx, and Kathy Glidden.

About the Authors

Benjamin Mako Hill is a Seattle native working out of Boston, Massachusetts. Mako is a longtime free software developer and advocate. He was part of the founding Ubuntu team and one of the first employees of Canonical Ltd. In addition to some technical work, his charge at Canonical was to help grow the Ubuntu development and user community during the project's first year. With the community off the ground, Mako left Canonical to return to graduate school at the MIT Media Lab, where he is helping out with One Laptop per Child's $100 Laptop Project. Mako has continued his involvement with Ubuntu as a member of the Community Council governance board, through development work, and through projects such as this book.

Jono Bacon (www.jonobacon.org) is an established author and consultant who works for the United Kingdom's government-funded OpenAdvantage (www.openadvantage.org) center in England. Jono spends each of his days working with businesses, education and charitable organizations, and individuals to help them move to Open Source software and Open Standards. Jono is also an experienced public speaker who has spoken around the world about Open Source, usability, and desktop and is known for his honest, humorous, and entertaining talks. In addition to this, Jono is a regular contributor to Open Source on a range of projects, has authored more than 400 articles for more than fifteen magazines and Web sites, and is the cocreator of the popular LugRadio podcast (www.lugradio.org).

Corey Burger lives in Victoria, British Columbia, Canada, and is a long-term user and contributor to Ubuntu. He is a member of the Ubuntu Documentation Team, the Laptop Testing Team, and has been involved with Ubuntu since its first release. Corey currently works with the Secure Internet Live Conferencing (SILC) Project to help deploy Ubuntu at nongovernmental organizations across Vancouver Island. Also active in promoting Ubuntu and Open Source, he has given several talks to conferences and Linux User Groups (LUGs) about Ubuntu. Corey's day job involves sales for Userful, a multiseat Linux vendor in Canada.

Jonathan Jesse is unusual in that he is a Microsoft Windows Network Administrator with a day job in Grand Rapids, Michigan, who also has a strong interest in Linux and Open Source software. He had looked at many different Linux distributions but had not found one that "just works" until Ubuntu and Kubuntu filled that bill. Since he is not a developer or a programmer, he struggled to find a way to give back to the Open Source community. Beginning with the Hoary Hedgehog release, Jonathan joined the Ubuntu Documentation Team by proofreading and submitting patches to the mailing list. He then started working on the Kubuntu documents. He has started testing builds for the Laptop Testing Team, works on bugs for the Kubuntu team, and helps out on the wiki as well. Ubuntu and Kubuntu have given Jonathan a way to give back to the community without having to be a developer, and he encourages everyone to come help him out.

Ivan Krstić is a software architect and journalist currently on leave of absence from Harvard University. Ivan has been using Debian Linux since late 1994. He switched to Ubuntu with its first release, and is now one of the administrators of the Ubuntu Server Team. He previously served as Director of Research at the Medical Informatics Laboratory at Zagreb Children's Hospital, where he depended on Ubuntu Server for mission-critical backend tasks. Ivan is presently building the user stack architecture and worrying about security for the One Laptop Per Child project.

Introduction

WELCOME to *The Official Ubuntu Book*!

In recent years, the Ubuntu operating system has taken the Open Source and IT worlds by storm. From out of nowhere, the Little Operating System That Could has blossomed into a full-featured desktop and server offering that has won over the hearts of users around the world. Aside from the strong technical platform and impressive commitment to quality, Ubuntu also enjoys success due to its sprawling community of enthusiastic users who have helped to support, document, and test every millimeter of the Ubuntu landscape.

In your hands you are holding the official authorized guide to this impressive operating system. Each of the authors selected to work on this book has demonstrated a high level of technical competence, an unbridled commitment to Ubuntu, and the ability to share this knowledge in a simple and clear manner. These authors were gathered together to create a book that offers a solid grounding to Ubuntu and explains how the many facets and features of Ubuntu work.

About This Book

At the start of every book, on every bookshelf, in every store, is a paragraph that sums up the intentions and aims for the book. In some cases, this paragraph turns into an introspective philosophical lesson with the author on the brink of claiming the book will help the reader cure disease and open up a donkey sanctuary. *The Official Ubuntu Book* is different. We have one very simple, down-to-earth aim: to make the Ubuntu experience even more pleasant for users. The Ubuntu developers and community have gone to great lengths to produce an easy-to-use, functional, and flexible operating system for doing, browsing, and creating all kinds of interesting things. This book augments that effort. With such an integrated and flexible operating system, this guide acts as a tour de force for the many things you can do with Ubuntu.

The Scope of the Book

With such an extensive and flexible operating system to cover, we had our work cut out for us to write a book that could cover the system in sufficient detail. However, if we were to write in detail about every possible feature in Ubuntu, you would need to buy a new bookcase to store the sheer amount of content that would need to be written. The authors would also need to continue writing until they were skeletons. Unlikely, some may say.

Part of the challenge in creating *The Official Ubuntu Book* was selecting the topics and content that can be covered within a reasonably sized book. As such, we have identified the most essential content to be covered and written about it. These chosen topics not only include coverage of installation, using the desktop, applications, multimedia, system administration, and software management but also include a discussion of the community, online resources, and the philosophy weaved into Ubuntu and Open Source. In addition to this, we managed to squeeze in a chapter full of useful troubleshooting recipes that you can use when you need to troubleshoot problems. All in all, the book provides an ideal one-stop shop for getting started with Ubuntu.

The Menu

Let's take a look at the range of chapters included in the book and what each covers.

- Chapter 1—Introducing Ubuntu: Spirited introduction to the Ubuntu project, its distribution, its development processes, and some of the history that made it all possible.

- Chapter 2—Installing Ubuntu: Run through the installation process one step at a time, and get Ubuntu ready to run on your computer.

- Chapter 3—Using Ubuntu on the Desktop: Take a whistle-stop tour of the Ubuntu desktop, the applications included, and explore ways to configure your desktop.

- Chapter 4—Advanced Usage and Managing Ubuntu: Explore some of the advanced ways to use Ubuntu, including managing the system. Learn how to install and manage software, use hardware devices and printers, interact with remote computers, use the terminal, and run some Windows programs under Ubuntu.

- Chapter 5—The Ubuntu Server: Introduces Ubuntu Server installation and administration, including coverage of console-line package management, basic security topics, and advanced installer features such as logical volume management (LVM) and RAID.

- Chapter 6—Support and Typical Problems: Packed to the seams with lots of small, independent recipes so you can learn how to solve common problems or meet requirements.

- Chapter 7—Using Kubuntu: The most popular spin-off project from Ubuntu is Kubuntu. This chapter provides a solid primer for getting started.

- Chapter 8—The Ubuntu Community: Understand the breadth of the Ubuntu community, including what folks do to build, promote, distribute, support, document, translate, and advocate Ubuntu—and find out what you can do to join in the fun.

- Chapter 9—Ubuntu Related Projects: Explore the universe of other distributions that surround Ubuntu, including Edubuntu and nUbuntu.

- Appendix A—Welcome to the Command Line: Take advantage of the power of the command line with the clear, easy-to-use examples in this brief primer.

- Appendix B—Core Ubuntu Documents: Review some of the key documents that define Ubuntu, including the Code of Conduct, the Ubuntu Licensing Policy, the Ubuntu Philosophy, and the Description of Ubuntu Components.

- Appendix C—Creative Commons Attribution-ShareAlike 2.0 Open Publication License.

- Appendix D—Ubuntu Equivalents to Windows Programs.

The Ubuntu team offers flexible installation options for Ubuntu users with three CD images available: the "Desktop CD," "Alternate Install CD," and "Server Install CD." These three CD images are conveniently combined onto one DVD included in the back of this book, allowing you to install Ubuntu for different configurations from just one disk. There is also an option to test the DVD for defects as well as a memory test option to check your computer.

The first boot option on the DVD, "Start or install Ubuntu" will cover most users' needs. For more comprehensive information, check the Help feature by selecting F1 on the boot menu. You can also refer to Chapter 2, which covers the Ubuntu installation process in detail.

You can find the DVD image, the individual CD images (for those of you without DVD drives), and Kubuntu and Edubuntu images on http://www.ubuntu.com/download.

## CHAPTER 1

Introducing Ubuntu

- **A Wild Ride**
- **Free Software, Open Source, and GNU/Linux**
- **A Brief History of Ubuntu**
- **What Is Ubuntu?**
- **Ubuntu Promises and Goals**
- **Canonical and the Ubuntu Foundation**
- **Ubuntu Subprojects, Derivatives, and Spin offs**
- **Summary**

THIS CHAPTER INTRODUCES THE UBUNTU PROJECT, its distribution, its development processes, and some of the history that made it all possible. If you are looking to jump right in and get started with Ubuntu, turn right away to Chapter 2, Installing Ubuntu. If you are interested in first learning about where Ubuntu comes from and where it is going, this chapter will provide a good introduction.

A Wild Ride

In April 2004 Mark Shuttleworth brought together a dozen developers from the Debian, GNOME, and GNU Arch projects to brainstorm. Shuttleworth asked the developers if a better type of operating system (OS) was possible. Their answer was "Yes." He asked them what it would look like. He asked them to describe the community that would build such an OS. That group worked with Mark to come up with answers to these questions, and then they decided to try to make the answers a reality. The group named itself the Warthogs and gave itself a six-month deadline to build a proof-of-concept OS. They nicknamed their first release the Warty Warthog with the reasonable assumption that their first product would have its warts. Then they got down to business.

It's difficult, particularly for those of us who were privileged to be among those early Warthogs, to imagine that the brainstorming meeting behind the Ubuntu project took place less than two years ago. Far from being warty, the Warty Warthog surpassed our most optimistic expectations and *everyone*'s predictions. Within six months, Ubuntu was in the Number 1 spot on several popularity rankings of GNU/Linux distributions. Ubuntu has demonstrated the most explosive growth of any GNU/Linux distribution in recent memory and had one of the most impressive first years of any free or Open Source software project in history.

It is staggering to think that after less than two years, *millions* of individuals are using Ubuntu. As many thousands of these users give back to the Ubuntu community by developing documentation, translation, and code, Ubuntu improves every day. As many thousands of these users contribute to a thriving advocacy and support community—both online and in their local communities—Ubuntu's growth remains unchecked. Ubuntu subprojects, a list of efforts that contains the now-maturing Kubuntu and Edubuntu projects, are extending the reach and goals of the Ubuntu project into new realms.

Meanwhile, millions of pressed Ubuntu CDs have been shipped at no cost to universities, Internet cafés, computer shops, and community centers around the world. You can find Ubuntu's familiar brown background and title bars almost anywhere people use computers. I have personally seen strangers running Ubuntu on trains in Spain, libraries in Boston, museums in Croatia, high schools in Mexico, and in many more places too numerous to list here.

In two years, Ubuntu has begun to mature. The release of Ubuntu 6.06—the Dapper Drake—provides a polished release with long-term support for both desktops and servers. However, while Ubuntu begins to settle in for the long term, the project maintains its youthful vigor, its ambitious attitude, its commitment to its principles, and its community-driven approach. As the project ages, it is proving that it can learn from its failures as well as its successes, and that it can maintain growth without compromising stability. We've come a long way—but we're still only getting started.

Free Software, Open Source, and GNU/Linux

While thousands of individuals have contributed in some form to Ubuntu, the project has only succeeded through the contributions of many thousands more who have indirectly laid the technical, social, and economic groundwork for Ubuntu's success. While introductions to free software, Open Source, and GNU/Linux can be found in many other places, no introduction of Ubuntu is complete without a brief discussion of these concepts and the people and history behind them. It is around these concepts and within these communities that Ubuntu was motivated and born. Ultimately, it is through these ideas that it is sustained.

Free Software and GNU

In a series of events that have almost become legend through constant repetition, Richard M. Stallman created the concept of "free software" in 1983. Stallman grew up with computers in the 1960s and 1970s, when computer users purchased very large and extremely expensive mainframe computers, which were then shared among large numbers of programmers. Software was, for the most part, seen as an add-on to the hardware, and every user had the ability and the right to modify or rewrite the software on their computer and to freely share this software. As computers became cheaper and more numerous in the late 1970s, producers of software began to see value in the software itself. Producers of computers began to argue that their software was copyrightable and a form of intellectual property much like a music record-ing, a film, or a book's text. They began to distribute their software under licenses and in forms that restricted its users' abilities to use, redistribute, or modify the code. By the early 1980s, restrictive software licenses had become the norm.

Stallman, then a programmer at MIT's Artificial Intelligence Laboratory, became increasingly concerned with what he saw as a dangerous loss of the freedoms that software users and developers had up until that point enjoyed. He was concerned with computer users' ability to be good neigh-bors and members of what he thought was an ethical and efficient computer-user community. To fight against this negative tide, Stallman articulated a vision for a community that developed liberated code—in his words, "free software." He defined "free software" as software that had the following four characteristics—labeled from zero through three instead of one through four as a computer programmer's joke:

- The freedom to run the program for any purpose (freedom 0)
- The freedom to study how the program works and adapt it to your needs (freedom 1)
- The freedom to redistribute copies so you can help your neighbor (freedom 2)
- The freedom to improve the program and release your improvements to the public so that the whole community benefits (freedom 3)

Access to source code—the human-readable and modifiable blueprints of any piece of software that can be distinguished from the computer-readable version of the code that most software is distributed as—is a prerequisite to freedoms one and three. In addition to releasing this definition of free soft-ware, Stallman created a project with the goal of creating a completely "free" OS to replace the then-popular UNIX. In 1984, Stallman announced this project and called it "GNU"—another joke in the form of a recursive acronym for "GNU's Not UNIX."

Linux

By the early 1990s, Stallman and a collection of other programmers working on GNU had developed a near-complete OS that could be freely shared. They were, however, missing a final essential piece in the form of a "kernel"—a complex system command processor that lies at the center of any OS. In 1991, Linus Torvalds wrote an early version of just such a kernel, released it under a "free" license, and called it "Linux." Linus' kernel was paired with the GNU project's development tools and OS and with the graphical windowing system called X. With this pairing, a completely free OS was born—free both in terms of price and in Stallman's terms of freedom.

All systems referred to as "Linux" today are, in fact, built on the work of this collaboration. Technically, the term "Linux" refers only to the kernel. Many programmers and contributors to GNU, including Stallman, argue emphatically that the full OS should be referred to as "GNU/Linux" in order to give credit not only to Linux but also to the GNU project and to highlight GNU's goals of spreading software freedom—goals not necessarily shared by Linus Torvalds. Many others find this name cumbersome and prefer calling the system simply "Linux." Yet others, such as the Ubuntu project, attempt to avoid the controversy altogether by referring to GNU/Linux only by using their own project's name.

Open Source

Disagreements over labeling did not end with discussions about the naming of the combination of GNU and Linux. In fact, as the list of contributors to GNU and Linux grew, a vibrant world of new free software projects sprouted up, facilitated in part by growing access to the Internet. As this community grew and diversified, a number of people began to notice an unintentional side effect of Stallman's free software. Because free software was built in an open way, *anyone* could contribute to software by looking through the code, finding bugs, and fixing them. Because software ended up being examined by larger numbers of programmers, free software was higher in quality, performed better, and offered more features than similar software developed through proprietary development mechanisms. In many situations, the development model behind free software led to software that was *inherently better* than proprietary alternatives.

As the computer and information technology industry began to move into the dot-com boom, one group of free software developers and leaders, spearheaded by two free software developers and advocates—Eric S. Raymond and Bruce Perens—saw the important business proposition offered by a model that could harness volunteer labor or interbusiness collaboration and create intrinsically better software. However, they were worried that the term "free software" was problematic for at least two reasons: First, it was highly ambiguous—the English word "free" means both gratis, or at no cost (e.g., free as in free beer) and liberated in the sense of freedom (e.g., free as in free speech). Second, there was a feeling, articulated most famously by Raymond, that all this talk of "freedom" was scaring off the very business executives and decision makers whom the free software movement needed to impress in order to succeed.

To tackle both of these problems, this group coined a new phrase—Open Source—and created a new organization called the Open Source Initiative. The group set at its core a definition of Open Source software that overlapped completely and exclusively with both Stallman's four-part definition of free software and with other community definitions that were also based on Stallman's.

One useful way to understand the split between the free software and Open Source movements is to think of it as the opposite of a schism. In religious schisms, churches separate and do not work or worship together because of relatively small differences in belief, interpretation, or motivation. For example, most contemporary forms of Protestant Christianity agree on *almost* everything but have separated over some small but irreconcilable difference. However, in the case of the free software and Open Source movements, the two groups have fundamental disagreements about their motivation and beliefs. One group is focused on freedom, while the other is focused on pragmatics. Free software is most accurately described as a social movement, while Open Source is a development methodology. However, the two groups have no trouble working on projects hand-in-hand.

In terms of the motivations and goals, Open Source and free software diverge greatly. Yet in terms of the software, projects, and the licenses they use, they are completely synonymous. While people who identify with either group see the two movements as being at odds, the Ubuntu project sees no conflict between the two ideologies. People in the Ubuntu project identify with either group and often with both. In this book, we may switch back and forth between the terms as different projects and people in Ubuntu identify more strongly with one term or the other. For the purposes of this book, though, either term should be read as implying the other unless it is stated otherwise.

A Brief History of Ubuntu

Born in April 2004 and at just under two years old at the time of this writing, a history of Ubuntu may seem premature. However, the last two years have been full ones for Ubuntu. With its explosive growth, it is difficult even for those involved most closely with the project to track and record some of the high points. Importantly, there are some key figures whose own history must be given to fully understand Ubuntu. This brief summary tries to quickly give you the high points of Ubuntu's history to date and the necessary background knowledge to understand where Ubuntu comes from.

Mark Shuttleworth

No history of Ubuntu can call itself complete without a history of Mark Shuttleworth. Shuttleworth is, undeniably, the most visible and important person in Ubuntu. More important from the point of view of history, Shuttleworth is also the originator and initiator of the project—he made the snowball that would eventually roll on and grow to become the Ubuntu project.

Shuttleworth was born in 1973 in Welkom, Free State in South Africa. He attended Diocesan College and obtained a business science degree in finance and information systems at the University of Cape Town. During this period, he was an avid computer hobbyist and became involved with the free and Open Source software community. He was at least marginally involved in both the Apache project and the Debian project and was the first person to upload the Apache Web server, perhaps the single most important piece of server software on GNU/Linux platforms, into the Debian project's archives.

Seeing an opportunity in the early days of the Web, Shuttleworth founded a certificate authority and Internet security company called Thawte in his garage. Over the course of several years, he built Thawte into the second largest certificate authority on the Internet, trailing only the security behemoth Verisign. Throughout this period, Thawte's products and services were built and served almost entirely from free and Open Source software. In December 1999, Shuttleworth sold Thawte to Verisign for an undisclosed amount that reached into the hundreds of millions in U.S. dollars.

With his fortune made at a young age, Shuttleworth might have enjoyed a life of leisure—and probably considered it. Instead, he decided to pursue his lifelong dream of space travel. After paying approximately U.S. $20 million to the Russian space program and devoting nearly a year to preparation, including learning Russian and spending seven months training in Star City, Russia, Shuttleworth realized his dream as a civilian cosmonaut aboard the Russian Soyuz TM-34 mission. On this mission, Shuttleworth spent two days on the Soyuz rocket and eight days on the International Space Station, where he participated in experiments related to AIDS and genome research. In early May 2002 Mark Shuttleworth returned to Earth.

In addition to space exploration and a less-impressive jaunt to Antarctica, Shuttleworth played an active role as both a philanthropist and a venture capitalist. In 2001, Shuttleworth founded the Shuttleworth Foundation (TSF)—a nonprofit organization based in South Africa. The foundation was chartered to fund, develop, and drive social innovation in the field of education. Of course, the means by which TSF attempts to achieve these goals frequently involved free software. Through these projects, the organization has been one of the most visible proponents of free and Open Source software in South Africa and even the world. In the venture capital area, Shuttleworth worked to foster research, development, and entrepreneurship in South Africa with strategic injections of cash into start-ups through a new venture capital firm called HBD—an acronym that stood for "Here Be Dragons." During this period, Shuttleworth was busy brainstorming his next big project—the project that would eventually become Ubuntu.

The Warthogs

There has been no lack of projects attempting to wrap GNU, Linux, and other pieces of free and Open Source software into a neat, workable, and user-friendly package. Mark Shuttleworth, like many other people, believed that the philosophical and pragmatic benefits offered by free software put it on a course for widespread success. That said, none of the offerings were particularly impressive. Something was missing from all of them. Shuttleworth saw this as an opportunity. If someone could build *the* great free software distribution that helped push GNU/Linux into the mainstream, he would come to occupy a position of strategic importance.

Shuttleworth, like many other technically inclined people, was a huge fan of the Debian project (discussed in depth later in this chapter). However, there were many things about Debian that did not fit with Shuttleworth's vision of an ideal OS. For a period of time, Shuttleworth considered the possibility of running for Debian project leader as a means of reforming the Debian project from within. With time though, it became clear that the best way to bring GNU/Linux to the mainstream would not be from within the Debian project—which in many situations had very good reasons for being the way it was. Instead, Shuttleworth would build a new project that worked in symbiosis with Debian to build a new, better GNU/Linux system.

To kick off this project, Shuttleworth invited a dozen or so Debian developers he knew and respected to his flat in London in April 2004. It was in this meeting (alluded to in the first paragraphs of this introduction) that the groundwork for the Ubuntu project was laid. By that point, many of those involved were excited about the possibility of the project. During this meeting, the team—which would in time grow into the core Ubuntu team—brainstormed a large list of the things that *they* would want to see in their ideal OS. The list is now a familiar list of features to most Ubuntu users. Many of these traits will be covered in more depth later in this chapter. The group wanted

- Predictable and frequent release cycles

- A strong focus on localization and accessibility

- A strong focus on ease of use and user-friendliness on the desktop

- A strong focus on Python as the single programming language through which the entire system can be built and expanded

- A community-driven approach that worked with existing free software projects and a method by which the groups give back as they go—not just at the time of release

- A new set of tools designed around the process of building distributions that allowed developers to work within an ecosystem of different projects and that allowed users to give back in whatever way they could.

There was consensus among the group that actions speak louder than words, so there were no public announcements or press releases. Instead, the group set a deadline for itself—six short months in the future. Shuttleworth agreed to finance the work and pay the developers full-time salaries to work on the project. After six months, they would both announce their project and reveal the first product of their work. They made a list of goals they wanted to achieve by the deadline, and the individuals present took on tasks. Collectively, they called themselves the Warthogs.

What Does *Ubuntu* Mean?

At this point, the Warthogs had a great team, a set of goals, and a decent idea of how to achieve most of them. The team did not, on the other hand, have a name for their project. Shuttleworth argued strongly that they should call the project "Ubuntu."

Ubuntu is a concept and a term from several South African languages, including Zulu and Xhosa. It refers to a South African ideology or ethic that, while difficult to express in English, might roughly be translated as "humanity toward others," or "I am because we are." Others have described ubuntu as "the belief in a universal bond of sharing that connects all humanity." The famous South African human rights champion Archbishop Desmond Tutu explained ubuntu in this way:

> A person with ubuntu is open and available to others, affirming of others, does not feel threatened that others are able and good, for he or she has a proper self-assurance that comes from knowing that he or she belongs in a greater whole and is diminished when others are humiliated or diminished, when others are tortured or oppressed.

Ubuntu played an important role as a founding principle in post-apartheid South Africa and remains a concept familiar to most South Africans today.

Shuttleworth liked the term Ubuntu as a name for the new project for several reasons. First, it is a South African concept. While the majority of the people who work on Ubuntu are not from South Africa, the roots of the project are, and Shuttleworth wanted to choose a name that represented this. Second, the project emphasizes the definition of individuality in terms of relationships with others and provides a profound type of community and sharing—exactly the attitudes of sharing, community, and collaboration that are at the core of free software. The term represented the side of free software that the team wanted to share with the world. Third, the idea of personal relationships built on mutual respect and connections describes the fundamental ground rules for the highly functional community that the Ubuntu team wanted to build. Ubuntu was a term that encapsulated where the project came from, where the project was going, and how the project planned to get there. The name was perfect. It stuck.

Creating Canonical

In order to pay developers to work on Ubuntu full time, Shuttleworth needed a company to employ them. He wanted to pick some of the best people for the jobs from within the global free and Open Source communities. These communities, inconveniently for Shuttleworth, know no national and geographic boundaries. Rather than move everyone to a single locale and office, Shuttleworth made the decision to employ these developers through a "virtual company." While this had obvious drawbacks in the form of high-latency and low-bandwidth connections, different time zones, and much more, it also introduced some major benefits in the particular context of the project. On one hand, the distributed nature of employees meant that the new company could hire individuals without requiring them to pack up their lives and move to a new country. More important, it meant that *everyone* in the company was dependent on IRC, mailing lists, and online communication mechanisms to do their work. This unintentionally and automatically solved the water-cooler problem that plagued many other corporately funded free software projects. Namely, that developers would casually speak about their work in person and cut the community and anyone else who didn't work in the office out of the conversation completely. For the first year, the closest thing that Canonical had to an office was Shuttleworth's flat in London.

With time, the company was named Canonical. The name was a nod to the project's optimistic goals of becoming the canonical place for services and support for free and Open Source software and for Ubuntu in particular. "Canonical" of course, refers to something that is accepted as authoritative. It is a common word in the computer programmer lexicon. It's important to note that being "canonical" is like being standard—it is not coercive. Unlike holding a monopoly, becoming the canonical location for something implies a similar sort of success—but *never* one that cannot be undone, and *never* one that is exclusive. Other companies will support Ubuntu and build operating systems based on it—but as long as Canonical is doing a good job, its role will remain central.

What Is Ubuntu?

The Warthogs' goal and Canonical's flagship project is Ubuntu. If you've gotten this far, you already have some idea of what that means. That said, this section tries to offer a little bit of background that is helpful in understanding exactly *what* Ubuntu is and what its goals are.

What Is a Distribution?

It's clear to most people that Ubuntu is an OS. The full story is a little more complex. Ubuntu is what is called a distribution of GNU/Linux—a "distro" for short. Understanding exactly what that means requires, once again, a little bit of history. In the early days of GNU and Linux, users needed a great deal of technical knowledge. Only geeks needed to apply. There were no Linux "operating systems" in the sense that we usually use the term— there was no single CD or set of disks that one could use to install. Instead, the software was dozens and even hundreds of individual programs—each built differently by a different individual, and each distributed separately. Installing each of the necessary applications would be incredibly time consuming at best. In many cases, incompatibilities and the technical trickery necessary to install software made getting a GNU/Linux system on a hard disk prohibitively difficult. A great deal of knowledge of configuration and programming was necessary just to get a system up and running. As a result, very few people who were not programmers used these early GNU/Linux systems.

Early distributions were projects that collected all of the necessary pieces of software from all of the different places and put them together in an easier-to-install form with the most basic configuration already done.

These distributions aimed to make using GNU/Linux more convenient and to bring it to larger groups of users. Today, almost nobody uses GNU/Linux without using a distribution. As a result, distribution names are well known. Ubuntu is such a project. Other popular distros include Red Hat, Novell's SuSE, TurboLinux, Linspire, Gentoo, and Debian.

Most distributions contain a similar collection of software. For example, they all contain most of the core pieces of GNU and a Linux kernel. They also almost all contain the X Window System and a set of applications on top of it that may include a Web browser, desktop environment, and an office suite. While distributions started out distributing only the core pieces of the OS, they have grown to include an increasingly wide array of applications as well. A modern distribution includes all of the software that "comes with an OS," that is, several CDs or DVDs containing anything that most users might want and the distribution is legally allowed to distribute.

Ubuntu, like other contemporary distros, offers a custom installer, a framework including software and servers to install new software once the system has been installed, a standard configuration method through which many programs can be configured, a standard method through which users can report bugs in their software, and much more. Frequently, distributions also contain large repositories of software on servers accessible through the Internet. To get a sense of scale, Ubuntu includes on the order of 17,000 pieces of software on its central servers—each piece of software is customized slightly and tested to work well with all of the other software on the system. That number grows daily.

What's important to realize is that distributions do not, for the most part, write or create the applications you use. The Ubuntu team did not write Linux, and it did not write GNU—although individuals on the team have contributed to both projects. Instead, Ubuntu takes GNU, Linux, and many thousands of other applications, and then tests and integrates them to be accessible under a single installer. Ubuntu is the glue that lets you take a single CD, install hundreds of separate pieces of software, and have them work together as a single, integrated desktop system. If you were to pick up a CD of another distribution such as Debian, Red Hat, or Novell, the software installed would be nearly identical to the software in Ubuntu. The difference would be in the way the software is installed, serviced, upgraded, and presented and the way it integrates with other pieces of software on the system.

An Ecosystem of Distributions

There are many hundreds of GNU/Linux distributions in active use today. A quick look at Distrowatch's (www.distrowatch.com) database demonstrates the staggering number and growth of distributions. One of the first GNU/Linux distributions was called Softlanding Linux System, or SLS. For a number of reasons, a programmer named Patrick Volkerding thought he could improve on SLS. Because SLS was free software, Volkerding had the freedom to make a derivative version of SLS and distribute it. Volkerding did just this when he took SLS's code and used it as the framework or model upon which to create his own variant called Slackware. Subsequently, Slackware became the first widely successful GNU/Linux distribution and is maintained to this day.

With time, the landscape of GNU/Linux distribution has changed. However, the important role of derivation that made Slackware possible has remained fully intact and is still shaping this landscape. Today, the hundreds of GNU/Linux distributions serve a multitude of users for a myriad of purposes: There are distributions specially designed for children, dentists, and for speakers of many of the world's languages. There are distributions for science, for business, for servers, for PDAs, for nonprofit organizations, for musicians, and for countless other groups.

Despite this diversity, the vast majority of derivatives can be traced back to one of two "parent" distributions: Red Hat and Debian. While it is not necessary to understand the details of how these projects differ, it's useful to know that Red Hat and Debian offer two compelling, but frequently different, platforms. Each project has strengths and weaknesses. For almost every group making a Linux-based OS one of these projects acts as square one (with a few notable exceptions, such as the Gentoo project).

However, while the process of deriving distributions has allowed for a proliferation of OS platforms serving a vast multiplicity of needs, the derivative process has, historically, been largely a one-way process. New distributions based on Red Hat—Mandriva and Novell's SuSE, for example—begin with Red Hat or a subset of Red Hat technology and then customize and diverge. Very few of these changes ever make it back into Red Hat and, with time, distributions tend to diverge to the point of irreconcilable incompatibility. While the software that each system includes remains largely consistent across all distributions, the way that it is packaged, presented, installed, and configured becomes increasingly differentiated. During this process, inter-distribution sharing and collaboration was growing in difficultly.

This growing divergence is indicative of a more general problem faced by distributions in getting changes upstream. Frequently, the users of GNU/Linux distributions find and report problems in their software. Frequently, distributions fix the bugs in question. While sometimes these bugs are in changes introduced by the distribution, often these bugs exist in the upstream version of the software and the fix applies to *every* distribution. What is not uncommon, but is unfortunately *much* less frequent, is for these bug fixes to be pushed upstream so that every distribution and user get to use them. This lack of collaboration is rarely due to malice, incompetence, or any tactical or strategic decision made by developers or their employers. Instead, tracking and monitoring changes *across* distributions and in relation to upstream developers is complicated and difficult. It's a fact of life that sometimes changes fall on the floor. These failures are simply the product of distribution-building processes, policies, and tools that approach distributions as products in and of themselves—not processes within an ecosystem.

Like many other distributions, Ubuntu is a derivative of Debian. Unlike many derivatives, Ubuntu has made it one of its primary goals to explore the possibility of a better derivation process with Debian, with Debian and Ubuntu's common upstreams (e.g., projects such as Linux or GNU), and with Ubuntu's *own* derivatives. A more in-depth discussion of Debian can help explain how Ubuntu positions itself within the free software world.

The Debian Project and the Free Software Universe

Debian is a distribution backed by a volunteer project of 1,000 official members and many more volunteers and contributors. It has expanded to encompass nearly 17,000 packages of free and Open Source applications and documentation. Debian's history and structure make it very good at certain things. For example, Debian has a well-deserved reputation for integrated package management and access to a large list of free software applications. However, as a voluntary and largely nonhierarchical organization, there are also several things that Debian has trouble providing. Frequent and reliable releases, corporate support and liability, and a top-down consistency on the desktop have each proved to be difficult for Debian to offer.

Each new distribution exists for a reason. Creating a new distribution, even a derivative, is far from easy. In large part, Ubuntu exists to build off of the many successes of the Debian project while solving some of the problems it struggles with. The goal is to create a synthetic whole that appeals to users who had previously not been able or willing to use Debian.

In building off the great work of the Debian project, as well as GNU, Linux, and other projects that Debian is built on, Ubuntu wanted to explore a new style of derivation that focused on a tighter interproject relationship within an ecosystem of different developers. While Ubuntu tries to improve and build on Debian's success, the project is in no way trying to replace Debian. On the contrary, Ubuntu couldn't exist without the Debian project and its large volunteer and software base, and the high degree of quality that Debian consistently provides. This symbiotic relationship between Ubuntu and Debian is mirrored in the way that both Ubuntu and Debian depend heavily on projects such as GNU and Linux to produce great software, which they can each package and distribute. Ubuntu sets out explicitly to build a symbiotic relationship with both Debian and their common "upstream."

The relationship between Ubuntu and Debian has not been simple, straightforward, or painless and has involved patience and learning on both sides. With time, both groups have found ways to work together that seem to offer major benefits over the traditional derive-and-forget model. It is through a complex series of technological, social, and even political processes—many of which will be described in the rest of this chapter—that Ubuntu tries to create a better way of building a free software distribution.

The Ubuntu Community

If you've read up until this point, you may have noticed a theme that permeates the Ubuntu project on several levels. The history of free software and Open Source is one of a profoundly effective *community*. Similarly, in building a GNU/Linux distribution, Ubuntu has tried to focus on an ecosystem model—an organization of organizations—in other words, a community. Even the definition of the term *ubuntu* is one that revolves around people interacting in a community.

It comes as no surprise then that an "internal" community plays heavily into the way that the Ubuntu distribution is created. While the Ubuntu 4.10

version (Warty Warthog) was primarily built by a small number of people, Ubuntu only achieved widespread success through contributions by a much larger group that included programmers, documentation writers, volunteer support staff, and users. While Canonical employs several dozen active contributors to Ubuntu, the distribution has, from day one, encouraged contributions from *anyone* in the community and rewards and recognizes contributions by all. Rather than taking center stage, paid contributors are *not* employed by Ubuntu—instead they are employed by Canonical Ltd. These employees are treated simply as another set of community members. They must apply for membership in the Ubuntu community and have their contributions recognized in the same way as anyone else. All nonbusiness-related communication about the Ubuntu project occurs in public and in the community. Volunteer community members occupy seats on the two most important governing boards of the Ubuntu project, the Technical Board, which oversees all technical matters and the Community Council, which approves new Ubuntu members and resolves disputes. Seats on both boards are approved by the relevant community, developers for the Technical Board and Ubuntu members for the Community Council.

In order to harness and encourage the contributions of its community, Ubuntu has striven to balance the important role that Canonical plays with the value of empowering individuals in the community. The Ubuntu project is based on a fundamental belief that great software is built, supported, and maintained only in a strong relationship with the individuals who use the software. In this way, by fostering and supporting a vibrant community, Ubuntu can achieve much more than it could through paid development alone. The people on the project believe that while the contributions of Canonical and Shuttleworth have provided an important catalyst for the processes that have built Ubuntu, it is the community that brought the distribution its success to date. The project members believe that it is only through increasing reliance on the community that the project's success will continue to grow. We won't outspend the proprietary software industry. As a community, though, we are very much more.

The nature of the Ubuntu community will be described in depth in Chapter 8, which is wholly devoted to the subject. Finally, it is worth noting that, while this book is official, none of its authors are Canonical employees. This book, like much of the rest of Ubuntu, is purely a product of the project's community.

Ubuntu Promises and Goals

So far, this book has been about the prehistory, history, and context of the Ubuntu project. After this chapter, the book will focus on the distribution itself. Before proceeding, it's important to understand the goals that motivated the project.

Philosophical Goals

The most important goals of the Ubuntu project are philosophical in nature. The Ubuntu project lays out its philosophy in a series of documents on its Web site that are important enough that we've included many of them verbatim in Appendix B of this book. In the most central of these documents, the team summarizes their charter and their major philosophical goals and underpinnings

> Ubuntu is a community-driven project to create an OS and a full set of applications using free and Open Source software. At the core of the Ubuntu Philosophy of Software Freedom are these core philosophical ideals
>
> 1. Every computer user should have the freedom to run, copy, distribute, study, share, change, and improve their software for any purpose without paying licensing fees.
>
> 2. Every computer user should be able to use their software in the language of their choice.
>
> 3. Every computer user should be given every opportunity to use software even if they work under a disability.

The first item should be familiar by now. It is merely a recapitulation of Stallman's free software definition quoted above in the section on free software history. In it, the Ubuntu project makes explicit its goals that every user of software should have the freedoms required by free software. This is important for a number of reasons. First, it offers users all of the practical benefits of software that runs better, faster, and more flexibly. More important, it gives every user the capability to transcend their role as a user and a consumer of their software. Ubuntu wants software to be empowering and to work in the ways that users want it to work. Ubuntu wants every user to have the ability to make sure it works for them. To do this, software *must* be free, so Ubuntu makes this a requirement and a philosophical promise.

Of course, the core goals of Ubuntu do not end with the free software definition. Instead, the project articulates two new, but equally important, goals. The first of these is that every computer user should be able to use their computer in the language of their choice as a nod to the fact that the majority of the world's population does not speak English while the vast majority of software interacts only in that language. To be useful, source code comments, programming languages, documentation, and the texts and menus in computer programs must be written in *some* language. Arguably the world's most international language is a reasonably good choice. However, there is no language that everyone speaks, and English is not useful to the majority of the world's population that does not speak it. Computers can be a great tool for empowerment and education, but *only* if the user can understand the words in their computer's interface. As a result, Ubuntu believes that it is the project's—and community's—responsibility to ensure that *every* user can easily use Ubuntu to read and write in the language with which they are most comfortable.

The ability to make modifications—a requirement of free software and of Ubuntu's first philosophical point—makes this type of translation possible. This book is a case in point. While it only helps explain Ubuntu to the relatively small subset of the world that already speaks English, the choice to write this book in English was made to enable it to have the widest impact. More important, it is distributed under a license that allows for translation, modification, and redistribution. The authors of this book cannot write this book in all of the world's languages—or even more than one of them. Instead, we have attempted to eliminate unnecessary legal restrictions and other barriers that might keep the community from taking on the translation work.

Finally, just as no person should be blocked from using a computer simply because he does not know a particular language, no user should be blocked from using a computer because he has a disability. Ubuntu must be accessible to users with motor disabilities, vision disabilities, and hearing disabilities. It should provide input and output in a variety of forms to account for each of these situations and for others. A significant percentage of the world's most intelligent and creative individuals have disabilities. Ubuntu's impact should not be limited to any subset of the world when it can be fully inclusive. More important, Ubuntu should be able to harness the ability of these individuals as community members to build a better and more effective community.

Conduct Goals and Code of Conduct

If Ubuntu's philosophical commitments describe the why of the Ubuntu project, the Code of Conduct describes Ubuntu's how. Ubuntu's Code of Conduct (CoC) is, arguably, the most important document in the day-to-day operation of the Ubuntu community and sets the ground rules for work and cooperation within the project. Explicit agreement to the document is the only criterion for becoming an officially recognized Ubuntu activist—an "Ubuntero"—and is an essential step toward membership in the project. Signing the Ubuntu Code of Conduct and becoming an Ubuntu Member is described in more depth in Chapter 6.

The CoC, which can be read in full in Appendix B, covers "behavior as a member of the Ubuntu Community, in any forum, mailing list, wiki, Web site, IRC channel, install-fest, public meeting or private correspondence." The CoC goes into some degree of depth on a series of points that fall under the following headings:

- Be considerate
- Be respectful
- Be collaborative
- When you disagree, consult others
- When you are unsure, ask for help
- Step down considerately

Many of these headings seem like common sense or common courtesy to many, and that is by design. Nothing in the CoC is controversial or radical, and it was never designed to be.

More difficult is the fact that nothing is easy to enforce or decide because acting considerately, respectfully, and collaboratively is often very subjective. There is room for honest disagreements and hurt feelings. These are accepted shortcomings. The CoC was not designed to be a law with explicit prohibitions on phrases, language, or actions. Instead, it aims to provide a constitution and a reminder that considerate and respectful discussion is *essential* to the health and vitality of the project. In situations where there is a serious disagreement on whether a community member has violated or is violating the code, the Community Council—a body which will be discussed in depth in Chapter 8—is available to arbitrate disputes and decide what action, if any, is appropriate.

Nobody involved in the Ubuntu project, including Shuttleworth and the other members of the Community Council, is above the CoC. The CoC is *never* optional and *never* waived. Of course, it was in no way designed to eliminate conflict or disagreement. Arguments are at least as common in Ubuntu as they are in other projects and online communities. However, there is a common understanding within the project that arguments should happen in an environment of collaboration and mutual respect. This allows for *better* arguments with *better* results—and with less hurt feelings and fewer bruised egos.

While it is sometimes incorrectly used as such, the CoC is not a stick to be wielded against an opponent in an argument. Instead, it is a useful point of reference upon which we can assume consensus within the Ubuntu community. Frequently, if groups in the community feel a member is acting in a way that is out of line with the code, the group will gently remind the community member, often privately, that the CoC is in effect. In almost all situations, this is enough to avoid any further action or conflict. Very few CoC violations are ever brought before the Community Council.

Technical Goals

While a respectful community and adherence to a set of philosophical goals provide an important frame in which the Ubuntu project works, Ubuntu is, at the end of the day, a technical project. As a result, it only makes sense that in addition to philosophical goals and a project constitution, Ubuntu also has a set of technical goals.

The first technical goal of the project, and perhaps the most important one, is the coordination of regular and predictable releases. In April 2004, at the Warthogs meeting, the project set a goal for its initial proof-of-concept release six months out. In part due to the resounding success of that project, and in larger part due to the GNOME release schedule, the team has stuck to a regular and predictable six-month release cycle and has only now—two years later—chosen to extend the release schedule by six weeks and only after obtaining community consensus on the decision. Frequent releases are important because it means that users are able to use the latest and greatest free software available—something that is essential in a development environment that is as vibrant and rapidly changing and improving as the free software community. Predictable releases are important, especially to businesses, because it means that they can organize their business plans around Ubuntu. Through consistent releases, Ubuntu can provide a platform that businesses and derivative distributions can rely upon to grow and build.

While releasing frequently and reliably is important, the released software must then be supported. Ubuntu, like all distributions, must deal with the fact that *all* software has bugs. Most bugs are minor, but fixing them may introduce even worse issues. Therefore, fixing bugs after a release must be done carefully or not at all. Ubuntu only engages in major changes, including bug fixes, *between* releases when the changes can be extensively tested. However, some bugs risk the loss of users' information or are a serious security vulnerability. These bugs are fixed immediately and made available as updates for the released distribution. Ubuntu works hard to find and minimize all types of bugs before releases and is largely successful in squashing the worst. However, because there is always the possibility that more of these bugs will be found, Ubuntu commits to supporting *every* release for 18 months after it is released. In the case of Ubuntu 6.06 (Dapper Drake), the project is going well beyond even this and committing to support the release for three full years on desktop computers and for five years in a server configuration.

This bipartite approach to servers and desktops implies the third major technical commitment of the Ubuntu project: support for both servers and desktop computers in separate but equally emphasized modes. While Ubuntu is more well known, and perhaps more popular, in desktop configurations there exist teams of Ubuntu developers focused both on server and desktop users. The Ubuntu project believes that both desktops and servers are essential and provides installation methods on every CD for both types of systems. Ubuntu provides tested and supported software appropriate to the most common actions in both environments and documentation for each. This book contains information on running Ubuntu both on the desktop and on a server.

Finally, Ubuntu is committed to making it as easy as possible for users to transcend their role as the consumers and users of software and to take advantage of each of the freedoms central to our philosophy. As a result, Ubuntu has tried to focus its development around the use and promotion of a single programming language, Python. The project has worked to ensure that Python is widely used throughout the system. By ensuring that desktop applications, text-based or console applications, and many of the "guts" of the system are written in or extensible in Python, Ubuntu is working to ensure that users need only learn one language in order to take advantage of, automate, and tweak many parts of their computer systems.

Bug #1

Of course, Ubuntu's goals are not only to build an OS that lives up to our philosophy or technical goals and to do it on our terms—although we probably would be happy if we only achieved that. Our *ultimate goal,* the one that supersedes and influences all others, is to spread our great software, our frequent releases, and the freedoms enshrined in our philosophy to as many computer users in as many countries as possible. Ubuntu's ultimate goal is not to become the most used *GNU/Linux distribution* in the world, it is to become the most widely used OS in the world.

The first bug in Malone, a bug-tracking system that Ubuntu uses, illustrates this fact. The bug, filed by Shuttleworth at severity "critical," remains open today and can be viewed online at https://launchpad.net/distros/ubuntu/ + bug/1. The text of the bug reads:

> Microsoft has a majority market share | Non-free software is holding back innovation in the IT industry, restricting access to IT to a small part of the world's population and limiting the ability of software developers to reach their full potential, globally. This bug is widely evident in the PC industry.
>
> Steps to repeat:
>
> 1. Visit a local PC store.

What happens:

1. Observe that a majority of PCs for sale have non-free software preinstalled.

2. Observe very few PCs with Ubuntu and free software preinstalled.

What should happen:

1. A majority of the PCs for sale should include only free software such as Ubuntu.

2. Ubuntu should be marketed in a way such that its amazing features and benefits would be apparent and known by all.

3. The system shall become more and more user friendly as time passes.

Many have described Ubuntu's success in the last two years as amazing. For a new GNU/Linux distribution, the level and speed of success has certainly been unprecedented. During this period, Ubuntu has lived up to both its philosophical and technical commitments, achieved many of its goals, and built a vibrant community of users and contributors who have accomplished monumental amounts while collaborating in a culture of respect and understanding fully in line with the Ubuntu code of conduct. However, Bug #1 demonstrates that the Ubuntu project will only be declared a complete success when Ubuntu's standards of freedom, technical excellence, and conduct are the norm *everywhere* in the software world.

Canonical and the Ubuntu Foundation

While Ubuntu is an organization driven by a community, several organizations play an important role in its structure and organization. Foremost among these are Canonical Ltd., a for-profit company introduced as part of the Ubuntu history description, and the Ubuntu Foundation, which is introduced below.

Canonical Ltd.

As mentioned above, Canonical Ltd. is a company founded by Shuttleworth with the primary goal of developing and supporting the Ubuntu distribution. Many of the core developers on Ubuntu—although no longer a majority of them—work full-time or part-time under contract for Canonical Ltd. This funding by Canonical allows Ubuntu to make the type of support commitments that it does. Ubuntu can claim that it will release in six months because releasing, in one form or another, is something that the paid workers at Canonical can ensure. As an all-volunteer organization, Debian suffered from an inability to set and meet deadlines—volunteers become busy or have other deadlines in their paying jobs that take precedence. By offering a subset of developers paying jobs, Canonical can set support and release deadlines and ensure that they are met.

In this way, Canonical ensures that Ubuntu's bottom-line commitments are followed through on. Of course, Canonical neither funds all Ubuntu work, nor could it. Canonical can release *a distribution* every six months, but that distribution will be *much* better and more usable through contributions from the community of users. Most features, most new pieces of software, almost all translations, almost all documentation, and much more are done outside of Canonical. Instead, Canonical ensures that deadlines are met and that the essential work, regardless of whether it's fun, gets done.

Canonical Ltd. was incorporated on the Isle of Man—a tiny island nation between Wales and Ireland that is mostly well known as a haven for international businesses. Since Canonical's staff is sprinkled across the globe and no proper office is necessary, the Isle of Man seemed like as good a place as any for the company to hang its sign.

Canonical's Service and Support

While it is surprising to many, fewer than half of Canonical's employees work on the Ubuntu project. The rest of the employees fall into several categories: business development, support and administration, and development on the Bazaar and Launchpad projects.

Individuals involved in business development help create strategic deals and certification programs with other companies—primarily around Ubuntu. In large part, these are things that the community is either ill-suited for or uninterested in as a whole. One example of business development work is the process of working with companies to ensure that their software (usually proprietary) is built and certified to run on Ubuntu. For example, Canonical worked with IBM to ensure that their popular DB2 database would run on Ubuntu and, when this was achieved, worked to have Ubuntu certified as a platform that would run DB2. Similarly, Canonical worked with HP to ensure that Ubuntu could be installed in the factory on their laptops for sale in Europe as an option for their customers. A third example is the production of this book, which, published by Pearson's Prentice Hall imprint, was a product of work with Canonical.

Canonical also plays an important support role in the Ubuntu project in three ways. First, Canonical supports the development of the Ubuntu project. For example, Canonical system administrators keep servers that support development and distribution of Ubuntu up and running. Second, Canonical helps support Ubuntu users directly. Canonical does this by offering phone and e-mail support to users and by arranging for support contracts with larger companies and organizations. This support is over and above the free (i.e., gratis) support offered by the community—this "commercial support" is offered at a fee, and is either part of a longer-term flat-fee support contract, or is pay-per-instance. Finally, Ubuntu supports other support organizations. Canonical does not seek or try to enforce a monopoly on Ubuntu support; it proudly lists *hundreds* of other organizations offering support for Ubuntu on the Ubuntu Web pages. Instead, Canonical offers what is called second-tier support to these organizations. Because Canonical employs many of the core Ubuntu developers, the company is very well suited to taking action on many of the tougher problems that these support organizations may run into. With its concentrated expertise, Canonical can offer this type of backup, or secondary support, to these organizations.

Bazaar and Launchpad

In addition to support and development on Ubuntu, Canonical Ltd. funds the development of Bazaar-NG, a distributed version control tool, and the Launchpad project. Bazaar-NG is a tool for developing software that is used heavily in Ubuntu and plays an important role in the technical processes through which Ubuntu is forged. However, the software, which is similar in functionality to other version control systems such as CVS, Subversion, or BitKeeper, is useful in a variety of other projects as well. More important, Bazaar-NG acts as the workhorse behind Launchpad.

More than half of Canonical's technical employees work on the Launchpad project. Launchpad is an ambitious Web-based superstructure application that consists of several highly integrated tools. The software plays a central role in Ubuntu development but is also used for the development of other distributions—especially those based on Ubuntu. The Launchpad consists of the following pieces:

- **Rosetta:**

  A Web-based system for easily translating almost any piece of free software from English into almost any language. Rosetta is named after the Rosetta Stone, which helped linguists finally crack the code of Egyptian hieroglyphics.

- **Malone:**

  The bug-tracking system that Ubuntu uses to manage and track bugs. It both tracks bugs across different versions of Ubuntu and allows the Ubuntu community to see the status of that bug in other places, including other distributions and potentially upstream. Malone is a reference to the gangster movie musical *Bugsy Malone.*

- **Soyuz:**

  The distribution management part of Launchpad that now controls the processes by which Ubuntu packages are built, tested, and migrated between different parts of the distribution. Soyuz is a reference to the type of Russian rocket that took Mark Shuttleworth to space. The word *soyuz,* in Russian, means "union."

Launchpad and its components are discussed in more depth in Chapter 9. The importance of Launchpad in the Ubuntu project cannot be overstated. In addition to handling bugs, translations, and distribution building, Launchpad also handles Web site authentication and codifies team membership in the Ubuntu project. It is the place where all work in Ubuntu is tracked and recorded. Any member of the Ubuntu community and any person who contributes to Ubuntu in almost any way will, in due course, find themselves creating an account in Launchpad.

The Ubuntu Foundation

Finally, in addition to Canonical and the full Ubuntu community, the Ubuntu project is supported by the Ubuntu Foundation, which was announced by Shuttleworth with an initial funding commitment of

$10 million. The foundation, like Canonical, is based on the Isle of Man. The organization is advised by the Ubuntu Community Council.

Unlike Canonical, the Foundation does not play an active role in the day-to-day life of Ubuntu. At the moment, the foundation is little more than a pile of money that exists to endow and ensure Ubuntu's future. Because Canonical is a young company, many companies and individuals find it difficult to trust that Canonical will be able provide support for Ubuntu in the time frames (e.g., three to five years) that it claims it will be able to. The Ubuntu Foundation exists to allay those fears.

If something bad were to happen to Shuttleworth or to Canonical that caused either to be unable to support Ubuntu development and maintain the distribution, the Ubuntu Foundation exists to carry on many of Canonical's core activities well into the future. Through the existence of the foundation, Ubuntu is able to make the types of long-term commitments and promises it does.

The one activity that the foundation can, and does, engage in is receiving donations on behalf of the Ubuntu project. These donations, and only these donations, are then put into action on behalf of Ubuntu in accordance with the wishes of the development team and the technical board. For the most part, these are spent on "bounties" that are given to community members who have achieved important feature goals for the Ubuntu project.

Ubuntu Subprojects, Derivatives, and Spin offs

Finally, no introduction of Ubuntu is complete without an introduction to a growing list of Ubuntu subprojects and derivatives. While Ubuntu was derived from Debian, the project has, over the last two years, already developed a number of derivatives of its own.

First and foremost among these is Kubuntu—a version of Ubuntu that uses KDE instead of GNOME as the default desktop environment. Kubuntu is described in depth in its own chapter (Chapter 7, Using Kubuntu), and so will not be explored in any serious depth here. However, it is important to realize that the relationship between Kubuntu and Ubuntu is different than the relationship between Ubuntu and Debian. From a technical perspective, Kubuntu is *fully* within the Ubuntu distribution. Organizationally, the Kubuntu team works fully within Ubuntu as well.

A similar organization exists with the Edubuntu project, which aims to help develop Ubuntu so that a configuration of the distribution can be easily and effectively put into use in schools. That project has a dual focus on both educational and school-related software and on a Linux Terminal Server Project (LTSP) setup that allows schools to run many students' computers using one or more powerful servers and many "dumb" terminals that connect to the server and run software off it. This relatively simple technical trick translates into huge cost savings in educational settings.

However, while both Kubuntu and Edubuntu work closely and within the larger Ubuntu project and both are partially funded by Canonical, there are many other derivatives which have begun to appear that do not fit this model. The first "outside" derivative was Guadalinex, a distribution created and maintained by the government of Andalusia in Spain. Other distributions include a lightweight version of Ubuntu for use on slower computers called Xubuntu and a system called nUbuntu, or Network Ubuntu, designed for network security testing. There is work on a host of other systems both inside and outside of the project.

In a way, it is through these derivatives that the work and goals of the Ubuntu project come together and are crystallized. It is only through the free and Open Source software movements' commitment to freely accessible source code that Ubuntu could be built at all. Similarly, it is only through Ubuntu's continued commitment to these ideals that derivatives are able to spring from Ubuntu. As a derivative with a view of distributions within an ecosystem, Ubuntu does not see the process of derivation as an insult or criticism. Far from it. Ubuntu thinks derivation is the highest form of compliment.

Outside of Ubuntu, Canonical Ltd.'s work is largely based around software such as Launchpad and Bazaar that are designed to facilitate precisely this sort of derivative process. This process, when practiced right, is one that describes an ecosystem of development in which *everyone* benefits—the derivative, Ubuntu, and Ubuntu's upstreams. It is only through this derivative process that everyone gets what they want.

Derivation, done correctly, allows groups to diverge where necessary while working together where possible. Ultimately, it leads to more work done, more happy users, and more overall collaboration. It is through this enhanced collaboration that Ubuntu's philosophical and technical goals will be achieved. It is through this profound community involvement that Bug #1 will be closed. It is through this type of meaningful cooperation, internal and external to the project itself, that the incredible growth of Ubuntu in its first two years will be sustained into the next two and the next twenty.

Summary

This chapter introduced you to the phenomenon that is Ubuntu. It began with some free software and Open Source history and then moved on to the history of Ubuntu. It then covered the Ubuntu products, philosophy, and goals, and the relationship between Canonical Ltd. and the Ubuntu Foundation. It finished with some discussion of the various Ubuntu sub-projects, derivatives, and spin offs.

## CHAPTER 2

Installing Ubuntu

- **Choosing Your Ubuntu Version**
- **Getting Ubuntu**
- **Installing from the Desktop CD**
- **Installing Using the Alternate Install CD**
- **Post-Installation**
- **Summary**

IF YOU ARE READING THIS, it is fairly safe to assume that you have made the decision to give Ubuntu a try. What a wise choice. Ubuntu is a cutting-edge Linux distribution with a dedication to freedom, ease of use, and flexibility. This flexibility not only manifests in creating a powerful and extensible operating system (OS) for your computer but also in how you evaluate and install it.

Trying out Ubuntu is simple. The Ubuntu desktop CD is a special live CD. You can use this disc to run Ubuntu from the CD itself, without it ever coming into contact with your hard disk. This is ideal if you are already using Windows; you can try out Ubuntu by running it from the CD, and you don't have to worry about it overwriting your Windows hard disk.

Choosing Your Ubuntu Version

The developers behind Ubuntu have worked to make the software as easy and flexible to install as possible. They understand that people will be installing Ubuntu on different types of computers (desktops, servers, lap-tops, etc.) and using different types of computers (PCs, 64-bit computers, Macs, etc.). To cater to everyone, there are two Ubuntu CDs that can be used. The DVD with this book includes the desktop CD and alternate install CD images.

- **Desktop:** The desktop CD is the one recommended for *desktops* and *laptops*. With this CD, you can boot Ubuntu from the CD and, if you like it, install it. Note this is the default option on the DVD or CD.

- **Alternate Install:** The alternate install CD is recommended for use when installing on a server. With this CD you boot into an installer and then run Ubuntu when the installation is complete.

When you have decided which type of CD to use, you now need to choose the correct computer architecture. Both the live and install disks support each of the following types of computer.

- **PC:** If you have an Intel 386, 486, Xeon, or Pentium class processor, you should choose the PC version. You can also use this for all AMD processors other than AMD64.

- **AMD64:** If you are using a 64-bit AMD processor, select this version.

▪ **PowerPC:** If you are using a PowerPC-based processor (common in many Apple Macs, PowerBooks, and Mac Minis), use this version.

So, as an example, if you want to install Ubuntu on your Intel Pentium IV laptop, choose the PC desktop CD. If you want to install Ubuntu on your Xeon server, choose the PC alternate install CD.

Other Ubuntu Distributions

In addition to the official Ubuntu release, there are some additional distributions that are based on Ubuntu but are slightly different, including the following:

▪ **Kubuntu:** Kubuntu is Ubuntu, but instead of using the GNOME desktop, Kubuntu uses the KDE desktop. See www.kubuntu.org/ for more information.

▪ **Edubuntu:** The Edubuntu distribution is a version of Ubuntu that has been customized for educational use. This includes, among other things, a range of educational software that looks and feels customized for kids. This distribution is particularly useful for those of you who want to run Ubuntu in a school or college environment or on a young child's computer. See www.edubuntu.org/ for more.

▪ **Xubuntu:** The Xubuntu distribution replaces the GNOME desktop environment with the Xfce 4 environment. Xubuntu is particularly useful for those of you who want to run Ubuntu on older hardware. See https://wiki.ubuntu.com/Xubuntu for more.

With a range of different distributions and options available, Ubuntu is flexible enough to be used in virtually all situations.

Is It Still Ubuntu?

Some of you may be reading about Kubuntu, Edubuntu, and Xubuntu and wondering how different they are from the regular Ubuntu release. These distributions differ mainly in which applications and desktop interface are included. As such, they differ quite a bit, but the underlying OS and software install system is the same.

Getting Ubuntu

Ubuntu is an entirely free OS, and when you have a copy of it you can give it to as many people as you like. This free characteristic of Ubuntu means that it is devilishly simple to get a copy. If you have a DSL or better Internet connection, head over to www.ubuntu.com/download, and select your country from the list of download sites. You can then select a desktop or alternate install CD based on your platform and download it.

NOTE   See the Burning a CD section below for details on how to create your Ubuntu CD from the file you just downloaded.

If you are willing to wait for a CD, you can get a physical Ubuntu CD mailed to you free of charge. To do this, go to https://shipit.ubuntu.com/, and log in. You will need an account on the Launchpad site to use the ShipIt service. If you don't have one, just click on the "create a new account" link to create one. To use ShipIt, fill in the simple form and submit it. Your CDs will then be sent out.

Burning a CD

When you download an Ubuntu CD, you download a special .iso file, which is the same size as a CD (around 650MB). To run the CD you need to convert this file into an installation CD. The file that you downloaded contains a detailed map of what the CD should look like, complete with all the different files that are part of Ubuntu. When you burn the .iso file to the CD-ROM, the original CD layout is restored, and you have a complete installation CD all ready to go.

TIP   **Which Image?**
When you are reading about .iso files, you will often see them referred to as *CD Images*. The term "image" here does not refer to a visual image such as a photo or picture but instead refers to a snapshot of a CD.

You need to use a CD-burning application to burn your .iso file to the CD correctly. Inside the application there should be a menu option called "Burn from Disk Image" or something similar. You then select the .iso file, insert a CD, and after a few minutes, out pops a fresh Ubuntu installation CD.

To give you a head start, the following sections present instructions for burning a CD in some popular tools.

In Windows with ISO Recorder   To burn your .iso with the freely available ISO Recorder, first go to http://isorecorder.alexfeinman.com/, and then download and install ISO Recorder. To burn your image, follow these steps:

1. Insert a blank CD into your CD writer.

2. Locate the .iso file you downloaded, right-click it, and select Copy Image to CD.

3. Click Next, and the recording process begins.

4. When the image has been written, click Finish to exit ISO Recorder.

In Windows with Nero Burning ROM   To burn your image using Nero Burning ROM, follow these steps:

1. Insert a blank CD into your CD writer.

2. Start Nero Burning ROM.

3. Follow the wizard prompts, and select Data CD.

4. When the wizard finishes, click Burn Image on the File menu.

5. In the Open dialog box, select the .iso file, and then click Open.

6. In the wizard, click Burn to create the Ubuntu CD. When completed, click the Done button to exit.

In Linux with GNOME   To burn your image using Linux with GNOME, follow these steps:

1. Insert a blank CD into your CD writer.

2. In Nautilus, right-click on the file you just downloaded, and choose Write to Disk. The Write to Disk dialog box opens.

3. In the dialog box, choose your CD writer and speed, and then click on Write. The Writing Files to Disk Progress dialog box opens, and Nautilus begins writing the disk.

Burning with Mac OS X   To burn your image using Mac OS X, follow these steps:

1. Load the Disk Utility application (found in your Utilities folder).

2. Insert a blank CD, and then choose Images > Burn and select the .iso file.

TIP   **Use the Right Option**
You need to ensure you use the Burn from Disk Image or similar option rather than just copy the .iso image onto the CD to be burned. If you just burn the file directly you will have a CD containing the single .iso file. This is no good.

The Burn from Disk Image function takes the .iso file and restores all the original files from the installation CD onto the disk. This ensures you have a proper installation CD.

Installing from the Desktop CD

So let's assume you are playing with Ubuntu running from the desktop CD, and you decide you like it. You decide you like it so much, in fact, that you want to install it on your computer. Does this mean you need to get a separate CD and install it? Heck, no. The new and improved Ubuntu lets you install to the hard disk by simply clicking a single icon and following the instructions—one disk to run them all.

If you don't already have the desktop CD running, pop it into your DVD/CD drive, and reboot your computer. If your computer does not boot from the CD, you should enter your computer's BIOS and change the boot order to ensure that your CD-ROM drive is tried first and the hard disk is tried next. Save your BIOS changes, and then restart again. The disk should boot now.

TIP   **BIOS Problems**
If you have problems configuring your BIOS to boot from the CD, you should consult the manual. If you don't have the manual, visit the manufacturer's Web site, and see if you can download the manual.

After a few seconds the Ubuntu logo appears and the top option is Start Ubuntu. Click Enter to select this option, and Ubuntu will begin to boot. After a minute or so the Ubuntu desktop will appear, and you can use the system right away. Under this scenario, the system is running from the CD and will not touch your hard disk. Do bear in mind, however, that because

Ubuntu is running from the CD, it will run slower than if it were installed to your hard disk.

If you decide you want to install the system permanently on your computer's hard disk, double-click the Install System Permanently icon located in the top left corner of the screen. An installer application appears that walks you through the different steps to permanently install your Ubuntu system. We will run through each of these pages in turn now.

TIP   **Time to Back It Up!**
Clicking the Install System Permanently icon will install Ubuntu on your hard disk. It is recommended that you back up any important files before you perform the installation.

Language

In the screen shown in Figure 2-1 you select the language for your Ubuntu system.

Ubuntu supports a huge range of different languages. Select your language from the list on the left, and then click Forward to continue.

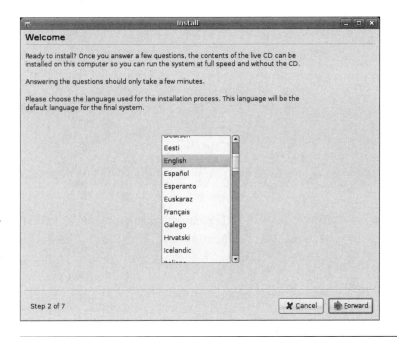

Figure 2-1 Pick your language.

Figure 2-2 Select the correct keyboard to ensure the symbols on the keys work correctly.

Configure Your Keyboard

The next screen (shown in Figure 2-2) configures your keyboard.

Choose your country from the list to select your keyboard layout. You can also use the box at the bottom of the window to test whether your keyboard layout works. Try typing some of the symbols on your keyboard (such as ", /, |) to make sure they work. If you press a symbol and a different one appears, you have selected the wrong keyboard layout.

Location

Now you can tell the installer where in the world you live (see Figure 2-3).

You can select your location in one of several ways. First, you can hover your mouse over the red dots in your part of the world to select the nearest location. When you are happy with the location, click it, and the map zooms in. You can then select the city nearest to you. Alternatively, use the Nearest City combo box to find the city nearest to you.

When you are done, click Next to continue.

Figure 2-3 Clicking the map zooms in, allowing you to select a location more easily.

Identification

The next step is to add some details about you that can be used to create a user account on the computer (see Figure 2-4).

First fill in the Real Name box. The information from this box is used in different parts of the system to indicate who the user is behind the account.

Next add a username in the Username box. Your username should be something easy to remember. Many people use either their first name or add an initial (such as jbacon or jonob). Each username on your computer must be unique—you cannot have two accounts with the same username.

Next add a password in the Password box, and then enter it again in the Verify Password box. This password is used when logging in to your computer with the username that you just created. When choosing a password, follow these simple guidelines:

- Make sure you can remember your password. If you need to write it down, keep it somewhere secure. Don't make the *WarGames* mistake of putting the password somewhere easily accessible and known to others.

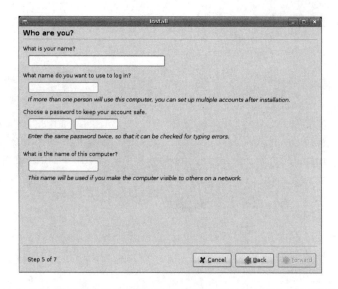

Figure 2-4 This user account is also used as the main system administrator.

- Try not to use dictionary words such as "chicken" or "beard" when choosing a password. One nifty way of keeping a password secure is to use a dictionary word but replace letters with numbers (e.g., "chicken" becomes "ch1ck3n").

- Your password should ideally be longer than six letters and contain a combination of letters, symbols, and numbers. The longer the password and the more it mixes letters, numbers, and symbols, the more secure it is.

Finally, add a hostname in the Hostname box. The hostname is a single word that identifies your current machine. This is used on a local network so that you can identify which machine is which.

Believe it or not, hostnames can be great fun. Many people pick themes for their hostnames, such as superheroes, and name each computer on their network after a superhero (Superman, Batman, Spiderman, etc.). Think of a fun hostname theme you can use.

When you have added all the information, click Next to continue.

Disk Space

The next part of the installation process prepares your hard disk for the software. This involves creating a number of *partitions* that store the Ubuntu system and your files. Hard disks are divided into partitions. Each partition reserves a specific portion of the hard disk for use by a particular OS. As an example, you may use the entire hard disk for your new Ubuntu system, or you may share the disk so that both Windows and Ubuntu are installed. This shared scenario is known as dual-booting. In a dual-booting situation, your hard disk typically has Windows partitions as well as Linux partitions, and when it boots it gives you a little menu so you can select whether to boot Windows or Linux.

In this part of the installer you create the partitions for your new system. This is the trickiest part of the installation, and also the most dangerous. If you have existing partitions (such as a Windows installation) on the disk, it is highly recommended that you back up your important files.

TIP   **Seriously, We Mean It**
Really, really, really do back up any important files. If you make a mistake in this part of the installation, you could lose your files and stop your system from booting.

Deciding on Your Partitions   Before you create your partitions, you should get an idea of what you want to do. If you have a clear idea of how your hard disk should be partitioned, it is easier to get everything working and up and running quickly.

These are the common methods of partitioning:

- **Only Ubuntu on the Disk:** If you are only installing Ubuntu on the disk and are happy to wipe the *entire disk,* your life is simple. Ubuntu can do all the work for you.

- **Dual-Booting:** If you want to dual-boot your system with Windows or Mac OS X and Ubuntu, you can share the disk among your Ubuntu and Windows or Mac OS X partitions.

Irrespective of whether you only install Ubuntu or dual-boot, you will need to decide how Ubuntu is partitioned. Ubuntu requires at least two partitions (one for the system and one for virtual memory swap space), but you can use additional partitions if you want to.

Using the Entire Disk   If you are happy to erase your entire hard disk, just select the Erase Entire Disk option, and click Forward. You are then asked to confirm the actions. Click Yes to continue. That's it!

Manually Partitioning   Click the Manually Edit Partition Table option, and click Forward to continue. You will see the screen shown in Figure 2-5.

This screen has a number of controls that are used to create your partitions. First, the combo box in the top right of the screen allows you to select which hard disk to partition. Select the relevant disk to add partitions to. The disks are listed by device name in alphabetical order. As such, disk A (such as /dev/hda) is the first disk in the system. If you only have one hard disk in your computer, the disk is already selected for you.

The large rectangle in the middle of the screen shows the current partition setup on the disk. If you are installing on a blank disk you will not see anything, as no partitions have been added. Click this rectangle, and you are ready to go.

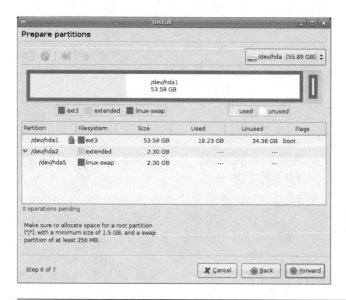

Figure 2-5 Main partitioning view.

Before you begin, you should prepare the disk for your partitions. Click New, and a box appears asking if you want to create an MS-DOS disk label. Click Create to continue. You are then asked if it is fine to destroy the data on the disk—click OK to continue. The disk is now filled with unallocated data. Now you can add your Ubuntu partitions.

To add a partition, click the unallocated space in the large rectangle, and then click New. A new window appears like that shown in Figure 2-6.

This window lets you configure a partition. The easiest way to do this is to use your mouse to move it around visually, and use the arrows on either side of the partition to stretch it to the correct size. If you would prefer to enter specific values, you can use the controls on the left side of the dialog box.

The Filesystem combo box is used to select which one of the many filesystem types you want the partition to use. The default filesystem included with Ubuntu is ext3, and it is recommended that you use ext3 for any Ubuntu partitions. Although ext3 is a good choice for Ubuntu, you cannot read an ext3 partition in Windows. If you need to create a partition that is shared between Windows and Ubuntu, you should use the FAT32 filesystem.

Add each of your partitions, and then click Forward.

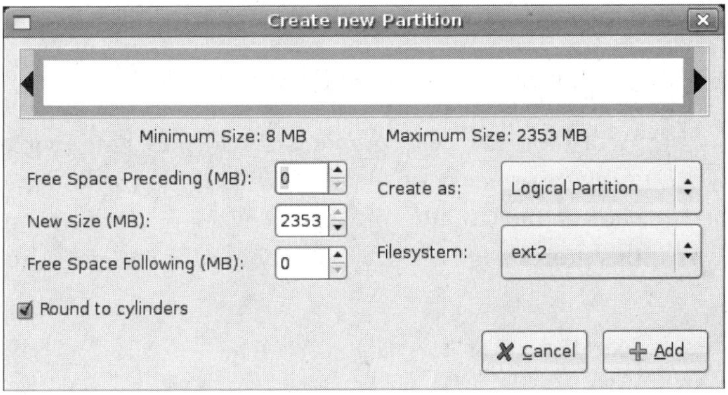

Figure 2-6 Configuring a partition.

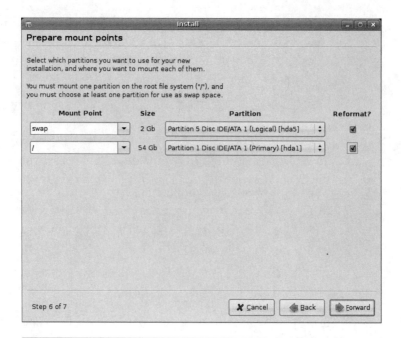

Figure 2-7 Mount points.

With the partitions added, you now need to specify what each one is used for. You will see the screen shown in Figure 2-7 next.

Use the Mount Point combo box to select one of the different mount points, and then use the Partition combo box to select the partition to which it applies.

Finishing Up

With the partitions complete, the installation is virtually done. You are given a summary of the choices that you made. When you accept these choices, the Ubuntu software is installed on your computer. At the end of this process, you are asked to reboot your computer. You are now finished!

TIP   **Better Use of Your Valuable, Valuable Time**
One of the great benefits of the desktop CD installer is that while the files are being copied from the disk, you can still use the system. Instead of sitting at your computer staring at the progress bar, you can play a few games to while away the time.

Installing Using the Alternate Install CD

Although the desktop CD is ideal for installing Ubuntu, you may want to use the traditional installer method to install the system. This method involves booting the alternate install CD, running through the installer, and then starting the system. This kind of installer is ideal for server installation or installation on older hardware.

To get started, put the CD in the drive, and restart your computer. When the CD boots you will see the menu shown in Figure 2-8.

Select the Install to the Hard Disk option with the arrow keys, and click Enter. After a few minutes, the installation process begins by asking you to choose a language. Select from the different languages by using the up and down arrow keys, and then use the Tab key to jump to red buttons to continue through the setup.

TIP   **Installing a Server**
If you choose to use the Install a Server Option, Ubuntu will install the software tools required for a typical server. This will not include any of the graphical applications or interface that come with the typical desktop installation. This makes Ubuntu ideal for running headless servers. See Chapter 5 for more details about running Ubuntu as a server.

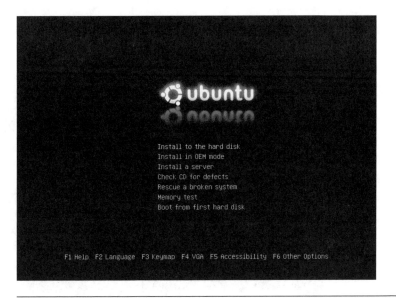

Figure 2-8 Alternate install CD menu.

Choosing Your Spot in the World

Next you are asked to choose your location (see Figure 2-9).

Pick which country you are in, and click Enter. This information is used to configure your time zone.

The next screen configures the layout of your keyboard. Keyboard layouts vary across the world to take into account the many and varied symbols and letters used in different countries. Even if you are using the typical Latin character set (as used in most European countries, America, Africa, and Australia), there are variations and additions (e.g., German umlauts). A keyboard layout is selected for you (e.g., British English if your location was set to United Kingdom), but the dialog box includes some additional options.

- **Find your layout by pressing some keys:** When you select this option you are asked to type in different letters, numbers, and symbols, and a keyboard layout is selected for you.

- **Select from full keyboard list:** Select your keyboard layout from the list.

- **Test whether this layout is correct:** This option allows you to type some letters, numbers, and symbols to double-check that the keyboard you have selected is the correct one.

With the language selected, your CD-ROM drive is then detected and scanned, and additional components are loaded.

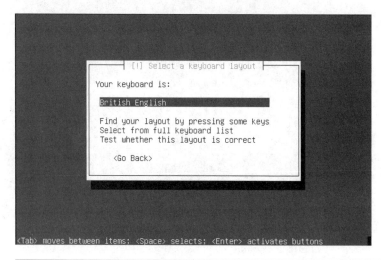

Figure 2-9 Select your keyboard layout.

Networking

Next an attempt is made to detect any network hardware and configure your network access. If you are connected to a wireless or wired network and are automatically assigned an IP address with DHCP, your network settings are automatically configured. If you are connecting wirelessly and need to enter a password for the WEP key, you are asked for one.

TIP   **WEP Passwords**
If you are entering an ASCII WEP password, prefix it with s: (e.g., s:theboinggreed).

In some cases there is a problem, and your network hardware or network settings cannot be automatically configured. This can be either because your network card is not supported by Ubuntu or because Ubuntu could not connect to a network. Don't worry too much about this at the moment as you can configure the network later when you boot your computer. See Chapter 6 for details about solving networking problems.

QUCIK TIP   The wpa, atheros (madwifi), ndiswrapper, and bcm43xx modules are not supported during the installation but do work afterward.

You are next asked for a hostname for the computer (see Figure 2-10).

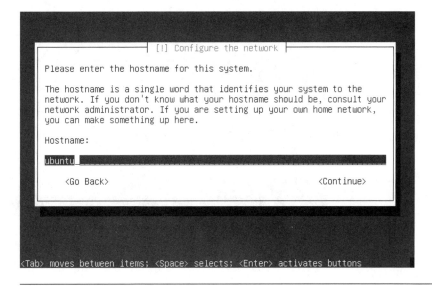

Figure 2-10 The hostname is used to identify you on your local area network.

Use the text box to add your own hostname, or use the default Ubuntu hostname if required. Feel free to let your imagination go wild, and create a theme for your hostnames (such as superheroes). Each host on your network can be related to that theme (e.g., Superman, Batman, Spiderman).

Creating Partitions

Creating partitions is the most challenging part of the installation routine. Before you partition your disk, think about how your partitions should be organized. You will see the screen in Figure 2-11.

You are given a number of partition options:

- Erase entire disk

- Erase entire disk, and use LVM

- Manually edit partition table

In the majority of cases, you probably want to use the Erase Entire Disk option. This will erase everything on the hard drive in your computer and set everything up for you. The second option, Erase entire disk, and use LVM, allows you to use Logical Volume Management (LVM). Finally, if

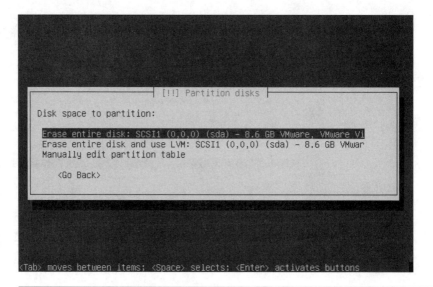

Figure 2-11 Partitioning disks.

you want to set up specific partitions, use the Manually Edit Partition Table option.

Let's look at each of these options in turn and how they are used.

Erase Entire Disk When you select this option, your entire disk is partitioned automatically. The installer will tell you that a primary and logical partition will be created, and then it asks if you want to go ahead and create the partitions. Click Yes, and you are done.

Erase Entire Disk and Use LVM Configuring LVM is covered in Chapter 5.

Manually Edit Partition Table Select this option if you want to create your own partitions manually. Here you can create a number of different types of partitions, set their size, and configure their properties. Creating these partitions is not done in the same graphical way as the live CD installer, and so it is a little more complex. However, doing so is still largely a process of selecting something and clicking Enter.

You are given a number of options with which to kick off:

- Configure software RAID
- Configure the Logical Volume Manager
- Guided Partitioning

QUICK TIP Discussion of software RAID and Logical Volume Manager is covered in Chapter 5.

Your disk is listed below these options, and it may display a few existing partitions. If you want to delete the existing partitions, select each one, click Enter, and select Delete the Partition. When you have deleted some partitions, you should see a FREE SPACE line. The FREE SPACE line is used to create new partitions. If the disk was empty already and you don't see a FREE SPACE line, select the hard disk, and click Enter. When it asks if you want to create an empty partition table, click Yes. You should now see the FREE SPACE line.

To create a new partition, select the FREE SPACE line, and click Enter. In the next screen, click Create a New Partition, and click Enter. Now enter the size the partition should be. You can use gigabytes (GB) and megabytes (M) to indicate size. For example, 4.2GB is 4.2 gigabytes, and 100M is 100 megabytes. You can also use a percentage or just add max to use the entire disk. Add the size, and then press the Tab key to select Continue. Click Enter. You are next asked whether the partition should be primary or logical. It is likely that you will want a primary partition. Make your choice, and continue.

If this is the first partition, you are asked if the partition should be at the beginning or end of the disk. It is recommended that when creating the root partition (known as /) on older computers, it should be placed at the beginning of the disk. This gets around some potential BIOS problems on older hardware. On newer computers, this is no longer a problem, and you can put the partition where you like on the disk.

On the next screen to display (see Figure 2-12) you can configure some settings for the partition.

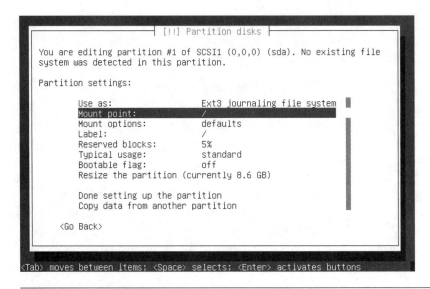

Figure 2-12 Setting partition options.

Table 2-1 Partition Settings

Setting	Description	Example
Use as	This is the type of filesystem. For a normal Ubuntu system, ext3 is recommended.	ext3
Mount point	This specifies what lives on the partition. See earlier in this chapter for details about the kind of partitions you should set up.	/
Mount options:	A number of options can be passed to the mount point, although the default setting should be fine.	defaults
Label	A text label describing the partition. Usually set to the same value as the mount point.	/
Reserved blocks	This is the percentage of the filesystem reserved for the super-user; 5% is a good default.	5.00%
Typical usage	This option can be used to optimize how the filesystem is organized, although the standard setting is typically used.	standard
Bootable flag	Does this partition contain the kernel and bootloader? If this is the root partition (known as /), set this to *on*.	off

The settings are run down for you in Table 2-1.

With the partition configured, click the Done Setting Up the Partition option.

You can now select FREE SPACE again (if there is free space left, of course) to create another partition. When you have finished partitioning, click Finish Partitioning and Write Changes to Disk option.

Configuring a User

The next part of the installation routine configures a user for the computer. This user role is important as it cannot only be used as a normal user but also has the ability to use *sudo* to perform system administrator tasks.

You are first asked to enter a full name for the user (such as Alan Clement). Next you are asked for a username, and one will be picked for you from your full name (such as alanc). If you want another username, enter it there. Finally, you are asked to enter a password for the user and asked to repeat the password for verification.

Finishing Up

At this point, the installation routine can now go away and install the system for you. After this the computer will reboot, and the installation is complete.

Post-Installation

Configuring the Login Screen

Although the default login screen is fine for most people, you may want to customize it. This could include changing the artwork to show your organization's logo instead of the Ubuntu logo, providing automatic login, or another type of customization. You can configure this screen by clicking System > Administration > Login Window.

The window that appears allows you to configure a number of different aspects of the login screen. Instead of discussing what each button does in exhaustive detail, it is more productive to cover how to configure particular tasks. By far the most important tasks are changing the artwork, automatic logins, and remote access.

Changing the Artwork   To change the artwork to your own you first need to create an image for your resolution. Find out your resolution by clicking Preferences > Screen Resolution, and then create an image for that size. Note where you save the image (such as in /home/jono), and then click Add in the Local tab to select the new image. The image is added to the list box. Now select the new image.

Enabling Automatic Logins   Click the Security tab, and tick the Enable Automatic Login checkbox. Now select the user to log in under from the User combo box.

TIP   **The Big S Word**
Always remember that automatic logins are a security risk. Someone could use your computer without you knowing it. If you are happy taking this risk, or if the risk is low because this is your personal computer, using this feature is fine.

Enabling Remote Graphical Logins One of the most powerful features in the X window system (the graphical engine that drives the Ubuntu desktop) is the ability to run graphical applications from a separate computer on your own computer.

By default, Ubuntu has this feature disabled. To enable it, click the Remote tab, and select Same as Local from the combo box.

You can connect to the computer with the following command (change the IP address to the relavant one):

```
foo@bar~$ X -query 192.168.0.2
```

This will run the remote connection on your current X server. To run it on another server, run this command:

```
foo@bar~$ X :1 -query 192.168.0.2
```

Setting Up Printers

Ubuntu has good support for printers, and the drivers for many common printers are already included. Printers come in two forms—local or remote—and Ubuntu supports both.

Remote printers are hosted somewhere on the network, and you can typically scan for these printers and have them configure automatically. To do this, click Global Settings and then Detect LAN Printers. A warning box will appear, indicating that a port will be opened on your computer that could potentially be used for malicious purposes. It is recommended you only run this scan on a trusted local network. If you don't trust the network 100 percent, cancel the scan. If you are willing to go ahead, click "OK," and after a minute or so the printers will appear in the box.

Local printers are printers that are attached to your computer. The vast majority of printers come with USB connectors now, and setup should just be a case of plugging in the printer and it being recognized and configured automatically. Plug in your printer, and then click the New Printer icon. If your printer is detected, you can select the Use a Detected Printer radio button, and then select the printer from the list. If the printer is not detected, select the port for the Printer Port combo box, and then click

Forward. On the next screen select the manufacturer and model of your printer, and then click Forward. Finally, click Apply.

To test whether or not a printer works, whether it is local or remote, right-click the printer icon, and click Properties. In the dialog box that pops up, click Print a Test Page. A page should then be sent to the printer.

If you have problems with printing, refer to Chapter 7 or visit http:// help. ubuntu.com/ or www.ubuntuforums.org/, and ask for help.

Summary

Congratulations on your new Ubuntu system. Whether you used the desktop CD or the traditional alternate install CD approach to get Ubuntu on your computer, you now have a powerful, extensible, and easy-to-use OS with a huge array of available software. Unlike other operating systems, Ubuntu includes a complete end-to-end software selection with a range of tools for office productivity, system configuration, Internet access, e-mail, and more. In addition to this impressive array of desktop software, your new system also includes an incredibly powerful underlying architecture that can be heavily customized. Those of you with a fondness for code and programming will also get a kick out of the millions and millions of lines of code that are freely available and spread among the different applications included. Ubuntu also provides extensive development tools for creating desktop applications, Web applications, and more.

You are at the start of an exciting journey, so let's get going. . . .

CHAPTER 3

Using Ubuntu on the Desktop

- Taking Your Desktop for a Ride
- Using Your Applications
- The Ubuntu File Chooser and Bookmarks
- Ubuntu in Your Language
- Customizing Ubuntu's Look and Feel
- Managing Your Files
- Ubuntu and Multimedia
- Summary

WITH UBUNTU INSTALLED and ready to rock, its time to get started using your new desktop. The stock install of Ubuntu provides a very complete and flexible system. Unlike other operating systems (OS), Microsoft Windows for example, Ubuntu includes everything you need to get started, such as an office suite, media tools, a Web browser, a graphics package, an e-mail client, and more. With the installation complete, you are up and running right away.

Using a computer is a rather individual process, and different people use their computers in different ways. To help promote this choice, Linux has the capability to use any one of a number of different graphical interfaces. This flexibility, combined with the ballooning popularity of Linux and Open Source, has resulted in literally hundreds of different graphical environments springing up, each covering these different types of users and ways of working.

Despite this huge range of different environments available, there are two clear leaders in KDE and GNOME. Both environments provide a comprehensive and easy-to-use desktop, but they differ in how that desktop is used. The KDE system is more akin to Windows and aims for complete configurability of your desktop. The competing GNOME desktop shows inspiration from both Windows and Mac OS X and sets as a priority simplicity and ease of use. Luckily, Ubuntu users are blessed with the choice of either desktop—the default desktop in stock Ubuntu is GNOME, and the Kubuntu distribution uses the KDE desktop. Kubuntu is covered in Chapter 7.

In this chapter, you get started with GNOME and use it to do the normal and not-so-normal things you face every day with your computer. This includes opening and running applications, managing your files, adjusting the look and feel, using applications, managing your media, and more. Buckle up and get ready to take your shiny new desktop for a drive!

TIP   **The Ubuntu Desktop is GNOME**
When reading about Ubuntu you often see the terms *Ubuntu desktop* and *GNOME* used interchangeably. Both of these terms refer to the same thing—the Ubuntu desktop uses GNOME itself. There is, however, the Xubuntu distribution, which takes the Ubuntu OS and replaces it for the lightweight Xfce environment. This is particularly useful for those of you who want to run Ubuntu on a lower-performance computer.

Taking Your Desktop for a Ride

When you start your Ubuntu system, you are asked for a username and password to log in with. In the last chapter you specified a user account when installing the system, so use that to log in. First type in your username and press enter, then your password and press enter.

TIP   **Language? Sprache? Langue? Lingua?**
Click the Options > Select Language button to change the language of the desktop. If you click the button and the selection does not include your language, jump to the Ubuntu in Your Language section on page 100 to add new language packs.

After a few seconds you will see the Ubuntu desktop appear (see Figure 3-1). The desktop comprises three main areas

- At the top of the screen is the *panel*. This bar contains the desktop menu options and application shortcut icons on the left side as well as the notification area on the right side. You use this bar to load applications and to see the status of certain activities on your system. The panel is always visible when you use your desktop.

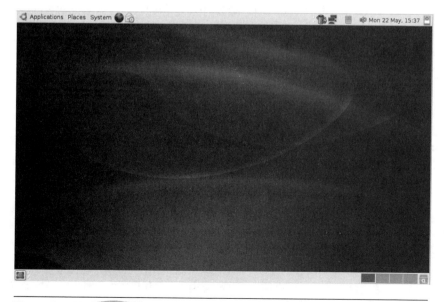

Figure 3-1 The Ubuntu desktop is simple, uncluttered and . . . brown.

▪ The large middle part of the screen is the *desktop*. This part of the screen is normally covered by the applications that you use, but you can also put icons and shortcuts on the desktop, too.

▪ The bottom part of the screen is called the *taskbar*. This area displays a rectangle for each application open just like in Windows.

You may have noticed that, unlike other OS, there are no icons on the desktop. The reason for this is that your icons typically get covered by applications, and, as such, you can't get at them. If you need to start applications, you typically use the Applications menu or the shortcuts.

TIP   **Device Icons**
Although there are no applications on the desktop, when you plug in USB devices such as portable music players, key rings, or digital cameras a device icon will appear on the desktop.

Starting Applications and Finding Things

Starting applications is simple. Just click on the Applications menu on the left side of the panel. Inside this menu are a number of submenus for different types of applications. Hover your mouse over each category, and then click the application that you want to load. As an example, click on Applications > Internet > Firefox Web Browser. After a few seconds the browser will pop up.

When applications are loaded, the brown window border has three buttons on the right-hand side:

▪ **Left button (thin white line):** This is used to minimize the application and put it in the taskbar.

▪ **Middle button (white square):** This maximizes the window to take up the full desktop area.

▪ **Right button (white cross):** This button closes the application.

Every application has an entry in the taskbar at the bottom of the screen. You can click these entries to minimize or maximize the application and right-click to see some other options.

Changing Your Menu Layout   Although the main Applications, Places, and System menus are logical by default, you may want to further customize them by moving entries into different submenus, not displaying certain items, and other tweaks. All of this is easily done with the built-in menu editor.

To edit the menus, right-click on a menu, and select Edit Menus. The menu editor now appears, as seen in Figure 3-2.

The menu editor is fairly intuitive. To adjust which items are shown, click on a submenu and deselect the items that you don't want to display. To add a new item, select the submenu the item should appear in, and then select File > New Entry. The box from Figure 3-3 will appear.

Figure 3-2 The menu editor lets you easily change the Ubuntu menus.

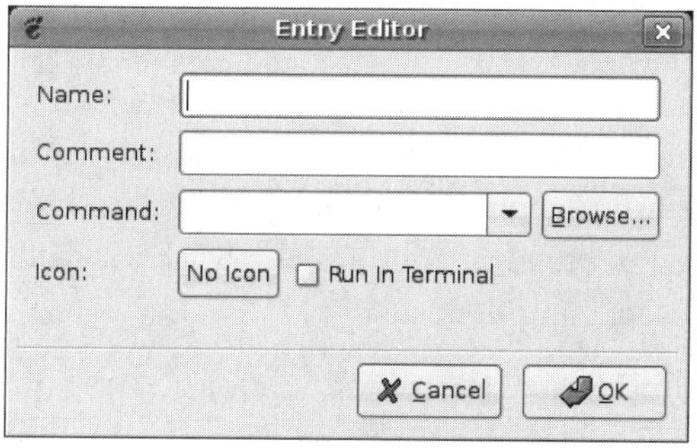

Figure 3-3 Feel free to add your own menu items.

In the Name box enter the name of the application you are adding. In the Comment box enter a brief description of the application, and then add the command to run the application in the Command box. You can also use the Browse button to select the application to run. Finally, click No Icon, and select an icon for the item. Click OK to finish adding it.

Find Your Files and Folders

When using your computer you often need to save and open files and folders, move them around, and perform other tasks. The Places menu contains a bunch of entries to access different parts of your computer and the network. These include

- **Home Folder:** Your home folder is used to store the files and work for each user who is logged in. This is the most important folder on the system, and you can think of it as the equivalent of My Documents in Windows—virtually everything you save lives here. Each user has a separate home folder.

- **Desktop:** The desktop folder is inside your home folder and contains files that visually appear on your desktop as icons. As such, if you drag a file onto your desktop, it will appear in the desktop folder and vice versa.

- **Computer:** Clicking this item displays the different drives attached to your computer as floppy drives, CD/DVD drives, and USB keys or sticks. This is the equivalent of the My Computer icon in Windows.

- **Network Servers:** This option accesses servers that are available on your local network. This is the equivalent of the Network Neighborhood in Windows.

- **Connect to Server:** Click this to run a wizard to create a connection to a network server. You can use this to add an icon to the desktop that, when clicked, provides a list of remote files in the desktop file manager. You can then treat this window like any other file manager window and drag files back and forth. This is really useful for copying files to other computers.

- **Search for Files:** Use this to search for files on your computer.

- **Recent Documents:** Click this submenu to display the most recently used documents.

Configure Your System

The third and final menu, System, is used to configure the system and customize your desktop. Inside the menu are two submenus.

- **Preferences:** This submenu contains items for customizing the look and feel of your desktop. Each of these settings applies only to the desktop of a user who is logged in. If you log in as another user, the settings change to that user's preferences.

- **Administration:** This submenu is used to configure systemwide settings such as networking, users, printing, and more. To use these menu items you need to know the system administrator password.

TIP   **Feel the Power**
When you installed Ubuntu, you were asked for a username and password for the system. This password not only provides access to your normal user account but also accesses the all-powerful Administration features. As such, when you access the menu options and are asked for the password just enter your normal password, and you can use them.

This feature only applies to the first user that you created on the system. If you add another account, the user cannot access the Administration options unless you explicitly give him or her access.

Shortcut Icons

On the panel there are a number of shortcut icons next to the menus. These small icons are always visible and can be single-clicked to gain immediate access to your favorite applications. Ubuntu comes with some stock shortcuts on the panel, but you are welcome to add your own.

Adding your own icon is as simple as finding the application you want to add in the menu and then dragging it to the panel. You can then right-click the new shortcut icon and select Move to move it to the right place.

Applets

One of the most useful features in Ubuntu is the ability to run small programs called applets on the panel. These small programs are useful for a variety of different tasks, and provide quick and easy access via the panel.

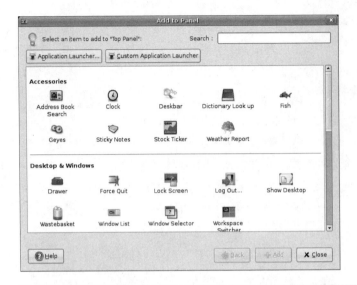

Figure 3-4 Ubuntu comes bundled with a selection of applets.

To add an applet, right-click the panel and select Add to Panel. The window shown in Figure 3-4 pops up. Select one of the many applets, and click Add. When the applet appears on the panel, you can press the middle mouse button (or the left and right buttons together) to move it around.

The Notification Area

In the top right-hand part of the panel is the notification area and the clock. The notification area is similar to the Windows system tray in that it provides a series of small icons that indicate something specific. A good example of this is the battery monitor. This small icon displays how much power your laptop has left, and when you hover the mouse over it you can see how much time is left before your computer gives up the ghost.

You can fiddle with the notification area items by right-clicking them to view a context menu. Some icons (such as the volume control) allow you to left-click on them to view them. Try clicking the little speaker icon and adjusting the slider.

QUICK TIP   Right-click the volume icon, and select Open Volume Control to access the mixer settings for your sound card. These settings configure the speakers, microphone, line-in, and any other sound card input or outputs.

The Clock

Next to the notification area is the clock. Click on the clock to view a calendar. Later, when you use Evolution, items that are added to your calendar appear in the clock applet too. Instead of opening up Evolution to find out when your dreaded dentist appointment is, just click on the clock to see it immediately.

QUICK TIP   Customize your clock by right-clicking it and selecting Preferences.

The Taskbar

The taskbar sits at the bottom of the screen. This small bar is always visible and indicates which applications are currently open. In addition to this, the taskbar also sneaks in a few other handy little features.

To the far left of the taskbar is the Hide/Show Desktop button. Clicking this button hides all of your open applications and shows the desktop. Clicking it again redisplays them. This button is useful when you need to quickly access something on your desktop.

Next to this button is the applications area, which shows each of the currently open applications. For each application, an entry is added, and you can right-click it to view a context menu. This menu is used to minimize, maximize, resize, close, and do other things to the application.

QUICK TIP   You can switch between multiple applications in Ubuntu just like in Windows by pressing Alt-Tab. When you press this key combination, a small window appears that can be used to switch between active applications.

To the right of the applications area are four small rectangles called the workspaces. Each of these rectangles represents another screen in which you can view an application. As an example, you may use your Web browser and e-mail client on the first desktop, talk to your friends on IRC and instant messenger on the second desktop, listen to your music in your audio player on the third desktop, and make notes in a text editor on the fourth one. You can then just click each virtual desktop to switch to it to access your different applications. Another useful tip is when moving applications between virtual desktops—if you have an application on the first desktop, just right-click the brown window or the taskbar entry, select Move to Another Workspace, and pick the relevant workspace number. The menu also has Move to Workspace Left and Move to Workspace Right options, too. This makes moving applications between your workspaces quite simple.

To the right of the workspaces is the wastebasket. Files that are dragged onto this icon are destined to be deleted. To fully delete these files, right-click the wastebasket and select Empty the Wastebasket.

TIP   **Usability and the Ubuntu Desktop**
Throughout the development of the Ubuntu desktop, great care and attention has gone into usability. As an example, the four corners of the screen are established as areas that are simple to access—you don't need to carefully mouse over the area and can instead just throw your mouse to the corner. This is why each corner has an important feature. It makes accessing each feature that little bit easier.

Ubuntu is filled with tiny usability improvements such as this that help make it as intuitive as possible.

Shutting Your Computer Down and Logging Out

To lock your screen, shut your computer down, log out, hibernate or suspend, and then click System > Log Out. You then will see the dialog box displayed in Figure 3-5.

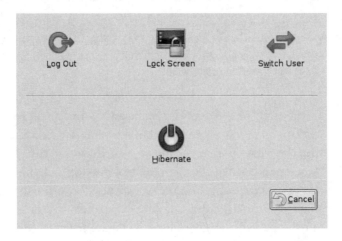

Figure 3-5 Who knew that logging out had so many possibilities?

There are a number of options here available upon log out.

- **Log Out:** This option lets you log out of the current session and go back to the main login screen.

- **Switch User:** When you click this option, your user account remains logged in, but another user account can be used. When the second account logs out, Ubuntu reverts to the original one.

- **Lock Screen:** This option locks the screen. This is useful when you need to use the bathroom or grab some lunch. It will lock the computer and ask for your password to reenable the desktop.

- **Sleep:** If your computer supports suspend, click this icon to suspend the power. The next time your computer is turned on, the desktop will be resumed.

- **Hibernate:** When you click this option, the current state of the system is saved to the hard disk and can be switched off. This is like the Sleep option, but slower and works on all computers.

- **Restart:** Click this to restart the computer.

- **Shut Down:** Click this to shut down your computer.

Using Your Applications

Now that you have gotten used to the desktop, let's explore some of the many applications included on your new system. By default, Ubuntu comes with a wide range of popular and established applications to listen to music, watch videos, create documents, browse the Web, manage your appointments, read your e-mail, create images, and much more. These applications have been vetted by the developers to ensure they are the best-of-breed Linux applications available.

Although Ubuntu includes a range of different software applications, it is likely you will want to install extra applications and explore other software that is available. Fortunately, the Ubuntu system is built on a powerful foundation which makes software installation as simple as pointing and clicking. Click Applications > Add Applications and a dialog box appears that you can use to install new applications. Just browse through the different categories and check the applications to install. Click the Apply button and the application is downloaded and installed for you.

This tool provides a simple way of accessing a limited core set of popular applications, but there are actually more than 16,000 packages available to your Ubuntu system. Software installation is discussed in detail in Chapter 4.

TIP   **Another Way of Running Applications**
Although you will most typically start your applications by selecting them from the Applications menu, you can also press Alt-F2 to bring up a box to type in the name of an application and run it.

Browsing the Web with Firefox

Firefox is the default Ubuntu Web browser and provides you with a simple, safe, and powerful browsing experience. Firefox has become one of the most successful Open Source projects in the world and continues to garner huge popularity. With more than 150 million downloads and rapidly increasing browser share, Firefox has been an unparalleled success. It really is that cool.

Fire up Firefox by clicking the blue earth shortcut icon on the panel or by selecting Applications > Internet > Firefox Web Browser. After a few seconds you are presented with the main Firefox window (See Figure 3-6).

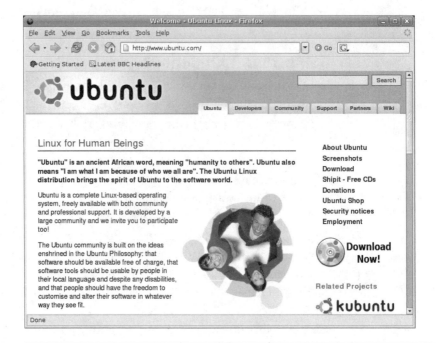

Figure 3-6 The Firefox interface is sleek but extensible.

The Firefox window looks similar to most Web browsers and includes the staple back, forward, reload, and stop buttons, an address bar, and some menus. These familiar-looking elements help you become familiar with Firefox, and if you have used Internet Explorer, Opera, Netscape, or Safari before, you are sure to pick it up in no time.

Navigating your way around the Internet is no different in Firefox than any other browser—just type the Web address into the address bar, and hit Enter. Firefox also has a few nice features that make it easy to access your favorite sites. As an example, if you want to visit the Ubuntu Web site, you can just enter www.ubuntu.com (leaving off all that http:// nonsense). Alternatively, you can just type in "Ubuntu," and Firefox will go off to Google, enter "Ubuntu" as the search term and take you to the first result in the search. This feature is incredibly handy for popular sites that are likely to be at the top of the search results page.

QUICK TIP The search box next to the address bar can be used to do a search on Google. Just type in your search term and press Enter. You can also choose other places to search (such as Amazon, eBay, etc.) by clicking the small icon and selecting a different option.

This search box can be used to search just about anything. To add more search engines, click the small icon and then select Add Engines.

Tabbed Browsing If you are anything like any of the authors behind this book, you look at a number of different Web sites each time you use the Internet. It is not uncommon to have your Webmail open as well as eBay, some discussion forums, news sites, blogs, and more. Before long, your desktop is littered with browser windows, and your taskbar is full to the brim.

Firefox has a nimble solution to this problem in the form of *tabbed browsing*. If you are looking at your friend's Web site about raccoons and decide you want to check out your favorite sports player's Web site, just click File > New Tab or press Ctrl-T and—ta-da!—a new tab is unveiled in your browser window. You can now load another page inside this tab.

The tabbed browsing fun doesn't stop though—oh no! When you are reading the Web and you see a link that you are interested in viewing, right-click the link, and select Open Link in New Tab. The page will load in the new tab, and you can continue reading the article and view the link afterward.

Bookmarking Your Favorite Sites   To bookmark the page you are viewing, click Bookmarks > Bookmark This Page. In the dialog box that pops up, use the combo box to select the folder to store the bookmark in. If you want to create a new folder, click the small arrow button on the right side of the box, and the box will expand. To create a main folder, select the bookmarks folder, and click New Folder. You can also create subfolders by clicking an existing folder and again clicking New Folder. When you have finished selecting or creating a new folder, click Add to add the bookmark.

Save Time with Live Bookmarks   Firefox also includes a special feature called *live bookmarks* that automatically grabs content from a Web site without your needing to visit it. As an example, go to http://fridge. ubuntu.com/ (a popular Ubuntu news site), and you will see a small orange icon on the right side of the address bar. Click this orange square, and a dialog box pops up to select where to store your bookmark. Use the default option (the toolbar folder), and click Add. A new toolbar button is added, and when you click on it a list of the items from the Web site are displayed. Each time you start Firefox, it will quietly go away and update this list so that you don't need to visit the site yourself.

TIP   If You Liked the Fridge
You may also like Planet Ubuntu at http://planet.ubuntu.com/. This site collects together the personal Weblogs of a number of different Ubuntu developers. Planet Ubuntu gives a unique insight into what the developers are working on.

Bolt It On, Make It Cool   Although Firefox is already a powerful and flexible Web browser, it can be extended even further using special plug-in extensions. These extensions not only cover typical browsing needs such as the Macromedia Flash plug-in but also cover other more specialized extras that extend the browser itself.

To install normal Web plug-ins, just visit a site that requires the plug-in. A yellow bar will appear indicating that you are missing a plug-in. Click the Install Missing Plug-ins button to grab the required plug-in. By default, Ubuntu does not come with the Macromedia Flash plug-in, so you will need to install this separately.

To extend the browser itself with additional features, go to https://addons. mozilla.org/, and browse for an extension that you are interested in. When you find something you would like to install, click the Install link. A dialog box will pop up asking you to confirm the installation. Click Install Now. Your new extension will now download and install automatically. Typically this requires a restart of Firefox, and then your extension is available.

TIP   **Be Careful Where You Download**
When browsing for extensions, it is recommended you only download extensions from http://addons.mozilla.org. If you do need to install an extension from another site, make sure it is a site you trust. Otherwise the extension may contain unsafe software, viruses, or spyware.

Creating Documents with OpenOffice.org

Included with Ubuntu is a full office suite called OpenOffice.org. This comprehensive collection of applications includes a word processor, spreadsheet, presentations, database, drawing editor, and math editor. The suite provides an extensive range of functionality, reads and writes Microsoft Office file formats, and can also export documents as Web pages, PDF files, and Macromedia Flash animations.

Let's give OpenOffice.org a whirl by creating a letter with it. Start Open Office.org Writer by selecting it from the Applications > Office menu. When it has loaded, you will be presented with the interface shown in Figure 3-7.

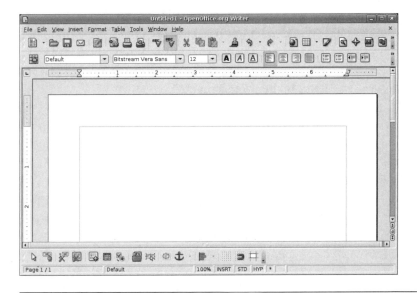

Figure 3-7 OpenOffice.org looks similar to Microsoft Office and is therefore quite simple to migrate to.

If you have used a word processing program before, much of the common interface elements such as the font type and size, bold, italic, underline, and alignment buttons look and behave the same. The OpenOffice.org developers have designed the suite to be easy to migrate to if you have used something such as Microsoft Office before. After a few hours playing with Open Office.org you are sure to know how to do what you need.

Start your letter by first choosing a nice font. In the font combo box you should see Nimbus Roman selected by default. Click the box and instead choose the lovely Bitstream Vera Sans font. Change the font size by clicking the combo box to the right of the font box and select 10 as the size. With the cursor currently on the left side of the page, add your home address to the letter.

Now press Enter to leave a blank line under the address and click the Align Right toolbar button (the icon looks like some lines aligned to the right). If you are unsure of what each button does, hover your mouse over it, and a tool tip pops up. Now add the address of the recipient.

Press enter again to leave a blank line, and type the main body of the letter. Feel free to use the bold, italic, and underline buttons to add emphasis to your words. You can also use other toolbar buttons to add items such as bullet points and numbered lists and change the color of the font. If you want to add features such as graphics, tables, special characters, and frames, click the Insert menu and select the relevant item. Each item that is added to the page can be customized by right-clicking it and using the items in the context menu.

When your letter is complete you can now save it by selecting File > Save, clicking the floppy disk toolbar icon or by pressing Ctrl-S. The default file format used by OpenOffice.org is the OpenDocument Format. This open standard file format is an official open standard and is used across the world. The file format is slightly different for the different types of application (.odt for word processor files, .ods for spreadsheets, etc.), but each format provides an open standard free from vendor lock-in. You can also save in a variety of other formats, including Microsoft Office.

TIP **Vendor Lock-In?**

In the proprietary software world, it is common for each application to have its own closed file format that only the vendor knows how to implement. When a person uses the software to create documents, the closed format means that only that specific tool can read and write the format. As long as you want to access your documents, you need that tool. This is known as vendor lock-in.

To combat this problem, the OpenOffice.org suite (and the vast majority of other Open Source applications) uses an open file format that is publicly documented. This means that other applications can implement the OpenDocument file format, and you can be safe in the knowledge that your documents will always be available and you are not locked in to any specific tool.

Another useful feature wedged into OpenOffice.org is the capability to save your documents in the Adobe PDF format. PDF files have been increasingly used in the last few years and are useful for sending people documents that they should not change (such as invoices). PDF files provide a high-quality copy of the document and are well supported across all OS. This makes PDFs ideal for creating catalogs, leaflets, and flyers. To save as a PDF file, click the PDF button on the main toolbar (next to the printer icon). Click the button, enter a filename, and you are done. Simple.

Managing Your E-Mail and Calendars with Evolution

Evolution has been modeled around the all-in-one personal information management tool. Within Evolution you can read your e-mail, manage your schedule, store contact details, organize to-do lists, and more in a single place. This makes evolution particularly useful for businesspeople who want easy access to this information.

Setting Up Your E-Mail Account To use evolution to read your e-mail you need to find out the following settings for connecting to your e-mail server (you can get these details from your ISP or system administrator):

- Your type of e-mail server (such as POP or IMAP)

- Your mail server name (such as mail.chin.com)

- Your mail account's username and password

- Authentication type (typically "password")

- Your outgoing mail server type (typically SMTP)

- Your outgoing mail server name

TIP   **Evolution and Webmail**
You can't use Evolution to read Webmail such as Gmail, Yahoo! Mail, or Hotmail unless you configure your Webmail to output as POP and use SMTP to send e-mail. Consult your Webmail provider for more details.

Load Evolution by clicking the envelope and clock shortcut icon from the panel (hover your mouse over the shortcuts to see what they are) or by clicking Applications > Internet > Evolution Mail. When the application loads you are taken through a wizard to set up your e-mail server (as shown in Figure 3-8).

Click Forward to continue the setup, and you will then be asked for your identity. Fill in your e-mail address in the E-Mail Address box, and add the optional information if you want to. The additional details are not essential for using Evolution. Click Forward to continue.

You are next asked to choose what kind of e-mail server you have from the drop-down box. When you make your selection, some additional settings

Figure 3-8 Setting up Evolution is simple so long as you know the details for your mail server.

are displayed. Fill in the server name and the username. You may need to adjust the Security and Authentication Type settings, but for most accounts the default settings should be fine. Click Forward to continue.

The next page configures some options for receiving your e-mail. None of these options are essential, although you may want to check the first box to automatically check for new mail. Click Forward to continue. The next screen configures sending e-mail. In the combo box select the Server Type (typically SMTP) and add the server name to the Server box. Click Forward to continue.

In the next screen enter a name to describe the account. The default entry (your e-mail address) is fine, but you may want to add something more meaningful such as "Work E-Mail" or "Home E-Mail." When you have added this, click Forward to continue. Finally, select your location from the map. If you click on your area of the world, the map will zoom in. Once you have done this, click Apply to complete the process and close the wizard.

With the wizard completed, the main Evolution interface will appear as shown in Figure 3-9.

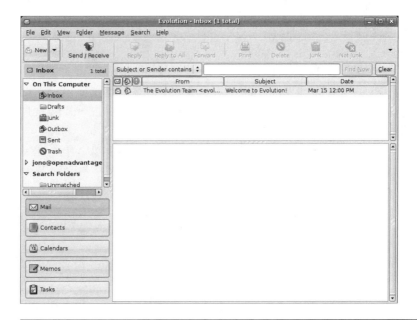

Figure 3-9 Those of you who have used Microsoft Outlook should find the interface very similar.

On the left sidebar you can see a number of buttons to access the mail, contacts, calendars, memos, and tasks components in Evolution. When you click each button, the interface adjusts to show you the relevant information about that component.

Working with Your E-Mail   Inside the e-mail component you can see the e-mail folders in the left panel and the list of messages in the top pane. When you click on a message, it is displayed in the bottom pane where you can read it. With your new account set up you will first want to go and grab the e-mail from your mail server. Click Send/Receive, and the mail is retrieved from your server and any unsent mail is sent.

TIP   **Problems?**
If you cannot connect to your mail server, there may be an error in your account configuration. To edit your account settings again, click Edit > Preferences, select the account from the list, and click Edit.

With you messages loaded, new e-mails are shown in bold in the top pane. Move through the different e-mails using the up and down arrow keys, and each message will be displayed. You can reply to a message by clicking the Reply or Reply To All toolbar buttons. New e-mails can be sent by clicking the New toolbar button. By default, new e-mails and replies are sent automatically when you click the Send button in the compose window. This way you don't need to click the Send/Receive button to deliver them.

Managing Your Calendar   Inside calendar mode, Evolution provides a convenient way of managing your schedule, adding new events, and viewing your calendar in different ways. When you click the Calendar button to enable this mode, you can see the timetable for today as well as the month view. The month view shows a couple of months in which the bold dates have events.

There are two types of events you can add to your calendar.

▪ **Meetings:** These are events with a specific group of people.

▪ **Appointments:** These are general events.

To add a new appointment, find the date for the event in the month view, right-click the Today view, and select New Appointment. In the box that pops up, fill in the Summary, Location, Time, and Description boxes. You can also use the Calendar combo box to select which calendar the event appears on.

TIP   **Multiple Calendars**
Evolution supports multiple calendars. This is useful if you want different calendars for different types of events such as personal and work-related activities. To create a new calendar, right-click the calendar list in the left sidebar and select New Calendar.

To add a new meeting, again find the date, right-click the Today view, and select New Meeting. Inside the dialog box that pops up, you need to add the participants who are attending the meeting. You can add participants in two ways: Use the Add button if they are not in your address book, or use the Attendees button if they are in your address book.

When you click Attendees, a new dialog pops up with a list of attendees down the left, and you can use the Add and Remove buttons to select a contact and add them to the different categories of Chairpersons, Required Participants, Optional Participants, and Resources. Now, you probably don't have any contacts in there as you are just starting to use Evolution, so use the main Contacts button on the left side of the main Evolution window to add some.

You can view your calendar in lots of different ways by clicking the different toolbar buttons such as Week, Month, and List. Play with them and see which ones are most useful to you.

QUICK TIP   Remember, your appointments can be accessed without opening Evolution by clicking on the clock in the panel.

Create Graphics with the GIMP

The GNU Image Manipulation Package, affectionately known as the GIMP to its friends, is a powerful graphics package. The GIMP provides a comprehensive range of functionality for creating different types of graphics. It includes tools for selections, drawing, creating paths, masks, filters, effects, and more. It also includes a range of templates for different types of media such as Web banners, different paper sizes, video frames, CD covers, floppy disk labels, and even toilet paper. Yes, toilet paper. You can load the GIMP by clicking Applications > Graphics > GIMP Image Editor.

Unlike Adobe Photoshop, the GIMP does not place all of its windows inside a single large window, and instead has a number of separate child windows. This can be a little confusing at first for new users. To get you started, let us run through a simple session in the GIMP.

An Example   Start the GIMP by clicking Applications > Graphics > GIMP Image Editor.

When the GIMP loads you will see a collection of different windows as shown in Figure 3-10.

Close the Tip of the Day window, and you are left with two other windows. The one on the left in the screenshot is the main tool palette. This window provides you with a range of different tools that can be used to create your images. The window on the right provides details of layers, brushes, and other information. The GIMP provides a huge range of different windows that are used for different things, and this is just one of them.

To create a new image click File > New. The window shown in Figure 3-11 will appear.

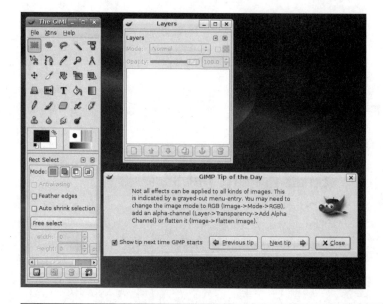

Figure 3-10 The GIMP does not put everything in one window like Adobe Photoshop.

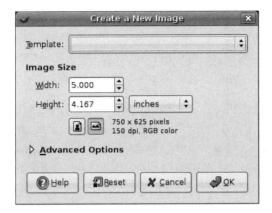

Figure 3-11 There are lots of templates available, including one for toilet paper!

The easiest way to get started is to select one of the many templates. Click the Template combo box and select 640×480. If you click the Advanced Options expander you can also select the type of color used in the image with the Colorspace box and how the background is filled. The Fill combo box is useful for either selecting a fill color or having a transparent background.

Click OK, and you will see your new image (Figure 3-12).

Figure 3-12 Use the right mouse button on the image to access lots of GIMP options and features.

To work on your image, use the tool palette to select which tool you want to use on the new image window. Each time you click on a tool in the palette, you see options for the tool appear at the bottom of the palette window.

When you click the T button in the palette, it selects the text tool. At the bottom of the palette you see the different options. Click the Font button, and select the Sans Bold font. Now click the up arrow on the Size box, and select the size as 45. Move your mouse over to the empty image, and you will see the mouse pointer changes to a text carat. Click in the image, and a box pops up in which you can enter the text to add to the image. Type in "Ubuntu." With the text entry still open, click the up arrow on the Size box so the text fills most of the window. As you can see, you can adjust the text while it is in the image. When you are happy with the formatting click Close on the text entry box. Your image should look a little like Figure 3-13.

Now click the button in the palette with four arrows on it. You can use this to move the text around. Click the black text, and move the mouse.

Let's now add an effect filter. The GIMP comes with a range of different filters built in. You can access these by right-clicking the image and selecting the Filters submenu. The GIMP also allows you to create scripts that combine filters together to create interesting combinations. Again, a number of

Figure 3-13 Ubuntu comes with a range of attractive fonts for use in your images.

these scripts are included, and you can access them by right-clicking the image and selecting the Python-Fu and Script-Fu submenus.

For our image, right-click the image and select Filters > Blur > Gaussian Blur. In the Horizontal and Vertical boxes select 20 as the value. Click OK to apply the effect. After a few seconds the blur is applied to your text. Anything in the GIMP can be undone by clicking Edit > Undo or typing Ctrl-Z. Your image should now look like Figure 3-14.

Now we are going to create another layer and put some text over our blurred text to create an interesting effect. In your image window, click Dialogues > Layers. The layers window now appears (Figure 3-15).

Layers are like clear plastic sheets that can be stacked on top of each other. They allow you to create some imagery on one layer and then create another layer on top with some other imagery. When combined, layers can create complex-looking images that are easily editable by only editing the layer you want. Currently, our blurred text is on a layer. Add a new layer by clicking the paper icon in the layers dialog box. Another window appears to configure the layer. The defaults are fine (a transparent layer the size of your image), so click OK.

Figure 3-14 There are lots of filters and effects bundled with the GIMP on your computer.

Figure 3-15 Layers are essential when creating complex images with lots of parts.

Now double-click the black color chip in the palette window and select a light color. You can do this by moving the mouse in the color range and then clicking OK when you find a color you are happy with. Now click the text button from the palette and again add the Ubuntu text. When the text is added it will be the same size as before. Now use the move tool and position it over the blurred text. Now you have the word "Ubuntu" with a healthy glow as shown in Figure 3-16!

Figure 3-16 Combining steps as we have done can result in interesting effects such as this.

The final step is to crop the image to remove the unused space in the image. Click Tools > Transform Tools > Crop > Resize and use the mouse to draw around the Ubuntu word. You can use the black pins on the outside of the selection to move it more precisely. Click Crop, and the image is now cropped. To save your work, click File > Save, and enter a filename. You can use the Select File Type expander to select from one of the many different file formats.

Communicate with Gaim

With the Internet steamrolling its way across the world, the ubiquitous global network has become a part of everyday life and something that you can reasonably assume people have access to. This has in turn spawned a range of Web-based services and interestingly, a variety of methods of communicating with each other.

Included with Ubuntu is Gaim, a cornucopia of different methods of instantly messaging your friends from within a single program. Instead of having to install a separate client application to talk to your friends on MSN, AIM, ICQ, and Jabber, Gaim can do it all in one place.

Gaim is available by clicking Applications > Internet > Gaim Instant Messenger.

Setting Up Your Accounts When you start Gaim, the first step is to create an account for each different type of network you want to use. Click the Accounts button on the main screen and the Accounts dialog box will appear. Click the Add button to add a new account, and the Add Account box appears (Figure 3-17).

This window adjusts which text boxes are available depending on the protocol chosen. The different networks available are listed as options in the Protocol box. To create an account you will need to have an existing account on one of the networks. Gaim allows you to have different accounts on different networks running together—you just create a new account for each protocol.

When you have selected a protocol, fill in the remaining boxes. The Screen Name box needs to contain your registered username (or e-mail address for MSN), and the password box needs the respective password to be added. You can also use the Alias box to add an interesting name that is

Figure 3-17 Many different types of account (MSN, AIM, Jabber, ICQ, IRC, etc.) are supported in Gaim.

displayed when other people see you online. If you want to configure any other options, click the Show More Options expander.

Using Instant Messaging   With your account(s) set up, click Sign On to log on. When you are logged in, your friends list (known as buddies in Gaim) are displayed (Figure 3-18).

Figure 3-18 Gaim provides quick and easy access to your buddies—just click them to talk!

You can use the Buddies menu option to add more buddies to the list with the Add Buddy option. To speak to a buddy, double-click the name, and a window will pop up.

Using IRC   Included in Gaim is support for IRC channels, and it has a very nice interface for IRC discussion. To use the IRC feature, first create an account. Next, sign on, and then click Buddies > Add Chat and enter the IRC channel name in the Channel box. Finally, double-click on the channel name to go to it.

Cutting-Edge Voice Over IP with Ekiga

Included with Ubuntu is a simple-to-use yet powerful Internet phone called Ekiga. Formally known as GNOME Meeting, Ekiga lets you make voice and video calls with other people across the Internet. In addition to the traditional Microsoft Netmeeting support, Ekiga now supports SIP, a protocol that is commonly used to allow people with software phones such as Ekiga to communicate with people using hardware Voice Over IP phones. SIP is an industry standard that many hardware phones, software phones, services, and providers support.

If you choose to use SIP, calls from one phone to another across the Internet are free. In addition to this, many providers allow you to make calls to normal landline phones for very little. Ekiga offers you the possibility to call anyone in the world directly from your computer with little fuss.

You can access Ekiga by clicking Applications > Internet > Ekiga Softphone.

Setting Up   When you first start Ekiga, you are guided through a setup wizard (Figure 3-19).

Click Forward to get started, and you see the next page (Figure 3-20).

In this box, enter your first and last name (such as Susan Curtis). Click Forward to continue.

You can now configure an Ekiga.net account (Figure 3-21).

At Ekiga.net, a free SIP service is offered. If you don't have an account (which is likely if this is the first time you have used Ekiga), click the Get an

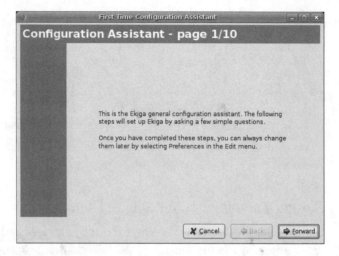

Figure 3-19 Setting up Ekiga is simple with the setup wizard.

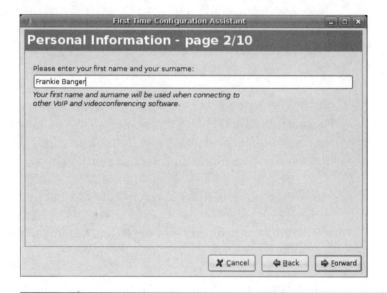

Figure 3-20 Adding your name makes it easier for people to find you online.

Ekiga.net SIP account button. Firefox is then loaded, and you can use the online form to sign up. If you don't want an account, just select the checkbox in the wizard saying you don't want to sign up. If you do sign up, add your username and password, and then click Forward.

Now you can configure your connection speed (Figure 3-22).

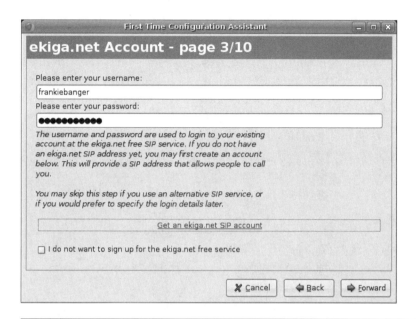

Figure 3-21 Ekiga.net offer a free SIP service.

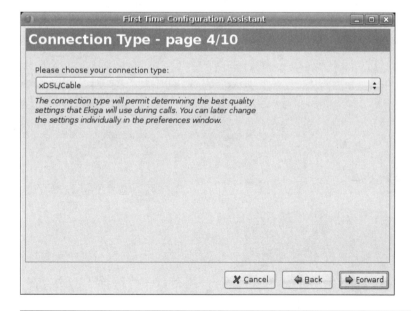

Figure 3-22 Be honest here—selecting a faster speed won't make it any quicker!

Just select the type of connection you have, and then click Forward.

Traditionally, one of the problems in the past with Internet phones has been that you need to modify your firewall (if you are running one) to get it working. This typically involved configuring your Network Address Translation (NAT) settings. Luckily, Ekiga can detect the type of NAT settings that you need (Figure 3-23).

After a few seconds of detecting your type of NAT it will propose an option. Click Yes to continue, and then click Forward.

Next, configure your audio (Figure 3-24).

Select ALSA from the box and click Forward to continue.

You can now select the audio input and output devices (Figure 3-25).

These settings are used to ensure that you can hear and record the audio. To test your settings, click Test Settings. If all is fine, click Forward to continue.

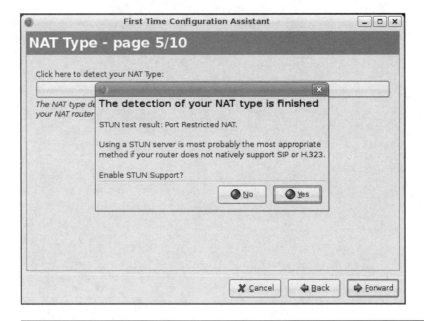

Figure 3-23 Traditionally, setting up NAT with Internet phones was a pain—until now.

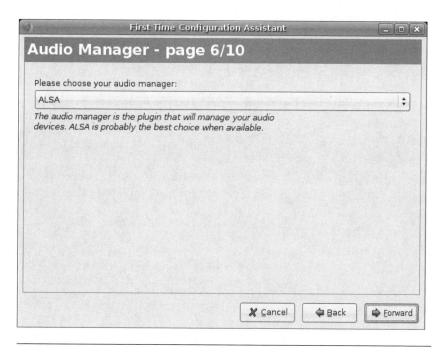

Figure 3-24 Ubuntu supports different types of audio frameworks, but the Advanced Linux Sound Architecture (ALSA) is the most common.

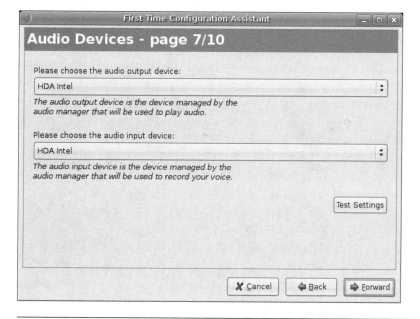

Figure 3-25 Make sure you get these settings right, or you won't hear anything.

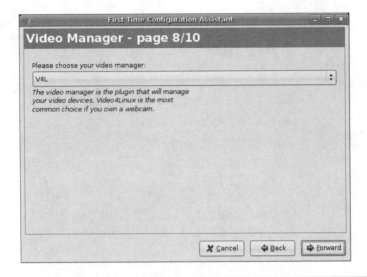

Figure 3-26 Ubuntu supports different types of video, but V4L is the most common.

Next select the type of video manager (Figure 3-26).

The video manager ensures that video is displayed correctly on your screen. Select V4L from the list, and click Forward to continue.

The final setting to configure is your Web camera (Figure 3-27).

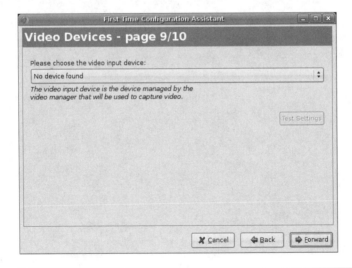

Figure 3-27 Remember to look your best online!

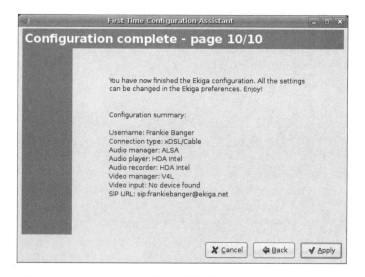

Figure 3-28 Now you are all set to make calls.

Ensure your camera is plugged in, and select a device from the combo box. If you can't see any options, you will need to configure your camera driver first. When you have selected a device, click Test Settings to verify that it works.

Finally, a summary of your options is displayed (Figure 3-28).

Ekiga is now configured.

Making a Call   With the configuration wizard complete, the main Ekiga window is displayed (Figure 3-29).

You are now ready to make a call. To do this, simply enter the phone number or SIP address of the person you want to call, and click the Connect button next to the address bar. The call is then connected, and you can begin talking.

On the left side of the window are a number of icons that do different things.

- **Text Chat:** When in a chat, click this icon to open the text chat window. You can use this to send text messages to the user.

- **View Mode:** Click this icon to select which view mode Ekiga is in. You typically need this when in a video chat with someone.

Figure 3-29 The Ekiga window is simple and sleek.

- **Address Book:** Click this icon to access the address book. Here you can save your contacts and you can also access the ekiga.net online white pages to see who else is online.

- **View Webcam:** This icon switches on the Webcam so that you can see the person you are speaking to.

In addition to these icons, there are some tabs located below the numeric keypad. Click these tabs to configure the audio and video settings for Ekiga.

Exploring the Ubuntu Landscape

Unlike many other OS, Ubuntu includes a comprehensive suite of applications right inside the system. This range of tools has been selected to allow you to install Ubuntu and get your work done, communicate with other people, read and create documents, watch and/or listen to media, and more. Unfortunately, due to space restrictions this book can only skim over the surface of available applications.

To help remedy this a bit, here is a quick summary of many of the applications included on the Applications menu in Ubuntu, including how to find the applications and a brief description

- **Text Editor**

  Applications > Accessories > Text Editor

  This simple, yet powerful, text editor is ideal for editing documents, making quick notes, and for programming. Included is a range of plug-ins for spell checking, statistics, file listings, and more.

- **Calculator**

  Applications > Accessories > Calculator

  For those times when you need to figure out a percentage or calculate whether you are getting a raw deal from your employer, the calculator is there. It provides a range of functionality for simple and scientific calculations.

- **Terminal**

  Applications > Accessories > Terminal

  Underpinning the desktop is an incredibly powerful command line core. This application puts a window around a command line interface and allows you configure transparency, fonts, behavior, and more. Essential for the command line junkies among you.

- **Dictionary**

  Applications > Accessories > Dictionary

  The dictionary provides a great way to find out how to spell a word or discover what the meaning is. The dictionary uses the latest definitions from an online dictionary. For those of you who spent hours as a child looking up rude words in the dictionary, hours of fun are guaranteed.

- **Gnometris**

  Applications > Games > Gnometris

  If you have too much time on your hands, a sure-fire way of wasting it is to play this version of Tetris. If you decide that single-player Tetris is not enough, go and download gtetrinet.

- **Nibbles**

  Applications > Games > Nibbles

  The classic worm game comes to Ubuntu. Another surefire way of whiling away an afternoon.

- **Mahjongg**

  Applications > Games > Mahjongg

  For those of you who actually understand the rules of Mahjongg, this application provides a great implementation of the game.

- **FreeCell Patience**

  Applications > Games > FreeCell Patience

  There is a body of thinking that suggests that FreeCell may be responsible for untold hours of lost productivity. If you are impatient about playing Patience, select FreeCell Patience.

- **Internet Phone**

  Applications > Internet > Ekiga Softphone

  Formally known as GNOME Meeting, Ekiga has experienced a raft of new features and been rebranded. You can use Ekiga for Voice Over IP and talk to your friends for virtually no cost across the Internet. With most Voice Over IP services and phones using the SIP protocol, the recent SIP integration in Ekiga means that you can join in on the fun. If you then roll in the video calling support, you are sure to spend hours with this great application.

- **Internet Relay Chat**

  Applications > Internet > XChat-GNOME IRC Chat

  Internet Relay Chat (IRC) provides a way of talking to other people on the Internet by typing text into discussion channels. There are literally thousands of users online and thousands of channels available. IRC has proven to be a truly useful tool for getting help about Ubuntu and Linux, too. Be sure to log onto the Freenode network, and visit #ubuntu.

- **Terminal Server Client**

  Applications > Internet > Terminal Server Client

  If you need to connect to a remote terminal server, this is how you do it.

- **Movie Player**

  Applications > Sound & Video > Movie Player

  Although listed as a movie player, this application actually plays a range of different types of media, including both video and audio.

- **Sound Recorder**

  Applications > Sound & Video > Sound Recorder

  If you need to record something, such as your voice for a podcast or audio message, you can use this simple tool.

- **Audio CD Creator**

  Applications > Sound & Video > Serpentine Audio-CD Creator

  If you have a collection of sound files that you would like to convert to an audio CD, this is the tool for you. This is particularly handy if you have a long drive and want to burn a CD with some music or podcasts to listen to.

- **CD Ripper**

  Applications > Sound & Video > Sound Juicer CD Extractor

  This application is the reverse of the previous one, allowing you to convert songs on a CD into songs that live on your hard disk or portable music player.

- **System Administrator Terminal**

  Applications > System Tools > Root Terminal

  If you want to run a number of commands as the system administrator, load this terminal, and you won't need to constantly use sudo.

- **System Monitor**

  System > Administration > System Monitor

  To get an idea of the current performance of your computer, click on this tool. The System Monitor lets you know which applications are running and how much memory/processing power they are using, and it also allows you to kill or restart processes that are hogging the resources.

Other Applications to Try   There are literally thousands of available packages that can be installed on your Ubuntu computer. These packages span a range of different areas, and this section covers some of the popular ones. Coverage of software installation appears in Chapter 4. Try these useful applications:

- **Blender**

  Package to install: Blender

  Blender (see Figure 3-30) is an incredibly powerful 3D modeling, animation, rendering, and production studio. Blender amasses an impressive range of functionality for creating photorealistic scenes, animations, and real-time virtual walkthroughs. Blender is also fully scriptable in Python.

- **Inkscape**

  Package to install: Inkscape

  Inkscape (see Figure 3-31) is a drawing package for creating Scalable Vector Graphics (SVG). Ever since the SVG format was introduced, it has taken the design world by storm and allows the creation of graphics that can scale to any size. Inkscape is a hugely flexible tool for creating such graphics, and a huge range of icons and artwork in Open Source projects are made in Inkscape.

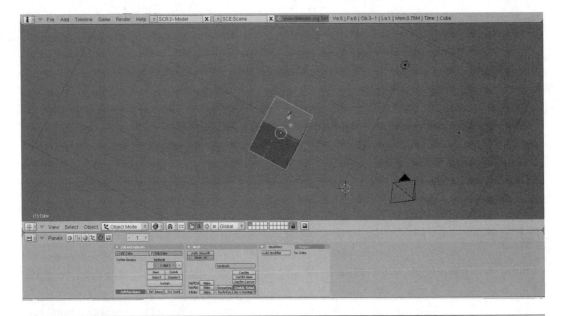

Figure 3-30 Blender.

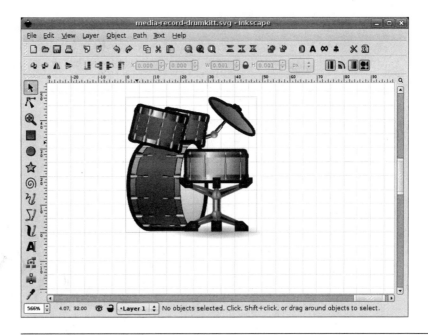

Figure 3-31 Inkscape.

- **Beagle**

  Package to install: Beagle

  Beagle (see Figure 3-32) is a search system that indexes virtually everything. When you install Beagle, you can search for "campfire," and it would return documents, images, Web pages, blog entries, instant messaging conversations, and more that contain that term. Beagle is still very much in development but is an incredibly useful tool.

- **F-Spot**

  Package to install: F-Spot

  F-Spot (see Figure 3-33) is a complete photo management application. With it you can import photos from your digital camera or USB stick, tag them with familiar terms, do touch-ups, and edit them in different ways. In addition to this, F-Spot can upload photos easily to Flickr and other online photo galleries. F-Spot is particularly useful for those of you who are trigger happy with a digital camera.

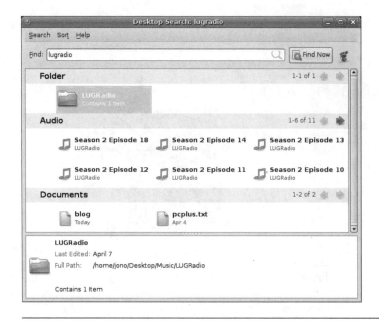

Figure 3-32 Beagle.

Figure 3-33 F-Spot.

Figure 3-34 NVU.

- **NVU**

  Package to install: NVU

  NVU (see Figure 3-34) is a complete What You See Is What You Get (WYSIWYG) Web page editor. NVU is ideal if you want to create Web pages visually without having to learn HTML and CSS code. NVU lets you create your pages and upload them easily.

- **Bluefish**

  Package to install: Bluefish

  For those of you who want to create Web pages but prefer to write code, Bluefish (see Figure 3-35) is an excellent Web editor. Bluefish is a lightweight but feature-rich editor with support for a range of languages as well as HTML and CSS.

- **Eclipse**

  Package to install: Eclipse

  If you are a developer and want an entire development environment, Eclipse (see Figure 3-36) is a good choice. Eclipse includes support for a huge range of languages by using plug-ins. This includes support

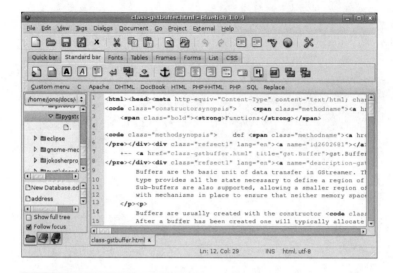

Figure 3-35 Bluefish.

for C, C++, Java, Python, Perl, Ruby, PHP, and more. Eclipse also has built-in support for source control (CVS or Subversion) and debugging, and automatically handles its own (and the plug-in's) software updates.

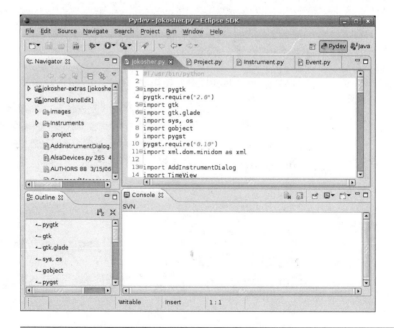

Figure 3-36 Eclipse.

The Ubuntu File Chooser and Bookmarks

One area in which the GNOME developers have worked hard is to create an intuitive and useful file chooser that is accessed in applications with File > Open. You may be wondering why they have spent so much time on such a small and seemingly insignificant part of the desktop. In reality, however, finding files is one of the most frustrating aspects of using computers and often involves digging through folder after folder to find what you need. Luckily, the GNOME file chooser helps cut down much of this file hunting significantly.

The file chooser is shown in Figure 3-37.

The listing of files on the right-hand side is used to find the file you need, and you can click on folders in this listing to traverse deeper into your subfolders. Note how each folder is displayed above the listing in a series of buttons. You can click these buttons to easily jump back to parent folders when needed.

Aside from manually picking files, the chooser also supports *bookmarks*. On the left side of the chooser there is a list of devices and bookmarks. These include Home (your home directory), Desktop (the files on your desktop), File system (the entire hard drive), as well as devices such as CD drives, floppy drives, and USB sticks.

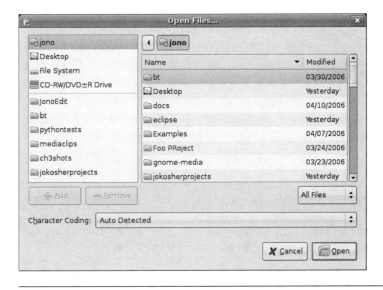

Figure 3-37 The file chooser has a number of subtle features such as bookmarks.

To create your own bookmark, use the listing on the right to find the folder that you want to bookmark, single-click it, and then click Add below the bookmarks box. The folder now appears in the bookmarks. Now whenever you need to access that folder, just click the bookmark! In addition to putting the bookmark in the file chooser, it is also available in other parts of the desktop such as the Places menu and in the file manager.

Ubuntu in Your Language

When you installed Ubuntu, you were asked which language the system should use. Although this sets the initial language for the system, you may want to change the language at a later date. To do this click System > Administration > Language Selector.

Ubuntu supports a huge range of different languages, and many applications include a Translate This Application menu option in the Help menu so that normal Ubuntu users can contribute translations in their language. If you would like to help with this effort, it is a fantastic contribution to the Ubuntu project.

When the language selector first loads, it may ask you to update your Language Packs. Just click Yes to continue. Inside the dialog box a number of languages are listed, each of which has Translations and Writing Aids checkboxes. For each language that you want available on the system, check the relevant boxes. The Translations box should be checked for menus, labels, and buttons to be translated, and the Writing Aids box should be checked to install dictionaries and grammar checkers.

When you have selected the boxes, click the Apply button, and the appropriate language packs are downloaded and installed. Now use the Default Language combo box to choose the new language. You need to log out and log back in for the changes to take effect.

TIP   **Choosing a New Language**
When you see the login screen, you can use the Language button to choose a language for that specific login session. When you select the language you are asked if you want to make it the default language or use it just for that specific session.

Customizing Ubuntu's Look and Feel

Whenever I have put someone in front of Ubuntu for the first time, there seems to be a uniform natural desire to tweak the look and feel of the desktop. In our increasingly diverse society, everyone is different, and everyone's tastes are equally individual and unique. It can be fun tweaking our desktops so they look just right, and Ubuntu has great support for all kinds of adjustments to your desktop. Do you want different-looking applications with a lime green background and crazy fonts? No problem, just don't show it to anyone else. . . .

Changing the Background

To change the background of your desktop right-click it and select Change Desktop Background. Inside the dialog box that appears, choose your wallpaper by clicking on an image, and the desktop background will automatically change. Ubuntu comes with a limited range of preinstalled wallpapers, so it is likely that you will want to add your own wallpaper. To do this, save your wallpaper somewhere on your computer, and then use the Add Wallpaper button to select it. The new wallpaper can be selected from the list.

If you are not really a wallpaper kind of person and would prefer just a color for the background, you can use the Desktop Colors controls at the bottom of the dialog box. The combo box provides three different types of background: Solid Color, Horizontal Gradient, and Vertical Gradient. Next to the combo box, click on the color chip to select the relevant color(s).

Changing the Theme

When you are using your applications, the visual appearance of the buttons, scroll bars, widgets, and other bits and pieces are controlled by the Theme. The built-in theming system can make your applications look radically different, and Ubuntu ships a number of themes with it that you can try.

Choosing a New Theme To choose a new theme click System > Preferences > Theme. Inside the dialog box that pops up are a number of themes that you can choose. Just click on a theme and the desktop will be adjusted automatically. You can further customize your theme by clicking the Theme Details button. A new dialog box appears that has tabs for the different parts of the theme you can configure. Click each tab and select an entry from the list to create your own perfect theme.

Installing New Themes To install a new theme, first head over to http://art.gnome.org/, and find a theme that you like. You need to look for Application Themes when browsing the site. When you find a theme that you like, download it to your computer. Now Click System > Preferences > Themes and click the Install Theme button. Using the file chooser, find the theme that you just downloaded and it will install automatically. Now select your new theme from the list.

Configuring a Screensaver

To choose a different screensaver click System > Preferences > Screensaver. The screensaver configuration tool then loads (Figure 3-38).

On the left side of the window is a list of available screensavers. Click on a screensaver and you will see a preview appear in the space to the right of the list. You can then use the slider to select how long the computer needs to be idle before the screensaver kicks in.

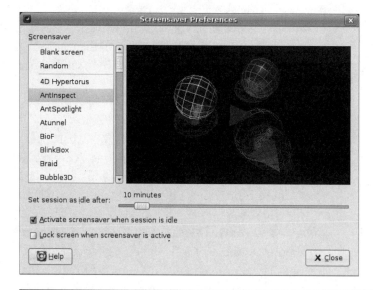

Figure 3-38 A number of screensavers are bundled with Ubuntu.

The Lock Screen When Screensaver Is Active checkbox can be selected to lock the screen when the screensaver starts and, as such, require the users to enter their passwords to reactivate the desktop. This is useful if you work in an office and want to ensure that no one tampers with your computer when you are away.

Managing Your Files

Files are the meat and potatoes of any computer, and they need to be managed, copied, moved, renamed, grouped, and loaded. Included with Ubuntu is a powerful yet simple file manager called Nautilus that integrates tightly into your desktop.

Nautilus makes extensive use of drag and drop. Unlike the kind of file manager used in Windows with its tree view and listing of files, Nautilus displays files in a series of windows in which you can drag files around easily. For those who just can't say goodbye to the tree view, Nautilus also supports that. Aside from providing a simpler user interface, Nautilus also includes a number of useful features such as video and image previews, emblems, bookmarks, permissions management, and more.

How Linux Stores and Organizes Files

Before we use Nautilus it would be worthwhile to have a crash course in how files and folders are organized on a Linux system. If you have not used Linux before, this is likely to be new to you as the layout is quite different from Windows and Mac OS X.

TIP   **Folder and Directories**
When reading about file management, don't get confused by the terms "folders" and "directories"—both words describe the same thing.

In the Windows world each disk drive is labeled with an identifying letter such as C: for your hard disk and A: for the floppy drive. In the Linux world, however, everything is part of the same file system organization. As such, if you have two or three hard disks, a CD drive, and USB stick all plugged in, they will all be part of the same folder structure.

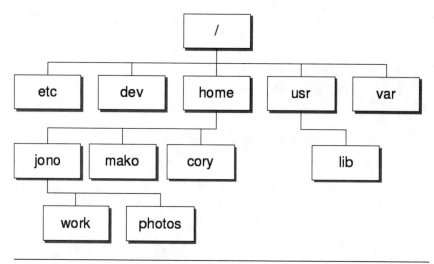

Figure 3-39 Linux file system organization.

The diagram shown in Figure 3-39 should give you an idea of how everything hangs together.

Right at the top of the tree is the root folder, referred to as /. Inside this folder there are a number of special system folders, each with a specific use. As an example, the /home folder contains a number of home directories for each user on the system. As such, the jono user account has the home folder set to /home/jono.

Which Folder Does What?   The folder structure in a modern Linux distribution such as Ubuntu was largely inspired by the original Unix foundations that were created by men with large beards and sensible sweaters. Although you don't really need to know what these folders do, since Ubuntu looks after the housekeeping for you, some of you may be interested in the more important folders. For your pleasure, we present the Linux folder hit list in Table 3-1.

Configuration Files   In the table, /etc is described as storing systemwide configuration files for your computer. Aside from these files that affect everyone, there are also configuration files for each specific user. Earlier,

Table 3-1 Linux Folders

Folder	Use
/boot	Contains important files to boot the computer including the bootloader configuration and the kernel.
/dev	Each device on your system (such as sound cards, Webcams, etc.) has an entry in this folder. Each application accesses the device by using the relevant items inside /dev.
/etc	Systemwide configuration files for the software installed on your system are stored here.
/home	Each user account on the system has a home directory, and they are stored here.
/lib	Important system software libraries are stored here. You should never need to delve into this world of the unknown.
/media	Media devices such as CD drives and USB sticks are referenced here when they are plugged in. More on this later.
/mnt	Other devices can be mounted later. Again, more on this later.
/opt	Optional software can be installed here. This folder is usually used when you want to build your own software. If you don't build your own software, you ignore this folder.
/proc /sys	Information about the current running status of the system is stored here.
/root	This is the home directory for the main superuser.
/sbin	Software that should only be run by the superuser is stored here.
/usr	General software is installed here.
/var	This folder contains log files about the software on your computer.

when you customized Ubuntu's look and feel, the settings were only applied to your current user account. So where are those settings stored?

Inside your home directory there are a number of folders that begin with a dot (.) such as .gnome2 and .openoffice2. These folders contain the configuration settings for specific applications for that specific user. By default these dot folders are hidden in Nautilus, as you rarely need to access them. For future reference you can view these hidden files and folders by clicking View > Show Hidden Files.

You can start Nautilus from a number of different places such as Applications > Accessories > File Browser or more commonly by clicking Places >

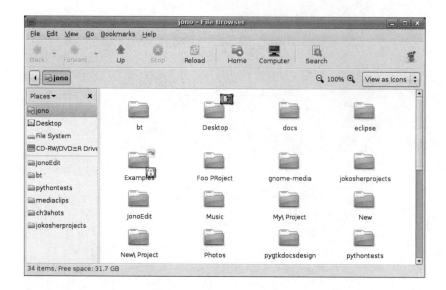

Figure 3-40 Accessing your home folder files is as simple as clicking Places > Home Folder.

Home Folder to load your home folder. When the folder loads, you should see something similar to what is shown in Figure 3-40.

The Nautilus window is split into two different parts. The sidebar shows categories of information such as bookmarks, folders, emblems (more on these later), and more. In the main part of the window you can see the sub-folders and files in the current folder. By default, Nautilus displays your bookmarks in the left sidebar and displays the contents of your home folder.

So, let's play with Nautilus and see what you can do with it. The first important skills to learn are general file management. Many of the tasks you need to do can be achieved by right-clicking your file/folder and selecting the relevant option. There are also a number of options in the Edit menu.

First create a folder. Do this by right-clicking the main part of the window and selecting Create Folder. A folder is added, and you can type in the name of it. If you change your mind about the name, rename it by right-clicking and selecting Rename. If you double-click on a folder, you can access it and perform the same operations in that subfolder.

Nautilus is also flexible in how your files are displayed. You can view the files and folders as either the default collection of icons or as a list. To switch to the list view, select View > View As List. You can also configure the organization of how your files and folders are displayed by right-clicking the main part of the window and selecting one of the options in the Arrange Items menu. Play with each of these options to see which ones work best for you.

QUICK TIP   Just like in the file dialog, Nautilus displays each of the different parts of the path as different buttons. As an example, /home/jono/work would have three buttons: home, jono, and work.

Selecting, Copying, and Moving Files/Folders

Copying and moving files and folders are simple with Nautilus and can be done in a number of different ways. To test this, create two folders in your home directory called Work and Invoices. Save some files inside each folder. You can quickly create empty files by double-clicking the folder to go into it, right-clicking, selecting Create Document > Empty File, and renaming the file to something useful. With a couple of folders now complete with files in them, let's move them around.

One method is to use two windows. Right-click the Work folder, and select Open in New Window. You now have two windows open, one with the contents of Work and one with the contents of your home directory. Now copy the Invoices folder to the Work folder by clicking it and dragging it over to the second window (which shows the contents of Work). By default, dragging from one window to another copies the item.

Another option is to select what you want to copy and paste it. Selecting items can again be done in a number of ways. One method is to click each file/folder while holding down the Shift or Ctrl keys to make multiple selections. The difference between the two keys is that Shift will allow you select a number of files/folders next to each other and Ctrl selects independent files and folders from anywhere in the folder-listing view. When you have selected what should be copied, right-click and select Cut or Copy. Cut will copy the original files but remove them and Copy will just copy them while leaving the original files intact. Now go to the destination folder, right-click it, and select Paste. The files/folders are now added.

Using the Sidebar

The sidebar in Nautilus can be changed to a variety of different views that should cater to virtually all tastes. Each of these different sidebar views has a range of different functions. Table 3-2 explains each one.

Although you will no doubt stick with one in particular, it is not uncommon to switch between options to achieve a particular task. For this reason, the flexibility provided by the range of sidebar options is useful.

TIP   **Drag and Drop**
If you want to put something in the Places view, drag and drop the item. The Ubuntu Desktop is filled with drag and drop shortcuts like this. If you think something could be dragged and dropped, try it!

Using Emblems

Emblems give you the ability to tag files and folders to indicate something. These small graphical icons are used to say that the file/folder falls into a particular category, visually signified by the emblem. As an example, you may want to tag a file to indicate it is a draft.

Table 3-2 The Different Nautilus Sidebar Options

Option	Feature
Places	This is the default view and includes the devices and bookmarks in the sidebar that you typically see in the file chooser.
Information	Displays some limited information about the current folder.
Tree	Displays a tree view similar to Windows/Mac OS X. Those of you who love the way Windows/Mac OS X works may want to use this.
History	Displays a history of the folders that you have clicked on.
Notes	This useful little feature allows you to write notes in the sidebar that are stored in the folder. This is handy when you need to explain or make comments about the current folder.
Emblems	List the files and folders that have specific emblems attached. Emblems are discussed separately.

When you select the Emblems sidebar, a range of different emblems appears. To apply an emblem to a file/folder, just drag the emblem onto it. You can drag multiple emblems onto the files to indicate multiple things.

Ubuntu and Multimedia

In recent years, multimedia has become an essential part of computing. Watching DVDs and videos and listening to CDs and music have become part and parcel of the modern desktop computer experience. These multimedia capabilities have been further bolstered by the huge popularity of legal music downloading. With a range of online stores for a variety of different types of music, it is not uncommon to listen to the majority of your music without ever seeing a little shiny silver disk.

Installing Codecs

Multimedia files and disks come in a variety of different types, and each type uses a special Codec to compress the content to a smaller size while retaining a particular level of quality. To play this media, you need to ensure that you have the relevant Codecs installed.

Unfortunately, Codecs have traditionally been something of a problem with Open Source software due to the legal restrictions placed upon them. The problem is that many Codecs (including MP3, Windows Media Format, QuickTime, and Realmedia) are proprietary and have restrictions placed on their use, distribution, and licensing.

Although developers in the Open Source community have gone away and created free implementations of these Codecs, the licensing that surrounds them conflicts with the legal and philosophical position that Ubuntu has set. Not only are these Codecs not included because they are legally iffy, but because they disagree with Ubuntu's ethic of creating a distribution that is entirely comprised of free software in the freest sense of the word.

QUICK TIP   If you want to find out more about installing these Codecs, see https://wiki.ubuntu.com/RestrictedFormats.

To work toward resolving these problems, a number of developers are working on free Codecs such as Ogg Vorbis and Ogg Theora that provide high-quality results and open licensing. The Ogg Vorbis Codec is used on audio and can provide better results than MP3 at a smaller file size. The Ogg Theora Codec is used for video and competes with the MPEG-4 Codec. Ubuntu includes the Ogg Vorbis and Ogg Theora Codecs, and you can encode and play back any media that uses those Codecs.

Although the world would be a better place if all Codecs were free, the reality is different, and many Ubuntu users still want to play their media on their new desktops. Table 3-3 shows the most typical Codecs used to encode and play back media, and lists their support in Ubuntu.

Listening to Audio Files

Ubuntu includes a powerful music player called Rhythmbox to organize and play your music file collection. Before you fire up Rhythmbox though, you need to create a folder to store your music files in. This folder can be anywhere, but putting it on the desktop makes sense, since it will then be easily accessible when you want to add new songs to it.

Right-click your desktop, and select Create Folder. A new folder is created, and you should enter a name for it. Call it "Music" for now. Within this

Table 3-3 Codec Support

Codec	File Type	Included	Supported
MP3	.MP3	No	Yes
Ogg	.ogg	Yes	N/A
Windows Media Audio	.wma	No	Yes*
Wave	.wav	Yes	N/A
MPEG-1	.mpg	No	Yes
MPEG-2	.mpg	No	Yes
Raw DV	.dv	Yes	N/A
Quicktime	.mov	No	Yes*
Windows Media Video	.wmv	No	Yes*
Realmedia	.rm	No	Yes*

*These Codecs involve the installation of nonfree software that may or may not be legal in your country.

directory, organize your music in a way that makes sense to you. A good system that many people use is to first give each artist/band a folder and then inside each folder have a subfolder for each album that contains the songs. So, as an example, inside the Music folder you would have an Overkill folder inside of which there would be a Horrorscope folder that contains the individual songs. You don't need to use this system if you don't want to, but as your music collection builds it makes sense to organize it this way. Many CD rippers also store songs in this way, so you should not need to reconfigure your CD ripper later.

QUICK TIP   Why not add your new music folder as a bookmark so it appears in the file chooser, Places menu, and elsewhere?

Using Rhythmbox   Load Rhythmbox (See Figure 3-41) by clicking on Applications > Sound & Video > Rhythmbox Music Player. When Rhythmbox first starts it asks you to select the directory where your music is stored, so select your Music folder. To import your music, right-click the Library entry in the left panel and select Import Folder. Your songs are added to your music collection.

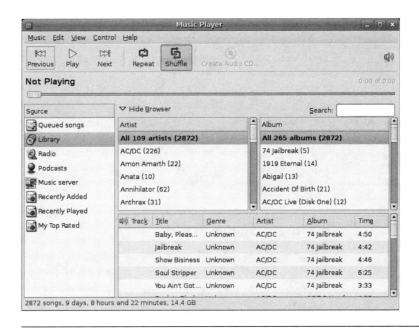

Figure 3-41 Rhythmbox is a great place to look after your music collection.

The Rhythmbox window is split into a number of different panes, each displaying different details about your music collection. The left pane (Source) lets you select the source of the music such as your media library, podcasts, and Internet radio. Each of these options has a browser pane available to display the source of the content. As an example, when you use the Library, a pane displaying the artists and one displaying the albums are displayed. You can use this to navigate your music.

Listening to Podcasts   Podcasts are audio shows that you can subscribe to, and they are increasingly becoming the new way to listen to audio and music. When you subscribe to a podcast, each new release is automatically downloaded for you. This makes it extremely convenient to regularly listen to audio shows.

If you are new to podcasting you should go and grab yourself a podcast feed of something you like. A site such as www.podcast.net is a good place to start. Go to the site in Firefox, and when you see a link saying podcast feed or RSS feed, right-click it, and select Copy Link Location.

Rhythmbox has good support for Podcast feeds, and subscribing to a feed is simple. In the sidebar, right-click the Podcast entry and click New Podcast Feed. Paste in the feed by right-clicking the box and selecting Paste. The files are automatically downloaded, and you can listen to them by double-clicking on them. Each time you start Rhythmbox a check is made to see if any new episodes exist, and if so, they are downloaded.

NOTE   **Rhythmbox and iPods**
Rhythmbox can also read songs from your iPod—just plug it in and it will display in Rhythmbox.

Unfortunately Rhythmbox can only read from the iPod at the moment and not write to it.

Playing and Ripping CDs

When you pop a CD into your CD drive, an application called Sound Juicer automatically loads to play your CD. If you are connected to the Internet, the CD is looked up on the Internet, and the album details and song titles are displayed.

Ripping Songs as Oggs   Sound Juicer is not just a CD player, but a ripper too. Using a ripper you can convert the songs on the CD into files that you can play on your computer. By default, Sound Juicer rips the files in the Ogg format, which provides better sound quality than MP3 at a smaller size. Before you rip the CD, click Edit > Preferences, and use the Music Folder combo box to select the Music folder that you created earlier to store your music files. If you have not set this folder to be a bookmark, you will need to click the combo box and then click Other to bring up the file chooser. By default the ripped files are stored in the format discussed earlier with each artist as a folder and then albums as subfolders.

To rip the songs just select the checkboxes of the songs you want ripped (by default all songs are selected), and then click Extract. Each song is then stored in your Music folder, and the song titles are used as the names of the files.

Ripping Songs as MP3s   Although the default Ogg support is recommended in most situations, you may prefer to rip MP3 files if you have a digital audio player that does not support Ogg files. To do this you need to configure Sound Juicer to enable MP3 support.

You should first install the gstreamer-10-ugly-multiverse package (from the Multiverse repository). Next, in Sound Juicer click Edit > Preferences and click the Edit Profiles button. In the dialog box that pops up, click New, call the profile MP3, and then select it from the list and click Edit.

Now fill in the settings with the following information:

- **Profile Description:** MP3 Encoder
- **GStreamer Pipeline:** audio/x-raw-int,rate=44100,channels=2 ! lame name=enc
- **File Extension:** MP3

Check the Active box, and click OK. Now close the Profiles dialog box, and click Close to close the Preferences box. Restart Sound Juicer, and you can now select MP3 from the Format combo box in the Preferences box.

TIP   **A Word of Caution**
Always, always remember that ripping CDs that are not yours is piracy. It's not fair, so don't do it!

Watching Videos

To watch videos in Ubuntu you need to ensure that you have the correct Codecs installed. As discussed earlier, some of these Codecs are available separately due to the legal implications of including them with the Ubuntu system. Refer to the Ubuntu wiki at http://wiki.ubuntu.com/ for details of how to install them.

Using Totem   To watch videos in Ubuntu, you use the Totem media player (see Figure 3-42). Load it by clicking Applications > Sound & Video > Totem Media Player.

To watch a video on your hard disk, click Movie > Open and select the file from the disk.

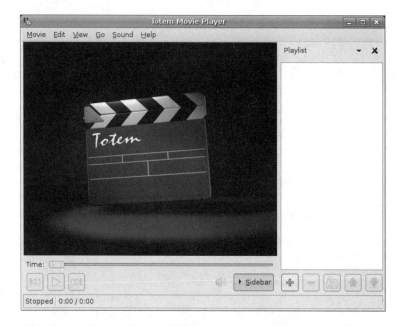

Figure 3-42 Totem is a simple and flexible media player.

TIP   **Another Way to Load Files into Totem**
You can also load multimedia files into Totem by double-clicking them on your desktop or in the file manager.

Totem also supports video streams. To watch a stream, click Movie > Open Location, and enter the Internet address for the stream. The video feed is then loaded and displayed.

Getting DVDs to Work   Ubuntu comes with DVD support for unencrypted DVDs. With the DVD industry being what it is, the majority of DVDs come encrypted, and if you want to watch them you need to ensure that a library that can decrypt these DVDs is installed. Unfortunately this library needs to be installed separately and is not included with Ubuntu. Refer to the Ubuntu wiki restricted formats page at https://wiki.ubuntu.com/RestrictedFormats for details.

With the library installed, insert a disk into your computer, and Ubuntu will automatically start Totem to view the disk. Alternatively, fire up Totem, and click Movie > Play Disk to play the DVD. Totem fully supports DVD menus and you can use the mouse to select the different menu options.

If you are settling down to watch a movie, there a few other settings you may want to configure. First click View > Aspect Ratio to select the correct aspect ratio for your screen, and then select View > Fullscreen to switch to full screen mode. To exit full screen, just move your mouse, and some on-screen controls will appear.

TIP   **Control Totem with a Remote Control**
Totem supports the Linux InfraRed Control (LIRC) library so you can use a remote control while watching your media.

Summary

In this chapter you've learned how to start using the core features of your new desktop. The concepts you have learned here should allow you to perform most of the day-to-day tasks when using your computer and provide a base from which to explore the other applications that are installed on your system. This solid grounding in the desktop paves the way for you to meander through the rest of the book, learning about the more advanced uses of your new system and exploring the enormous flexibility that Ubuntu provides.

Always remember that there is a wealth of help and documentation available online. If you ever find yourself stuck, take a look at the Ubuntu Web site at www.ubuntu.com/ or the Ubuntu documentation at http://help.ubuntu.com/ and make use of the forums, wiki, mailing lists, and IRC channels.

## CHAPTER 4

Advanced Usage and Managing Ubuntu

- Adding and Removing Programs and Packages
- Keeping Your Computer Updated
- Moving to the Next Ubuntu Release
- Using and Abusing Devices and Media
- Configuring a Printer in Ubuntu
- Graphically Access Remote Files
- The Terminal
- Working with Windows
- Summary

AS YOU'VE SEEN SO FAR, Ubuntu is relatively straightforward to set up and use for the common day-to-day types of uses. With time though, most users want to change their software, add and experiment with other software that Ubuntu has to offer, install and use hardware devices and printers, access remote files, use the famous (and sometimes feared) terminal, and may even want to run some Windows programs. Ubuntu provides many ways to do each of these things. While they are a little more complex than the material covered in previous chapters, the Ubuntu community has worked hard to make them as easy as possible, and this chapter shows you how to do all of them.

Adding and Removing Programs and Packages

While Ubuntu already includes most of what people need, sometimes you need something extra such as a desktop publishing application for school or a game to pass the time. The easiest way to add these is with Add Applications, which is extremely simple to use but has a few limitations.

Installing and Using Add Applications

By far the easiest way to install desktop applications is Add Applications, available at the bottom of the Applications menu. Like Synaptic and the other tools discussed in this chapter, Add Applications installs from the same online repositories. Thus, using one tool will cause the other tools to be able to recognize the same change.

To launch Add Applications, simply click on it like any other program in the menu. When it first runs, and occasionally afterward, it will initialize itself. This may take a few moments, so be patient. Eventually you will see the main screen shown in Figure 4-1.

The interface is divided into three parts. On the left is a list of all the various types of applications, laid out in the same way as the menu. Select a category to see a list of all the applications in that category in the upper right. Selecting an application in the upper right section will display a description of what that program does in the lower right section.

Add Applications also allows you to search, either by the program name, the "package" name, or in the description of the program. Enter the search

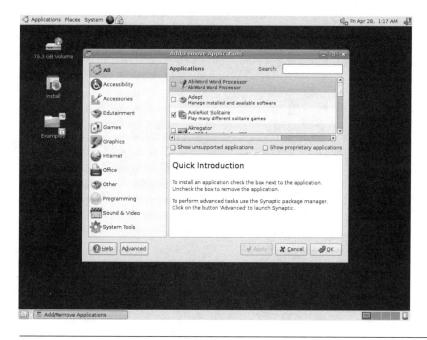

Figure 4-1 Add Applications main screen.

term into the text box in the upper right, and hit Enter. Figure 4-2 shows an example of search bar results.

By default, Add Applications will only show applications that are supported. These are applications in the main and restricted component (see Appendix B for an explanation of the different components of Ubuntu). While this is a large list, there are even more to find. By checking the box labeled Show Unsupported Applications in the lower left you will be able to see all the programs in the community-supported sections. After checking this option, the applications are available to view but will still need the actual online repository to be turned on. Simply selecting an application in the community-supported section will turn the repository on. Figure 4-3 presents the sequence of events involved in installing a universe application.

Additionally, Add Applications can list proprietary applications: those applications that are not released under a free Open Source license. Check the box, and they will become visible both via the listing and through search. As with any other application they can be clicked to install.

Figure 4-2 Search bar with results.

Figure 4-3 Sequence of events involved in installing a universe application.

Terminology

There are a few terms you might need to know before you start, such as words used to describe how the software gets installed on your machine as well as how the system works.

- **APT:** Advanced Package Tool, or APT, describes the entire system of online repositories and the parts that download them and install them.

- **Repository or Software Channel:** A giant online warehouse of software. In the Ubuntu world, these are divided between official Ubuntu repositories and nonofficial ones.

- **Packages:** Applications are stored in packages that not only tell about the program that you want to install but also what it needs to run and how to safely install and uninstall it.

Installing Using Synaptic

Synaptic is a powerful graphical tool called a package manager. While Add Applications deals with packages that contain applications, Synaptic deals with all packages, including applications, system libraries, and other pieces of software. Changing the system on this level is more difficult but allows more detailed control. For instance, you can choose to install a specific library if you need it for a program not available in a package format.

To find Synaptic, look under the System menu and then the Administration menu. It is listed as Synaptic Package Manager. Start the program, and you will see the main window, as shown in Figure 4-4.

TIP　**What's in a Name?**
Why the name Synaptic? Synaptic is a play on words, based on the word apt, which is the Debian package management system. Ubuntu is based on Debian and also uses APT.

Synaptic is a graphical package manager and works slightly differently than Add Applications. Unlike Add Applications, Synaptic deals directly with packages, which allows for a greater level of control while exposing the details of how package management works.

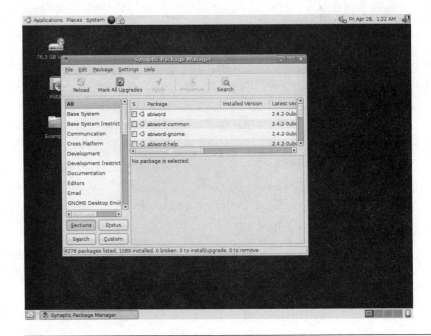

Figure 4-4 Synaptic main window.

Installing a Package   As with Add Applications, installing packages with Synaptic is fairly easy. After you find the package you wish to install, click on the gray box on the right, and choose Mark for Installation. A dialog box will pop up (see Figure 4-5) showing you what needs to be installed (if anything else is needed). After you have selected the packages you wish to install, click Apply to start downloading and installation.

Removing a Package   To remove a package, click on the green box, and choose Mark for Removal (see Figure 4-6). If you wish to remove all the configuration files too, choose Mark for Complete Removal. After you have selected the packages you wish to remove, click Apply on the toolbar to start the actual process of removing the package.

Updating Your System   Synaptic provides an easy way to update your system. Look in the toolbar, and first click Reload to make certain the package information is up-to-date. Then click Mark All Upgrades to mark all new versions for updating. Finally, click Apply to actually download and install the updates (see Figure 4-7).

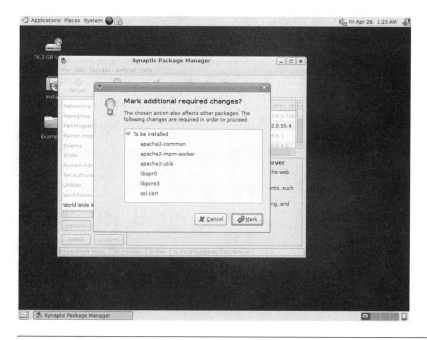

Figure 4-5 Pop-up on Mark for Installation.

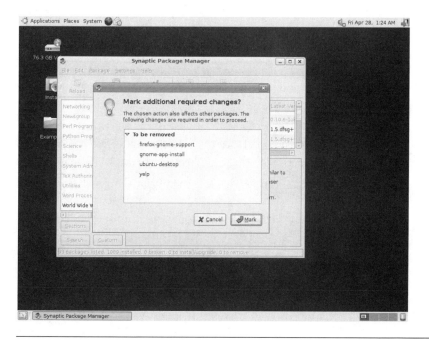

Figure 4-6 Mark for Removal.

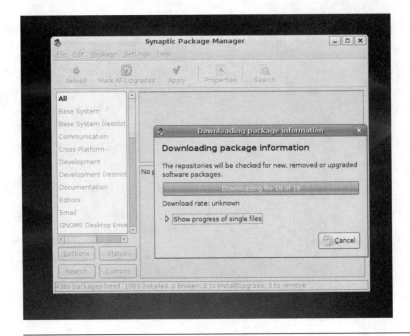

Figure 4-7 Updating takes three button clicks.

Finding That Package   So you are looking for a package but don't know where to start? The fastest and easiest way is to simply click the Search button on the toolbar or type Ctrl-F. That will launch a search dialog box. By default it searches both the package name and description, but it can also search just by name or a number of other fields.

If you know what section the package is in, select it in the left pane (you may need to go back to the Sections pane). Select the button in the lower right labeled Sections, and browse through the packages in that section. The upper right pane also has a neat feature called Type-ahead (see Figure 4-8). Simply select any package, and then start typing the first few letters of the package name. The cursor should jump right to that section.

Often a package will require other packages, called dependencies, in order to install. (See the beginning of this chapter for a more detailed look at programs, packages, and dependencies.) If more packages are needed, a pop-up will come up and list what changes are to be made. Sometimes installing a package can cause another package to be removed. Accept the changes by clicking Mark. Synaptic will not actually change anything until

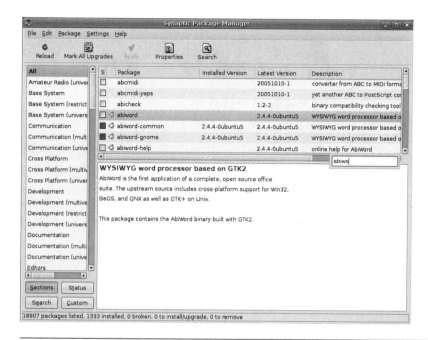

Figure 4-8 Type-ahead.

you click Apply on the toolbar. This is to allow you to line up a number of changes and then apply them all at once. After you click Apply, you will be warned about which packages are going to be changed. Click the Apply button, and watch Synaptic install what you want.

Keeping Your Computer Updated

No piece of software or operating system (OS) is perfect. What this means for you is that there will be a number of security and other updates that will be released by the Ubuntu developers. These come as needed and are quite easy to install.

Most of the updates to your machine will be security related. This means that the developers have found a flaw in a particular program in Ubuntu and have released a fix for it. There will also be a small number of updates to fix some critical bugs. For a home user, there is generally no reason not to install these right away, as not installing them might leave your computer open to security breaches, virus infection, or worse. Ubuntu developers also have a very strict policy about not putting new versions of

Figure 4-9 The security update icon.

programs into stable versions of Ubuntu, which keeps your system more stable by not introducing new problems.

Installing Updates

Helpfully, Ubuntu will tell you when you need to update your machine. Simply look for the icon shown in Figure 4-9 in the upper right of your screen.

In addition, a small bubble will pop up to alert you to new updates (Figure 4-10).

Click on the bubble or the icon to launch the update program. It will ask you for your password, and then show you a list of what you need to update. To start the update, click on the install button. The update window is shown in Figure 4-11.

Learning about What Was Updated

The update window will also show you specifically what is going to be fixed. In the details pane, it will show you what got fixed and how. It

Figure 4-10 The bubble making you aware of new updates.

Figure 4-11 The update window.

might also list a CVE number. The CVE number is a unique identifier for a security vulnerability. You can look it up on http://cve.mitre.org to see what the exact flaw was. However, in general you don't need to worry about these details.

Using Synaptic to Check for Updates

Synaptic need not only be used to manage packages but also to check for updates. When you launch Synaptic, it will ask you for your password. After it starts, first click on the Reload button in the upper left. This will prompt Synaptic to check the repositories for new updates. After it has finished, click Mark All Upgrades. This will prompt Synaptic to mark all software upgrades as those you want to install. If Synaptic does not tell you there are any updates to be made, everything is already up-to-date. If something requires updating, it will tell you which packages need to be updated. Close the window, and then click Apply. This will install any needed upgrades.

Figure 4-12   Synaptic preferences.

Sometimes the updater will tell you that it cannot update certain programs. This is because updating those programs would require the removal or addition of certain packages on the system. This is where Synaptic comes in. Synaptic is able to do what is called a smart update, which will figure out what needs to be added or removed. Synaptic will use smart update by default, and then you can just update as described in the previous paragraph. You can confirm that smart update is activated by going to Settings > Preferences (see Figure 4-12). Make certain that the system upgrade option is set to Smart Upgrade.

Moving to the Next Ubuntu Release

So now your system is up-to-date. But then you learn of a new Ubuntu release. Should you move to it, and if so, how do you do it? Well, to answer the first question you have to understand that Ubuntu 6.06, which comes with this book, is a little bit special. Ubuntu currently releases a new version every six months and supports those releases for 18 months. However, 6.06

is going to be supported for three years on the desktop. That means that you don't need to move from 6.06 until 2009 when security support runs out. However, 6.10 (due for release in October 2006) is only going to be supported for the normal 18 months.

So what does this mean for you? If 6.06 works for you and you don't like upgrading to a new version of Ubuntu every six months or so, I would recommend you stay with it until April 2009 when you can upgrade to the next long-supported version of Ubuntu. But if you like to see the latest stable versions, you can keep upgrading every six months.

Doing the Actual Upgrade

Until Ubuntu 6.06 came along, upgrading was not quite as easy as it sounds. There were a few text files you had to edit and then some manual tweaking to be done. The upgrade from 5.10 to more recent versions should be easier as there is now a graphical tool that tells you when a new version of Ubuntu is available, and it walks you through the upgrade process. Note that if you already know or want to learn the manual method that is fine, too. Both means will achieve the same result.

When a new release is available, the update manager will tell you that a new version is available. Click on the Upgrade button to start the process. You will first be shown the release notes, which mention new features or any outstanding bugs. After you click on the Upgrade button on this screen, the necessary changes to your software repositories are made and then the program will download and install the new distribution. You may be prompted if you have changed any configuration files. After the actual installation is complete, you will be told which packages are no longer supported (have moved to universe). Last, all you need to do is restart your computer when prompted, and you will shortly be enjoying the new release.

Using and Abusing Devices and Media

With increasingly cheap prices of hardware and media, typical computer users are burning more and more CDs, using more USB sticks, and rarely reverting to the old floppy disks that have dogged computing for so long.

The lack of floppy drives in modern computers has really symbolized the death of the rather limited, slow, and restrictive floppy disk.

Using these kinds of devices in Ubuntu is simple and intuitive. In many cases you just plug them in and work. Each device needs to be mounted before it can be used, but Ubuntu automatically mounts it for you. The main point to remember is to always unmount the device before you remove it. Even floppy disks should be properly unmounted before they are removed. Unmounting a device ensures all data has been copied to it before you pull it out.

TIP   **Problems Unmounting**
If you have problems unmounting a device, make sure that you are not currently using it. As an example, if you have a file manager window open looking at the files on the device, it is currently being used and, as such, cannot be unmounted. As a general rule, just make sure you close everything down from the device and everything will be fine.

If at any time you are unsure which devices are plugged into your computer, click Places > Computer to see a list of the drives available.

Using USB Key Rings

In the last few years, USB key rings, pens, and sticks have taken over as the commonplace solution for moving files between different computers. These cheap and often high-capacity little devices offer a simple and efficient way of carrying your files around with you. Although these USB storage devices come in many different shapes and forms, they all basically work the same way in Ubuntu.

Using USB storage devices in Ubuntu is a piece of cake. Just plug them in, and an icon to the device appears on your desktop. A file manager window to display the contents of the device also appears. You can interact with the device and the files as you would with the files on your hard disk.

When you have finished using your USB device, right-click the device icon that appeared on your desktop and select Unmount. When the icon disappears from your desktop you can safely remove it from the USB port.

TIP   **Copy Your Files to the Hard Disk**
USB comes in two major forms: USB1 and USB2, with the latter being far quicker. If you have a multimedia file such as an audio or video clip or another large file, you may want to copy it to a hard disk before you load it. Hard disks provide far faster load times than these other media.

Burning CDs

Burning files is simple in Ubuntu with its built-in support for CD writers. Simply pop a writable CD into the drive and an icon appears on the desktop. Double-click the icon, and an empty file manager window appears. Now drag the files to be burned into this window. When you are ready to burn the CD, click File > Write to Disk.

A dialog box appears, and you can configure a few items before the disk is burned. Enter a name for the disk in the Disk Name box and use the Write Speed combo box to select the best write speed for your drive. If you have an old or unreliable CD writer, you may want to select a slower speed to prevent a burn error. Finally, click the Write Disk button to start the burn.

TIP   **Quick Tip**
You can also access the burner by clicking Places > CD/DVD Burner.

Creating Audio CDs   Creating an audio CD from a number of audio files on your computer is simple with Serpentine. Load Serpentine by clicking Applications > Sound and Video > Serpentine Audio-CD Creator.

When the application loads, click Add, and navigate to your Music folder and click on the file(s) that you want to burn to the CD. To select multiple files, hold down the Shift or Ctrl keys while selecting.

With your songs added, click the Write to Disk button to burn the CD.

Burning a CD from an Image   With more and more people downloading Open Source software, installation disks are often released as downloadable .iso files. When you burn these files to a CD the files from the disk image are restored and the resulting CD just looks like a normal CD.

To burn an .iso file to a CD, simply right-click it and select Write to Disk.

Using Floppy Disks

To use a floppy disk in Ubuntu insert the disk in the drive and then select Places > Computer. Now double-click on your floppy drive to mount it and display the files. When you have finished using the disk right-click the floppy drive and select Unmount.

Using Digital Cameras

When you plug a digital camera into your computer, a device icon automatically appears on your desktop and Ubuntu pops up a window asking if you want to view the photos from your camera. You can then view the photos and drag them from the photo viewer window over to a file manager window to save the photo.

Always remember that the majority of digital cameras are just USB devices, and you can access the photos like any other USB device from within the file manager.

Configuring a Printer in Ubuntu

In the Linux world, configuring a printer has traditionally been a challenge. For years, newcomers to Linux have been repeatedly challenged and even bludgeoned with terms, commands, and phrases such as "CUPS," "lpd," "Edit /etc/cups/printers.conf as root." Users often had to edit fairly complex text files by hand and spend a good deal of time learning how to insert arcane instructions just to get a printer to work. Things have changed with Ubuntu, however.

Making It Easier with GNOME CUPS Manager

Although you will still encounter some challenges, Ubuntu has made configuring a standard home printer much easier with the GNOME CUPS Manager application. Using CUPS Manager, you can configure both locally attached printers as well as those that reside on a remote networked system. You can run this application by pointing your mouse to the System > Administration menu, and then clicking on the Printing option, as shown in Figure 4-13, below.

Selecting this option will bring up the Printers window, as shown in Figure 4-14.

Notice that no printers are defined. You are about to change this.

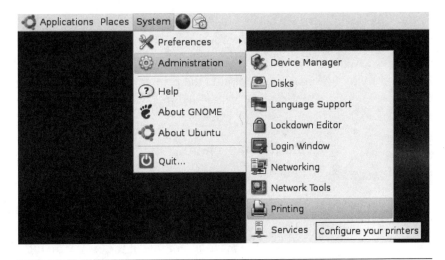

Figure 4-13 Selecting the Printing application from the Administration menu in Ubuntu.

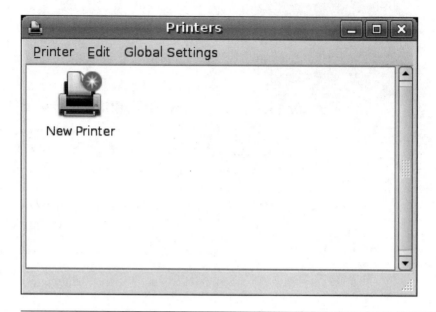

Figure 4-14 The GNOME Printers dialog box.

Note about Using GNOME

This section discusses using GNOME tools.

The GNOME CUPS Manager application allows you to add printers, as well as modify their settings. You can also use this application to monitor existing jobs, disable the printer, or restart it. In the example below, you will add a new printer and then view its settings.

Gathering Information

The most important thing to remember when configuring a printer is to not get ahead of yourself. Before you start clicking on icons and running anything, make sure that you have completed the following steps:

1. Obtain the make and model of the printer. In the example below, a Lexmark Z33 will be added.

2. Plug the printer in, and turn it on.

Sometimes you may not find the exact driver for your exact printer, as this case shows. For example, the printer being used is a Lexmark Z33, but the

Z32 driver is selected as no Z33 driver exists. Generally, if the driver does not exist for your exact model, choose the closest one, and then test it. If that doesn't work, try other drivers.

Launching the Wizard

Once you have properly prepared to install your printer, right-click New Printer, then click Add. If the Add icon does not appear, click on the Printer icon, then select Add. You will see the Add a Printer wizard, shown in Figure 4-15.

This discussion assumes that you are installing a local printer. Installing a network printer requires you to select the Network Printer radio button, then choose a networking protocol. If you have connected your printer to the computer and turned it on, it will be automatically detected, as shown above.

Once you have selected a printer or a port, click Forward. At this point, you will have to choose a printer driver. If your printer has been automatically

Figure 4-15 Step 1 for adding a printer in Ubuntu.

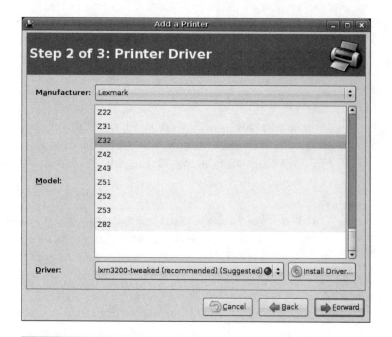

Figure 4-16 Selecting a driver.

detected, the wizard will choose a driver for you. This driver should work. You can always change it later. If no driver is selected, scroll through the list of options by manufacturer. Figure 4-16 shows how a driver for the Lexmark 33 (using the 32 driver) has been selected.

Click Apply, and the driver will be installed. If you need to install a custom driver, click the Install Driver button. You can see this button in Figure 4-16, above.

Finally, you can enter in a description and location for your printer, as shown in Figure 4-17.

Remote Printing

You can also configure your Ubuntu system to send print jobs to a remote print server. If, for example, you have a Windows system with a printer

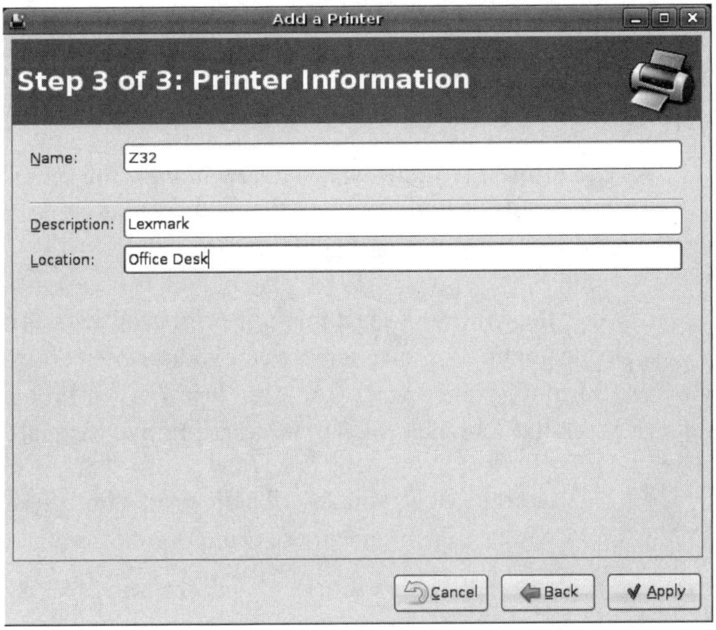

Figure 4-17 Entering printer location and description.

attached on your network, simply choose the Network Printer radio button and specify the host name or IP address of the Windows system. You will then have to specify a connection protocol.

If your Windows system is sharing a printer, you will have to specify Samba, which is the standard way to get Linux and Windows systems to communicate with each other. You will still have to specify a print driver, as described above.

Mission Accomplished!

After you click Apply, you will be able to print out a test page. Do so, and make sure that the page prints correctly. If you find that the page prints well, then you are finished. You can now print from the applications you have installed. For example, you can print from OpenOffice, Mozilla, or even the command line.

The Printers Window

Figure 4-18 shows the Printers window now populated with the printer you have just configured, in this case, a Lexmark Z33.

The Printers window will also let you view the status of printing jobs. If you double-click on the icon, you will see how you can view each printing job as it sits in a queue, ready for printing.

Once the window is open for your printer, click on Printer > Properties to bring up the Properties window for your printer. From here, you can check and modify the settings for your printer. The Properties window comprises five tabs. Below is a brief description of each tab:

- **General:** Allows you describe the printer and give its location. In some cases, you can choose printer resolution.

- **Paper:** Allows you to select paper size and type (e.g., A4, standard) and the paper source.

- **Advanced:** Settings that allow you to further customize page, resolution, and printing choices, including the number of copies to print per request, manual feed options, and toner usage (Figure 4-19).

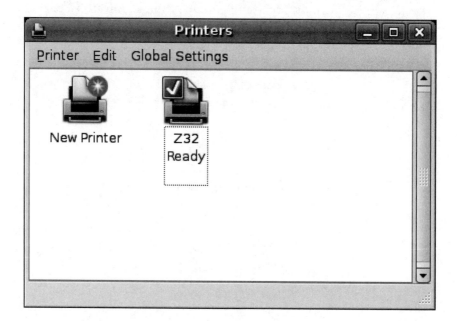

Figure 4-18 The Printers window showing the newly added Lexmark Z33.

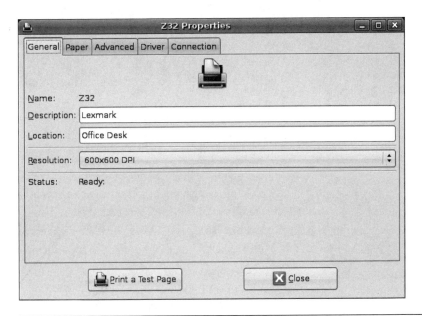

Figure 4-19 The printer Properties window, showing the Advanced tab.

- **Driver:** Allows you to specify the driver used by the printer. You can change values manually.

- **Connection:** Allows you to determine the particular connection type used. In the above example, a USB connection was chosen. If you move your printer to another port or connection type, you can change the settings here. You can even specify a network connection.

You can use these tabs to modify various settings. It might be easier to delete an existing printer icon and then start over rather than to edit all of these settings, especially if you plan on making a big change to your printer configuration. Still, editing these settings will help you fine-tune your printing needs.

Graphically Access Remote Files

Within the Ubuntu desktop, you can use the same powerful file manager to manage files that are on a remote server, either on your local network or in far-flung parts of the world via the Internet. This feature is incredibly useful when you need to transfer lots of files around, such as when you work on

Web pages or need to make your work remotely available to someone else. To access these files, you can connect to the server in various ways, each of which requires a connection profile. This profile configures the connection, and you will need to gather your server's settings to create it.

To set up the connection, click Places > Connect to Server and you will see the dialog shown in Figure 4-20.

When the dialog box appears, select the type of connection from the combo box. The box then adjusts to display the settings required, and you should make sure the Name to Use for Connection box contains a descriptive name for the connection such as : "Work Server" or "Web Site." When you have added the settings, click the Connect button to continue.

An icon now appears on your desktop for the connection. Double-click the icon, and you are asked for a password to the server. Enter this password, and you are then asked if you would like to store your passwords in the key ring. The desktop key ring provides a convenient place to store all of your connection passwords, and you only need to remember the password for the key ring itself. If you choose to store the password in the key ring, you are asked for a password for it. In the future, whenever you double-click the icon to access the server, you will be asked for the key ring password.

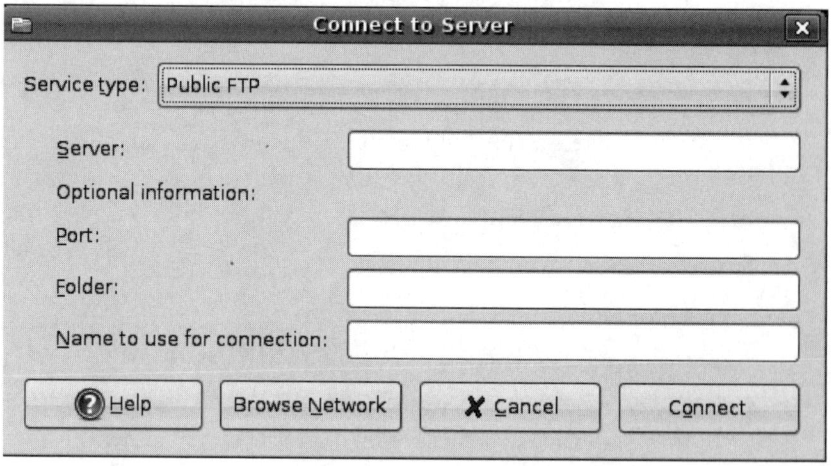

Figure 4-20 Access your remote server's files graphically on your desktop.

When you have been authenticated to access the server, your files appear in a file manager window, and you can use the file manager as normal.

The Terminal

Although Ubuntu is a desktop-driven OS, the system is running on a powerful and incredibly flexible command line core. Inspired by more than 20 years of UNIX heritage, the command line environment present on Linux systems enables you to perform some incredibly powerful tasks by stringing different commands together in different ways.

The philosophy behind UNIX is to create a large number of small tools, each of which is designed to do one task but do it incredibly well. As an example, there is a command called ls which does nothing more than list files in a folder. Although listing files is its singular function in life, it has every option imaginable for listing files.

Although ls is limited by itself, it can be combined with other commands that have equal levels of flexibility to create impressively powerful combinations. To do this a *pipeline* is created using the > symbol to hook these different commands together. Pipelines can be constructed in any number of different ways, and once the user has the knowledge of what the different commands do, stringing a pipeline of commands together can solve virtually any task you can imagine.

It should be made 100 percent clear that using the command line is *not* an essential skill required to use Ubuntu, but it is a skill that can increase the flexibility of your computer for more advanced, customized tasks.

Crash Course in the Terminal

Fire up the terminal by clicking Applications > Accessories > Terminal. You will see a terminal window similar to the one shown in Figure 4-21.

In the terminal window you can see the terminal prompt and a black cursor. The prompt shows your current username, the name of the host, and the name of the folder you are currently in. When you first fire up the terminal, the folder is shown as a tilde (~) which is shorthand for your home directory.

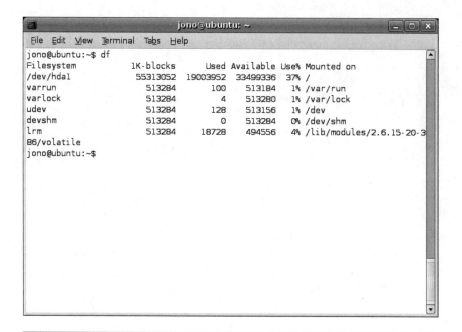

Figure 4-21 It is handy to drop in to the terminal when you need to tweak something in particular.

Getting Started First have a look at the files in your home folder by running the following command:

```
foo@bar~$ ls
```

The ls command lists the files in your current folder. The default command just displays a collection of items that are in your folder. To make ls more useful, you can pass it options:

```
foo@bar~$ ls -al
```

The -al parts are options that can be passed to the command. In this example, two options, a (list all files), and l (use a long display format to display file permissions, dates, sizes, and more) are used with ls to display all of the files (including hidden files) and their details.

TIP   **To Dash or Not to Dash?**
In many command lines tools, options are added following a dash (-). Some tools, however, don't need the dash.

Now jump to a different directory:

```
foo@bar~$ cd Desktop
```

The cd command changes the directory to the place you specify after the command (in this case, the desktop directory). A nice shortcut that you can use when typing files and folders is to type the first few letters and then press the Tab key to fill in the remainder of the file/folder. As an example, in the previous command you could type cd Des and press the Tab key to fill the rest of Desktop in.

When inside a directory, you may want to have a quick look at the contents of a text file. To do this, use the cat command:

```
foo@bar~$ cat myfile.txt
```

This command outputs the contents of the file to the screen.

As you can imagine, there are hundreds and hundreds of different commands available on the system, and we don't have the space to cover them here. There are a number of superb Web sites and books that you can use to find out about the many different commands.

Building Pipelines   The power of the command line really comes into its own when you start combining commands together into pipelines. A pipeline uses the pipe symbol (|) to string together a number of commands to perform a specific task. As an example, if you use the cat command to display the contents of a file to the screen, but the file scrolls past you, create a pipeline and use the less command to be able to browse the file:

```
foo@bar~$ cat foo.txt | less
```

To see how this works, break the command into parts, each separated by the pipe. The output of the part on the left (cat'ing the file) is fed into the less command on the right, which allows you to browse the file with the arrow keys.

Pipelines can be useful for finding specific information on the system. As an example, if you want to find out how many particular processes are running, run a command like this:

```
foo@bar~$ ps ax | grep getty | wc -l
```

Here you count how many "getty" processes are running (getty is the software that runs a console session). The `ps ax` command on the left lists the processes on the system, and then the `grep` command searches through the process list and returns any lines with the letters getty in them. At this point, only the lines with `getty` in them are returned. Finally, these lines are fed into `wc`, which is a small tool to count the number of words or lines. The `-l` option specifies that the number of lines should be counted.

Running Commands as the Superuser   When you log in to your computer, the account you use is a normal user account. This account is restricted from performing various system administration tasks. The security model behind Ubuntu is that you should run as a normal user all the time and only dip into the system administrator account when you need to.

To jump to this superuser account when using the terminal, use the `sudo` command. The command works by putting it before the command you want to run. As an example, if you want to restart the networking system from the command line, run:

```
foo@bar~$ sudo /etc/init.d/networking restart
```

The command to the right of `sudo` is the command that should be run as the administrator, but `sudo` lets you run the command as the current user. When you run the above command you are asked for the administrator password. This is the same password as the one you established for the first user you added when you installed Ubuntu on the computer. If you are using that user's account just enter your normal password.

When you have authenticated yourself to `sudo` you will not be asked for the password again for another 15 minutes.

Finding Help   Each command on your computer includes a manual page—or man page—that contains a list of the options available. Man pages are traditionally rather terse and only intended for referencing the different ways the command should be used. For a friendlier introduction to using commands a Google search is recommended.

To view a man page (such as the man page for `ls`), run:

```
foo@bar~$ man ls
```

The man page command itself has a number of options (run `man man` to see them), and one of the most useful is `-k`. This option allows you to search the man pages for a particular word. This is useful when you don't remember the command. As an example, you could find all commands related to processes by running:

```
foo@bar~$ man -k processes
```

Working with Windows

Although the Linux platform offers an increasingly compelling platform for the desktop, there are sometimes situations when there is just no alternative application available. This is often the case with specific business applications, educational tools, and games. Luckily, you can run many of these applications right on top of your Ubuntu desktop.

For the last twelve years, the members of the Wine project have been beavering away to create a free software implementation to run Windows applications on Linux. They have made great strides in getting more and more applications to run. Although there are often still quirks here and there, there are many programs that run perfectly under Wine. It is recommended that you try the applications you want to run before you use them for important work.

Install the Wine package with the Synaptic package manager. When the package has downloaded and installed, run the `winecfg` tool. To do this, press Alt-F2, and type `winecfg`. This small program sets up your Wine environment and provides some options for configuring how your Wine system is run. The default settings should be suitable for most applications.

Running Applications

To run an application right-click it, and select Open with Wine Windows Emulator. Most Windows applications need to be installed before use, so first right-click the setup program, and run it under Wine. When the program is installed, you can find it in the .wine/c_drive/Program Files folder in your home folder. Navigate to that directory (making sure you turn on hidden file viewing in Nautilus), and run any files with an .exe extension.

Using Windows Files on Another Partition

For those of you with a considerable amount of your life present on Windows partitions, you may want to be able to access these partitions from Ubuntu. This is no problem, although you will need to edit a special configuration file to do this. Luckily, you only need to edit this file once, and then everything will be set up.

You should first load Administration > Disks and write down the partition numbers and filesystem for your Windows partitions. The partition number will look something like /dev/hdb1 or /dev/sdb1, and the filesystem will be either FAT, VFAT, or NTFS. If you have a FAT or VFAT filesystem, you are in luck—you can read and write the partition. If you have an NTFS partition, you will unfortunately only be able to read from it.

The next step is to create some mount points. When your Windows partitions are enabled, they are accessed via a particular folder in Ubuntu. This is called a mount point. So, as an example, if you have a mount point as /media/win1 and on your Windows partition you want to access your Work folder, you would access it from Ubuntu as /media/win1/work.

Mount points usually live in the /media folder. Create a different mount point for each windows partition. As an example, if you have three Windows partitions, run the following commands:

```
foo@bar:~$ sudo mkdir /media/win1
foo@bar:~$ sudo mkdir /media/win2
foo@bar:~$ sudo mkdir /media/win3
```

Now open up the following configuration file:

```
foo@bar:~$ sudo gedit /etc/fstab
```

The /etc/fstab file maps partition numbers to mount points. At the bottom of the file add a line like this for each mount point:

```
/dev/hdb1 media/win1 vfat users,rw,owner,umask=000 0 0
```

You will need to change the partition number (the first column), mount point (second column), and filesystem (third column) for your relevant partitions.

Now reload /etc/fstab to enable the partitions:

```
foo@bar:~$ sudo mount -a
```

Some hard disk icons for the new partitions now appear.

Summary

In this chapter we looked at a variety of different advanced subjects related to running and managing your Ubuntu system. Installation, removal, and upgrade of software using the Add Programs dialog and using Synaptic were discussed. We've also discussed the installation and use of several different types of hardware devices, including an in-depth look at printing. We've perused some of the methods of accessing remote files and offered a crash course in the powerful Ubuntu terminal. Finally, we've looked at a possibility for running certain programs written for Microsoft Windows under Ubuntu.

## CHAPTER 5

The Ubuntu Server

- **What Is Ubuntu Server?**
- **Installing Ubuntu Server**
- **Ubuntu Package Management**
- **Ubuntu Server Security**
- **Summary**

UBUNTU 4.10, LOVINGLY KNOWN AS WARTY WARTHOG, was the first public version of Ubuntu. Its installation media provided no obvious way to install the barebones operating system (OS) without a full desktop environment. The system administrator crowds, easily irritable and feisty by nature, were greatly annoyed: They proclaimed Ubuntu was just a desktop distribution, and sauntered back to their caves in contempt.

The next version of Ubuntu that came out, Hoary Hedgehog, rectified the problem and allowed for trivial installation of a minimal Ubuntu suitable for servers. Yet the myth of Ubuntu as a purely desktop-oriented distribution stuck.

Luckily, the sentiment is just that—a myth. Ubuntu is a world-class server platform today, providing everything you'd expect from a server OS and with the human flavor that makes Ubuntu different. The dedicated hackers on the Ubuntu Server Team tend to the minutiae of hardware support and testing, and mercilessly beat on the latest versions of server software to make sure it's up to snuff for inclusion in the distribution. They are available to users like you to field feedback, questions, and cries of anguish.

That said, setting up a server is no small task. Server administrators constantly deal with complex issues such as system security, fault tolerance, and data safety, and while Ubuntu makes these issues more pleasant to deal with, they're not to be taken lightly. The aim of this chapter is thus not to teach you how to be a system administrator—we could easily fill a dozen books attempting to do that—but to give you a quick crash course. We'll also highlight the specific details that set Ubuntu Server apart from other server platforms, offer tips on some of the most common server uses, and give you pointers on where to find other relevant information. Let the mischief begin!

What Is Ubuntu Server?

By far the most common reaction from users first encountering Ubuntu Server is one of utter and hopeless confusion. People are foggy on whether Ubuntu Server is a whole new distribution or if it's an Ubuntu derivative like Kubuntu (only for servers) or perhaps something else entirely.

Let's clear things up a bit. The primary software store for Ubuntu and official derivatives is called the Ubuntu archive. The archive is merely a collection of software packages in Debian "deb" format, and it contains every single package that makes up distributions such as Ubuntu, Edubuntu, Xubuntu, Kubuntu, and Ubuntu Server. What makes Kubuntu separate from Ubuntu, then, is only the set of packages from the archive that its installer installs by default and that its CDs carry.

Ubuntu Server is no different. It depends on the very same archive as the standard Ubuntu distribution, but it installs a distinctive set of default packages. Notably, the set of packages comprising Ubuntu Server is very small. The installer will not install things such as a graphical environment or many user programs by default. But since all the packages for Server come from the same official Ubuntu archive, you can install any package you like later. In theory, there's nothing stopping you from transforming an Ubuntu Server install into a regular Ubuntu desktop installation or vice versa (in practice, this is tricky, and we don't recommend you try it). You can even go from running Kubuntu to running Ubuntu Server. The archive paradigm gives you maximum flexibility.

We've established that Ubuntu Server just provides a different set of default packages than Ubuntu. But what's important about that different set? What makes Ubuntu Server a server platform?

The most significant difference is a non-preemptible server kernel with an internal kernel timer frequency of 100 Hz instead of the desktop default of 1 kHz. We'll spare you the OS theory: the idea is to offer some extra performance and throughput for server applications. In addition, the server kernel supports SMP and basic NUMA. SMP, or symmetric multiprocessing, is the code that allows you to utilize more than one processor in your server, and NUMA is a memory design used in some multiprocessor systems that can dramatically increase multiprocessing performance.

TIP   **The Big Iron Kernel**
In addition to the standard server kernel, Ubuntu Server offers a so-called Big Iron kernel, which is for those very, very few people out there running enormously expensive supercomputing systems. You almost certainly don't want to run the Big Iron kernel. As one Ubuntu developer put it, if you can count the number of processors in your server on your fingers, don't use this kernel. If you ordered your server online by typing a "1" in a "Quantity" box, this is not the kernel for you. If your server didn't require the Occupational Safety and Health Administration to inspect the install location for proper structural support, don't use this kernel. If your BIOS boot sequence takes less than ten minutes and involves fewer than five screens, don't use this kernel. If turning on the server doesn't require a manual and doesn't dim the lights in the entire building, don't use this kernel. If . . . well, you get the idea.

So what else is different in Ubuntu Server? Other than the server kernel and a minimal set of packages, not too much. Though Ubuntu has supported a minimal installation mode for a number of releases, spinning off Ubuntu Server into a proper derivative distribution is still a young effort, and many neat features are planned for the future but aren't available just yet.

Ubuntu Server 6.06 LTS, known as Dapper, does offer officially supported packages for the Red Hat Cluster Suite, Red Hat's Global File System or GFS, Oracle's OCFS2 filesystem, and the Linux Virtual Server utilities: keepalived and ipvsadm. Combined with the specialized server kernel, these bits already let you use your Ubuntu Server for some heavy lifting. Recognizing the wild popularity of the LAMP (Linux, Apache, MySQL, PHP) stack, the Ubuntu Server CD offers a LAMP installation option right at the boot screen. And there's a great lineup of upcoming features: Among other things, we're hoping to throw in a resource manager for cluster folks, automatically place system configuration files under version control, ship with out-of-the-box support for server farm monitoring and hard drive replication over the network, and provide an integrity checker for installed systems directly on Ubuntu CDs.

Installing Ubuntu Server

So you've downloaded your Ubuntu Server CD from http://releases. ubuntu.com/ubuntu-server, burned it, eagerly placed it in your CD drive, and rebooted the machine to be greeted by the friendly Ubuntu menu. The first option, Install in Text Mode, installs an Ubuntu server. The second option, Install a LAMP Server, runs the same installer as the first, but will also automatically install and set up Apache, MySQL, and PHP for you. However, if you installed from the DVD then you select Install a Server to get started.

For the most part, server installation is identical to installing a regular Ubuntu machine. This is because Ubuntu takes extra care to ask only the most fundamental questions in the installer, and it turns out those don't differ much between a desktop and a server system. For a quick review of the installation procedure, turn back to Chapter 2. Here, we'll be looking at some of the advanced installer gadgetry that that chapter leaves out, and which is particularly geared toward server users.

The neat stuff begins when you arrive at the partitioning section of the installer. With a desktop machine, you'd probably let the installer configure a basic set of partitions by itself and go on its merry way. But with servers, things get a bit more complicated.

A Couple of Installer Tricks

As we'll explore below, in terms of partitioning and storage, server installations can be quite a bit more complex than desktop ones. There's a small bag of useful tricks with the installer that can help when things get hairy.

The installer itself runs on virtual console 1. If you switch to console 2 pressing Alt+F2, you'll be able to activate the console by hitting Enter and land in a minimalistic (busybox) shell. This will let you explore the complete installer environment, and take some matters into your own hands if need be. You can switch back to the installer console pressing Alt+F1. Console 4 contains a running, noninteractive log file of the installation, which you can inspect by pressing Alt+F4. Finally, it's sometimes useful to be able to connect to another server during installation, perhaps to upload a log file or to gain access to your mailbox or other communication. By default, the shell on console 2 will not provide you with an ssh client, but you can install one by running `anna-install openssh-client-udeb` after the installer configures the network. Now you can use the ssh and scp binaries to log in or copy data to the server of your choice.

Partitioning Your Ubuntu Server

Deciding how to partition the storage in your server is a finicky affair, and certainly no exact science. Generally, it's a good idea to have at least three partitions separate from the rest of the system

- /home—where all the user files will live
- /tmp—temporary scratch space for running applications
- /var—mail spools and log files

TIP   **Partition Security and Separating Logs and Spools**
There are several options that you can turn on for specific system partitions that afford you extra security. We'll explain them later in this chapter, in the section dealing with security.

As an aside, if this server will keep extensive mail and news spools, you might want to further separate /var into partitions for /var/log and /var/spool. Having them both on the same partition might cause severe I/O congestion under heavy use.

Keeping data on separate partitions gives you, the administrator, a fine-grain choice of filesystem you use for a particular purpose. For instance, you might choose to put /tmp on ReiserFS for its superior handling of many files in a directory and excellent performance on small files, but you might keep /home and /var on ext3 for its rock-solid robustness.

In addition, a dedicated /home partition lets you use special options when mounting it to your system, such as imposing disk space quotas or enabling extended security on user data. The reason to keep /tmp and /var separate from the rest of your system is much more prosaic: These directories are prone to filling up. This is the case with /tmp because it's a scratchpad, and administrators often give users very liberal quotas there (but have a policy, for example, of all user data in /tmp older than two days getting purged), which means /tmp can easily get clogged up. /var, on the other hand, stores log files and mail spools, both of which can come to take up massive amounts of disk space either as a result of malicious activity or a significant spike in normal system usage.

Becoming a system administrator means you have to learn how to think like one. If /tmp and /var are easy to fill up, you compartmentalize them so that they can't eventually consume all the disk space available on your server.

The Story of RAID

If you've only got one hard drive in your server, feel free to skip ahead. Otherwise, let's talk about putting those extra drives to use. The acronym RAID stands for redundant array of inexpensive disks, although if you're a businessman, you can substitute the word "independent" for "inexpensive." We forgive you. And if you're in France, RAID is short for *recherche assistance intervention dissuasion*, which is an elite commando unit of the National Police—but if that's the RAID you need help with, you're reading the wrong book. We think RAID is just a Really Awesome Idea for Data: When dealing with your information, it provides extra speed, fault tolerance, or both.

At its core, RAID is just a way of replicating the same information across multiple physical drives. The process can be set up in a number of ways, and specific kinds of drive configurations are referred to as RAID levels. These days, even low- to mid-range servers ship with integrated hardware RAID controllers, which operate without any support from the OS. If your new server doesn't come with a RAID controller, you can use the software RAID functionality in the Ubuntu kernel to accomplish the same goal.

Setting up software RAID while installing your Linux system was difficult and unwieldy only a short while ago, but it is a breeze these days: the Ubuntu installer provides a nice, convenient interface for it, and then handles all the requisite backstage magic. You can choose from three RAID levels: 0, 1, and 5.

RAID 0   A so-called striped set, RAID 0 allows you to pool the storage space of a number of separate drives into one large, virtual drive. The important thing to keep in mind is that RAID 0 does not actually concatenate the physical drives—it actually spreads the data across them evenly, which means that no more space will be used on each physical drive than can fit on the smallest one. In practical terms, if you had two 250GB drives and a 200GB drive, the total amount of space on your virtual drive would equal 600GB; 50GB on each of the two larger drives would go unused. Spreading data in this fashion provides amazing performance, but also significantly decreases reliability. If any of the drives in your RAID 0 array fail, the entire array will come crashing down, taking your data with it.

RAID 1   This level provides very straightforward data replication. It will take the contents of one physical drive and multiplex it to as many other drives as you'd like. A RAID 1 array does not grow in size with the addition of extra drives—instead, it grows in reliability and read performance. The size of the entire array is limited by the size of its smallest constituent drive.

RAID 5   When the chief goal of your storage is fault-tolerance, and you want to use more space than provided by the single physical drive in RAID 1, this is the level you want to use. RAID 5 lets you use n identically sized physical drives (if different-sized drives are present, no more space than the size of the smallest one will be used on each drive) to construct an array whose total available space is that of $n-1$ drives, and the array tolerates the failure of any one—but no more than one—drive without data loss.

TIP   **The Mythical Parity Drive**

If you toss five 200GB drives into a RAID 5 array, the array's total usable size will be 800GB, or that of four drives. This makes it easy to mistakenly believe that a RAID 5 array "sacrifices" one of the drives for maintaining redundancy and parity, but this is not the case. Through some neat mathematics of polynomial coefficients over Galois fields, the actual parity information is striped across all drives equally, allowing any single drive to fail without compromising the data. Don't worry, though. We won't quiz you on the math.

Which RAID to Choose?   If you're indecisive by nature, the past few paragraphs may have left you awkwardly hunched in your chair, mercilessly chewing a No. 2 pencil, feet tapping the floor nervously. Luckily, the initial choice of RAID level is often a no-brainer, so you'll have to direct your indecision elsewhere. If you have one hard drive, no RAID for you. Do not pass Go, do not collect $200. Two drives? Toss them into RAID 1, and sleep better at night. Three or more? RAID 5. Unless you really know what you're doing, avoid RAID 0 like the plague. If you're not serving mostly read-only data without a care about redundancy, RAID 0 isn't what you want.

TIP   **Other RAID Modes**
Though the installer only offers the most common RAID modes—0, 1, and 5—many other RAID modes exist and can be configured after the installation. Take a look at http://en.wikipedia.org/wiki/RAID for a detailed explanation of all the modes.

Setting Up RAID

After carefully studying the last section, maybe reading a few books on abstract algebra and another few on finite field theory, you finally decided on a RAID level that suits you. Since books can't yet read your mind, we'll assume you chose RAID 1. So how do you set it up?

Back to the installer. When prompted about partitioning disks, you'll want to bravely select the last option, Manually Edit Partition Table. The very first option in the new dialog box is Configure Software RAID, but don't go there just yet. You need to prepare the physical partitions first.

Below the top four options on the screen (RAID, Logical Volume Manager, Guided Partitioning, and Help), you'll find a list of the physical drives in your server that the Ubuntu installer detected.

TIP   **Avoiding the "Oh, No!" Moment**
We've said this before, and we'll say it again: It's very easy to mistakenly erase valuable data when partitioning your system. Since you're installing a server, however, we'll assume you're comfortable deleting any data that might already exist on the drives. If this is not the case, back up all data you care about now! We mean it.

Indented below each drive, you'll find the list of any pre-existing partitions, along with their on-disk ordinal number, size, bootable status, filesystem type, and possibly, their mount point. Using the arrow keys, highlight the line summarizing a physical drive (not any of its partitions), and hit Enter—you'll be asked to confirm replacing any existing partition table with a new one. Select Yes, and the only entry listed below that drive will be FREE SPACE. In our fictional server, we have two 80GB drives—hda and hdb—so we'd follow this process for both drives, giving each a fresh partition table. Say we've decided on a 20GB /home partition. Arrow over to the free space, hit Enter, and create the partition—look back to Chapter 1 if you need a refresher on all the options. Once you've entered the size for the new partition, you'll be brought to a dialog where you can choose the filesystem and mount options. Instead of plopping a filesystem on the raw partition, however, you'll want to enter the Use As dialog, and set the new partition to be a physical volume for RAID.

Still with us? Now rinse and repeat for the other drive—create the exact same partition, same size, and set it as a RAID volume. When you're done, you should be back at the initial partitioning screen, and you should have an identically sized partition under each drive. At this point, choose Configure Software RAID at the top of the screen, agree to write out changes to the storage devices if need be, and then choose to create an MD (multidisk) device. After selecting RAID 1, you'll be asked to enter the number of active devices for the array. In our fictional two-drive server it's two. The next question concerns the number of spare devices in the array, which you can leave at zero. Now simply use the spacebar to put a check next to both partitions that you've created (hda1 and hdb1), and hit Finish in the Multidisk dialog to return to the basic partitioner.

If you look below the two physical drives that you used to have there, you'll notice a brand new drive, the Software RAID device that has one partition below it. That's your future /home partition, sitting happily on a RAID array. If you arrow over to it and hit Enter, you can now configure it just as you would a real partition.

The process is the same for any other partitions you want to toss into RAID. Create identical-sized partitions on all participating physical drives, select to use them as RAID space, enter the multidisk configurator (software RAID), and finally, create an array that utilizes the real partitions. Then create a filesystem on the newly created array.

TIP   **Array Failure and Spare Devices**

When a physical drive fails in a RAID array that's running in a level that provides redundancy—such as 1 or 5—the array goes into so-called degraded mode (never verbally abuse or be cruel to your RAID arrays!). Depending on the number of devices in the array, running in degraded mode might just have performance downsides, but it might also mean that another physical drive failure will bring down the whole array and cause total data loss. To recover the array from degraded mode, you need to add a working physical drive to the system (the old one can be removed) and instruct the array to use the new device to "rebuild."

In order to minimize the amount of time an array spends in degraded mode, and to prevent having to power off the machine to insert new physical drives if the server doesn't support hot-swapping, you can put extra physical drives into the machine and flag them as hot spares, which means the system will keep them active but unused until there's a drive failure. Cold spares, as the name implies, are just extra drives that you keep around on a shelf until there's a failure, at which point you manually add them to the array.

That's it! The Ubuntu installer will take care of all the pesky details of configuring the system to boot the RAID arrays at the right time and use them, even if you've chosen to keep your root partition on an array. Now let's look at another great feature of the Ubuntu installer: the Logical Volume Manager (LVM).

The Story of the Logical Volume Manager

Let's take a step back from our RAID adventure and look at the bigger picture in data storage. The entire situation is unpleasant. Hard drives are slow and fail often, and though abolished for working memory ages ago, fixed-size partitions are still the predominant mode of storage space allocation. As if worrying about speed and data loss weren't enough, you also have to worry about whether your partition size calculations were just right when you were installing a server or if you'll wind up in the unenviable position of having a partition run out of space, even though another partition is maybe mostly unused. And if you might have to move a partition across physical volume boundaries on a running system, well, woe is you.

RAID helps to some degree. It'll do wonders for your worries about performance and fault tolerance, but it operates at too low a level to help with the partition size or fluidity concerns. What we'd really want is a way to push the partition concept up one level of abstraction, so it doesn't operate directly on the underlying physical media. Then we could have partitions that are trivially resizable or that can span multiple drives, we could easily take some space from one partition and tack it on another, and we can juggle partitions around on physical drives on a live server. Sounds cool, right?

Very cool, and very doable via logical volume management (LVM), a system that shifts the fundamental unit of storage from physical drives to virtual, or "logical" ones (although we harbor our suspicions that the term "logical" is a jab at the storage status quo, which is anything but). LVM has traditionally been a feature of expensive, enterprise Unix operating systems, or was available for purchase from third-party vendors. Through the magic of free software, a guy by the name of Heinz Mauelshagen wrote an implementation of a logical volume manager for Linux in 1998, which we'll refer to as LVM. LVM has undergone tremendous improvements since then, is widely used in production today, and just as you'd expect, the Ubuntu installer makes it easy for you to configure it on your server during installation.

LVM Theory and Jargon   Wrapping your head around LVM is a bit more difficult than with RAID because LVM rethinks the whole way of dealing with storage, which expectedly introduces a bit of jargon that you need to learn. Under LVM, physical volumes, or PVs, are seen just as providers of disk space without any inherent organization (such as partitions mapping to a mount point in the OS). We group PVs into volume groups, or VGs, which are virtual storage pools that look like good old cookie-cutter hard drives. We carve those up into logical volumes, or LVs, that act like the normal partitions we're used to dealing with. We create filesystems on these LVs, and mount them into our directory tree. And behind the scenes, LVM splits up physical volumes into small slabs of bytes (4 Mb by default), each of which is called a physical extent, or a PE.

Okay, so that was a mouthful of acronyms, but as long as you understand the progression, you're in good shape. You take a physical hard drive and set up one or more partitions on it that will be used for LVM. These partitions are now physical volumes (PV), which are split into physical extents (PE), and then grouped in volume groups (VG), on top of which you finally create logical volumes. It's the LVs, these virtual partitions, and not the ones on the physical hard drive, that carry a filesystem and are mapped and mounted into the OS. And if you're really confused about what possible benefit we get from adding all this complexity only to wind up with the same fixed-size partitions in the end, hang in there. It'll make sense in a second.

The reason LVM splits physical volumes into small, equally sized physical extents is that the definition of a volume group (the space that'll be carved into logical volumes) then becomes "a collection of physical extents" rather than "a physical area on a physical drive," as with old-school partitions. Notice that "a collection of extents" says nothing about where the extents are coming from, and certainly doesn't impose a fixed limit on the size of a volume group. We can take PEs from a bunch of different drives and toss them into one volume group, which addresses our desire to abstract partitions away from physical drives. We can take a VG and make it bigger simply by adding a few extents to it, maybe by taking them from another VG, or maybe by tossing in a new physical volume and using extents from there. And we can take a VG and move it to different physical storage simply by telling it to relocate to a different collection of extents. Best of all, we can do all this on the fly, without any server downtime.

Do you smell that? That's the fresh smell of the storage revolution.

Setting Up LVM

By now, you must be convinced that LVM is the best thing since sliced bread. Which it is—and, surprisingly enough, setting it up during installation is no harder than setting up RAID. Create partitions on each physical drive you want to use for LVM just as you did with RAID, but tell the installer to use them as "physical space for LVM." Note that in this context, PVs are not actual physical hard drives; they are the partitions that you're creating.

You don't have to devote your entire drive to partitions for LVM. If you'd like, you're free to create actual filesystem-containing partitions alongside the storage partitions used for LVM, but make sure you're satisfied with your partitioning choice before you proceed. Once you enter the LVM configurator in the installer, the partition layout on all drives that contain LVM partitions will be frozen.

Let's look back to our fictional server, but let's give it four drives, which are 10GB, 20GB, 80GB, and 120GB in size. Say we want to create an LVM partition, or PV, utilizing all available space on each drive, and then combine the first two PVs into a 30GB volume group, and the latter two into a

200GB one. Each VG will act as a large virtual hard drive on top of which we can create logical volumes just as we would normal partitions.

As with RAID, arrowing over to the name of each drive and hitting Enter will let us erase the partition table. Then hitting Enter on the FREE SPACE entry lets us create a physical volume—a partition which we set to be used as a physical space for LVM. Once all three LVM partitions are in place, we select Configure the Logical Volume Manager on the partitioning menu.

After a warning about the partition layout, we get to a rather Spartan LVM dialog that lets us modify VGs and LVs. According to our plan, we choose the former option, and create the two VGs we want, choosing the appropriate PVs. We then select Modify Logical Volumes and create the LVs corresponding to the normal partitions we want to put on the system—say one for each of /, /var, /home, and /tmp.

You can already see some of the partition fluidity that LVM brings you. If you decide you want a 25GB logical volume for /var, you can carve it out of the first VG you created, and /var will magically span the two smaller hard drives. If you later decide you've given /var too much space, you can shrink the filesystem, and then simply move some of the storage space from the first VG over to the second. The possibilities are endless.

TIP   **LVM Doesn't Provide Redundancy**
The point of LVM is storage fluidity, not fault tolerance. In our example above, the logical volume containing the /var filesystem is sitting on a volume group that spans two hard drives. Unfortunately, this means that either drive failing will corrupt the entire filesystem, and LVM intentionally doesn't contain functionality to prevent this problem.

Instead, when you need fault tolerance, build your volume groups from physical volumes that are sitting on RAID! In our example, we could have made a partition spanning the entire size of the 10GB hard drive, and allocated it to physical space for a RAID volume. Then, we could have made two 10GB partitions on the 20GB hard drive, and made the first one also a physical space for RAID. Entering the RAID configurator, we would create a RAID 1 array from the 10GB RAID partitions on both drives, but instead of placing a regular filesytem on the RAID array as before, we'd actually designate the RAID array to be used as a physical space for LVM. When we get to LVM configuration, the RAID array would show up as any other physical volume, but we'd know that the physical volume is redundant. If a physical drive fails beneath it, LVM won't ever know, and no data loss will occur. Of course, standard RAID array caveats apply, so if enough drives fail and shut down the array, LVM will still come down kicking and screaming.

You're Done—Now Watch Out for Root!

Whew. With the storage stuff out of the way, the rest of your server installation should go no differently than installing a regular Ubuntu workstation. And now that your server is installed, we can move on to the fun stuff. From this point on, everything we do will happen in a shell.

When your Ubuntu server first boots, you'll have to log in with the user you created during installation. Here's an important point that bites a number of newcomers to Ubuntu: Unlike most distributions, Ubuntu does not enable the root account during installation! Instead, the installer adds the user you've created during installation to the admin group, which lets you use a mechanism called sudo for performing administrative tasks. We'll show you how to use sudo in a bit. In the meantime, if you're interested in the rationale for the decision to disable direct use of the root account, simply run man sudo_root after logging in.

TIP   **Care and Feeding of RAID and LVM Arrays**
If you've set up some of these during installation, you'll want to learn how to manage the arrays after the server is installed. We recommend the respective how-to documents from The Linux Documentation Project at www.tldp.org/HOWTO/Software-RAID-HOWTO.html and www.tldp.org/HOWTO/LVM-HOWTO.

The how-tos sometimes get technical, but most of the details should sound familiar if you've understood the introduction to the subject that we have given in this chapter.

Ubuntu Package Management

Once your server is installed, it only contains the few packages it requires to boot and run properly. To get it to do some actual serving, we'll have to install specific server software. In the comfort of the GNOME graphical environment on an Ubuntu desktop, we could launch Synaptic and point and click our way through application discovery and installation. But on a server, we must be shell samurai.

The Ubuntu Archive

Before we delve into the nitty-gritty of package management, let's briefly outline the structure of the master Ubuntu package archive, which we mentioned in the introduction to this chapter. Each new release has five repositories in the archive, called main, restricted, backports, universe, and multiverse. A newly installed system comes with only the first two enabled (and the security update repository, but we'll talk about that later). Here's the repository breakdown

Main: This includes all packages installed by default; these packages have official support.

Restricted: These are packages with restricted copyright, often hardware drivers.

Backports: These are newer versions of packages in the archive, provided by the community.

Universe: The universe includes packages maintained by the Ubuntu community.

Multiverse: The multiverse includes packages that are not free (in the sense of freedom).

The term "official support" is a bit of a misnomer, as it doesn't refer to technical support that one would purchase or obtain, but speaks instead to the availability of security updates after a version of Ubuntu is released. Standard Ubuntu releases are supported for 18 months, which means that Ubuntu's parent company, Canonical Ltd., guarantees that security updates will be provided, free of charge, for any vulnerabilities discovered in software in the *main* repository for 18 months after a release. No such guarantee is made for software in the other repositories.

Of particular note is that certain Ubuntu releases have longer support cycles. These releases are denoted by the acronym LTS (long-term support) in their version number. Ubuntu 6.06 LTS, Dapper, will be supported for five years on servers!

APT Sources and Repositories

You're now aware of the structure of the Ubuntu archive, but we didn't explain how to actually modify the list of repositories you want to use on your system. In Debian package management parlance, the "list of repositories" is part of the list of Advanced Package Tool (APT) sources (keep your eyes peeled: many of the package tools we'll discuss below begin with the prefix "apt"). These sources tell APT where to find available packages: in the Ubuntu archive on the Internet, on your CD-ROM, or in a third-party archive.

The APT sources are specified in the file /etc/apt/sources.list. Let's open this file up in an editor—if you're not used to vim, substitute nano for it, which is an easier-to-use, beginner-friendly editor:

```
$ vim /etc/apt/sources.list
```

The lines beginning with a hash, or #, denote comment lines and are skipped over by APT. At the top, you'll see the CD-ROM source that the installer added, and following it these two lines:

```
deb http://us.archive.ubuntu.com/ubuntu/ dapper main restricted
deb-src http://us.archive.ubuntu.com/ubuntu/ dapper main restricted
```

We can infer the general format of the APT sources list by looking at these lines. The file is composed of individual sources, one per line, and each line of several space-separated fields. The first field tells us what kind of a source the line is describing, such as a source for binary packages (deb) or source code packages (deb-src). The second field is the actual URI of the package source, the third names the distribution whose packages we want (dapper), and the remaining fields tell APT which components to use from the source we're describing—by default, main, and restricted.

If you look through the rest of the file, you'll find it's nicely commented to let you easily enable two extra repositories: the very useful universe and the bleeding-edge backports. In general, now that you understand the format of each source line, you have complete control over the repositories you use, and while we strongly recommend against using the backports repository on a server, enabling universe is usually a good idea.

With that in mind, let's get you acquainted with some of the basic command-line package management tools on an Ubuntu system. Ubuntu inherits its package management from Debian, so if you're familiar with Debian, the utilities we'll discuss are old friends.

dpkg

Our first stop is the Debian package manager, dpkg, which sits around the lowest levels of the package management stack. Through a utility called dpkg-deb, dpkg deals with individual Debian package files, referred to as "debs" for their .deb filename extension.

dpkg is extensively documented in the system manual pages, so you can read up about the various options it supports by entering man dpkg in the shell. We'll point out the most common dpkg operations: listing and installing packages. Of course, dpkg can also remove packages, but we'll show you how to do that with the higher-level tool called apt-get, instead.

Listing Packages   Running dpkg -1 | less in the shell will list all the packages on your system that dpkg is tracking, in a six-column format. The first three columns are one letter wide each, signifying the desired package state, current package status, and error status, respectively. Most of the time, the error status column will be empty.

The top three lines of dpkg output serve as a legend to explain the letters you can find in the first three columns. This lets you use the grep tool to search through the package list, perhaps to look only at removed packages, or those that failed configuration.

Installing a Package Manually

There are more than 17,000 packages in the Ubuntu archive for each release. Only a small percentage of those are officially supported, but all the other packages are still held to reasonably rigorous inclusion requirements. Packages in the Ubuntu archive are thus almost universally of high quality and are known to work well on your Ubuntu system.

Because of this, the archive should be the very first place you look when you choose to install new software. In rare instances, however, the software you want to install won't be available in the archive, either because it's new or because there are redistribution restrictions which prevent it from being included. In those cases, you might have to either build the software from source code, run binaries that the vendor provides, or find third-party Ubuntu or Debian packages to install.

TIP **Practice Safe Hex**

That's a terrible pun. We apologize. But it probably got your attention, so follow closely: Be very, very cautious when dealing with third-party packages. Packages in the Ubuntu archive undergo extensive quality assurance and are practically certain to be free from viruses, worms, Trojan horses, or other computer pests. If you only install software from the archive, you'll never have to worry about viruses again.

With third-party packages, you just don't know what you could be installing. If you install a malicious package, you've given the package creator full control of your system. So ideally, don't install third-party packages at all. And if you must, make absolutely sure you trust the source of the packages!

Impatience is a hallmark virtue of programmers and system administrators alike, so if you were too impatient to read the warning note, do it now. This is serious business. Let's continue: Say you've downloaded a package called "myspecial-server.deb." You can install it simply by typing:

```
$ sudo dpkg -i myspecial-server.deb
```

dpkg will unpack the deb, make sure its dependencies are satisfied, and proceed to install the package. Remember what we said about the root account being unusable by default? Installing a package requires administrator privileges, which we obtained by prefixing the command we wanted to execute with sudo and entering our user password at sudo's prompt.

TIP **A Quick Note on Shell Examples**

In the dpkg example above, the dollar sign is the standard Unix shell symbol, so you don't need to actually type it. We'll use it in the rest of the chapter to indicate things that need to be entered in a shell. On your Ubuntu system, the shell prompt won't be just a dollar sign, but will look like this:

```
user@ server:~$
```

User and server will be replaced by your username and the hostname you gave the server during installation, respectively, and the part between the colon and dollar sign will show your working directory. A tilde is Unix shorthand for your home directory.

apt-get and apt-cache

Now let's jump higher up in the stack. Whereas dpkg deals mostly with package files, apt-get knows how to download packages from the Ubuntu archive or fetch them from your Ubuntu CD. It provides a convenient, succinct interface, so it's no surprise it's the tool that most system administrators use for their package management on Ubuntu servers.

While apt-get deals with high-level package operations, it won't tell you which packages are actually in the archive and available for installation. It knows how to get this information behind the scenes from the package cache, which you can manipulate using a simple tool called apt-cache. Let's see how these two commands come together with an example. Say we're trying to find and then install software that lets us work with extended filesystem attributes.

Searching the Package Cache and Showing Package Information   We begin by telling apt-cache to search for the phrase "extended attributes":

```
$ apt-cache search "extended attributes"
attr - Utilities for manipulating filesystem extended attributes
libattr1 - Extended attribute shared library
libattr1-dev - Extended attribute static libraries and headers
python-pyxattr - module for manipulating filesystem extended attributes
python2.4-pyxattr - module for manipulating filesystem extended
attributes
rdiff-backup - remote incremental backup
xfsdump - Administrative utilities for the XFS filesystem
xfsprogs - Utilities for managing the XFS filesystem
```

The parameter to apt-cache search can be either a package name or a phrase describing the package as above. The lines following our invocation are the output we received, composed of the package name on the left, and a one-line description on the right. It looks like the attr package is what we're after, so let's see some details about it.

```
$ apt-cache show attr
Package: attr
Priority: optional
Section: utils
Installed-Size: 192
Maintainer: Nathan Scott <nathans@debian.org>
Architecture: i386
Version: 2.4.25-1
Depends: libattr1, libc6 (>= 2.3.4-1)
Conflicts: xfsdump (<< 2.0.0)
Filename: pool/main/a/attr/attr_2.4.25-1_i386.deb
Size: 34192
MD5sum: fc71e19f1fff7017998332d96459baba
Description: Utilities for manipulating filesystem extended attributes
```

```
A set of tools for manipulating extended attributes on filesystem
objects, in particular getfattr(1) and setfattr(1).
An attr(1) command is also provided which is largely compatible with
the SGI IRIX tool of the same name.
Bugs: mailto:ubuntu-users@lists.ubuntu.com
Origin: Ubuntu
```

Don't be daunted by the verbose output. Extracting the useful bits turns out to be pretty simple. We can already see from the description field that this is, in fact, the package we're after. We can also see the exact version of the packaged software, any dependencies and conflicting packages it has, and an e-mail address to which we can send bug reports. And looking at the filename field, the pool/main snippet tells us this is a package in the main repository.

Installing a Package So far, so good. Let's perform the actual installation:

```
$ sudo apt-get install attr
```

apt-get will track down a source for the package, such as an Ubuntu CD or the Ubuntu archive on the Internet, fetch the deb, verify its integrity, do the same for any dependencies the package has, and, finally, install the package.

Removing a Package For didactic purposes, we're going to keep assuming you're very indecisive and that right after you installed the attr package, you realized it wasn't going to work out between the two of you. To the bit bucket with attr!

```
$ sudo apt-get remove attr
```

One confirmation later and attr is blissfully gone from your system, except for any configuration files which it may have installed. If you want those gone, too, you'd have to instead run the following:

```
$ sudo apt-get--purge remove attr
```

Performing System Updates Installing and removing packages is a common system administration task, but not as common as keeping the system up to date. This doesn't mean upgrading to newer and newer versions of the software (well, it does, but not in the conventional sense), because once a given Ubuntu version is released, no new software versions enter the repositories except for the backports repository. On a server, however, you're strongly discouraged from using backports, because they receive a very limited amount of quality assurance and testing, and because there's usually no reason for a server to be chasing new software features. New features bring new bugs, and as a system administrator, you should value stability and reliability miles over features. Ubuntu's brief, six-month development cycle means that you'll be able to get all the new features in half a year anyway. But by then they will be in the main repositories and will have received substantial testing. Keeping a system up to date thus means making sure it's running the latest security patches, to prevent any vulnerabilities discovered after the release from endangering your system.

Luckily, `apt-get` makes this process amazingly easy. You begin by obtaining an updated list of packages from the Ubuntu archive:

```
$ sudo apt-get update
```

and then you simply run the upgrade:

```
$ sudo apt-get upgrade
```

After this, `apt-get` will tell you either that your system is up to date or what it's planning to upgrade, and it will handle the upgrade for you automatically. How's that for cool?

Running a Distribution Upgrade

When a new Ubuntu release comes out and you want to upgrade your server to it, you'll again use `apt-get`. We'll discuss apt sources in a bit, but for now, here's what an upgrade from Breezy to Dapper would look like:

```
$ sudo sed -i "s/breezy/dapper/" /etc/apt/sources.list
$ sudo apt-get update
$ sudo apt-get dist-upgrade
```

Let's dissect what we've done. The first line uses a tool called `sed`, or the stream editor, to exchange every occurrence of the word "breezy" with the word "dapper" in the file called /etc/apt/sources.list, or the apt sources file. We then tell `apt-get` to reload the list of packages from the archive, which downloads the list of packages available in Dapper because of our change to the apt sources. `dist-upgrade` is the smug older brother of `upgrade` who knows how to deal with dependencies in the face of new package versions.

So apt-get will figure out the order in which to replace packages with the versions from the new release, and then just run through it like a regular upgrade.

Except when it doesn't.

Trivial to use and rather powerful, it's no wonder that apt-get is one of Ubuntu's most beloved features. It's a time-tested tool that deals well with most package situations and makes the system administrator's life a breeze when dealing with software maintenance. But every once in a while, apt-get will paint itself into a corner, and a lot of times that'll happen when trying to upgrade to a new release.

In Dapper, a lot of work has gone into making the release upgrade a smoother process. Some improvements have been made, but apt-get is only so flexible, and it's not known whether the deeper issues with it can be fixed at all if we stay within its framework. This is why Ubuntu has its sights set on another package manager, appropriately called Smart, to maybe take over from apt-get. Smart is written in a high-level, dynamic language, has superior dependency graph resolution capabilities, and would still offer all the ease of use of apt-get while better handling the corner cases. Smart is experimental software, though, so its inclusion for such a chief role as package management is still very uncertain and has no known timeline. We're really just giving you a heads up; apt-get should still be your best friend.

Building Packages from Source   The Ubuntu archive, unlike Debian's, doesn't permit direct binary uploads. When Ubuntu developers want to add a piece of software to the archive, they prepare its source code in a certain way and put it in a build queue. From there it's compiled, built automatically, and—if those steps succeed—pushed into the archive.

Why go through all the trouble? Why not just have the developers build the software on their machines? They could upload binaries to the archive, bypassing the build queue, which can take hours to build software. Here's the catch: Ubuntu officially supports three hardware platforms (Intel x86, AMD64/EM64T, and PowerPC). Without the build queue, developers would have to build separate binaries of their software for each platform, which entails owning a computer running on each platform (expensive!) or creating complicated cross-compilation toolchains. And even then, sitting through three software builds is an enormous waste of precious developer time.

The build queue approach solves this problem, because the automatic build system takes a single source package and builds it for all the necessary platforms. And it turns out that the approach provides you, the system administrator, with a really nifty benefit: It lets you leverage the dependency-solving power and ease of use of apt-get, and apply it to building packages from source!

Now that you're excited, let's backtrack a bit. Building packages from source is primarily of interest to developers, not system administrators. In fact, as a sysadmin, you should avoid hand-built packages whenever possible, and instead benefit from the quality assurance that packages in the Ubuntu archive receive. Sometimes, though, you might just have to apply a custom patch to a piece of software before installing it. We'll use the attr package example, as before. What follows is what a session of building attr from source and installing the new package might look like—if you want to try it, make sure you install the dpkg-dev and devscripts packages.

```
$ mkdir attr-build
$ cd attr-build
$ apt-get source attr
$ sudo apt-get build-dep attr
$ cd attr-2.4.25
<apply a patch or edit the source code>
$ dch -i
$ dpkg-buildpackage -rfakeroot
$ cd ..
$ sudo dpkg -i *.deb
```

All of the commands we invoked are well-documented in the system man pages, and covering them in detail is out of the scope of this chapter. To briefly orient you as to what we did, though:

1. We made a scratch directory called attr-build and changed into it.

2. apt-get source attr fetched the source of the attr package and unpacked it into the current directory.

3. apt-get build-dep attr installed all the packages that are required to build the attr package from source.

4. We changed into the unpacked attr-2.4.25 directory, applied a patch, and edited the package changelog to describe our changes to the source.

5. `dpkg -buildpackage -rfakeroot` built one or more installable debs from our package.

6. We ascended one directory in the filesystem and installed all the debs we just built.

This is a super-compressed cheat sheet for a topic that takes a long time to master. We left a lot of things out, so if you need to be patching packages for production use, go and read the `man` pages of the tools we mention above first and get a better understanding of what's going on!

aptitude

Around the highest levels of the package management stack hangs aptitude, a neat, colorful textual frontend that can be used interchangeably with `apt-get`. We won't go into detail about aptitude use here; plenty of information is available from the system manual pages and the online aptitude help system (if you launch it as `aptitude` from the shell). It's worth mentioning, though, that one of the chief reasons some system administrators prefer aptitude over `apt-get` is its better handling of so-called orphan packages. Orphan packages are packages that were installed as a dependency of another package which has since been removed, leaving the orphan installed for no good reason. `apt-get` provides no automatic way of dealing with orphans, instead relegating the task to the `deborphan` tool, which you can install from the archive. By contrast, aptitude will remove orphan packages automatically.

Tips and Tricks

Congratulations. If you've gotten this far, you're familiar with most aspects of effectively dealing with packages on your Ubuntu server. Before you move on to other topics, though, we want to present a few odds and ends that will probably come in handy to you at one point or another.

Listing Files Owned by a Package   Sometimes it's really useful to see which files on your system belong to a specific package, say, `cron`. Here's `dpkg` to the rescue:

```
$ dpkg -L cron
```

Be careful, though, as dpkg -L output might contain directories that aren't exclusively owned by this package but shared with others.

Finding Which Package Owns a File   The reverse of the previous operation is just as simple:

```
$ dpkg -S /etc/crontab
cron: /etc/crontab
```

The one-line output tells us the name of the owner package on the left.

Finding Which Package Provides a File   Both dpkg -S and dpkg -L operate on the database of installed packages. Sometimes, you might need to figure out which—potentially uninstalled—package provides a certain file. We might be looking for a package that would install the bzr binary, or /usr/bin/bzr. To do this, first install the package apt-file (requires the universe repository), then execute:

```
$ apt-file update
$ apt-file search /usr/bin/bzr
```

Voilà! apt-file will tell you that the package you want is bzr, with output in the same format as dpkg -S.

That's it for our package management tricks—it's time to talk about security.

Ubuntu Server Security

As a system administrator, one of your chief tasks is dealing with server security. If your server is connected to the Internet, for security purposes, it's in a war zone. If it's only an internal server, you still need to deal with (accidentally) malicious users, disgruntled employees, and the guy in accounting who *really* wants to read the boss's secretary's e-mail.

In general, Ubuntu Server is a very secure platform. The Ubuntu Security Team, the team that produces all official security updates, has one of the best turnaround times in the industry. Ubuntu ships with a no open ports policy, meaning that after you install the machine—be it an Ubuntu desktop or a server—no applications will be accepting connections from the Internet by default. Like Ubuntu desktops, Ubuntu Server uses the sudo mechanism for system administration, eschewing the root account. And finally, security updates are guaranteed for at least 18 months after each release (five years for some releases, like Dapper), and are free.

In this section, we want to take a look at filesystem security, system resource limits, dealing with logs, and finally some network security. But Linux security is a difficult and expansive topic; remember that we're giving you a crash course here, and leaving a lot of things out—to be a good administrator, you'll want to learn more.

User Account Administration

Many aspects of user administration on Linux systems are consistent across distributions. Debian provides some convenience tools, such as the `useradd` command, to make things easier for you. But since Ubuntu fully inherits Debian's user administration model, we won't go into detail about it here. Instead, let us refer you to www.oreilly.com/catalog/debian/chapter/ book/ ch07_01.html for the basics. After reading that page, you'll have full knowledge of the standard model, and we can briefly talk about the Ubuntu difference: `sudo`.

As we mentioned at the end of the installation section (You're done—Now Watch Out for Root!), Ubuntu doesn't enable the root, or administrator, account by default. There is a great deal of security benefit to this approach and incredibly few downsides, all of which are documented at the `man` pages for `sudo_root`.

The user that you added during installation is the one who, by default, is placed into the admin group and may use `sudo` to perform system administration tasks. After adding new users to the system, you may add them to the admin group like this:

```
$ sudo adduser username admin
```

Simply use `deluser` in place of `adduser` in the above command to remove a user from the group.

One thing to keep in mind is that `sudo` isn't just a workaround for giving people root access. It can also handle fine-grain permissions, such as saying, "allow this user to execute only these three commands with superuser privileges."

Documentation about specifying these permissions is available in the "sudoers" man page, which can be a bit daunting—feel free to skip close to the end of it, until you reach the EXAMPLES section. It should take you maybe 10 or 15 minutes to grok it, and it covers a vast majority of the situations for which you'll want sudo. When you're ready to put your new knowledge to use, simply run:

```
$ visudo
```

Be careful here—the sudoers database, which lives in /etc/sudoers, is not meant to just be opened in an editor, because an editor won't check the syntax for you! If you mess up the sudoers database, you might find yourself with no way to become an administrator on the machine.

Filesystem Security

The security model for files is standardized across most Unix-like OS, and is called the POSIX model. The model calls for three broad types of access permissions for every file and directory: owner, group, and other. It works in exactly the same way on any Linux distribution, which is why we won't focus on it here. For a refresher, consult the man pages for chmod and chown, or browse around the Internet.

We want to actually look at securing partitions through mount options, an oft-neglected aspect of dealing with system security that's rather powerful when used appropriately. When explaining how to partition your system, we extolled the virtues of giving, at the very least, the /home, /tmp, and /var directories their own partitions, mentioning how it's possible to use special options when mounting these to the filesystem.

Many of the special mount options are filesystem-dependent, but the ones we want to consider are not. Here are the ones that interest us:

nodev A filesystem mounted with the nodev option will not allow the use or creation of special "device" files. There's usually no good reason to allow most filesystems to allow interpretation of block or character special devices, and allowing them poses potential security risks.

nosuid   If you read up about Unix file permissions, you know that certain files can be flagged in a way that lets anyone execute them with the permissions of another user or group, often that of the system administrator. This flag is called the setuid (`suid`) or the `setgid` bit, respectively, and allowing this behavior outside of the directories that hold the system binaries is often unnecessary and decreases security. If a user is able to, in any way, create or obtain a suid binary of his own choosing, he has effectively compromised the system.

noexec   If a filesystem is flagged as `noexec`, users will not be able to run any executables located on it.

noatime   This flag tells the filesystem not to keep a record of when files were last accessed. If used indiscriminately, it lessens security through limiting the amount of information available in the event of a security incident, particularly when computer forensics is to be performed. However, the flag does provide performance benefits for certain use patterns, so it's a good candidate to be used on partitions where security is an acceptable trade-off for speed.

Deciding which mount options to use on which partition is another fuzzy science, and you'll often develop preferences as you become more accustomed to administering machines. Here's a basic proposal, though, that should be a good starting point:

- /home—`nosuid, nodev`

- /tmp—`noatime, noexec, nodev, nosuid`

- /var—`noexec, nodev, nosuid`

System Resource Limits

By default, Linux will not impose any resource limits on user processes. This means any user is free to fill up all of the working memory on the machine, or spawn processes in an endless loop, rendering the system unusable in seconds. The solution is to set up some of your own resource limits by editing the /etc/security/limits.conf file:

```
$ sudoedit /etc/security/limits.conf
```

The possible settings are all explained in the comment within the file, and there are no silver bullet values to recommend, though we do recommend that you set up at least the nproc limit, and possibly also the as/data/memlock/rss settings.

TIP   **A Real-Life Resource Limit Example**

Just to give you an idea of what these limits look like on production servers, here is the configuration from the general login server of the Harvard Computer Society at Harvard University:

```
*     -       as        2097152
*     -       data      131072
*     -       memlock   131072
*     -       rss       1013352
*     hard    nproc     128
```

This limits regular users to 128 processes, with a maximum address space of 2GB, maximum data size and locked-in-memory address space of 128MB, and maximum resident set size of 1GB.

If you need to set up disk quotas for your users, install the quota package, and take a look at its man page.

System Log Files

As a system administrator, the system log files are some of your best friends. If you watch them carefully, you'll often know in advance when something is wrong with the system, and you'll be able to resolve most problems before they escalate.

Unfortunately, your ability to pay close attention to the log files dwindles with every server you're tasked with administering, so administrators often use log processing software that can be configured to alert them on certain events, or write their own tools in languages such as Perl and Python.

Logs usually live in /var/log, and after your server runs for a while, you'll notice there are a lot of increasingly older versions of the log files in that directory, many of them compressed with gzip (ending with the .gz filename extension).

Here are some log files of note:

- /var/log/syslog—general system log

- /var/log/auth.log—system authentication logs

- /var/log/mail.log—system mail logs

- /var/log/messages—general log messages

- /var/log/dmesg—kernel ring buffer messages, usually since system bootup

Your Log Toolbox   When it comes to reviewing logs, there are a few tools of choice that you should become familiar with. The tail utility prints, by default, the last ten lines of a file, which makes it a neat tool to get an idea of what's been happening last in a given log file:

```
$ tail /var/log/syslog
```

With the -f parameter, tail launches into follow mode, which means it'll open the file and keep showing you changes on the screen as they're happening. If you want to impress your friends with your new system administrator prowess, you can now easily recreate the Hollywood hacker movie staple: text furiously blazing across the screen.

Also invaluable are zgrep, zcat, and zless, which operate like their analogues that don't begin with a "z" but on gzip-compressed files. For instance, to get a list of lines in all your compressed logs that contain the word "warthog" regardless of case you would issue the following command:

```
$ zgrep -i warthog /var/log/*.gz
```

Your toolbox for dealing with logs will grow with experience and based on your preferences, but to get an idea of what's already out there, do an apt-cache search for "log files."

A Sprinkling of Network Security

Network security administration is another feature provided largely by the OS, so it's no different on Ubuntu than on any other modern Linux distribution. That means we won't cover it here but will leave you with a pointer.

The `iptables` command is the front end to the very powerful Linux firewall tables. Unfortunately, dealing with `iptables` can be rather difficult, particularly if you're trying to set up complex firewall policies. To whet your appetite, here's `iptables` in action, dropping all packets coming from a notorious time-sink domain:

```
$ sudo iptables -A INPUT -s www.slashdot.org -j DROP
```

Tutorials, how-tos, and articles about `iptables` are available on the Internet in large numbers, and the system `man` pages provide detailed information about all the possible options. Spending some time to learn `iptables` is well worth it, because it'll let you set up network security on any Linux machine, and will make it pretty easy for you to learn other OS firewall systems if need be.

Final Words on Security

We've barely even scratched the surface of system security in this subsection, though we've tried to give you good pointers on where to start and where to get the information you need to learn more. But let us give you some sage advice on security in general, since it's a painful truth to learn: There is no such thing as a fully secure system. Securing systems isn't about making it impossible for a breach to occur. It's about making the breach so difficult that it's not worth it to the attacker. This definition is pretty fluid, because if your attacker is a bored 14-year-old sitting in a basement somewhere chewing on cold pizza, you can bet that he'll leave your system alone if it's even marginally secure. But if you're keeping around top secret information, then it's a lot more difficult to have the system be secure enough that breaking into it isn't worth it, from a cost/benefit point of view, to the attackers.

Security is also neat because, as a concept, it permeates the entire idea space of computer science. Getting really good at security requires incredibly deep understanding of the inner workings of computer systems, which has the nonobvious advantage that if you're trying to get a deep understanding of computer systems but don't know where to start, you can start with security and simply follow the trail. Use this to your advantage! Good luck.

Summary

If you've never administered a system before, the transition from being a regular user will be difficult, regardless of which OS you choose to learn to administer. The difficulty stems from the wider shift in thinking that's required. Instead of just making sure your room is clean, now you have to run and protect the whole apartment building. But the difficulty is also educational and rewarding. (We realize they also told you this for your theoretical physics class in college, but we're not lying.) Learning to maintain Ubuntu servers is a great choice for you, because you'll benefit from a vibrant and helpful user community, and you'll be working with a top-notch OS every step of the way.

Just as we were in the final editing stages of this book, Ubuntu founder Mark Shuttleworth took the stage with new Sun Microsystems CEO Jonathan Schwartz in front of an audience of 15,000 at Sun's annual JavaOne conference. In 2001, Sun's previous CEO Scott McNealy famously compared running Linux on a mainframe to "having a trailer park in the back of your estate." But standing together in San Francisco, Schwartz and Shuttleworth announced that Sun plans to provide commercial support for Ubuntu Server on Sun's hardware. Meeting with reporters after his presentation, Schwartz called Ubuntu "one of the most important—if not *the* most important—Linux distribution out there," adding that "the odds are quite good that [Sun] will be aggressively supporting the work that Ubuntu is doing." While it's too early to make any predictions about exactly how Sun's collaboration with Ubuntu will play out, one thing is certain after the JavaOne announcement: the industry sees Ubuntu Server as a very powerful contender in the server OS arena.

If you're a seasoned administrator who came to see what all the Ubuntu Server fuss is about, stay tuned. The project, though rock-solid as far as stability goes, is still in its feature infancy, and the Server Team is working very hard at making it the best server platform out there. We're emphasizing advanced features. We already offer some great clustering primitives, and we will be expanding our clustering support to include resource management and Single System Image (SSI) clustering. We're working on integrating the phenomenal Xen hypervisor into Ubuntu Server. And we're being very fussy about getting all the little details just right.

In both cases, if you're installing a new server, give Ubuntu Server a try. It's a state-of-the-art system, and we're sure you'll enjoy using it. Get in touch, tell us what to do to make it better, and lend a hand. Help us make Ubuntu rock even harder on big iron and heavy metal!

TIP   **Getting in Touch**

If you want to tell us why you like Ubuntu Server, or why you hate it, or send us cookies, or just stalk us from a distance, come on in! Go to https://lists.ubuntu.com/mailman/listinfo/ubuntu-server to join the ubuntu-server mailing list, visit our page on Launchpad at https://launchpad.net/people/ubuntu-server or jump on IRC. We're on the #ubuntu-server channel on FreeNode. Hope to see you there!

## CHAPTER 6

Support and Typical Problems

- **Your System**
- **Applications**
- **Multimedia**
- **Networking**
- **Hardware**
- **System Administration**
- **Other**
- **Summary**

DESPITE THE FACT that the Ubuntu developers work tirelessly to make the Ubuntu user experience as fluid and problem-free as possible, there are always going to be bugs, glitches, and errors in software. This is nothing unique to Ubuntu; it is a characteristic that is applied to all software. Anything created by humans is subject to error.

One of the many benefits of the Open Source development process is that errors and bugs are typically reported, found, and fixed in a far shorter time frame than is the case with proprietary software. This ensures that the software included with Ubuntu is far more solid and stable than some proprietary alternatives.

Although bugs are typically fixed quickly, there is still the case of user error. Even if a piece of software is completely bug-free, it can be used incorrectly, be misconfigured, or otherwise not work as expected. This is perfectly normal, and the aim of this chapter is to discuss some of the most common problems faced by users and explore how to fix or otherwise resolve these issues.

This chapter is presented in a cookbook format, presenting each problem followed by a concise solution. If you have read through the other chapters in the book and not found the solution in this chapter, the next option is to try the superb Ubuntu Forums at www.ubuntuforums.org/. In recent years, the forums have proved to be a goldmine of useful information. Not only do they include discussion about problems and issues that other people have, they are also laden with community-contributed how-to articles that cover a wealth of different areas.

Your System

Your Ubuntu system is a little like an ecosystem. For certain things to work, other things must be already working. When you are new to any operating system (OS), it can often be a little difficult to get to know how some of these core system functions work.

In this section we cover the core system technology in Ubuntu and problems that can crop up when using it.

Ubuntu Won't Start!

When Ubuntu first starts, the GRUB bootloader loads an OS for you. If you only have Ubuntu installed on your computer, it is loaded automatically. Otherwise, if you have more than one OS (such as Ubuntu and Microsoft Windows), you can pick the relevant one from a menu. If you don't see the menu, restart your computer, wait until you see the word GRUB, and press Enter. Now use your arrow keys to select an option.

The core chunk of software that is loaded when Ubuntu starts is the kernel, and sometimes there are a few different kernels installed on your system. On the menu, each kernel version (such as 2.6.15) has two options: the stock kernel and one called "recovery mode." Try booting the newest non-recovery mode kernel, and see if your system starts.

The Bootloader   If your system still fails to start, it is likely that your bootloader is broken. When you use a bootloader such as GRUB, a tiny file (called the *boot* sector) is copied into the very first part of your hard disk. If this file is broken or corrupted, your system often won't boot. Don't worry, though, you can fix this! Restart your computer, and choose the newest rescue mode option. When using rescue mode, the system starts in a limited single-user command line mode. You can use this mode to fix any problems from the command line. In this case, you need to fix the GRUB bootloader.

To do this, go to /boot/grub, and load menu.lst in a text editor. Unfortunately we don't have the space to cover GRUB configuration here, so it is recommended that you consult the excellent documentation on the GRUB Web site at www.gnu.org/software/grub/.

Backing Up and Restoring Your Boot Sector   When GRUB runs, the boot sector part of your hard disk contains information about which OS you can boot. This sector sometimes gets corrupted due to a system crash or power loss and your computer won't boot. Luckily, with a few carefully chosen commands, you can back up and restore this important sector.

Back it up using this command:

```
foo@bar:~$ sudo dd if=/dev/hda of=MBR-backup bs=512 count=1
```

The dd command copies the sector from the first disk (/dev/hda—change this to your disk) and saves it as MBR-backup in the current directory.

QUICK TIP   When referring to boot sectors you may see it prefixed as MBR—this is short for *master boot record.*

To restore the sector, run this command:

```
foo@bar:~$ sudo dd if=MBR-backup of=/dev/hda bs=512 count=1
```

When you boot your computer in rescue mode, you can use these commands to manage your boot sector.

The Ubuntu Logo Appears Corrupted or Just Looks Odd While Booting

When your system starts it uses a special splash image to make the boot process more attractive, as shown in Figure 6-1.

If you have problems with this splash screen, you can disable it. To do this, load the /boot/grub/menu.lst file into a text editor, and scroll to the bottom of the file. You should see a line such as this:

```
kernel    /boot/vmlinuz-2.6.15-10-386 root=/dev/hda1 ro quiet
          splash
```

Just remove the splash word from the line and restart your computer. Now plain text boot messages are displayed when the system starts.

When I Start My Computer I Get Text Instead of a Graphical Interface

The graphical interface used in Ubuntu comes in two parts: X and GNOME. The X server is an underlying chunk of software that ensures your graphics card and monitor work, and it provides a base for GNOME

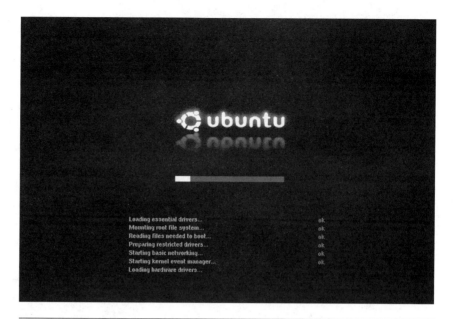

Figure 6-1 The graphical boot screen can be switched off if needed.

to run on. The GNOME desktop uses X as an engine to create the rich desktop platform you have been using. If you start the computer and you can only see text and no graphical interface, this is a problem with X.

First, reboot your computer to see if that fixes the problem. When your computer has booted, if you still have the same problem, Ubuntu may have told you that it cannot start X. If you did not see this message, press Ctrl-Alt-F7 to see if you can access the graphical interface. If this does not work, there is a configuration problem with X.

X stores its configuration in /etc/X11/xorg.conf. Before you fiddle with your configuration, it is always wise to make a backup of the file. Even if X is not starting, some other parts of the configuration may be working fine.

```
foo@bar:~$ cd /etc/X11
foo@bar:~$ sudo cp xorg.conf xorg.conf.old
```

First you move to the /etc/X11 directory and then you use the cp command to copy the existing file (xorg.conf) to a backup file (xorg.conf.old). You now have both an xorg.conf and an xorg.conf.old with the same information in them.

Now run the X configuration process:

```
foo@bar:~$ sudo dpkg-reconfigure xserver-xorg
```

A configuration routine will start, and you should experiment with different settings in the routine. Unfortunately, we don't have the space to cover X configuration in detail, so refer to https://wiki.ubuntu.com/debuggingxauto configuration.

TIP   **Restricted Drivers**
Ubuntu only ships with fully Open Source graphics drivers. There are, however, closed source drivers available for ATI and NVidea cards. For more information about these drivers, visit the respective manufacturer's Web site.

I Tried to Use a Word or PowerPoint Document, and the Fonts Are All Wrong

When loading Microsoft Office documents in OpenOffice.org, the document may require Windows fonts that are not on your system. Many of these fonts are available online and can be automatically downloaded with the msttcorefonts package from the multiverse repository.

When you install msttcorefonts, it automatically downloads and installs the following common Windows fonts:

- Andale Mono
- Arial Black
- Arial (Bold, Italic, Bold Italic)
- Comic Sans MS (Bold)
- Courier New (Bold, Italic, Bold Italic)
- Georgia (Bold, Italic, Bold Italic)
- Impact
- Times New Roman (Bold, Italic, Bold Italic)
- Trebuchet (Bold, Italic, Bold Italic)

- Verdana (Bold, Italic, Bold Italic)

- Webdings

With the installation complete, restart X, and the fonts are available.

How Do I Install a Package?

In Ubuntu, all components (applications, documentation, artwork, etc.) are split up into separate packages. Each package serves one purpose. For instance the package Firefox contains Mozilla Firefox, and Ubuntu-audio contains the Ubuntu default audio theme.

To install a program, select Applications > Add/Remove. When asked for a password, enter your login password. Select a category in the left pane. This corresponds to the Applications menu. Click an empty checkbox for any application you want in the upper right pane to select it for installation. Or deinstall an application by deselecting the application's checkbox. Nothing will actually happen until you click Apply or OK. A dialog box lists the pending changes, and if you click OK the required packages are downloaded and installed (or deinstalled if that's what you chose). When it's finished, click Close.

If you can't find what you're looking for, enter a word into the search box in the upper right corner. For instance if you enter "picture," it will show the GIMP, a powerful tool to edit pictures. You can also search for a specific application, such as Patience.

When you still can't find it, or you want to install a package not listed in Add/Remove, click the Advanced button. You can also open Synaptic by selecting System > Administration > Synaptic Package Manager. Enter your login password if prompted.

First click the Reload button on the toolbar to download the latest package lists. To search for a package, click Search on the toolbar. For example, enter "Tux Paint," and click Search. Successive search queries are stored in the left pane, and the results are shown in the right pane. To install a package, click the box to the left of the name. Select Mark for Installation from the list. Synaptic will warn when other packages (dependencies) have to be installed for the package you want to install. Click Mark to automatically mark the required packages for installation. The package you've selected is highlighted in green. Packages marked for removal appear in red. For Tux Paint, you see two other packages highlighted in green. Other required packages marked for installation do not appear in the search results for Tux Paint, because they are not specifically made for Tux Paint, and hence can also be used by other applications.

To browse for packages click Components in the lower left corner. The categories presented in the left pane are not corresponding to the Applications menu. The "universe" and "multiverse" categories hold packages not supported by Ubuntu. It is advisable only to install them if you know what you are doing.

When you have selected a package, a description is shown in the bottom pane. To obtain more detailed information (such as the download and installed size), click Properties on the toolbar.

When you are done marking packages, click Apply on the toolbar. This opens a dialog where you can see the pending changes. If you are sure, click Apply. The required packages are then downloaded and installed. When it's finished, click Close.

I Want to Install an Application That Is Not in Synaptic

Although Synaptic contains a huge selection of packages, sometimes the package you need is not included. The first thing you should check is that you have enabled the additional repositories such as universe and multiverse. Open Synaptic from System > Administration > Synaptic Package Manager. Now click Settings > Repositories > Add. Ensure that all of the Components check-boxes are selected. See https://wiki.Ubuntu.com/AddingRepositoriesHowto for more details.

The Repository Rundown

The *universe* repository contains the thousands of packages that are part of the Debian distribution, upon which Ubuntu is based. All of these packages are entirely free and supported by a community of Ubuntu contributors.

The *multiverse* repository contains a number of packages that are freely available to download but are not fully Open Source. If you only want to run Open Source software, you may not want to use this repository.

If you have enabled these extra repositories and your package is still not there, have a quick hunt around with a search engine to see if you can find a repository (known as a Debian or APT repository) for your package. If you find one, use the Repositories dialog box you have just played with to add the new repository, and then use Synaptic to install the package.

If no repository is available, look for a Debian package (.deb) for the application. If you find one, download it, and double-click it to install. If no Debian Package exists, look for an Autopackage. (Details about Autopackage installation are later in this chapter.)

Finally, if all else fails, download the source code and compile it.

Nautilus Is Painfully Slow—How Can I Make It Run Faster?

There are a number of options you can deactivate to make using Nautilus a faster process. First, click Edit > Preferences, find the tab marked Preview, and click on it. If Show Text in Icons (the first option) is enabled it will preview some of the contents of text documents in their icons. Set this option to Never. Next, there's an option called Show Thumbnails. This option will preview image files as thumbnails. Set this option to Never to further improve the speed of Nautilus browsing. If enabled, the option Preview Sound Files will make it possible to preview sound files without actually opening them. Set this to Never as well. The last option, Count Number of Items, shows how many items are within the folders listed in the directory you're currently browsing. Set this to Never.

If you are still not satisfied with the speed of Nautilus, you could check out some other file managers, such as Rox Filer or Thunar.

Add TrueType Fonts to Your Desktop Quickly

Fonts have a huge impact on how attractive and usable your desktop is. Although Ubuntu comes with a range of high-quality fonts, you may want to install some additional fonts. This is often the case when you need to use a specific company font. On modern OS, most fonts come in the form of TrueType fonts. Ubuntu offers full support for TrueType fonts, and it is simple to add new fonts.

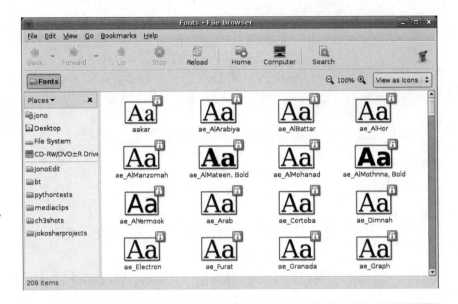

Figure 6-2 Installing fonts is as simple as dropping them in the font directory.

To add a font, press Alt+F2. In the resulting dialog box type fonts:///, and press Enter. A font folder opens up such as that seen in Figure 6-2. Drag and drop your new font(s) to the folder that opens up.

To check to see if the new fonts are installed, press Alt+F2, and in the dialog box type ~/.fonts. You should see your new font in the folder that appears. Try out the new font in an application such as GIMP. You will have to restart open applications before they detect the new fonts.

NOTE   If you perform these steps as an ordinary user, the fonts will only be available to your user account.

How Can I Test That an ISO File Works?

Whenever you download a Linux distribution such as Ubuntu, you will typically download an .iso file, a file that contains an image of a CD. This file is then used to create an installation CD that can be used to install the distribution. After downloading the file you may want to first check that the file works and, second, verify that the file is a legitimate download.

Checking That the ISO Works   Open a terminal, and then go to the folder where the ISO image has been downloaded. As an example, if you saved it to your disk in Firefox, it will have saved it to the Desktop folder in your home folder:

```
foo@bar:~$ cd Desktop
```

To test that the ISO image works, you are going to mount it and access the files in a particular folder. First, create this folder:

```
foo@bar:~$ mkdir test_iso
```

Now mount it on that folder:

```
foo@bar:~$ sudo mount -o loop -t iso9660 my_iso_file.iso test_iso
```

That's it! Now you can browse the folder test_iso.

Verifying the ISO   To verify the iso, fire up a terminal, and run the following command:

```
foo@bar:~$ md5sum my_iso_file.iso
```

Wait a little while and Ubuntu will print a "word" that is 33 characters long. Now go to the site from which you downloaded the file, and compare this word with the md5sum given by the owner of the iso file, usually a file named MD5SUMS. The words should match.

I Downloaded an Autopackage But I Don't Know How to Run It

Autopackages are software packages that install on any Linux distribution, including Ubuntu. Autopackages offer an ideal way of installing software on your system that is not available via Synaptic. If you need something Synaptic can't offer, Autopackages are a great alternative.

TIP   **Replacing an Application with an Autopackage**

If you are running an existing application that was installed via Synaptic, and you want to replace it with an Autopackage, make sure that you uninstall the application first with Synaptic. Autopackage does not work in conjunction with Synaptic, so ensure that you remove any applications before you install the Autopackage.

When you find an Autopackage that you want to install, download it to your desktop. Now, right-click the package, and select Properties. In the Permissions tab, select the Execute checkbox on the Owner row. Now close the dialog box, and double-click the package.

The installation program now begins, and you can just follow the onscreen instructions.

How Do I Compile an Application?

When a distribution package is not available, the source code is always available to compile with Open Source applications. Compilation is the process of converting programming code into a program that you can run and use. Although it sounds like a devilishly difficult process, it is typically fairly simple.

You should first have a look on the application's Web page, or in the INSTALL or README file that is included with the code to see what software the application needs to run. When you know what is required, use Synaptic to search for the required tools. Many of the requirements will be software libraries (software that applications require to run), and these libraries typically have "lib" at the start of the package name. As an example, if you need to have the Vorbis audio codec installed, do a search in Synaptic for Vorbis, and libvorbis will be one of the packages. You should also install with -dev at the end of the package name (such as libvorbis-dev). These packages allow you to compile software for that library.

The process of compiling software involves three steps: (1) configuration, (2) compilation, and (3) installation. Open a terminal, move into the directory from which you extracted the source code, and configure it:

```
foo@bar:yourapp$ ./configure
```

When you run ./configure, it checks to see that you have all the required software. If it throws an error, it is likely that a required tool or library is missing. Find out what it is, and install it. Typically, configure will tell you what you need to install.

If the configure script works fine, compile the code with this command:

```
foo@bar:yourapp$ make
```

If a problem appears when compiling the software, it may be a bug or problem in the source code. It is best to refer your problem to the author of the code for further help.

If the compile process was successful, install the application with this command:

```
foo@bar:yourapp$ sudo make install
```

The software is now fully installed.

QUICK TIP   If you want to ensure you have all the right tools installed to build your application, run the following command:

```
foo@bar:~$ sudo apt-get build-dep packagename
```

I Can't See the Hidden Dot Files and Folders in the File Manager

Files and directories that begin with a dot (such as .openoffice2) are typically used to store settings and configuration details for a particular application. By default, the file manager does not show these files. So how do you view, move, and copy them? Simple. Just click View > Show Hidden Files, or press Ctrl-H and your hidden files are displayed, as shown in Figure 6-3.

TIP   **Warning!**
Don't ever mess around with hidden files and directories unless you know exactly what you are doing. Making the wrong move with one of these files or directories could break something!

How Do I Restore Something I Deleted in the File Manager?

When you delete something in Ubuntu, the files are not deleted immediately and are instead moved to the wastebasket. If you accidentally deleted your important report and want to avoid limb removal by your boss, open the wastebasket by double-clicking the small wastebasket icon in the bottom right-hand corner of the screen, and then drag your files back into the file manager. The world now returns to the happy place it was before you accidentally deleted your files.

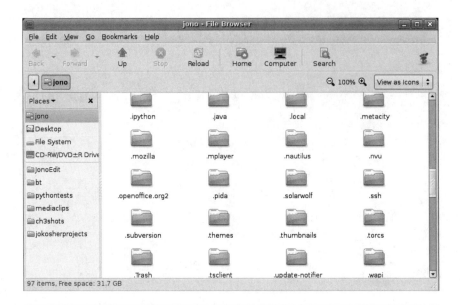

Figure 6-3 Displaying hidden files can be useful when you need to edit them.

The Desktop Has Hung—What Do I Do?

In the rare situation that the desktop hangs, first try to restart it by pressing Alt-Ctrl-Backspace at the same time. This kills and restarts the X server. Another method of killing the X server is to press Alt+F2 to jump to a terminal, log in, and then run this command:

```
foo@bar:~$ /etc/init.d/gdm stop
```

This command stops the graphical login screen, which in turn stops the X server. You can restart it with this command:

```
foo@bar:~$ /etc/init.d/gdm start
```

My Screen Resolution Is Wrong

If your screen resolution is incorrect, click System > Preferences > Screen Resolution, and select a new resolution from the combo box.

If the box does not show the resolution that you want, refer to the recipe that reconfigures your X server.

How Can I Automatically Login without Having to Enter My Login Details?

If logging in is a drag for you, click System > Administration > Login Screen Setup, and select the Login a User automatically on first bootup checkbox. In the checkbox below it, select the user who should be logged in automatically.

Be careful when automatically logging in—anyone will have access to the computer when it is started. If you would prefer certain people not have access to the computer, automatically logging in may not be such a good idea.

TIP   **Automatically Logging in Root**
In the Security tab of the window, you can allow root to login automatically. Although possible, this is *not recommended* due to the security implications. Automating a root login could allow anyone to tamper with your computer—so be careful!

I Tried to Upgrade My System, but I Get an Error

If you try to install some software or upgrade your computer, and you get an error, the package manager may have tied itself in a knot. To try to resolve this, open a terminal, and run the following commands:

```
foo@bar:~$ sudo apt-get update
foo@bar:~$ sudo apt-get -f install
```

The first command updates your package list, and the second command tries to fix your package manager. If this is successful the packages that failed will be installed correctly.

In addition to these commands, you can reconfigure any packages that have not yet been configured by running:

```
foo@bar:~$ sudo dpkg –configure –pending
```

I Am Running Out of Disk Space—How Do I Free Up Some Space?

If you are concerned you may be running out of disk space, there are a few techniques that you can use to clear some room. Before you do anything you should get a report of how much disk space is available. Load up a terminal, and run the following command:

```
foo@bar:~$ df -h
```

The df command prints a listing of the free space on your disk. By passing it the -h option, more readable file sizes are displayed (e.g., 9.5G as opposed to 9887776). In addition to the file size, a percentage of how much space is left is displayed. If the line with / in the Mounted On column is nearing 100 percent, you need to clear some room. The / partition is where most of the software is installed.

The first thing you should do is to clean out your package cache. Every time a package is downloaded with Synaptic or with the automatic upgrade manager, it is stored in /var/cache/apt/archives/. You can clean out these packages without affecting your system. Just run the following command:

```
foo@bar:~$ sudo apt-get clean
```

With the package cache cleaned, you should now look for the largest directories on your system. This is where the command line can really come into its own. Run the following command:

```
foo@bar:~$ du -h /home | sort -nr | less
```

The du command lists disk usage for the /home directory (where users store their files). Again, the -h option makes the sizes more readable. The output of this command is fed into sort which organizes the output numerically (-n) and reverses the order (-r) to display the largest files first. Finally, the output is fed into less, which lets you scroll up and down through the listing.

Find the largest directories, and remove any unwanted files by either using the graphical file manager or the rm command.

TIP   **A Graphical Option**
A useful little tool called Baobab can be installed to provide a graphical means of exploring hard disk usage. Baobab also includes a script for Nautilus so that you can right-click a folder to use Baobab to explore that folder. Baobab is packaged and ready to install for Ubuntu—just use Synaptic to download and install it.

I Deleted Something in the File Manager, but I Don't See the Extra Disk Space

When you delete files in the file manager, they are copied to the wastebasket. To finally delete them, right-click the wastebasket in the bottom right-hand corner of the screen, and click Empty the Wastebasket. A dialog box pops up asking you to confirm the deletion. Click the Empty the Wastebasket button, and the files are removed.

Another Version of Ubuntu Is Out—How Do I Upgrade to It?

If a new version of Ubuntu is released, the update manager will notify you via an upgrade notification pop-up bubble. To upgrade, click the Upgrade button, and follow the instructions.

If you want to manually upgrade, first find out the codename for the next version of Ubuntu (in the same vain as Warty, Hoary, Breezy, and Dapper). Now open /etc/apt/sources.list, and replace the word "dapper" with the new codeword. Now run:

```
foo@bar:~$ sudo apt-get updates
```

This command updated your package list. Now upgrade the system:

```
foo@bar:~$ sudo apt-get dist-upgrade
```

You are asked if you wish to continue. Press Y, and then press Enter to continue. Your entire system is now upgraded.

TIP   **As Usual . . .**
Remember to back up all your important files before doing a distribution upgrade!

Applications

Applications are the lifeblood of any desktop computer, but they are also packed with configuration options, different types of functionality, and other things that could possibly trip you up. This section covers some of the common application-oriented problems in Ubuntu.

When I Click the Close Window Icon, My Program Doesn't Go Away

If your application seems to hang, and the window won't go away, keep clicking the X icon. After a few seconds a dialog box should appear to indicate the program has become inactive and asking if you want to close it.

If this does not work, you can use xkill to stop it. Press Alt+F2, type xkill, and press Enter. Your mouse cursor changes to a small skull and crossbones. Click the offending application window, and it will finally be banished to that place where naughty applications wallow.

The Upgrade Notification Bubble Keeps Appearing, and I Want It to Stop

When your system detects new upgrades are available, a small bubble appears in the notification area. To switch this off, right-click the upgrades icon, and deselect the Show Notifications option.

Extending Nautilus with Scripts

The file manager driving your Ubuntu desktop is called Nautilus. This comprehensive tool is not only packaged with features out of the box, but also has the ability to be extended and improved with the use of special scripts.

A Nautilus script is just an executable shell script (usually using the default Ubuntu bash shell) that is placed in a special scripts directory so that the Nautilus graphical shell can find it. This is a really neat function of Nautilus, because it allows you to extend the functionality of the file browser to do just about anything.

Scripts are invoked by selecting a file or group of files and right-clicking with the mouse to bring up a Context menu. One of the options of this menu is the Scripts submenu, which allows you to select a script to invoke on the selected files.

Installing a Script   For a script to appear on the Script submenu, it must be placed in your scripts directory and be executable. If you place an executable script in your scripts directory, its name will not necessarily appear on the Scripts menu immediately. You first must visit the scripts directory with Nautilus by using the last option in the Scripts menu. Once the directory is visited, Nautilus will know about which scripts you have, and you will be able to use them. The current location of the scripts directory is .GNOME2/Nautilus-scripts in your home directory.

A Sample Nautilus Script To get you started with Nautilus scripts, we will look at an example script. This script pops up a window to ask for a folder location and then loads Nautilus at that location. It's a simple example, but it shows you how to create a script and run it.

Open your favorite text editor, and paste the following code into a new file:

```
#! /bin/bash
#
# GoTo script for Nautilus scripts
# by ardchoille
# This script is released under the GPL
# February 20, 2006
#
mylocation='zenity -entry -text="Enter the desired location:"
-width=300 -title="Nautilus location"'
Nautilus -no-desktop -browser $mylocation
exit
```

Save the new file to your Nautilus scripts directory with the filename of "GoTo." (You can use any filename really.) Now make the new script executable with:

```
foo@bar:~$ chmod a+x filename
```

Right-click in Nautilus, and choose Scripts > GoTo, and you will be presented with a zenity dialog that asks for a valid path. After entering the path, click the OK button, and Nautilus will open with the specified path.

TIP   **For More Fun and Games . . .**
Install the Nautilus-actions package to add an extension to Nautilus for configuring programs to be launched depending on Nautilus selections.

I Went to a Web Site in Firefox, and the Macromedia Flash Plug-in Is Missing

If you visit a Web site in Firefox and the flash plug-in is required, a small bar appears indicating that you need to install an additional plug-in. To do this, click the Install Missing Plug-ins button, and follow the instructions.

When the program has downloaded and installed the plug-in, restart Firefox, and you are all set.

Java Is Not Installed on My System

To run a Java application on your system or access a Java Web site in Firefox, you need to install the Java libraries first. To do this, fire up Synaptic, and install the j2re1.4 and j2re1.4-mozilla-plug-in packages.

If you want to run a version of Java not included with Ubuntu, refer to https://wiki.Ubuntu.com/RestrictedFormats.

I Have Heard Desktop Search Is Cool—How Do I Install It?

In recent months, desktop search has gained more and more coverage in different parts of the media. With the release of Mac OS X Tiger and speculation about WinFS in Windows Vista, more hype was piled onto the desktop search bonfire. You will be pleased to know that Linux users don't miss out either.

The idea behind desktop search is that all files on your desktop are automatically indexed. When you create or remove a file, the index is updated. With this kind of functionality, you can use a single search interface to look for anything on your system.

The Linux implementation of desktop search is called Beagle. Beagle is still very much in development and, as such, is not included by default in Ubuntu. To install Beagle select the Beagle package from Applications > Add/Remove Applications. Beagle not only indexes the name and contents of your files, it also indexes e-mails in Evolution, instant messaging conversations in Gaim, blogs, Web pages, and more.

To perform a search click Applications > Accessories > Beagle Search, and type in your search term. Press Enter, and you will see the results such as those displayed in Figure 6-4.

TIP   **All Hail the Deskbar**
If you install Beagle and find that you like it, you should also install the deskbar package. This small panel applet provides a convenient means to search for all kinds of different things on your computer. It is simple, convenient, and reliable.

Figure 6-4 Beagle is simple and useful.

My E-Mail Doesn't Work in Evolution

When you first run Evolution it runs through the setup procedure to configure your e-mail address. To do this successfully, you need to have the
following details available:

- Your type of e-mail server (such as POP or IMAP)

- Your mail server name (such as mail.chin.com)

- Your mail account's username and password

- Authentication type (typically password)

- Your outgoing mail server type (typically SMTP)

- Your outgoing mail server name

If you have configured your account and your e-mail doesn't work, click
Edit > Preferences, select the account from the list, and click the Edit button.

Ensure that the settings above are all correct. If you still cannot connect to your e-mail server, there is either a configuration problem or a network problem.

The latter problem would mean one of two things: your computer is not connected to the network, or the mail server is not connected to the network. To test this, run the following command in a terminal:

```
foo@bar:~$ ping mail.chin.com
```

Replace mail.chin.com with the name of your mail server. The ping command sends a few pieces of information to the server to see if it responds. If it does respond, a series of lines will be displayed with a response time. If you get this, your network is running fine, and the problem is likely to be a configuration error.

A configuration error can either be on your computer or the mail server itself, with your computer being the far more likely candidate. You should get in touch with the person who runs the mail server and confirm that your settings above are correct. Also check that the mail server is running fine. If the configuration error is on the mail server side, there is nothing you can do until it is fixed. In this case, ask the administrator to let you know when it is fixed.

When you find out the correct configuration settings, enter them into Evolution and try again.

Multimedia

Multimedia is playing an increasingly important role in modern desktops, and most people like to listen music, watch movies, and watch videos on their desktop. Unfortunately, multimedia has had something of a checkered history in the Linux world due to the licensing problems with the all important codecs that are required to view and hear your media. This section explores some of common problems faced with multimedia and your Ubuntu desktop.

TIP   **Restricted Formats**
You can get further help and guidance on restricted media formats that don't ship with Ubuntu by visiting https://wiki.Ubuntu.com/RestrictedFormats.

I Downloaded a Particular Media File, and It Won't Play

Included with Ubuntu are Open Source codecs such as Ogg Vorbis and Ogg Theora, but the vast majority of media on the Internet uses restrictively licensed codecs such as MP3, Windows Media, QuickTime, and others.

Ubuntu does not ship these Codecs for legal and philosophical reasons. Not only would shipping the Codecs possibly breach the original license, but Ubuntu is fundamentally oriented around a totally free and Open Source desktop.

There are methods for playing these media formats, and if you want to install them, refer to the Ubuntu Forums for more details.

My DVD Won't Play

As with the previous problem, DVD playback is also a somewhat restricted process that requires special software to be installed. The software is available if needed. Again, refer to the Ubuntu Forums for more details.

DVD Playback Is Jittery and Jumpy

When you watch DVD movies on your computer, you may find that they are jittery and unstable. In most cases the problem is that direct memory access (DMA) mode in your DVD drive is not enabled. By enabling this mode, your problems should disappear.

Check if DMA mode is enabled by running this command:

```
foo@bar:~$ sudo /sbin/hdparm /dev/hdc | grep dma
```

Most DVD drives are /dev/hdc, but change the letter if yours is different. If DMA mode is not enabled, you will see this:

```
using_dma = 1 (on)
```

To turn on DMA mode, run this command:

```
foo@bar:~$ sudo /sbin/hdparm -d1 /dev/hdc
```

Now try to play your DVD.

If this solves your problems, you should edit /etc/hdparm.conf and add the following block:

```
/dev/hdc {
     dma = on
}
```

When I Start Some Applications, Ubuntu Says I Don't Have Access to /dev/dsp

There are literally hundreds of thousands of applications for the Linux system, and many of them have different requirements and dependencies. One area in which this can be a problem is audio software. Each audio application relies on one of many sound servers: pieces of software that manage communication with the sound card. These sound servers come in many forms, including esd, gstreamer, arts, and jack.

In Ubuntu, esd is the default sound server. Although the multimedia applications included with your desktop work fine, some other applications (such as Audacity shown in Figure 6-5) may complain when you start them that something else has access to /dev/dsp. To solve this click Applications > System Tools > System Monitor. In the list of processes click on esd, and click the End Process button. By stopping esd you can now use the application.

TIP   **But Remember . . .**
Of course, by killing esd, those applications that require esd will not run. To use those applications (such as the default multimedia application included in Ubuntu) start esd by pressing Alt+F2 and typing esd into the textbox. You will hear some beeps to indicate esd is now running.

My Microphone Doesn't Work

Although it seems like an obvious first point to check, ensure that you have plugged your microphone into the right socket. Many computers include a number of audio inputs/outputs, and they can be easily confused. In recent years a number of hardware manufacturers seem to have gone out of their way to poorly mark these sockets, so don't worry if you get them mixed up. If in doubt, consult your manual.

With the microphone properly plugged in, load up the recording level monitor by clicking Applications > Sound and Video > Recording Level Monitor, and speak into your microphone. If you see nothing appearing

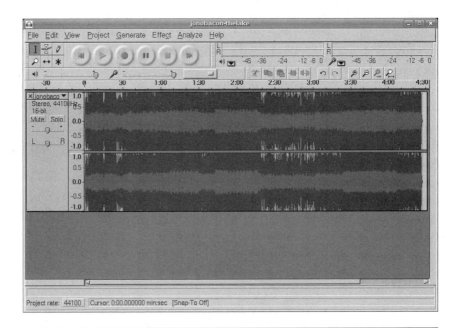

Figure 6-5 Audacity is a typical application that requires this recipe.

on the scale, you need to turn on and adjust the volume of your microphone. To do this, right-click the volume icon in the notification area, and select Open Volume Control. Inside the dialog that pops up, click the Capture tab, make sure the microphone sliders are near the top and that the small microphone icon does not have a red cross on it. This icon mutes the devices, and clicking it toggles it.

Now speak into the microphone, and you should see the recording level monitor flash. To record your voice click Applications > Accessories > Sound Recorder.

How Do I Change the Visual Theme?

To change the way your Ubuntu desktop looks, click System > Preferences > Theme, and you will see Figure 6-6.

From there, you can select predefined themes or click details to create a custom theme. Changes are applied immediately. If you click Details, you get a dialog box with three tabs. All themes are separated into three parts: the elements (buttons, text fields, etc.), the window frame (the title bar), and

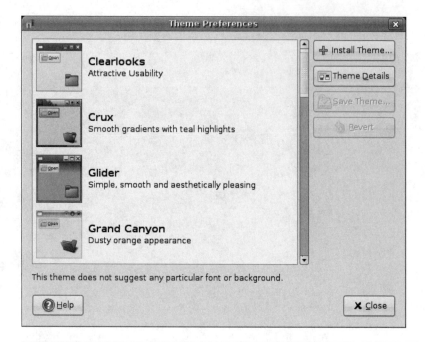

Figure 6-6 Changing themes is simple—click it, and it changes!

icons. If you have downloaded new themes, drag them into the theme details window, and click Install. When you are done, click Close.

How Do I Find and Install New Desktop Themes and Backgrounds?

We all love tweaking our desktops so they look individual to our own tastes and preferences. Luckily the desktop is very flexible in how it can be visually configured. To make this as simple as possible, the GNOME Art Web site was created to host a huge array of wallpapers and themes. You can use the site to spruce up your desktop.

TIP   **Art Web Sites**
There are a number of sites that help make your desktop look pretty. See http://art.ubuntu.com, http://art.gnome.org or http://gnome-look.org.

To make this even easier, there is a tool called art manager that can be used to find new themes and backgrounds, but it is not installed by default. To install it, use Synaptic to install GNOME-art. After it is installed, click System > Preferences > Art Manager to load it.

To find desktop backgrounds click Art > Backgrounds > All. If you don't want to see GNOME backgrounds, click Art > Backgrounds > Other. Alternatively, if you only want GNOME backgrounds, click Art > Backgrounds > GNOME. The art manager downloads thumbnails and descriptions of all available backgrounds. The latest backgrounds are at the bottom of the list. Select one from the list. To show the background in detail, click Preview. To install it, click Install. The change background window then shows the installed background. From there you can optionally change its style. When you're done, click Finish to get back to the art manager.

To find desktop theme elements click Art > Desktop themes > Application. The latest are at the bottom. To see a sample window displaying the selected theme, click Preview. To install the theme, click Install. Then from the Theme preferences window, click Theme-details, and select the new elements from the list. Click both Close buttons to go back to the art manager.

Finding new window borders and icon themes works similarly. You can also install splash screens and login screens, but the former are not used by default in Ubuntu (though they can be enabled in the session manager), and the latter cannot be installed directly. GTK+ engines are seldom used. None of the applications that are installed by default use it.

How Do I Turn My Ubuntu Computer into a MythTV Box?

MythTV is a collection of applications that can convert a computer into a full-fledged media center with the capability to pause live TV, record shows, play music, play videos, play DVDs, access weather information, and more. More details about MythTV are available at www.mythtv.org/. MythTV also goes to great lengths to look like a normal TV device and not like a computer plugged into a TV (see Figure 6-7 for an example).

To install a full MythTV system, install each of the mythtv packages that are available in Synaptic. You also need to install a few other packages:

- **xmltv:** This is used to grab TV listings in XML formatting

- **DVD support:** To watch DVDs you should refer to the Ubuntu Wiki and install the relevant packages

- **lirc:** Install this if you want to use a remote control

Figure 6-7 MythTV makes TV so much more fun!

MythTV comes in two major parts: the front end and the back end. The back-end is used to perform the grunt work such as recording and processing shows, and the front-end provides an attractive user interface. With this architecture you could run the back end on a bulky, noisy machine elsewhere in the house and run the front end on a fanless, attractive little machine in your living room.

Unfortunately, we don't have the space to cover the configuration of MythTV. Instead refer to the Ubuntu Forums.

Networking

There are few modern computers that are not on the Internet now. With such an important feature, having a networking problem can feel like a crippling blow, particularly for those of us who spend extended periods of time staring at a Web browser. This section identifies some of the common problems with wired and wireless networking.

I Can't Access My LAN

First check that the cables for your network are plugged in correctly. On many hubs, a small light appears when a cable is plugged into one of the sockets. Many Ethernet cards also display a connection light too.

Next check if the card has been recognized by the system. To find out, fire up the Networking tool by clicking System-Administration > Networking, and you should see an icon displayed in the window that represents your network card. If there is no icon, your card has not been detected and loaded by Ubuntu.

TIP   **How to Find Out If Your Device Is Supported**

If your device is not currently supported, search through the Ubuntu Wiki (http://wiki.Ubuntu.com/) and the Ubuntu Forums (http://Ubuntuforums.org/). Searching for the name and model of your device is most likely to return some results. Alternatively, do a Web search for your device and Linux or Ubuntu to see if any generic support is being worked on.

In the Networking tool, double-check that your settings are correct. You can check if your network card is working and has an interface by opening a terminal with Applications > Accessories > Terminal and typing:

```
foo@bar:~$ ifconfig
```

You should see a number of blocks such as eth0 or ra0. One of these blocks should have a local IP address. The format of this address depends on which IP range is on your network. The range 192.168.0.n where n is a number between 1 and 254 is commonly used. If you see an IP address in your ifconfig output, try pinging the IP that you set as the gateway. If you did not set a gateway (typically when you obtain your IP address automatically with DHCP), your IP address is likely to be 192.168.0.1. Try to send packets to this IP:

```
foo@bar:~$ ping 192.168.0.1
```

Change the IP address if your IP range is different. If you get a number of lines with a time = attribute at the end, your network card works.

If you have set up your network card to automatically grab an IP address with DHCP, you can get a new address by running the following command:

```
foo@bar:~$ sudo dhclient
```

Nameserver Problems

A common problem that users often face is that the connection to your network is working, but the addresses for the nameservers are incorrect. A nameserver (also known as a DNS server) converts Web addresses (such as www.Ubuntu.com) into the numeric IP address that is used to access the site.

If you have a working connection but cannot access domains, it is certainly a nameserver problem. To test this, you will need to know an IP address. You may have been given some IP addresses for different services from your ISP. Alternatively, you can use another computer to find an IP address with which to test. Try pinging the address, and if you get pings back you know it's a nameserver problem. To resolve this, specify the correct nameservers in the DNS tab.

How Do I Use ssh (Secure SHell) for Transferring Files across a Network?

Secure shell is a protocol for connecting to remote computers in a safe way. To connect on the client side to a remote computer, click Locations > Connect to Server, and choose SSH as the service type. In the first field, enter the host name or IP address of the remote computer.

The folder field can be left blank but can be used to go straight into a folder when you open the connection in the file manager. For instance, the home folder of user joe is typically /home/joe. Other folders are still accessible by clicking the Up button on the toolbar. Enter the username of the user on the remote computer in the username field. If it's the same as the local username, just leave it blank. Both the folder field and the username field are case sensitive. Click Connect to proceed.

The first time you connect, a question appears that says the identity of the remote computer is yet unknown. This is normal. Click the Login Anyway button to proceed. If you are asked for a password, enter the password of the user on the remote computer. Click on Remember Password for This Session and Connect. If the password was wrong or it took too long to enter the password, it is asked again.

The connection appears on the desktop. If you chose not to remember the password for the session or in the keychain, you may be asked again.

Now you can use the remote files the same way you use them locally. You can even copy files across different ssh connections and other network protocols such as FTP.

How Do I Use a Graphical Application Remotely with ssh (Secure SHell)?

To connect on the client side to the remote computer, first open a terminal. Click Applications > Utilities > Terminal Window. Now run this command:

```
foo@bar:~$ ssh -X user@host
```

where *user* is the user name on the remote computer, and *host* is the host name or IP address. If the user name is the same, leave out the *user@* part. -X here signals ssh that you want to run graphical applications. Make sure you use capitals exactly as shown. Usernames are also case sensitive.

If it's the first time you are connecting, you will get a warning similar to the following:

```
The authenticity of host '251.152.123.101' (251.152.123.101)' can't
be established.
RSA key fingerprint is
01:12:23:34:45:56:67:78:89:9a:ab:bc:cd:de:ef:ff.
Are you sure you want to continue connecting (yes/no)?
```

Type Yes, and press Enter. When asked for a password, enter the password of the user on the remote computer. Now you should have a shell on the remote computer, and it's possible to run commands remotely.

You can try, for example, Firefox to open up Mozilla Firefox, or Gaim to have a chat with yourself.

My Wireless Card Is Not Working

One of the greatest new features for laptop users in Ubuntu is network-manager. With this shiny new application it is finally easy to connect your Ubuntu system to any wireless network. Where previously you had to jump through hoops to do WPA or 802.1x authentication, network manager makes this completely transparent.

Simply click on the Network-Manager icon to see all available wireless networks, and click on the network to connect to it. If wireless authentication is needed, be it WEP, WPA, or 802.1x, a network-manager dialog will pop up asking for your authentication details.

Of course, these improvements are not limited to laptop or even desktop users. Even for machines without a GUI, networking has been made easy by the Debian and Ubuntu developers who integrated WPA authentication into the standard network configuration system.

If network manager does not solve the problem, the first step should be to see which driver your wireless card needs. Do a search for your card on Google and in the Ubuntu Forums to find out which driver you need. Many of the drivers are already included in Ubuntu, but some newer drivers may not be present.

Next, you need to find out if the driver is loaded. As an example, if you have an Intel Centrino and it uses the ipw2200 driver, run this command

```
foo@bar:~$ sudo lsmod | grep ipw2200
```

Replace ipw2200 with the relevant driver for your card. If you get some lines returned, the driver is loaded and working. If nothing is returned, your card is either not supported or the driver is not included in Ubuntu. You should refer to the Ubuntu Forums for further support.

With the card identified, you now need to get connected. The easiest way to do this is to select System > Administration > Networking. Inside this tool you should see an icon for your wireless card. Select it and click the Properties button. Now add the name of the wireless network and a password if applicable. If you are using a normal password such as s3cr3tpass, select Plain (ASCII) from the Key type box. If you are entering the long numeric password—use the Hexedecimal option.

QUICK TIP   If you don't have a password on your wireless network, leave the Key type and WEP key boxes empty.

If you are automatically assigned an IP address, use the Configuration box to select DHCP. Otherwise, select Static IP Address, and enter the details of your network in the boxes.

For more information, see https://wiki.Ubuntu.com/HardwareSupport ComponentsWirelessNetworkCards.

I Need to Use WPA or I Use WPA-PSK on My Wireless Access Point

To use WPA, you need a supported card. Such cards are listed on the WPA Supplicant Web site at http://hostap.epitest.fi/wpa_supplicant/. Common drivers that support WPA include ipw2200, ipw2100, and madwifi.

To use WPA (Wi-Fi Protected Access) with wireless cards in Ubuntu, the wpasupplicant package must be installed. After installing it, edit /etc/wpa_supplicant.conf. Networks are configured by adding network blocks to the configuration file. Each network block can also be assigned a priority so if both networks are seen, the higher priority network is chosen. Examples for common network configurations can be found in /usr/share/doc/wpasupplicant/examples/wpa_supplicant.conf.gz.

Some configurations require certificates that should be available from the network administrator. WPA Supplicant can also configure your wireless card to use unencrypted networks, as noted in the example file. After writing the file, edit /etc/default/wpasupplicant and change the ENABLED, DRIVER, and INTERFACE options. The DRIVER option should match the type of wireless device being used. Available drivers can be viewed by typing:

```
foo@bar:~$ wpa_supplicant -help
```

To start the Supplicant run:

```
foo@bar:~$ /etc/init.d/wpasupplicant start
```

Lastly, wpasupplicant should be added to STOP_SERVICES in /etc/default/acpi-support to ensure it functions properly after a system suspend or hibernation.

To check if the connection is working, run:

```
foo@bar:~$ sudo wpa_cli
```

This command gives information on the current connection along with scrolling logs to indicate the current status. By default wpa_cli must be run as root. Status will show what network the wireless card is currently connected to and parameters about the link. Scan causes the supplicant to look for a new access point while scan_results will display what access points are locally accessible to the machine. As soon as the supplicant authenticates, `ifplugd` should start the interface with `ifup`, and networking will be available shortly. If it seems that the supplicant is not working it may be that a different driver must be selected in the /etc/defaults/wpasupplicant configuration file. Also, some cards cannot operate in a mixed TKIP/CCMP (types of encryption) mode. If it appears the PTK listed in the log from wpa_cli is CCMP but that the GTK is TKIP, setting the pairwise and group entries of a network configuration block to TKIP may fix the issue.

Hardware

There are many, many different types of hardware available for computers, including Webcams, network cards, hard disks, video cards, sound cards, and more. For each of these devices to work, a driver needs to be loaded by the Linux kernel. Unlike systems such as Windows, you don't need to install a special driver that is included with the device. Instead, the driver should already be included in Ubuntu and ready to work out of the box.

Of course, this is not always the case, and sometimes hardware can be something of a beast to get working. In this section we tear apart some of the hardware-related problems and attempt to resolve them.

Ubuntu Has Not Detected My Old Sound Card

Many older devices are not automatically detected by the current 2.6 kernel series. This is done to avoid hardware issues such as crashes. Unfortunately if you have an older sound card, it means you need to roll your sleeves up and poke around to get it running. To do this you need to know which kernel module your card needs and then load the module yourself. Loading the correct module for your device will not cause your system to crash, but loading the wrong one may well do so. You may need to experiment with different modules.

Look for the model of sound card you have by referring to your computer's specifications, the name of the device in Windows (if applicable), or by opening the computer case and looking at the sound chip. You can use Google to match a chip's serial number with the chipset type. Here is a list of devices and the relevant kernel module (taken from www.icewalkers.com/linux/howto/bootprompt-howto-8.html):

- snd-dummy = Dummy soundcard
- snd-mpu401 = mpu401 UART
- snd-mtpav = MOTU Midi Timepiece
- snd-serial = Serial UART 16450/16550 MIDI
- snd-virmidi = Dummy soundcard for virtual rawmidi devices
- snd-ad1816a = ADI SoundPort AD1816A
- snd-ad1848 = Generic driver for AD1848/AD1847/CS4248
- snd-als100 = Avance Logic ALS100
- snd-azt2320 = Aztech Systems AZT2320 (and 2316)
- snd-cmi8330 = C-Media's CMI8330
- snd-cs4231 = Generic driver for CS4231 chips
- snd-cs4232 = Generic driver for CS4232 chips
- snd-cs4236 = Generic driver for CS4235/6/7/8/9 chips
- snd-dt019x = Diamond Technologies DT-019x
- snd-es168 = Generic ESS AudioDrive ESx688
- snd-es18xx = Generic ESS AudioDrive ES18xx
- snd-gusclassic = Gus classic
- snd-gusextreme = Gus extreme
- snd-gusmax = Gus Max
- snd-interwave = Interwave
- snd-interwave-stb = Interwave
- snd-opl3sa2 = Yamaha OPL3SA2
- snd-opti93x = OPTi 82c93x based cards
- snd-opti92x-cs4231 = OPTi 82c92x/CS4231

- snd-opti92x-ad1848 = OPTi 82c92x/AD1848

- snd-es968 = ESS AudioDrive ES968

- snd-sb16 = SoundBlaster 16

- snd-sbawe = SoundBlaster 16 AWE

- snd-sb8 = Old 8 bit SoundBlaster (1.0, 2.0, Pro)

- snd-sgalaxy = Sound galaxy

- snd-wavefront = Wavefront

- ad1848 = AD1848

- adlib = Adlib

- mad16 = MAD16

- pas2 = ProAudioSpectrum PAS16

- sb = SoundBlaster

- uart401 = UART 401 (on card chip)

- uart6850 = UART 6850 (on card chip)

- opl3 = Yamaha OPL2/OPL3/OPL4 FM Synthesizer (on card chip)

- opl3sa = Yamaha OPL3-SA FM Synthesizer (on card chip)

- opl3sa2 = Yamaha OPL3-SA2/SA3 FM Synthesizer (on card chip)

When you have found the name of the module required, try loading it into the kernel:

```
foo@bar:~$ sudo modprobe themodule
```

If there is no error message, it may just be the right one! Run alsamixer to see if there is a sound device for it to configure:

```
foo@bar:~$ alsamixer
```

If the module is the wrong one, alsamixer will not allow you to set the sound parameters. If you can, add the module name to the /etc/modules file so that it gets loaded every time you boot:

```
foo@bar:~$ sudo gedit/etc/modules
```

My Cardbus Adapter Is Not Being Recognized

If you have a cardbus adapter and are having difficulty getting it work, open a terminal and run this command:

```
foo@bar:~$ sudo gedit /boot/grub/menu.lst
```

Find the line `## ## End Default Options ##` below which you can see your kernel. As an example:

```
title       Ubuntu, kernel 2.6.12-10-686-smp
root        (hd0,0)
kernel      /boot/vmlinuz-2.6.12-10-686-smp root=/dev/sda1
                ro quiet splash
initrd      /boot/initrd.img-2.6.12-10-686-smp
```

Add this to the end of the third line, one space after `splash`:

```
pci=assign-busses
```

It should now look like this:

```
title       Ubuntu, kernel 2.6.12-10-686-smp
root        (hd0,0)
kernel      /boot/vmlinuz-2.6.12-10-686-smp root=/dev/sda1
                ro quiet splash pci=assign-busses
initrd      /boot/initrd.img-2.6.12-10-686-smp
```

Restart your computer, and your cardbus device should work.

I Plug in My USB Stick and Nothing Happens

When a USB stick is plugged in, it must be mounted before you can access it. This normally happens automatically, and you should see an icon on your desktop similar to that displayed in Figure 6-8.

Unfortunately, in some rare cases it doesn't work. To fix it, first check that your system is set to automatically mount USB sticks. Click System > Preferences > Removable Drives and Media and look in the Storage tab. The following checkboxes should be selected:

- Mount removable drives when hot-plugged
- Mount removable media when inserted
- Browse removable media when inserted

Figure 6-8 To use a USB storage device you just double-click the device icon that appears.

When you have selected the boxes, click Close, and try plugging your USB stick in again.

If you still have no luck, plug the USB stick in and then click Places–Computer. If there is an additional drive in the Computer window, right-click it, and select Mount Volume.

If you still have no luck, you need to manually mount the disk. First, click Applications > Accessories > Terminal, and then plug in your USB stick. Now run the following command:

```
foo@bar:~$ sudo mount -t vfat /dev/sda1 /mnt
```

To view your files use the file manager to access the /mnt directory. Before you finish with the disk, unmount it with:

```
foo@bar:~$ umount /dev/sda1
```

TIP   **Drive Names**
On some computers you may need to use /dev/sdb1 or /dev/sdc1. Type in the following command when you have plugged in your disk to see which drives are available:
```
foo@bar:~$ ls -l /dev/sd*
```

I Copied Some Files to/from My USB Stick, but When I Access It Later the Files Are Not There

When you plug in your USB stick, Ubuntu automatically mounts it. When you copy files to or from the stick, the files are copied over in bursts. Due to the way the kernel in Ubuntu works, sometimes there can be a slight delay before your files copy. If you remove the USB stick before they have finished copying, some or all of the files may not have copied over successfully.

To ensure that everything you do with the USB stick is complete before you remove it, you should unmount it. To do this right-click the Drive icon on your desktop or in Places > Computer, and select Unmount. Give it a few seconds. and when the light on the USB has stopped flashing, you can safely remove it from your computer.

My CD-ROM/DVD Is Not Working

If you are having problems accessing your CD-ROM/DVD drive, it is most likely because it is not mounted. Click Places > Computer and look at the CD-ROM/DVD drive icon in the window. If the drive is not mounted, the icon looks like a drive; otherwise it looks like a disk. If the drive isn't mounted, right-click it, and click Mount Volume.

My CD-ROM/DVD Drive Won't Eject

If you press the eject button on your CD-ROM drive and it won't eject, click Places > Computer, right-click the CD-ROM/DVD drive, and select Eject. If this doesn't work, load up a terminal by clicking Applications > Accessories > Terminal, and type:

```
foo@bar:~$ eject
```

I Bought a Device, but It Doesn't Work in Ubuntu

When you buy a hardware device such as a graphics card, sound card, DVD drive, or webcam the device needs to have a driver installed for it to work. In the Windows world this driver is included with the device, and you simply install it after you have plugged the device in.

In the Linux world things work a little differently. Your Ubuntu system includes an important piece of software called the kernel that manages how devices are used. The kernel includes a number of drivers that cover a huge range of hardware out of the box. The philosophy in the Linux world is that you should not even need to install a driver—just install the hardware, and the kernel will pick it up.

Although the kernel includes huge support for devices, there are occasions when a driver is not included. At this point you should find out if the device is actually supported in Ubuntu. To do this, search the Ubuntu forums wiki and do a general search on the Internet for your device and the keyword Linux. After a bit of hunting around you will probably find a driver that is available but obviously was not included with Ubuntu. Your first job should be to submit a bug report to say that the driver is not included in Ubuntu (see It Was Suggested I File a Bug Report but I Don't Know How later in this chapter). Include in your bug report the address of the Web site with the driver.

My Computer Says It Is Out of Memory

If you get memory errors and have a reasonable amount of memory (256MB or more) and a swap partition, your memory may be faulty. To check if your memory is working, restart your computer and when you see GRUB loading, press Escape to display the boot menu. Select the Memtest option, and a small tool will check your memory for errors.

The memtest utility tries its best to find problems with your memory, but there may be cases where memtest passes but the memory still has problems. To test against this, try swapping the memory with some that is known to work and see if the problems go away. If they do, the memory is certainly faulty.

How Can I Copy Photos from My Mobile Phone to My Ubuntu Computer with Bluetooth?

Ubuntu has built-in Bluetooth support, but you need to install the GNOME-Bluetooth package. Inside this package is a small tool called GNOME-obex-server. This application allows you to transfer files from your mobile to your computer.

When you have installed the package, hit Alt+F2, and enter GNOME-obex-server. A small blue icon appears in the notification area, and you can now send a file from your phone via Bluetooth.

I Can Read My USB Storage Device, but I Can't Write to It

If you are having trouble writing to a USB key or external USB hard drive, there are a number of possible causes of the problem.

The first and most simple to diagnose is that you may not have permission to write to the device. When you plug in the drive, right-click the icon that appears on your desktop, and select Properties. In the window that appears, click the Permissions tab and ensure that the Others line has the Write checkbox selected. If this is not selected, you don't have permission to access the drive.

QUICK TIP   If you do have sufficient permissions but still can't write to the drive, jump to the Filesystem Fun section below.

To change these permissions, fire up a terminal, and move to the /media folder:

```
foo@bar:~$ cd /media
```

Now take a look at which drives are in there:

```
foo@bar:~$ ls -al
```

In the output that appears you should see "usbdisk" as one of the entries. Now change the permissions so everyone can access it:

```
foo@bar:~$ sudo chmod a+w usbdisk
```

You should now be able to access the disk.

Filesystem Fun

If you have permissions to access the drive but still can't write to it, the problem is likely to be a filesystem issue. On a storage device such as a floppy disk, USB key, or hard drive, a specific type of filesystem is used to manage how the files are written to the physical disk. Ordinarily, you don't need to worry about this. But when things go wrong, it's time to figure out the details.

There are a number of different filesystems. The default Linux filesystem is ext3. In the Windows world, a few other filesystems are available such as FAT16, FAT32, and the NTFS system used by Windows NT.

Although FAT16 and FAT32 are fully supported in Ubuntu, an NTFS filesystem cannot yet be written to on a Linux computer. However, recent new code has gone in the Linux kernel to write to NTFS with FUSE or a kernel module. This code is still rather experimental and not included in a stock Ubuntu system, so be careful when playing with it.

To find out which filesystem the device uses, run the following command:

```
foo@bar:~$ sudo mount
```

In the output, look for the /dev/sda1 or /dev/sdb1 line. USB devices are usually located at either of these locations. You can see the filesystem next to where is says type. As an example, see the following:

```
/dev/sda1 on /media/usbdisk type ext3 (rw,noexec,nosuid,nodev)
```

In this example, the filesystem is ext3. You can also add the umask=0000 option if you want to allow any user to read the disk.

If the file system is supported (ext3, VFAT, FAT16, FAT32) but you still can't access the disk, the filesystem may be corrupted. In cases such as this it makes sense to format the disk with a new filesystem.

Before you format your disk, make *absolutely sure* that you are happy to remove the entire contents of the disk. If you need the files on the disk, have a look around the Internet and post to the Ubuntu forums to see if anyone else can help you before you format the disk. *Formatting really is the last option you have available!*

How Do I Format a Disk?

When most people think of formatting a disk, they think it is the process of deleting everything on the disk. Formatting a disk actually involves a little bit more, and it completely replaces the filesystem on the disk.

A side benefit to formatting a disk is making the disk work on different computers. Only certain types of filesystems are supported by each OS, and formatting a disk with a common filesystem can ensure that it works with these different OS. As an example, if you format a USB key with the ext3 filesystem, it won't work in Windows. If you use the VFAT filesystem, it will work in both Windows and Linux.

Formatting is fairly simple, and you just need to know the location of the device. USB storage devices (such as USB key rings and key fobs) tend to be located at /dev/sda1 or /dev/sdb1. Make sure that you have the right device, and then use one of the many `mkfs` commands to create the relevant filesystem. As an example, to create an ext3 filesystem, use the following command:

```
foo@bar:~$ sudo mkfs.ext3 /dev/sda1
```

There are a range of other `mkfs` commands that can be used to create other filesystems:

- `mkfs`
- mkfs.cramfs
- mkfs.ext2
- mkfs.ext3
- `mkfs.jfs`
- `mkfs.minix`
- mkfs.msdos
- `mkfs.reiser4`
- mkfs.reiserfs
- `mkfs.vfat`
- `mkfs.xfs`

Each of these commands is used in the same way.

The Keys on My Keyboard Spit Out the Wrong Letters/Symbols

Every keyboard on a computer has a particular keyboard layout and locale attached to it. The keyboard layout specifies how many keyboard keys you have, in what order, and the locale specifies what each key does.

The locale is particularly important as letters and symbols vary dramatically in different locales. Aside from different types of letters, common symbols are often placed in different areas. As an example, on some keyboards the double quote (") is on the key above the right shift key. On some keyboards it is Shift+2. Having the wrong keyboard settings can be incredibly frustrating, and if the symbols printed on your keys don't match up to the symbol that spits out when you press it, your keyboard settings are incorrect.

To fix this click System > Preferences > Keyboard. Click the Layouts tab, and next to the Keyboard model box click the . . . button to select your keyboard model if you know it. If you don't know it, use the default setting. Now click the Add button, and resize the window so you can see the keyboard layout diagram more easily. Choose a different locale that matches your keyboard, and then click OK.

Now click on the Keyboard tab, and use the Type to Test Settings box to test if your keyboard settings are correct.

My Serial Mouse Is Not Working

To get a non-USB serial mouse working, first run this command:

```
foo@bar:~$ sudo dpkg-reconfigure xserver-xorg
```

When asked for the mouse device, select /dev/ttys0 for COM1 or /dev/ttys1 for COM2.

My Mouse Scroll Wheel Does Not Work

To enable your scroll wheel, you need to run the X configuration program:

```
foo@bar:~$ sudo dpkg-reconfigure xserver-xorg
```

One of the questions asks if you would like to enable the scroll wheel. Enable this, and then restart your desktop. Your lovely little scroll wheel should work now.

My Remote Control Doesn't Work

If you want to use a remote control with your Ubuntu computer, you need to install the Linux Infra Red Control (LIRC) package in Synaptic. LIRC is the library, and it supports a wide range of remote-control units.

The first step is to determine which LIRC driver is required for your particular remote control. Take a look at the list of remotes on the LIRC site at www.lirc.org/ or use your favorite search engine if it is not listed on the site.

LIRC includes a number of built-in drivers, and you can see which ones are included by running the following command:

```
foo@bar:~$ lircd -driver=help
```

When you know which driver is required and you know your installed LIRC supports, you can edit the hardware.conf file in the /etc/lirc file to configure which one is used. Simply set the DRIVER line to the driver you selected. With this complete, restart LIRC:

```
foo@bar:~$ /etc/init.d/lirc restart
```

With LIRC ready and running, you can test it by running the following command:

```
foo@bar:~$ /etc/init.d/lirc restart
```

When you press the buttons on your remote control, a code should appear. This code can be mapped to a button on your remote by editing the lircd.conf file in /etc/lirc. For specific configuration details, see the LIRC Web site.

How Do I Find Out Which Hardware Works in Ubuntu before I Purchase It?

Currently, there is no centralized device database to search for hardware that works with Ubuntu, although work is going on to support this in a future version of Ubuntu.

A good place to start is to look at https://wiki.ubuntu.com/hardware support. You should then search the discussion forums and use Google to find out if anyone else has used it. Although not an ideal way of digging out the information, the forums and Google are likely to give you the information you need until the full device database is complete.

System Administration

Traditionally, Linux has been very popular with system administrators. This has not only been due to Linux's incredible flexibility and power, but also the Unix philosophy that drives much of the Linux platform. System administrators spend much of their day in the command line crafting strings of commands that hook together to do something interesting. With this powerful underlying command line platform, so much is possible.

System administration is sometimes fraught with its own fair share of problems though. This section lines up some of the problems and attempts to resolve them.

How Do I Schedule Things to Happen?

Built right into Ubuntu is a very powerful system to schedule things to happen at specific times or at regular intervals. This system, called cron, allows you to specify the timing details and the command to run in a special file called a crontab.

The crontab is a simple text file that holds a list of commands that are to be run at specified times. These commands, and their related run times, are controlled by the cron daemon and are executed in the system's background. More information can be found by viewing the crontab's man page, and we will run through a simple crontab example later to demonstrate how it is used.

The system maintains a crontab for each user on the system. In order to edit or create a crontab, you need to load it into a text editor. This text editor is opened when you use the -e option on the crontab command. To create a crontab, open a terminal and run the following command:

```
foo@bar:~$ crontab -e
```

The default nano text editor will open an empty crontab file. When adding crontab instructions, each line represents a separate crontab entry, also known as a cron job.

Crontab Sections   A typical line in a crontab looks like this:

```
00 1 3 5 10 ps ax
```

Each of the sections is separated by a space, with the final section having one or more spaces in it. No spaces are allowed within Sections 1–5, only between them. Sections 1–5 are used to indicate when and how often you want the task to be executed. This is how a cron job is laid out from the left to right:

- **minute:** (0–59)

- **hour:** (0–23, 0 = midnight)

- **day:** (1–31)

- **month:** (1–12)
- **weekday:** (0–6, 0 = Sunday)
- **command:** Code

If you read each line in the crontab from the left and use the above column descriptions, you can see how the instruction is built up. As an example:

```
01 04 1 1 1 /usr/bin/somedirectory/somecommand
```

The above example runs /usr/bin/somedirectory/somecommand at 4:01 A.M. on any Monday which falls on January 1. An asterisk (*) can be used so that every instance (every hour, every weekday, every month, etc.) of a time period is used. Code:

```
01 04 * * * /usr/bin/somedirectory/somecommand
```

The above example will run /usr/bin/somedirectory/somecommand at 4:01 A.M. on every day of every month.

Comma-separated values can be used to run more than one instance of a particular command within a time period. Dash-separated values can be used to run a command continuously:

```
01,31 04,05 1-15 1,6 * /usr/bin/somedirectory/somecommand
```

The above example will run /usr/bin/somedirectory/somecommand at 01 and 31 past the hours of 4:00 A.M. and 5:00 A.M. on the 1st through the 15th of every January and June.

The /usr/bin/somedirectory/somecommand text in the above examples indicates the task which will be run at the specified times. It is recommended that you use the full path to the desired commands as shown in the above examples. The crontab will begin running as soon as it is properly edited and saved.

Crontab Command Options   There are a number of options you can pass to the crontab command to make it do different things. Here are some common options:

- The -l option causes the current crontab to be displayed on standard output.

- The -r option causes the current crontab to be removed.

- The -e option is used to edit the current crontab using the editor specified by the VISUAL or EDITOR environment variables.

When you edit a crontab file, the modified crontab is checked for accuracy and, if there are no errors, installed automatically.

An Example   Below is an example of how to set up a crontab to run updatedb, which updates the slocate database: Open Konsole and type crontab-e and press Enter, and type the following line, substituting the full path for the one shown below, into the editor:

```
45 04 * * * /usr/bin/updatedb
```

Save your changes, and exit the editor. Crontab will let you know if you made any mistakes. The crontab will be installed and begin running if there are no errors. That's it. You now have a cron job setup to run updatedb, which updates the slocate database, every morning at 4:45.

Note that a semicolon (;) or the double-ampersand (&&) can also be used in the command section to run multiple commands consecutively:

```
45 04 * * * /usr/sbin/chkrootkit && /usr/bin/updatedb
```

The semicolon will cause both commands to be executed. The double ampersand will cause the second command to execute only if the first command does not fail. The above example will run chkrootkit and updatedb at 4:45 A.M. daily, providing you have all listed applications installed.

How Can I Copy a File from One Computer to Another?

The easiest way to copy files between machines is to use the Places > Connect to Server dialog box to make a connection using the graphical file manager. If you would prefer to do this on the command line, use the following command:

```
foo@bar:~$ scp file.txt jimmy@chin.com:/home/jimmy
```

The scp command works the same as the normal cp command, but it copies the file (file.txt) to another server (chin.com) using a specific user account (jimmy) and into a particular directory on the remote computer (/home/jimmy).

I Know an Application Is Available in Ubuntu but Synaptic Can't Find It

If you are browsing through Synaptic and can't find a package that you know is available for Ubuntu, it is likely that you have not enabled the additional repositories.

To fix this, load Synaptic and click Settings > Repositories. Click the Add button, and select the Community and Nonfree checkboxes. Click OK to accept the settings and then OK on the Repositories window. Finally, click the Reload button to refresh the package list. Your package should now be listed.

I Am Running Ubuntu on an Older Computer, and I Would Like a Faster Desktop

Unlike other OS, Linux has the flexibility to scale incredibly well across different computers with different levels of horsepower. With the huge range of Open Source available, you can tweak your system so that it can be optimized in lots of different areas. This is particularly useful for recycling PCs. A number of large organizations will throw out older hardware that is unable to run the latest OS from Microsoft. In many cases, these computers are actually perfectly usable if the software is optimized a little. Some Open Source groups have set up to take these old machines, install Linux, and provide them to their local communities.

The first aspect to optimize is the GUI. The default desktop in Ubuntu uses GNOME, and GNOME requires a reasonable degree of processing power. If you don't need many of the features in GNOME and literally just want to start applications, using something such as ICEWM may be a better choice. Load Synaptic, and ensure the Community repository is enabled. Install the icewm and menu packages. Now log out, and before you log back in, click the Options menu to change your session from the default one to the icewm one. A number of alternative desktop environments are available. For more functionality than icewm, try installing the xubuntu-desktop package and running the xfce session, also seen in Xubuntu (see Figure 6-9).

You may also want to explore applications that are more lightweight. As an example, instead of using OpenOffice.org for word processing, try

Figure 6-9 Also look at the Xubuntu distribution, which includes the lightweight xfce4 instead of GNOME.

Abiword. It is a featureful but lightweight word processor. Try the following alternatives:

- **Web Browser:** Instead of Firefox, use Galeon.

- **Terminal:** Use an xterm instead of the GNOME terminal.

- **Spreadsheet:** An alternative to OpenOffice.org for spreadsheets is Gnumeric.

I Have Reinstalled Windows, and Now Ubuntu Won't Start!

The first thing your computer does when you turn it on is read a special place on your hard disk called the master boot record (MBR). The information written there tells the computer what to do next. When you installed Ubuntu, it placed a boot menu on the MBR that lets you choose from which system to boot.

Unfortunately, when you reinstall Windows it will recreate the MBR, not taking into consideration that any other OS may exist and replacing it with an MBR that only boots Windows. This is no good, and you naturally want to be able to replace it with the menu that lets you choose which system to boot.

Grab the CD you used to install Ubuntu on your computer. If you don't have it anymore, download a CD image from www.Ubuntu.com/download, and burn it on a blank CD. If you used the desktop CD to install, you will need to use the alternate install CD with the traditional text mode installer.

Insert the CD in the drive, and restart your computer. It will boot on the CD instead of using the hard disk as usual. Now highlight the Rescue a Broken System line, and press Enter. Select your language and keyboard, and let the installer detect the network (for the computer name, you can leave the default Ubuntu) just like when you installed Ubuntu for the first time.

You will then be presented with a list of available partitions on your hard disks. Don't worry about the first line (/dev/disks/disk0/part1). Start looking at the other lines. You need to remember on which disk and on which partition Ubuntu is installed. Most of the time, you probably have just one disk. If you have Windows installed on it, it is probably located on the first partition of this disk, and Ubuntu should be on the second one. Therefore, you probably want to select /dev/disks/disk1/part2 (then press Enter), unless your situation is more complex.

On the last screen, select the first line `Execute a shell in. . . .` You can now enter commands. Start by mounting the disks on your system:

```
foo@bar:~# mount -a
```

Now type:

```
foo@bar:~# df
```

Look at the list printed on the screen. Search the last column for the single / character, and on the corresponding line look for the first column. It should say something such as /dev/hda2 (the last few characters may be different for you). Now type the following command, and replace /dev/hda with what you have just read, but without the last digit (/dev/hda instead of /dev/hda2 in the above example):

```
foo@bar:~# grub-install /dev/hda
```

Wait for the process to finish. It might take a few minutes. About a dozen lines should have appeared on the screen. Check whether you find the text "installation finished." If you do, everything went fine. You can now restart your computer by typing

```
foo@bar:~# exit
```

Eject the CD, and then select Reboot the System. Welcome back to Ubuntu!

How Do I Fix My Disk after a Power Failure?

Although the Ubuntu development team takes every care to ensure every possible situation is catered for, one of the most difficult problems is power outages. Computers rely on power, and when it is dramatically removed from the system, the whole Ubuntu world in your computer shuts down immediately. The problem with this is that sudden power failure causes your Ubuntu machine to shut down improperly. When you next start the computer you may then be prompted with a confusing fsck message. What is this and how do you fix it?

The fsck program is a little tool to fix hard disks that don't have consistent filesystems; filesystems typically made inconsistent by power failures. When the disk is inconsistent, Ubuntu automatically runs fsck to fix it. It asks you a bunch of questions that only a filesystem developer really understands, and you feel obliged to say Yes to each of them. As such, you sit there hammering the Y key over and over answering the questions.

There is a quick and simple fix to this problem. Instead of wearing out your Y key, you can simply edit one file and have any errors automatically fixed for you.

If your system is already running the desktop, open a terminal. and enter the following command:

```
foo@bar:~$ sudo gedit /etc/default/rcS
```

Now change the FSCKFIX line to the following:

```
FSCKFIX=yes
```

Save the file, and the next time you reboot fsck will fix any detected disk problems without you having to intervene.

If you are using the character-based login, use the following command:

```
foo@bar:~$ sudo nano /etc/default/rcS
```

Change the FSCKFIX line as above and then press Ctrl-O and Ctrl-X to save and exit.

Ubuntu Takes Up Too Much Disk Space on My Old Computer

If you are running Ubuntu on an older computer with a limited amount of disk space, you may want to choose software with more limited space requirements. Luckily, Ubuntu is incredibly flexible in choosing which software you want to install.

Install Ubuntu from the alternate install disk (not the desktop CD). When you have booted the installer, choose Install a Server, and install Ubuntu as usual. When you have rebooted into your minimal install, log in and type:

```
foo@bar:~$ sudo nano /etc/apt/sources.list
```

Press the down cursor until you reach the line

```
# deb http://archive.Ubuntu.com/Ubuntu/ dapper universe main
restricted multiverse
```

Press the X key twice to delete the # symbol at the beginning of that line. Save the file by typing :wq, and then hit Enter. Here you have enabled a repository. If you have enabled repositories in the past in Synaptic, this is what happens behind the scenes. You can manage your repositories by simply editing /etc/apt/source.list.

Now run the following commands:

```
foo@bar:~$ sudo apt-get update
foo@bar:~$ sudo apt-get install x-window-system-core xterm wdm icewm
menu
```

This whole system can be installed on a disk with less than 1G of free space.

My Computer Is Running Quite Slowly—How Can I Find Out What Is Going On?

If you are having performance problems, there may be a particular process on your computer gobbling up all of the memory. To find out what is happening, run the following command:

```
foo@bar:~$ top
```

The top command shows the current processes on your computer that are using the most system resources. If you see a particular program taking up an unusual amount of resources, that may be the culprit.

Some processes (such as the Apache Web server) fork and replicate themselves when used. Another useful technique is to see how many of these processes are running:

```
foo@bar:~$ ps ax | grep theprogram | wc -1
```

This command takes a listing of the processes running on the system, uses grep to search for a specific process and then counts the number of lines returned, thus indicating how many processes are running.

How Can I Find Out the Different Options for Commands?

Every command that is included in Ubuntu has a small reference card, called a man page, included. This page displays the range of options that are available. Access it by typing man, and then enter the command:

```
foo@bar:~$ man grep
```

Another method of listing the options is to use the -h or –help options:

```
foo@bar:~$ grep –help
```

How Do I Get My Root Account Back?

In a default Ubuntu installation, the root account is disabled. Instead, the user account that is created in the installation process is used with sudo to access administrator facilities. The sudo command is used extensively to temporarily take on root privileges when needed.

If you want to get the root account back, run the following command:

```
foo@bar:~$ sudo passwd root
```

Now enter your user account's password and then enter a new root password. You will be asked to verify the new root password.

TIP **Tired of Typing Sudo?**
If you want to type in a number of root commands and don't want to constantly prefix every command with sudo, run the following command:

```
foo@bar:~$ su -
```

This will upgrade your terminal to the root user. You can also use the -i switch in sudo:

```
foo@bar:~$ sudo -i
```

Everything you type in now is as the root user. To go back to your original user, use the following command:

```
foo@bar:~# exit
```

When using this command, note how when you are a normal user the prompt ends with a $ symbol, but when root it ends with a # symbol.

To disable the root account at a later date, run the following command:

```
foo@bar:~$ sudo passwd -l root
```

This will lock the root account.

I Forgot My System Password—What Can I Do?

Although passwords are indefinably essential and useful, they are also prone to being forgotten. With an increasing number of nasties out there on the Internet wanting to suck your password away, you need to think of more complex passwords, which are in turn harder to remember and easier to forget.

If you forget the system password, you need to jump through a few more hoops to reset your password. Reset your computer and when you see the word GRUB appear on the screen, press Escape to see the boot menu. Select the recovery mode option from the menu. When the computer boots it will present you with a root shell. At the prompt type:

```
foo@bar:~# passwd <username>
```

Follow the prompts to set a new password. Finally, reboot the computer with the following command:

```
foo@bar:~# reboot
```

How Do I Access My Windows Partitions?

If you are running Ubuntu on a computer with a Windows disk, you may want to read and write to the disk. Ubuntu can safely read the Windows NT NTFS partitions and can read and write to Windows 95/98/2000 FAT32 partitions.

First, load a terminal, and use the fdisk command to know what partitions you currently have:

```
foo@bar:~$ sudo fdisk -1
```

The output should be similar to this:

```
Disk /dev/hda: 81.9 GB
Device Boot     Start     End      Blocks      Id    System
/dev/hda1 *         1    1306    10490413+      7    HPFS/NTFS
/dev/hda2      1307    1311       40162+      83    Linux
/dev/hda3      1312    1344      265072+      82    Linux swap
/dev/hda4      1345    9964    69240150       f    W95 Ext'd (LBA)
/dev/hda5      1345    1606     2104483+      b    W95 FAT32
/dev/hda6      1607    2852    10008463+      83    Linux
 . . .
```

In this output, the /dev/hda1 partition (the first partition on the first disk) is a 10GB Windows NTFS partition (probably called C:) and /dev/hda5 is a 2GB FAT32 partition (probably called D:).

When you access a disk, you need to mount it first. To mount it, you need to indicate a directory where the files from the disk are accessed—this is called a mount point. Create mount points in /media for the Windows partitions. It is good to use /media/C for C: and /media/D for D:, etc. to make things easy to remember.

```
foo@bar:~$ sudo mkdir /media/C /media/D
```

To make the disks accessible when you boot the computer, you need to add a few lines to /etc/fstab. This file indicates which disks are available. Add the following two lines:

```
/dev/hda1      /media/C      ntfs      nls=utf8,umask=0222      0      0
/dev/hda5      /media/D      vfat      defaults,umask=0000      0      0
```

The fourth column lets you specify options for mounting the partition, and nls=utf8,umask=0222 means that any user can read the NTFS partition.

To mount the two partitions without restarting, run the following command:

```
foo@bar:~$ sudo mount -a
```

The two partitions are now available and will be automatically mounted the next time Ubuntu is restarted.

Ubuntu Is Slow on My AMD K7 Computer

The computer world is filled with different processors, including but not limited to Intel, AMD, Cyrix, Transmeta, Arm, Sun, and IBM processors. Although Linux supports each of these processors, the Linux kernel can often be optimized for specific processors.

First, load Synaptic. Click the Search button, and type in k7. Find and install the Linux-k7 package. Close Synaptic, and restart the computer. Hit Escape when you see GRUB appear to display the boot menu. Select the k7 kernel, and it will use the new kernel. Your system will work exactly the same as before, but it will be that little bit quicker.

TIP   **And for Intel**
You can also install a Linux-686 kernel for Pentium-class computers.

How Do I Add Users?

To add a new user to your computer select System > Administration > Users and Groups. When the window loads, click the Add User button, and then just fill in the details. To do this in the command line, use the adduser command:

```
foo@bar:~$ sudo adduser jimmy
```

This adds a user called Jimmy.

Other

And now, we'll finish with a collection of other common problems and quirks that don't fit neatly into any of the other categories in this chapter.

Running Another OS In Ubuntu

Some of you will have read the title of this recipe and wondered how on earth you can run another OS on an existing OS. Surely such a thing is not possible? Well, actually it is.

In recent years virtualization technology has been developed to simulate a computer in software. You can use this technology to boot a virtual computer in a window and run an OS on it, entirely in software. There have been some commercial applications to do this for a while, but recently the Open Source QEMU project has developed to such a point to make this viable to run a variety of different OS. It can run Windows, FreeBSD, Netware, and even other Ubuntu installations.

First of all, use Synaptic to install QEMU. When it has installed, use the file manager to create a folder in your home directory called "qemu." Now load a terminal and run the following commands:

```
foo@bar:~$ cd qemu
foo@bar:~qemu$ qemu-img create hd.img 350M
```

The last parameter (350M) indicates the size of the virtual drive in megabytes. Feel free to adjust this to your liking.

The next step is to boot an install CD in the virtual machine:

```
foo@bar:~$ qemu -boot d -cdrom /dev/cdrom -hda hd.img
```

When your installation has finished, reboot the virtual machine:

```
foo@bar:~$ qemu -boot c -fda /dev/fda -cdrom /dev/cdrom -hda hd.img
-user-net -pci -m 256 -k en
```

With the setup complete, you can add a link to the new OS on your panel. Right-click on the panel where you want to create the launcher, and choose Add to Panel > Custom Application Launcher. Enter the following details:

- **Name:** Win2000

- **Command:** qemu -boot c -fda /dev/fda -cdrom /dev/cdrom -hda /path/to/your/hd.img -user-net -pci -m 256 -k en

Choose an icon for your new OS.

It Was Suggested I File a Bug Report, but I Don't Know How

Ubuntu is a collaboratively developed system in which hundreds of developers from around the world work together to build a simple, yet powerful, distribution. With so much software involved in Ubuntu, bugs and problems can naturally creep into the system. If you believe that the problem you have is not a configuration or hardware error, it may well be a bug. Anyone can submit a bug report, and it is encouraged that regular users of Ubuntu contribute bug reports where possible.

Bug reports are handled on a special Web site called Launchpad, which resides at http://launchpad.net/ (see Figure 6-10).

Launchpad provides a complete environment in which bugs can be tracked and future features are merged into Ubuntu. Launchpad is not only designed to make bugs for Ubuntu easy to report, but to also support bugs for other systems too. This means that developers can work together to resolve problems.

To report a bug, click on the Help menu in the application for which you want to report the bug. Select Get Online Help. Firefox will now load, and you are taken to the Launchpad site. To use Launchpad, you need a user account, so click the Register link to register your account. Enter your e-mail address, and you will be e-mailed registration details. When you have completed the registration, log in to Launchpad. You can always access your application in Launchpad by using the Get Online Help menu item.

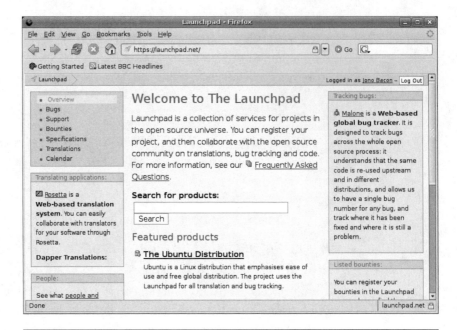

Figure 6-10 Launchpad is where the bug reports live.

TIP   Another Way into the Bug Tracking System
You can also access the bug tracking system by going to Launchpad, clicking the Bugs link in the right sidebar, and then entering the name of the application in the text box farther down the page. If possible, it is generally recommended that you use the Help menu approach as it will automatically pick the right application for you.

The first step is to check to see if the bug has already been reported. In the right sidebar of Launchpad are a series of menu options. Each bug that is added to the system is automatically given a unique ID for the bug, and you can search for this number if needed. You can alternatively search for something related to the problem. As an example, search for "crash" or "hang." If you find your bug has already been reported, you can keep updated with changes to do with the bug by clicking the Subscribe link in the right sidebar.

If no bug exists, you should report it yourself. To do this, click the Report a Bug in <application name> in Ubuntu link. Simply fill in the Summary box with a single-line description of the bug, and then use the Description box to fill in the details. You should be as detailed as possible and include your computer's specifications, any special steps you went through to trigger the bug, the effects of the bug, and how you expected the software to work. Try to be detailed, but keep everything you say relevant to the bug. If you would prefer to keep your bug report confidential, select the checkbox, but it is highly recommended you keep your bug reports public if possible. This means that as many people as possible can see the report and possibly act on it.

With the bug submitted, you will receive e-mail updates about the progress the developers are making to fix the bug. In some cases the developers may ask you to run commands or try different things to help nail down the bug so they can fix it.

Bug reporting is an essential process in which everyday users of Ubuntu can really help keep the software as bug-free and stable as possible. It is a truly valid contribution to the Open Source community.

TIP **Need a Hand?**
If you need help reporting a bug, ask for support on the Ubuntu-users list, IRC, or the forums. The community will be more than happy to help.

How Can I Monitor the Weather?

Besides looking out the window, you can add a weather applet to a panel that shows the current temperature along with an icon that indicates sunshine or rain. Right-click a panel, and select Add to Panel. Drag the weather applet (under Accessories) to an empty spot on the panel, and click Close. Now right-click the weather applet, select Preferences, and select the Location tab. From here you can select your city or a city in the vicinity. Click Close when you are done. If you want more detailed information, just click the applet.

How Do I Make Ubuntu Bread?

With so many recipes in this chapter to solve common problems or perform small tweaks and optimizations, it seems unfair not to include an actual recipe. This actual recipe was posted to the popular Ubuntu Forums to create some special Ukranian egg bread called Kalach, which is much like challah or any other egg bread. The twist of course is that it is shaped like our favorite distribution's logo (see Figure 6-11).

http://ubuntuforums.org/attachment.php?attachmentid=656&d=111283
4131)###

Figure 6-11 The Ubuntu loaf.

To create this bread you will need the following ingredients:

3 eggs

1 teaspoon of yeast

3/4 cup warm water (40 degrees Celsius)

pinch of salt

1/4 cup oil

1/4 cup sugar

3 to 5 cups flour

First put the yeast in the warm water while you gather the other ingredients.

Beat the three eggs in a bowl and save a teaspoon of the egg mixture for later. Add three cups of flour to a big bowl along with the egg, sugar, oil, and salt. When the yeast is bubbly, add it in too.

Knead. If it is crumbly, add water. If it is too sticky, add more flour. The dough should be firmer than your average bread dough to keep its shape.

Cover the bowl with a damp towel, and let the dough rise in a warm place. When it has doubled in size, punch it down, and roll it out into three ropes.

Make the ropes less than one inch thick (2.5cm) so that it will cook evenly. Do this on a large surface. You need a lot of room. Use a bit of oil if things are sticky. Your dough should be somewhat stiff, so this should not be a problem.

You should end up with three ropes that are a little less than three feet long (75 cm). Pinch them together on one end and then braid them.

Take the lowermost rope and place it in between the other two. The middle rope is now the lowest rope, move it into position by bringing it down to where the other rope (lowermost) used to be. Take the topmost rope and place it in between the other two. Take the rope that is now highest and pull it up to its position as topmost rope. Place the lowermost rope in between the two others. You get the picture. . . .

When you have a long braid, snip off the ends, and join the ends to form a circle. Try to join the individual ropes together as best as you can. Place it on an oiled cookie sheet. Take the snipped off bits and form two long strands. Intertwine them together by putting them side-by-side and holding one end while rolling the other end with the palm of your hand. Stretch this out around the bottom of the big braid and join the ends together.

Cover the kalach with a damp towel and let it double in size (about an hour, maybe less, on a hot day). Brush it with the egg mixture. You should have enough to cover it completely. Cook at 350° Fahrenheit until it becomes dark brown. Let it cool.

Be very careful. My dog jumps up on the table to eat this. I make this for special occasions, and it is embarrassing when guests find the dog with the half of the bread that she could not finish under the table.

How Can I Prevent the Pain I Am Getting in My Fingers When I Type?

If you feel pain or numbness in your fingers, you are likely suffering from repetitive strain injury (RSI). This common complaint typically afflicts those who work with computers for long periods every day. The constant movement of the fingers in such a repetitive fashion can cause swelling and pain in the fingers and wrists. RSI can also affect your neck, back, legs, and other areas.

If you suspect you have RSI you should first consult your doctor. RSI is a condition that requires treatment. This treatment can come in the form of physiotherapy, regular breaks, workspace adjustments, and in some extreme cases, medication or surgery.

One of the most common methods of reducing RSI is to take regular rest breaks. It is a good idea to break about once an hour. Your desktop can help with this. Click on System > Preferences > Keyboard, and select the Typing Break tab. You can use the settings in the tab to enforce a break once an hour.

Another type of break is a micropause. These breaks usually occur every couple of minutes, and the break lasts for only a few seconds. These breaks are intended to be less intrusive and give your hands a chance to regularly rest for a short period to allow the blood to flow. A useful little tool called Workrave has been developed to enforce regular micropauses. Use the Synaptic package manager to install Workrave.

TIP   **Remember!**
Always consult a doctor with any health problems. RSI in many cases is a treatable problem, but your doctor can best advise you on the recommended treatment.

Summary

Software by its very nature is subject to inaccuracies, bugs, and usability problems—and users by their very nature are subject to errors, mistakes, and misjudgments. Although every release of Ubuntu makes Linux and computing far easier to use and more flexible than the previous release, there are always going to be occasions when something just doesn't work.

Hopefully, this chapter has provided some useful solutions to some of the typical problems you may face when using Ubuntu. If this chapter still does not answer your questions though, head over to the incredible Ubuntu Forums at www.ubuntuforums.org/ to tap into a huge community of people who can help.

## CHAPTER 7

Using Kubuntu

- Introduction to Kubuntu
- Installing Kubuntu
- Customizing Kubuntu
- Systems Administration
- Managing Files with Kubuntu
- Common Applications
- Finding Help and Giving Back to the Community
- Summary

THE KUBUNTU PROJECT STRIVES to take the best of Ubuntu and the best of the K Desktop Environment (KDE) to produce a great Linux distribution. This chapter will cover information ranging from what exactly Kubuntu is to how to manage and keep your Kubuntu system up-to-date with the latest applications and fixes. The goal of Kubuntu is to provide a great Linux operating system (OS) that provides a simple and easy-to-use OS through great graphical tools and an OS that is easy to customize to your desire.

Introduction to Kubuntu

Kubuntu is an official project of Ubuntu—a complete implementation of the Ubuntu OS led by Jonathan Riddell (an employee of Canonical Ltd.) and an army of developers. However, Kubuntu uses KDE instead of GNOME for Ubuntu. The main goal of Kubuntu is to be a great integrated Linux distribution with all of the great features of Ubuntu, but based on KDE. Since Kubuntu is an official part of the Ubuntu community it adheres to the same Ubuntu manifesto: Great software should be available free of charge and should be usable by people in their own language regardless of disability. Also, people should be able to customize and alter their software in ways they deem fit.

Like Ubuntu, Kubuntu makes the following commitments: the very best translations and accessibility infrastructure that the free software community has to offer; Kubuntu will always be free of charge, and there is no extra cost for an "enterprise" version, and Kubuntu will always provide the latest and best software from the KDE community.

Looking for a certain piece of software? Kubuntu has it, with more then 1,000 pieces of software in its repositories including the latest kernel version and, of course, the latest KDE, which at the time of this writing is at version 3.5.2. The standard desktop applications (Web browsing, e-mail, word processing, and spreadsheet applications) allow Kubuntu to replace any current desktop OS. If you are running servers, whether it is a Web server, e-mail server, or database server, Kubuntu can do that as well.

History of KDE

In 1996, Matthias Ettrich posted a now famous newsgroup post that described some of the problems that he had with the Unix Desktop.

Unix popularity grows thanks to the free variants, mostly Linux. But still a consistent, nice looking, free desktop environment is missing. There are several nice either free or low-priced applications available, so that Linux/X11 would almost fit everybody's needs if we could offer a real GUI . . .

IMHO a GUI should offer a complete graphical environment. It should allow a user to do his everyday tasks with it, like starting applications, reading mail, configuring his dekstop . . . All parts must fit together and work together. . . .

The goal is NOT to create a GUI for the complete Unix-system or the System-Administrator . . . The idea is to create a GUI for an ENDUSER.

With this post he started building the KDE Project. KDE originally stood for Kool Desktop Environment but later was adapted to be K Desktop Environment. The mascot for KDE is a green dragon named Konqi, who can be found in various applications.

Matthias chose to develop KDE around the QT Toolkit, and by 1997 the first large complex applications were being released. In 1998, version 1.0 was released. However, there was much debate based on the fact that QT was not licensed around a free software license. Two projects came about from this debate, one named "Harmony" which would only use free libraries and another project called GNOME. In 1998, the QT toolkit was licensed under a new Open Source license called the Q Public License (QPL), and in 2000 QT was released under the Gnu General Public License (GPL).

KDE is primarily a volunteer effort. However, many companies employ developers to work on this project. Some of these companies include Novell (through the purchase of SUSE Linux), Trolltech (the company that produces the QT toolkit), and many others.

At the time of this writing the current version of KDE is 3.5.2. The next major release of KDE will be version 4 and will include many changes. For more information on KDE visit the project's Web site at www.kde.org. The project's homepage also provides information on how you can help out with the project and contribute back to the KDE community.

History of Kubuntu

When Ubuntu was first being discussed there were rumors that it would be only based on GNOME, and KDE would be left out. Jonathan Riddell, a KDE developer, posted an article on his Web log (blog) that soon became the No. 1 hit on Google for Ubuntu Linux. The article states:

> The signs are there that this could be something big, more so than the likes of Linspire, Xandros, or Lycrosis. Unlike those companies, they [Canonical Ltd. Software] understand Free Software and open development. It is likely to be a GNOME-based job, but maybe there is a KDE developer out there who is working for them without letting on. If not I'm always available.

This post started a flurry of activity both for Riddell and the others who wanted to participate.

A lot of changes needed to be made to get Kubuntu working correctly. A hardware-accessible library needed to be changed. Programs and packages needed to be created, along with a clean K-menu changed to fit the philosophy of Ubuntu. And along the way more people needed to join the project. It was a conscious decision to keep the default KDE colors and icons in order to remain as close to KDE as possible.

Once a preview release of Ubuntu (Hoary Hedgehog) came out, another flurry of activity ensued that had developers uploading last-minute changes—including some that broke almost everything they had set up—and the first CDs were released. Since this initial release Kubuntu has grown and changed. New items in the Breezy (5.10) release included system settings, automatic mounting when inserting a USB drive, and, of course, the latest KDE. In the next release, Dapper Drake (6.04), there are almost the same numbers of changes the latest version of KDE (version 3.5.2) along with featuring the addition of zerconf discovery, a new installer, Katapult enabled by default, and CJK (Chinese, Japanese, and Korean Language) support.

Kubuntu is quickly building up a sizable community of its own. Not only are there new package managers and a dedicated documentation team, but also many community and fan sites to help provide support and the most current information. Kubuntu has grown tremendously from just one developer to a large group as it continues to improve the quality of the distribution.

Navigating in Kubuntu

All of the applications in Kubuntu are stored in the K menu in the left-hand bottom corner of the task bar. This menu is organized in a manner that flows smoothly and makes sense. Items that involve a connection to the Internet are grouped under the Internet section while items that deal with music, videos, or pictures are grouped under Multimedia. Like everything else, this can be customized or changed to fit your needs. This will be discussed later. Any new application installed will find its appropriate spot in the K menu.

TIP   **Katapult**

Katapult is a great application that is enabled by default that will help you navigate Kubuntu. This handy program will change your computing ways. This is the one program you will miss the most if you ever need to return to the Windows world. Katapult is an application that can launch programs without the need for a shortcut or maneuvering through the K menu. Simply hit Alt-Space, and Katapult will launch. To run an application, simply start typing the name of the program, and Katapult will use tab-completion to fill in the rest of the name. A great feature is that Katapult will also work on files that are stored in the root of your home directory. Figure 7-1 shows Katapult in action.

The next three icons on the task bar are shortcuts to the System Menu, Konqueror, and Kontact. The system menu allows you to navigate quickly to places such as your home directory, a listing of attached media devices, and even remote places. The Konqueror shortcut launches the default file management tool. We cover this in more detail later in the chapter. Kontact

Figure 7-1 Katapult provides an easy way to open just about any application without wasting time searching for its location in the K menu.

Figure 7-2 The clean look of the Kubuntu desktop.

is the default Personal Information Manager (PIM) and will be discussed later on as well. To further emphasize the clean look of Kubuntu, there are no icons on the desktop, as Figure 7-2 shows.

The developers have spent a lot of time making Kubuntu easy to navigate and also very easy to customize.

Shutting Your Computer Down and Logging Out

To shut your computer down, log out, or switch users go to the K menu, and then select the option you would like. Kubuntu is a multiuser (many users per system) OS. You can either lock your session and switch to a new user or just start a new session. The other option is to lock the session so no one else can access your Kubuntu session without the password. The final choice at the bottom of the K menu is to End the Current Session.

Ending a session is the location you would choose to either turn off your computer, reboot, or end the current session (log out). See Figure 7-3, which depicts these options.

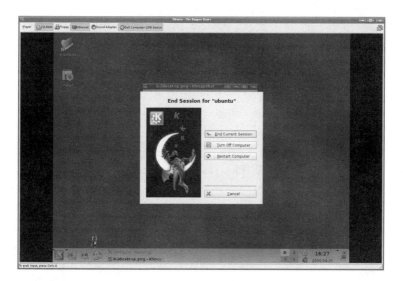

Figure 7-3 Logging out of Kubuntu.

Installing Kubuntu

Installing Kubuntu is just like installing Ubuntu. It is pretty much a snap. Let's start with where you find it.

Where to Find Kubuntu

Kubuntu is available at the same location as Ubuntu, www.kubuntu.org/download.php. An image file can be downloaded and then burned onto either a DVD or a CD-ROM. There are two different types of Kubuntu images that can be downloaded and used. The first is the Desktop CD that allows the user to test and run Kubuntu without changing any settings. The second is the actual installer.

New to Kubuntu 6.06, the Desktop CD will come with an installer so you will not have to download a separate version if everything tests successfully. A good way to demonstrate the power of Kubuntu is to show it off with the desktop CD, and when your friends like it install it for them.

Another way to get Kubuntu would be through ordering the free CD from Ubuntu (shipit.kubuntu.org). The beauty of this is there is no cost for shipping and handling, and you will then have an official CD complete with cover art and everything. This is also great for user groups or install parties where a group of people will be using Kubuntu.

Can I Switch to Kubuntu If I Have Ubuntu Installed Already?

If you have installed Ubuntu on your system already, it is extremely easy to install and configure Kubuntu. In Synaptic, find the package Kubuntu-desktop, which will provide all the necessary programs to have your system look and act like Kubuntu. Don't worry. You can still switch between Ubuntu with GNOME as the desktop manager and Kubuntu with KDE as the desktop environment. Once Kubuntu is installed, one can choose which desktop environment to use, either GNOME or KDE. Also if you wish to have Ubuntu, it is simple to switch; just install Ubuntu-desktop and you will be using the GNOME desktop.

Once you have installed the Kubuntu-desktop, end your GNOME session, and choose Session from the menu. Select KDE instead of GNOME as your window manager, and then select Make Default. From now on KDE will start for you when you sign on.

Guided Installation

Kubuntu follows the easy-to-use Ubuntu installer to set up and configure your system. Like Ubuntu, there is more than one way to install a new copy, including Expert and Normal modes. New to this version of Kubuntu is a way to rescue a broken system and get it up and working again. The Normal install, which is the easiest and most used, asks several basic questions such as host name, how the network is configured, username and password, and how the drives will be formatted. Once these questions are answered, the system will proceed with formatting your hard drive and installing Kubuntu. After logging in for the first time, the next step will be to make sure your system is up-to-date including any bug fixes or security patches. This is done through Adept, which is discussed later in this chapter.

Installing from the Desktop CD

New to this version of Kubuntu is the ability to install directly from the desktop CD. This removes the need to download separate CDs. Simply download the desktop CD, and show off how great Kubuntu is to your friends or give it a test run for the first time. Kubuntu's Live Installer program is called Ubiquity.

Figure 7-4 Ubiquity's welcome screen.

Upon choosing to install Kubuntu, Ubiquity will start guiding you through the installation process (see Figure 7-4).

Ubiquity will prompt you with basic questions about what language you would like to install (Figure 7-4) and then guide you in setting up the correct country and time zone (Figure 7-5).

Figure 7-5 Selecting the correct time zone.

Figure 7-6 Selecting the keyboard layout.

Once these have been set, Ubiquity will prompt you to select the correct keyboard layout (Figure 7-6), help you create a username and password, and help you assign a name for the install computer (Figure 7-7).

After filling out this information, Ubiquity will help you set and partition your disks (Figure 7-8). After everything is set up, Kubuntu will be installed.

Figure 7-7 Configuring the computer name and username.

Figure 7-8 Configuring disk partitions.

Once everything is finished, you will be prompted to reboot the computer (Figure 7-9). You are now ready to use your Kubuntu system.

Using Sudo

A large change, and one that many people stumble with before getting used to it, is the "lack" of a root account. Upon installation you are not prompted to provide with a root password. The password created with the first user is the password that will allow you to access the administrative functions. There will be many times when configuring the system or making global changes will require the sudo password to complete.

Customizing Kubuntu

A major feature of Kubuntu is the amount of customization that can be done. Due to the freedom of Open Source software, if there is an application you are looking to use, you can find it. Everything from the desktop background to the font size of applications to the order and arrangement of the K menu can be customized.

Figure 7-9 Finishing the installation.

Customizing the Desktop

By simply right-clicking on the desktop and selecting Configure Desktop a great deal of changes can be made. Kdesktop, as the application is called, is divided into five different sections: background, behavior, multiple desktops, screensaver, and display. As you can see from looking at Figure 7-10, the system looks a lot like the program used by Microsoft Windows to adjust the same properties.

Kubuntu comes with several backgrounds that are installed by default. Any of these may be selected from the list. Additional backgrounds can be selected from KDE.org by clicking on Get New Wallpapers. Since Kubuntu is a multidesktop system, each desktop can have the same background, a different one, or even be sized differently. This system offers many opportunities for great customization.

The behavior section allows the user to customize how the desktop behaves. Want icons on the desktop? Want a menu bar at the top of the

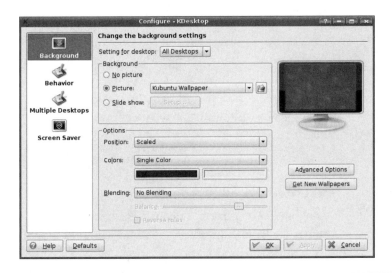

Figure 7-10 Kdesktop.

screen? How does the mouse behave? Along with these options the user can choose what types of icons are used for each application and association.

Interested in using multiple desktops? How about 20 of them? Any user can organize desktops based on tasks, thus grouping applications together based on the current task one is working. For example, this feature was applied specifically when this book was written. Day-to-day applications were open on one desktop while a word processing application, help applications, and a Web browser were all open on another desktop.

Another important item that can be changed is the screensaver and how it operates. This section, which is under Configure Desktop, allows the user to select any of the preinstalled options or those downloaded from the Internet. After the correct screensaver has been chosen, simply configure it to start automatically and decide if it will lock your screen as well.

The display section can help the user choose different screen sizes and refresh rates. In this section, you can also work with the power settings for your monitor, a great tool for laptop users. Power control allows the monitor to be suspended or powered off after a designated time period passes. These settings can also be applied upon startup if desired.

Choosing how the desktop looks can help make Kubuntu feel personalized. If the appearance seems to be lacking, further changes can be made by choosing System Settings > Appearance. This allows the user to further customize things such as colors, icons, and style. Kubuntu is all about customization, and there are many ways to change how the desktop appears. This almost guarantees that no two users will have identical desktops.

Get Hot New Stuff

Looking for the latest screensaver, desktop background, or other cool things for your Kubuntu installation? Kubuntu fully supports the Get Hot New Stuff (GHNS) framework of KDE. GHNS allows people to upload templates to a server and have other users download and use that template. In an interview posted on KDE.news (http://dot.kde.org/1110652641), Josef Spillner describes exactly how the process works.

> [U]ser A is using a spreadsheet application and modifies a template that comes with it. This template can then be uploaded to a server and eventually be downloaded by user B by checking the contents of the "Get Hot New Stuff" download dialogue.

The GHNS framework shows up in several places throughout Kubuntu.

One place where you can see this is when configuring the background for your desktop. On the right in this section is Get New Wallpapers. Upon selecting this, a new window will open up and display new wallpapers that you can use. These images come from www.kde-look.org. Figure 7-11 shows how this works.

Different applications have the capability to download information from the Internet and from KDE sites. Throughout applications in Kubuntu you will find references to "Get More."

Customizing Applets and the Kicker

The Kicker is the application launcher of KDE. The Kicker is also capable of running different docked applets such as the page, the task bar, or the

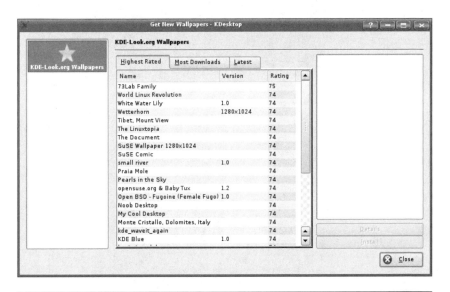

Figure 7-11 The GHNS framework at work.

clock. Applets are small applications that run inside the Kicker. The applet everyone is probably most familiar with is the task bar. It resides by default at the bottom of the screen and includes the K menu and programs that are currently up and running. The next applet over is also called the mini-pager. It shows a small preview of the different desktops and applications that are running in these desktops. Another applet that will be used on a regular basis is the Quick Launcher Applet. This allows the user to quickly start his or her favorite or most used programs.

Everything that is part of the Kicker can be customized to meet the user's needs. It may even be removed. To add new items to the Quick Launcher Applet simply right-click on this applet, and add the application to the panel. Find the program in the list or drag a shortcut from the desktop and access it at any time.

Customizing the K menu

The K menu makes adding, changing, and removing applications very easy to do. Upon installation, each application is placed in a certain location, but this may be altered. Simply right-click on the K menu, and select Menu Editor as shown in Figure 7-12.

Figure 7-12 Select menu editor.

In fact, the user can even change the location of the K menu or remove it altogether.

Upon selecting the menu editor a new window will open up that will allow the user to make the desired changes. One of the most noticeable aspects of this application is that there are more folders in this list than in the K menu. This is due to a decision the team made to only show folders that have programs installed in them. To customize the K menu, simply use the tools provided under the File menu.

A major benefit of Kubuntu is that if the user does not like the way the system looks, he or she may change it. Almost everything can be customized to truly personalize the system.

Systems Administration

As with any computer application, Kubuntu will occasionally need administrative support. Do not be afraid of personally administrating the Kubuntu system. While it is not completely foolproof, there have been a lot of changes to help make things easier. Knowledge of the command line will go a long way in configuring the system, but the developers have made sure to provide graphical interfaces when they make sense. Everything from changing the IP address from Dynamic Host Control Protocol (DHCP) to static to installing packages can all be done without having to drop down to the command line. This section will focus exclusively on system administration through the graphical interface.

Installing New Packages

As mentioned earlier, Kubuntu is built around some of the same applications and system as Ubuntu. All applications are installable through packages. Like Ubuntu, Kubuntu uses the Advanced Package Tool (APT) and also like Ubuntu has a wonderful graphical interface that makes it easier to use that is called Adept. Adept is becoming the de facto installer for the KDE environment on Debian-based systems. This program was sponsored by Canonical Ltd. to help further the project of Kubuntu and other Linux distributions. The old package manager, Kynaptic, was lacking many features and was not user-friendly. Adept seeks to solve this problem.

Adept is composed of four parts: the installer (Add/Remove Programs), the main program (Adept), adept update-notifier, and adept-updater. These programs will help you install packages and keep your system up-to-date with the latest and greatest changes.

To start Adept and begin installing new applications, open up the K menu and click on Add/Remove Programs, or simply type Add/Remove programs in Katapult. Once launched, the screen shown in Figure 7-13 will be displayed.

Add/Remove programs breaks programs into three groups: packages that can be installed with KDE, applications that can be installed with GNOME, and applications that can be installed on either desktop environment. Searching for that needed application is very simple. Just type in the application you are looking for, click on it, and select install. Figure 7-14 shows an example of this.

Once you click on Apply Changes, Add/Remove Programs will download the information from the repository and install the application. Easy and painless. Add/Remove programs will also download any dependencies to prevent any conflicts or broken programs.

Figure 7-13 Add/Remove Programs main window.

Figure 7-14 Installing an application with Add/Remove Programs.

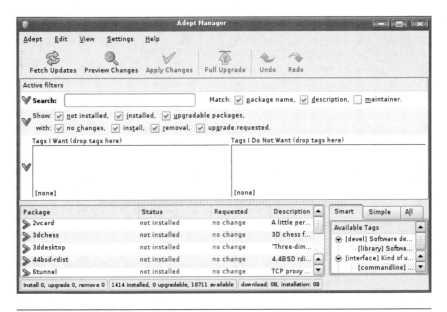

Figure 7-15 Adept.

The main Adept program is slightly more powerful than Add/Remove Programs. Not only can you can install programs and update your system, you can also manage the different repositories from which you can download programs.

To start Adept and begin to install new applications open up the K menu, and move through the System folder to Adept. The different sections can be seen in Figure 7-15.

Adept has an easy-to-use search feature that allows the user to quickly locate the application that needs to be installed. Simply locate the name of the application, click the drop down arrow, and select install. This will queue the package to be installed; simply clicking on apply changes will set up the application on the system. Unlike Microsoft Windows, Kubuntu is great about not forcing a system restart in order for the new application to work correctly.

NOTE   A restart could be required if the version of KDE is updated.

Packages are organized into four different groups or repositories: main, restricted, universe, and multiverse. A standard installation will set up the system to install packages from the main repository. This repository contains applications that are free software and programs that allow for complete redistribution and which are also fully supported by the Kubuntu team. When the user installs something from the main repository he or she is guaranteed to receive security updates and support through the various venues.

The restricted group of software is reserved for software that is commonly used and is supported by the Kubuntu team, even though they may not be able to change or update it. An example of software included here are binary videos drivers that some vendors publish.

Software in the universe repository is where almost every other known Open Source software application can be found. Software here comes with a variety of licenses, and some might have restricted use in various countries. Users should take care to ensure that they do not violate these restrictions. Items built and maintained in this group are put together by the Masters of the Universe (MOTU). However, there is no support from the core developers for these items.

Anything from the multiverse repository contains software that is not free, which is defined by the Kubuntu Main Component License Policy. Software here is used at the user's own risk.

Managing Repositories

With Adept, you do not need to know how to manually edit a sources.list. Adept can guide you through making these changes. From the File menu simply select Manage Repositories, and you will see a window that looks like the display in Figure 7-16.

To enable the universe repository, edit the repository labeled universe, and remove the comments by following these steps.

1. Double-click on the comment next to ##http://us.archive.ubuntu.com/ ubuntu, and change the comment field to "deb."

2. Double-click on the actual address and remove the ## which acts to comment out the repository.

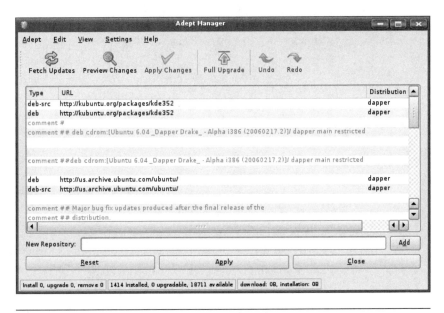

Figure 7-16 Editing your repositories in Adept.

3. Click on Apply at the bottom to save your changes, making your list look like that shown in Figure 7-17.

4. Close this window by clicking Close.

5. Reload your sources by clicking Fetch Updates.

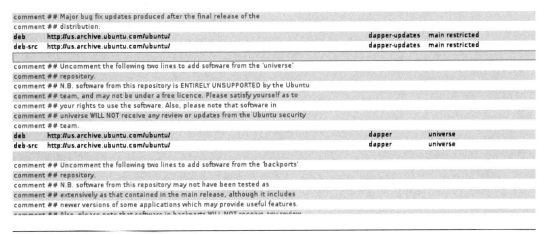

Figure 7-17 Repositories with universe enabled.

Sometimes there is the need to add repositories to your sources listing, and that is done just as easily as enabling a repository.

1. Open up Manage Repositories from the File Menu.

2. Add the necessary Repository.

3. Click on Apply and then Close to save your changes.

4. Reload your sources for the new repository by clicking on Fetch Updates.

Installing a Package

The easiest way to find the package you need to install on your system is to use the search function built into Adept. After opening up Adept and typing in the password, you will be presented with the main Adept screen. Just type the name of the package you are looking for, and Adept will display a listing of every package that includes what you are looking for (see Figure 7-18).

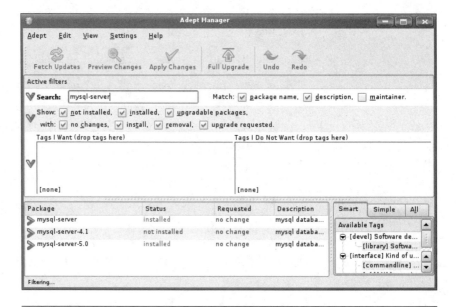

Figure 7-18 Using the search bar in Adept to find packages.

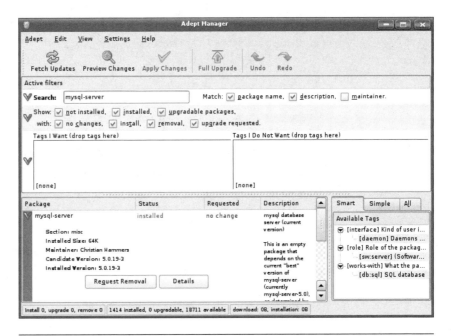

Figure 7-19 Expanded information regarding a specific package.

Through the use of filters, Adept will help limit the package listing you are searching for. These filters include: show packages that are not installed, show packages that are installed, and show packages that are upgradeable.

Once the package has been found, click on the name or drop-down arrow, and Adept will display the description of the program and current version (see Figure 7-19).

At this time you will be presented with two options: install the package and view the details of the package. Details will show more information including dependent packages and where the files will be installed.

Once an application is marked for installation, Adept will also mark all of the dependent files for installation as well. This will prevent what is referred to as "dependency hell" in which not all of the required files are installed to get an application to function correctly. Notice that the requested action will change from "no change" to "install." Figure 7-20 shows mysql-server (an Open Source database server) marked for installation.

A very important part of installation packages through Adept is to make sure you *always* preview the changes by clicking on Preview Changes at the top *before* clicking Apply Changes. Any changes marked can be undone up to the point of applying them simply by clicking Undo. Figure 7-21 shows the additional packages that will be installed along with the main package.

mysql-server	not installed	install	mysql database server (current version)
mysql-server-4.1	not installed	no change	mysql database server binaries
mysql-server-5.0	not installed	install	mysql database server binaries

Figure 7-20 Installing mysql-server with Adept.

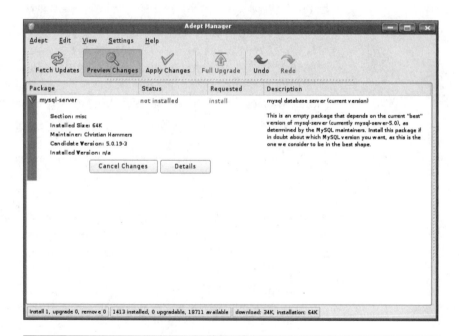

Figure 7-21 Previewing changes in Adept.

Upgrading Kubuntu

If you are using the last release of Kubuntu, Kubuntu 5.10 (the Breezy Badger), by simply editing the repositories you can upgrade to the most current version. To change from Breezy Badger to Dapper Drake, change all references to Dapper under Manage Repositories, and save the changes. Make sure you reload the repositories to get all the updates by selecting Fetch Updates. After the information is downloaded, select Full Upgrade. That is it. No need to purchase a new OS, no need to worry about how a new version will affect the budget. Simply upgrade to the latest and greatest Kubuntu. Now it is time to grab a cup of coffee, sit back, relax, and watch the system upgrade as it will take a while to download all the changed packages and install them on the system.

How to Keep the System Up-to-Date

Two parts of Adept, the Adept Updater and the Adept-Updater-Notifier, will help keep the system current with the latest fixes and updates. Open up the K menu, and under the System folder launch the System Updater Wizard (Adept Updater). After entering your password, the application will launch and will allow the user to install any needed updates for the system. Like any software package, there are updates. However, Adept updater will help keep you current with the latest and greatest. Just as when installing new packages, the system will rarely have to be restarted for these changes to take effect.

The Adept-Update-Notifier will periodically check for updates and will then allow the user to launch Adept-Updater and install the fixes. The application functions much like the Windows Update icon in Windows systems.

When there are updates available for your system a red triangle will appear in the taskbar. Clicking on it will launch Adept-Updater. After entering your password the necessary updates will be downloaded and the user will be prompted for installation.

System Settings

The System Settings application (see Figure 7-22) is a new addition to Kubuntu. This program allows users to make many changes to the system, including setting Sound, User Accounts, Mouse Behavior, and other settings

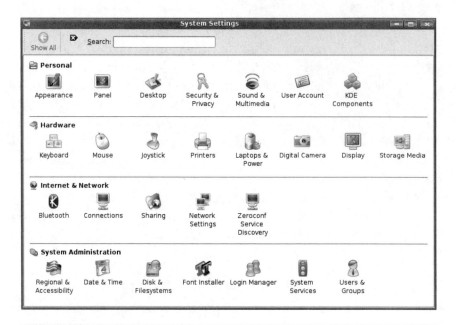

Figure 7-22 The System Settings application.

on the network. For those familiar with using KDE, System Settings replaces the K Control Center. However, the application is still there and can be run by hitting Alt+F2 for the run command and typing in Kcontrol or by typing Kcontrol in Katapult.

System Settings can be found in the K menu or by typing System Settings in Katapult.

When making changes, there will be times that you will be prompted to enter your password. These changes are system-wide and will affect all users of the Kubuntu system and can be made by entering Administration Mode. System Settings is divided into four sections: personal, hardware, Internet and network, and system administration. When migrating through the different options, to return to the main screen, be sure to select Show All instead of closing out the application. This is a common mistake and may take some getting used to. Selecting this option will return the user to the main System Settings window.

Personal Changes made to this section will only affect the current user signed in. The user can change the fonts, how the panel behaves, and various KDE components.

Under the personal section, you can change the panel, desktop, and even user information. Changing the desktop background and settings has already been addressed in this chapter. However, this is another way of accessing this information.

One area in the personal settings where a lot of changes can be made to customize your Kubuntu system, including changing your password, is the user account section. Another area is session management. It can help save your settings upon logging out. You can do a lot of customization to make Kubuntu your very own.

Hardware   This section explains changing how the mouse functions, how power control is set up, and other hardware-related tasks. It is through this section that the user will learn to set up the type of printer connected to the Kubuntu system. Upon selecting Printers, the Common Unix Print System (CUPS) will initialize and enable control of the printing subsystem. Figure 7-23 shows the printer window open.

To add a printer, select Add and follow the guide for configuring the printer. CUPS can print to a locally attached printer, a network attached

Figure 7-23 The printer window.

printer, or even a printer shared out through a Windows print server. For some of the changes made at this level, the user will need to enter administration mode through use of your password.

New to this version of Kubuntu (6.06) is the capability to change how the graphical system displays. Kubuntu provides an easy-to-use graphical tool (Display) to help manage the X window configuration. Now it is no longer a painful process to change your screen size or resolution, but can be easily done through the system settings window.

Internet and Network   In this section of System Settings, the user can make changes that affect how the system operates on a network. For those who use a wireless network, there is a good chance that the network card will be detected during installation. This can be managed here as well.

New to this release of Kubuntu is the capability to run Zeroconf Discovery. Zeroconf allows computers to communicate on a network without any kind of configuration. This utility will discover the different services that are running on any computer that is available on any of the network connections. For example, Zeroconf comes into play when multiple users want to connect two laptops to each other via a crossover cable to transfer a file or play a network game.

Kubuntu can also be set up to share files and sessions across the network. By selecting Sharing, a new window will open up, allowing the user to manage desktop sharing, file sharing, and even local network browsing. If desktop sharing is enabled, others can connect to the first user's Kubuntu and see what is happening on that desktop. This is a great utility for those trying to support and troubleshoot other computers. File sharing and local network browsing enable the system to act as mini file server and provide outside access to files on the system.

A lot of information can be modified under the Network section, but be careful. Users can drastically change how the system functions and may accidentally make a change that will prevent Internet access. See Figure 7-24 for an example of how this looks.

When installing Kubuntu, the installer asked some questions that set up basic networking, including whether or not the IP address would be static

Figure 7-24 The network section.

or dynamic, the default gateway, and other necessary information. All of these options can be changed here. Any changes made to this section require your user password. In this section the user can make changes to the network interfaces, the routes, how Domain Name System (DNS) is set up, and create additional network profiles (See Figure 7-25). Making all these changes used to require knowledge of the command line, but now it can all be managed within Kubuntu.

The first tab on the network settings window allows configuration of the different interfaces and determining if the addressing will be static or dynamic. Going left to right, the next tab allows changes to the default route and which interface to use. Instead of having to manually edit a host file, under the DNS tab you can set up different static host names and entries. This is all information that you set up during installation, but it can later be changed here.

Setting up and changing how your system works used to require knowledge of text files and the command line, scaring people away from using Linux. With the advent of different graphical tools and the intuitive grouping of programs, system administration has become a lot easier.

Figure 7-25 Configuring a network interface.

System Administration   The final section of System Settings deals with administrating your Kubuntu system. Changes made here will require that you enter your password. Items that can be changed in this section include date and time, users and groups, regional settings, services, and other options.

In the users and groups section you can manage who will be able to access the system and what groups they belong to. If you would like more then one person to be able to access the sudo account, add that individual to the admin group. However, you will need access to the sudo password to make any changes here.

The process of adding and changing users has been simplified to help you out. Figure 7-26 shows this process.

Is your newly installed Web server not starting automatically? Are you having problems setting up a service to run correctly? System services will

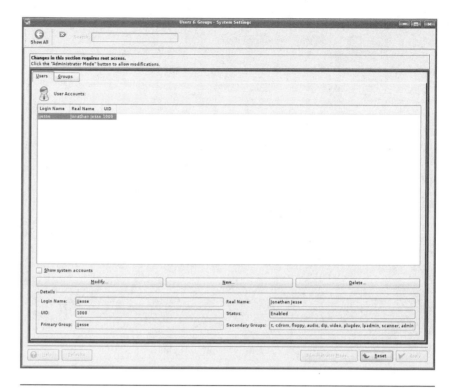

Figure 7-26 Adding users through system settings.

guide you through the different run levels and setting up when a service will start. Figure 7-27 shows an example of making such a change.

Managing Files with Kubuntu

Now that you have your system installed and set up the way you would like, it is time to understand how to navigate the different files and ways to access information in Kubuntu. That starts with the default file manager, Konqueror.

Introduction to Konqueror

Konqueror is a very powerful file manager that can do more than just browse your directories, it is also the second Web browser to pass the ACID2 test. As a file manager, Konquerer can do everything a "modern" file manager can (See Figure 7-28). Files can be browsed through either an

Figure 7-27 Configuring services.

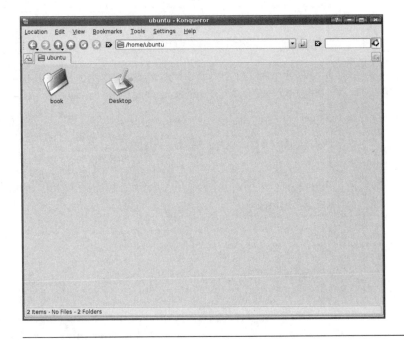

Figure 7-28 Konqueror.

icon view or a tree view. Copying, pasting, moving, and deleting files are all simple tasks that can be done through Konqueror. A nice feature of Konqueror is that directories automatically update. This means that if a file is created in a directory currently being viewed it is not necessary to refresh the directory to see the changes.

One of the great things about Konqueror is how much you can do within it. Need access to media files? Simply type media:/ and browse your media files. All other kinds of shortcuts, called kioslave, exist in Konqueror, including searching the Web with Google (gg: *KEYWORD*), or even browsing files via ssh through sftp://. Need help finding a file on your system? Simply use locate:/ to have Konqueror find it for you. You can visit the different system folders through system:/. There are all kinds of shortcuts and keywords like this built into Konqueror, including Google suggest in the search bar.

Another feature of Kubuntu is a built-in universal viewer. Click on a file, and it will show the file contents. This works for images, postscript files, and many other file types. Any new type of file just needs to register to work in this way.

Finding Files and Folders

Konqueror's built-in search capability allows you to find that file or folder you are looking for. One of the kioslaves is locate:, which will help you search for files. In the address type `locate:` followed by the file or folder name, and hit enter. Konqueror will then find what you are looking for. See Figure 7-29 for an example of locate: in action.

The search bar, which is located next to the address, can also help you find files and folders. This toolbar functions exactly like a search bar in a Web browser. Simply type the name of the file or folder you are looking for, hit enter, and Konqueror will then go out and find the files or folders requested.

Ripping Audio CDs

While AmaroK (discussed later in the chapter) can help you manage your music collection, Konqueror can help you add (rip) CDs into your collection so you can listen to them on your iPod or mp3 device. Simply place the CD in

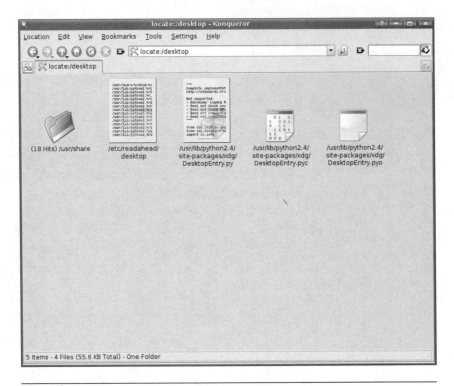

Figure 7-29 Using locate: to find files in Konqueror.

the CD-ROM drive, and, when prompted, open it up in a new window. There will be different folders labeled with different media formats. For example, if you are using the Ogg Vorbis format (the default format for media files in Kubuntu), open the folder and copy them to the directory where you store your collection. Another application to use to rip music is KaudioCreator, which is discussed later in the chapter.

Accessing Windows Partitions

A lot of people still have Windows partitions on their hard drives and would like to access the information stored there. Kubuntu can browse these files in read-only mode. Each Windows partition needs to be mounted before it can be accessed in Konquerer. This is a very simple process.

By default, Kubuntu mounts all its media in the /media directory, and your windows directory will be mounted in the same location. First, create a directory. Next, mount the partition to that directory. All of this work will be done from the command line, so open up Konsole, Kubuntu's terminal program (See Figure 7-30), and create the directory by typing sudo mkdir /media/windows. Enter your password. After the directory is created, mount the directory by typing the following sudo mount /devhda1 /media/windows -t ntfs -o nls=utf8,umask=0222. In simpler terms, this command will mount the directory in the correct folder with permissions that will allow you to access it in Konqueror. (Note: Read-only access is limited to NTFS partitions. Kubuntu can read and write to partitions formatted as FAT.)

Now you can browse files that are still stored on your Windows partition.

Accessing USB Drives

USB drives are everywhere these days, and Kubuntu handles them quite easily. Simply connect your USB drive, and it will auto-mount. These drives will then be available under Konqueror through the media folder. Before

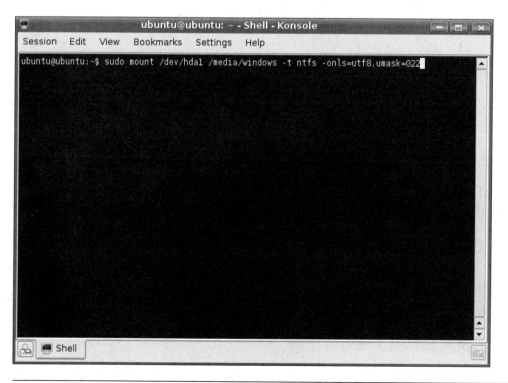

Figure 7-30 Konsole with commands.

removing the drive, make sure that you unmount it by right-clicking on the device and selecting Eject. The device can then be safely removed.

Managing Music

Kubuntu comes with a great program that can help manage all of your music files called amaroK (See Figure 7-31).

This application can serve as a full-fledged media library that can create playlists, track how often the user listens to a certain song, and even interact with your iPod. Looking for lyrics to the song that is currently playing? AmaroK can find them. Wondering what the CD cover of your favorite new album looks like? AmaroK can grab this information for the user as well. Along with media stored locally, amaroK can track podcasts and even let you listen to your favorite Internet radio station. Music is stored in a collection library that is arranged by artist, album, and song based on the tags built into the media. Each song can be rated, which can help determine the frequency of it appearing during "shuffle mode."

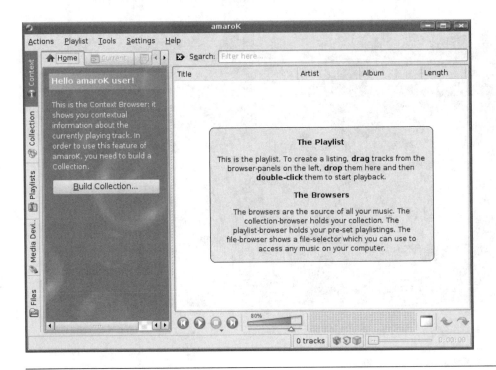

Figure 7-31 amaroK.

Upon launching amaroK for the first time there is a nice wizard that helps configure the user's collection. This First-Run Wizard will set up how the program will be displayed and the location of the folders that music is stored in. (Yes, a collection can be built across many different folders and sub folders.)

After setting these two options, amaroK will ask the user how the music will be stored. Since the application uses a database, this information can be stored in SQLIte, MySQL, or PostgreSQL depending on what is installed and your preferences. If at any time the user needs to make changes to how things are configured, the First-Run wizard can be rerun at anytime from the Tools menu. Figures 7-32 through 7-35 present several screenshots of the First-Run Wizard.

In order to listen to .mp3 files, an additional package will need to be installed from multiverse (see the section on Managing Repositories) through Adept. The package, libxine-extraodecs will also enable you to play some VI and some QuickTime videos, (S)VCDs, and most video files out there.

Now that your collection is configured, it time to create your playlists. Simply select the songs you would like to listen to, and drag them over to

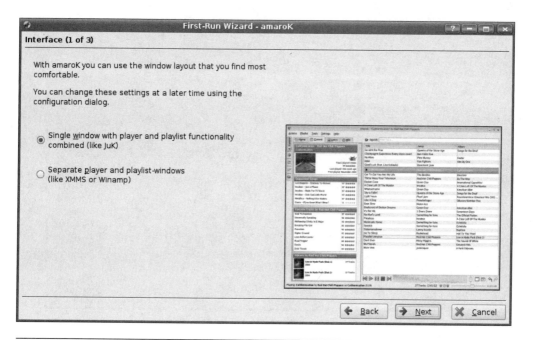

Figure 7-32 Welcome to the First-Run Wizard.

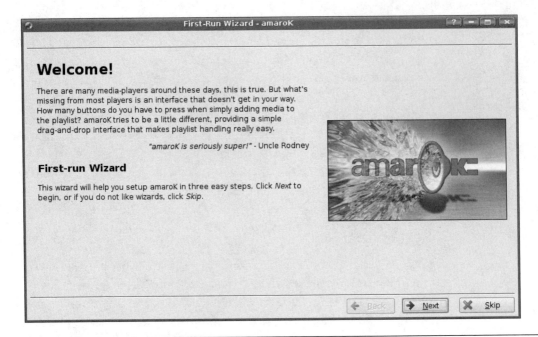

Figure 7-33 Choosing the default look of amaroK.

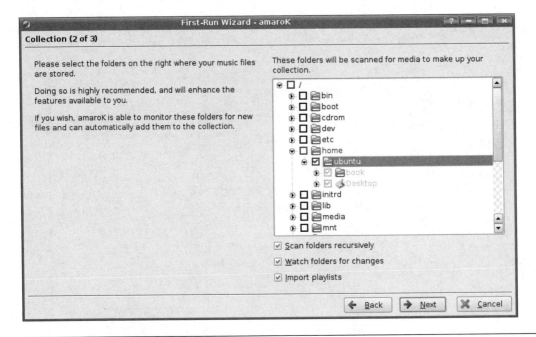

Figure 7-34 Selecting the location for your catalog.

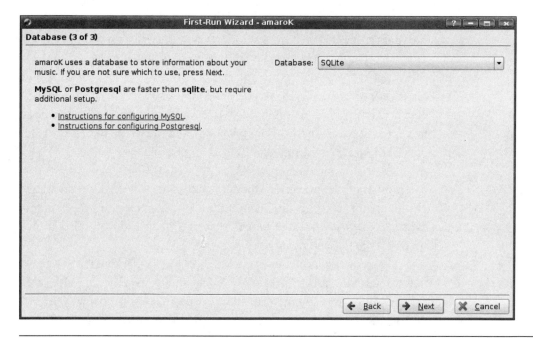

Figure 7-35 Choosing the type of database to store your collection in.

the playlist pane. If you would like to listen to all of your music, select dynamic mode, and it will create a playlist based on past listening habits. The more you listen to a certain song, the greater chance that song will repeat or a similar song will appear in the dynamic playlist.

Common Applications

Kubuntu comes with a large number of applications preinstalled and configured, including Web browsers, office applications, and e-mail. Remember, since choice is a huge factor in Kubuntu, if you do not like the default applications you can always change them. All of these applications are available through the K menu.

OpenOffice.org

The default office application for Kubuntu is OpenOffice.org 2.0. This version is the second major release of the suite that includes Writer, Calc, Draw, Impress, and Math. Each of these programs is easy to use and can help you switch from the Microsoft Office product line. In fact, the OpenOffice.org suite that can be installed on a Windows system comes on the installation CD to help you get comfortable and ready for a switch to Kubuntu. Each application corresponds to a similar application in the MS Product line. Calc is very similar to Excel, Writer is the same as Word, Impress is Power-Point, and Base functions similarly to Access. OpenOffice.org can handle all but Microsoft Access files without problems, and the whole suite is ready for use in a corporate environment as well as for personal use.

To demonstrate the power of OpenOffice.org, we will work on creating a new document. To open up OpenOffice.org Writer, open up the K menu, navigate to Office, and then OpenOffice.org Writer. You can also launch Katapult, type in Writer, and hit Enter.

Writer resembles any other word-processing software you have used before. Simply start typing your letter or paper as you normally would, and use the toolbar for formatting options that you require, including changing alignment, boldfacing, italicizing, and others.

When you are done working on a document, save the document through File > Save or by typing Ctrl+S. OpenOffice.org saves documents in the Open Document format. This file format is a standard across the world. You can also save documents in other formats, including Microsoft Office and Adobe PDF format. To save as a PDF file, just click the PDF button on the main toolbar (located next to the print icon), and enter a filename.

As mentioned before, Kubuntu CDs come with Open Source software that can be installed on Windows PCs so you can learn the OpenOffice.org suite before installing Kubuntu if you choose to do so.

Web Browsing

As mentioned earlier, Konqueror can function as a file manager as well as a Web browser. To launch Konqueror, open up the K menu, navigate to Internet, then Konqueror. Alternately, you can launch Katapult (Alt+Space) and type in Konqueror. Like other modern Web browsers, Konqueror provides tabbed browsing, the capability to have multiple Web pages open in the same window. To do this go File > New Tab or press Ctrl+T. A new tab will be created in your open Konqueror window. A cool feature is that you can be browsing the Web in one tab, browsing your home directory in another tab, and also browsing network folders in a third tab. All of these functions can help manage your taskbar and help keep your desktop looking clean and sharp.

As a Web browser, Konqueror enables you to set bookmarks, change your Home Page, and utilize all the other features you would expect from a Web browser.

Navigating around the Internet is no different in Konqueror than in any other Web browser, including Firefox, Opera, Netscape, or Internet Explorer. Just type the Web address into the address bar, and hit Enter. For example, type in www.kubuntu.com to visit the home page for Kubuntu.

To search using Google, simply move to the search bar, and directly to the right of the address bar type in what you are looking for. Konqueror will use Google to find it for you (see Figure 7-36 for an example).

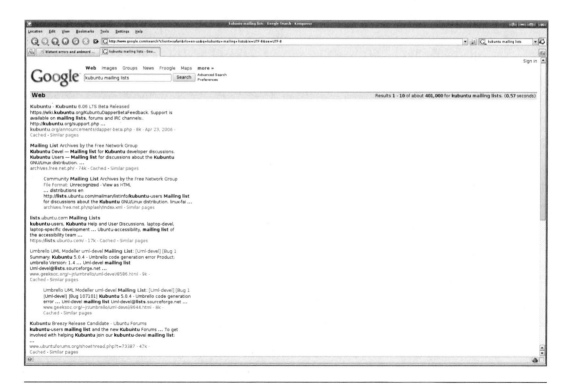

Figure 7-36 Using the Google search bar to search the Web.

TIP   If you are using Konqueror in the file manager mode, the Google search bar defaults to locate, which will search your hard drive.

Often when browsing the Web, you will see an orange icon at the bottom of Konqueror. This means there is an RSS (Really Simple Syndication) feed available. To track this feed, simply click on it, and Konqueror will add it to your subscribed feeds in Akregator. More information on Akregator will be provided later in this chapter.

Using Firefox for Browsing the Web

Allowing choice is a key feature of Ubuntu, and Kubuntu ships with the latest available version of Firefox (as of this writing 1.5.1). Firefox has taken the Web browser world by storm and is as good or even better then Internet Explorer. Firefox not only provides better features and a better browsing experience, it adheres better to Web standards. Like Konqueror, Firefox includes tab browsing (File > New Tab or Ctrl+T), bookmarks, and everything you would expect of a modern Web browser.

Firefox has a lot of different extensions that can be plugged in and allows greater flexibility for your Web browser. The most common plug-ins are Macromedia Flash and Java, which some Web pages require.

Installing a plug-in is as simple as visiting a Web site that requires it. A yellow bar will appear indicating you are missing a plug-in. Click on the Install Missing Plug-ins button to install the required plug-in.

Burning CDs—Audio and Data

Another common task is creating or burning CDs both for listening to music or for creating a backup of your system. Kubuntu's default CD creation program is K3b. K3b provides a very familiar (See Figure 7-37) interface for burning and copying CDs.

Simply click on one of icons from the main Kreator screen that describes the project you would like to create: a new audio CD, a new Data CD, a new data DVD project, or even copy a CD. After the new project has been started, simply drag the files from the top section to the lower section (See Figure 7-38).

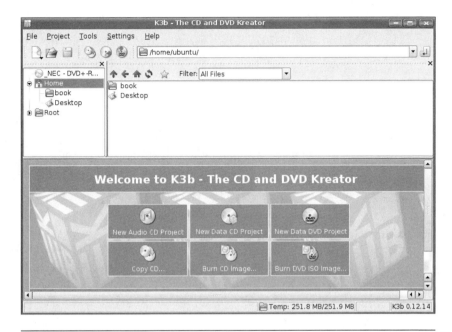

Figure 7-37 K3b.

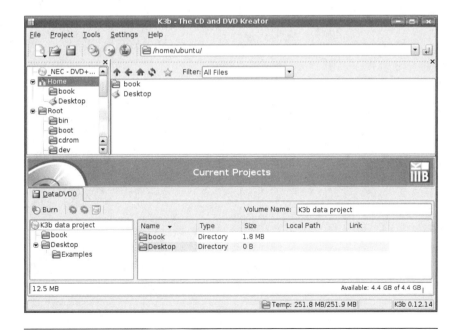

Figure 7-38 Just drag and drop the files.

Once the files have been selected, select Burn, and sit back while your new CD is created. K3b is a very easy-to-use utility that can help with the creation of backup CDs or even new music CDs.

KAudioCreator

KAudioCreator can be launched through the Multimedia section in the K menu or through Katapault by typing KAudioCreator. To rip music, you first need to configure the correct encoder. Simply use the wizard under Settings > Configure KAudioCreator to select the correct encoder, OggEnc or FLAC. To create mp3s out of files you will need to use Adept to install Lame from the universe repository. Upon selecting the encoder, the files will be placed automatically in /home/username/encoder. See Figure 7-39 for an example of Configure KAudioCreator.

KAudioCreator will automatically try to connect to CDDB to download the artist and track information. This will help you to better manage your music collection.

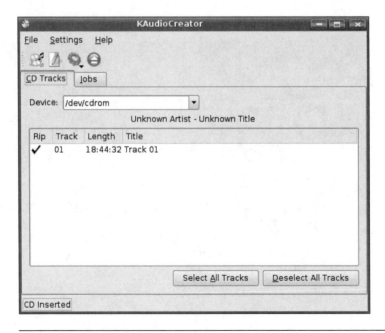

Figure 7-39 KAudioCreator in action.

Once the track information has been downloaded from CDDB (Compact Disk Database), simply click on the tracks you would like to rip, or click on Select All Tracks. Once the tracks have been selected, click on Rip Selection directly under the Settings menu, or go to File > Rip Selection.

KaudioCreator will help you convert the music from your CDs into a format that you can use with your iPod or other mp3 player.

Instant Messaging

Instant Messaging is another application that we almost cannot live without these days. Kopete, Kubuntu's default instant messaging client, handles this task very well. It is found under the Internet section in the K menu. You can also launch Kopete from Katapult by typing Kopete. The beauty of Kopete is that it can connect to all of the major service providers, so you do not have to have multiple programs open. Kopete can handle ICQ, MSN Messenger, Yahoo Messenger, and AIM. The newest version of Kopete, which is included with Kubuntu, can handle MSN Webcams as well. Because Gtalk (Google's Instant Message program) is built around the Jabber protocol, Kopete can handle that as well. Figure 7-40 shows a sample of Kopete in action.

Figure 7-40 Kopete.

The first time Kopete is launched the Configure Kopete wizard opens. First, set up the different accounts that you will use to connect. Kopete can save your passwords to these accounts and even automatically connect upon startup.

Once the accounts are configured correctly, you can change Kopete's behavior to fit your preferences. There are many options that can be selected, including away settings, what happens when a new message arrives, and even how the system starts up.

As mentioned previously, new in the latest version of Kopete is the capability to access MSN Webcam chats. Configuring how Kopete deals with Webcams is the last option that can be changed here.

Kontact

These days almost everyone uses e-mail, and almost everyone uses some form of calendar program to keep track of appointments and schedules. Kontact, Kubuntu's default personal information manager (PIM), will take care of all of these tasks plus more. Open up Kontact, and it will look like Figure 7-41.

Figure 7-41 Kontact.

From looking at the example, you can see that Kontact has a lot of different features, and we cover a lot of the program's options in the following sections. To start Kontact, go to K menu > Internet section. You can also start it from Katapult by typing Kontact.

Kmail is the program that handles e-mail. It can be run separately from Kontact if you choose. The first step in configuring Kontact is to set up Kmail to send and receive e-mail.

Setting Up Your E-mail Account There are several pieces of information that you will need to know in order to set up things. Your Internet Service Provider (ISP) or system administrator should be able to provide these details to you.

- Type of e-mail server (such as POP or IMAP)
- Mail server name (such as mail.domainname.com)
    - Mail account's username and password
    - Authentication type (typically "password")
- Outgoing mail server name

When Kontact is launched for the first time, a wizard will guide you through setting up this information. The first option will be to set up your identify with the e-mail address in the E-mail Address box and add any optional information that you would like. Click Forward to continue.

When you choose the type of e-mail server you are using, the options will vary. Fill in the server name and the username. The Security and Authentication Type settings may need to be changed, but for most accounts the default settings should be fine. Click Forward to continue.

The next screen does not have to be filled out, but decide what you want to do based on your preferences. However, the next screen will help you set up sending e-mail. Select the server type, typically SMTP, and add the server name to the server box. Click Forward to continue. Finally click on Finish to close the wizard and begin using Kmail.

Using Korganize   Korganize is included with Kontact. It will track your schedule and provide reminders of your appointments. Upon switching Kontact to calendar mode, you will see a month view on the right and actual dates on the right, as Figure 7-42 shows.

There are two different types of events that can be set up in Kontact:

■ **Meetings:** Events scheduled with different people

■ **Appointments:** General events

It is easy to add a new appointment. Find the date for the event in the month view, right-click, and select New Event. In the new window that opens up, fill out the Summary, Location, Time and Description boxes. You can also set up Kontact to remind you when it is time for the appointment.

Another great application that is a part of Kontact (or which can be used separately) is Akregator, an RSS (Really Simple Syndication) program that can track your favorite Web feeds. Due to the integration of Akregator and

Figure 7-42 Korganize, Kontact's in calendar mode.

Konqueror, any Web page that has an RSS feed will have an orange icon in the corner of the program (See Figure 7-43) that helps add it to your list.

Simply click on the icon and select Add to Akregator. Akregator will keep your feeds up-to-date by automatically checking for new content. Another bonus of the integration between Konqueror and Akregator is that Web pages can be opened up within Akgreator to post comments and view more information than what is provided by the Web feed.

Kontact is a great program that can help organize your life, track your favorite Web sites thru RSS, and be your e-mail application.

Krita

Kubuntu comes with a great program to help edit and create photos or drawings. Krita, which can be found under the Graphics section of the K menu or launched from Katapult by typing Krita, is a fully functional graphics program. Everything including photo retouching, image editing and creating original art can be done with Krita. Krita can handle almost any type of image file format including Photoshop files created with version 6.

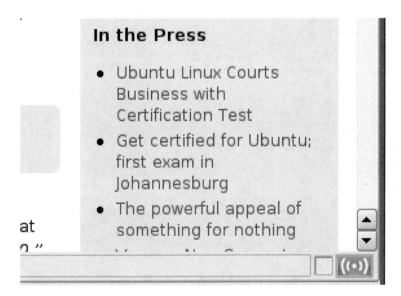

Figure 7-43 Using the RSS icon to add a feed to Akregator.

Creating a New Image   Upon starting Krita, you will be prompted to either start a new image or open up an existing one. Under Create Document, there is a group of templates that can be used to create this image, ordered by color model. As we will be creating a new image, just use the Empty Document, and you will be prompted with the New Image dialog box (Figure 7-44).

At this point you can name your document, specify the width, height, and resolution, and set the color mode and depth of your image.

The main screen for Krita is displayed, and it be somewhat confusing. There are toolbars on the left, right and top of the window, and the actual painting area is in the middle (Figure 7-45).

Manipulating an Existing Document   Another example of using Krita is cropping an existing document to a new size. This is easily done using the different tools. Open up an existing image, and use the Select a rectangular area tool located on the left in the Krita toolbar.

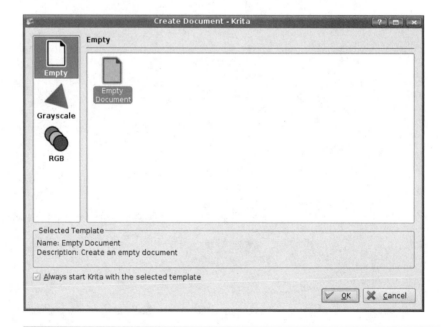

Figure 7-44 Custom document in Krita.

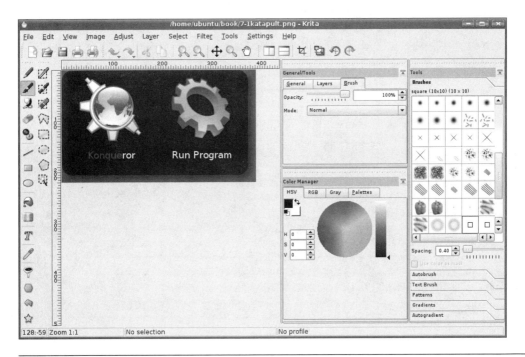

Figure 7-45 The main window for Krita.

After selecting the area you would like, Krita makes the outside area gray. Figure 7-46 shows what this looks like.

Once the portion of the image you would like has been selected, hit Ctrl-X to cut the image. A cool feature of Krita is that you can then paste what you cut into a new image by selecting Paste into New Image from the Edit menu (Figure 7-47).

Krita is a great image manipulation tool that can help you with all of your image needs. For more information on how to use Krita, refer to the Krita handbook included with Kubuntu as discussed later in the chapter.

Watching Movies and Playing CDs

The default media player for movies and also for listening to CDs is a great program called Kaffiene. Kaffiene can be found under the K menu under

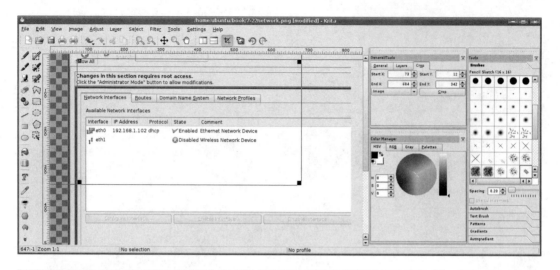

Figure 7-46 Selecting an area in Krita.

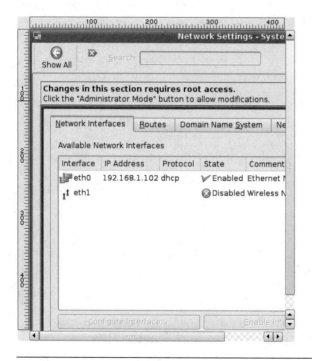

Figure 7-47 Paste into a new image in Krita.

Multimedia or launched from Katapult by typing Kaffiene. This program functions a lot like Windows Media Player for those coming from a Windows background.

Internet Relay Chat

A great place to find support for Kubuntu is Internet Relay Chat (IRC) through Konversation and the different IRC channels. Join irc.freenode.org, and then come over to #Kubuntu to get any of your support questions answered. The people there are full of great knowledge and can probably solve any issue or problem that you have.

Konverstation can be found in the Internet section under the K menu. Upon startup for the first time, a wizard will open and allow you to configure your identity, the account which you use to connect to the different channels. See Figure 7-48 for an example.

Remember #Kubuntu is a great place to find help with your Kubuntu installation, so set up Konverstation to automatically connect to that channel upon startup.

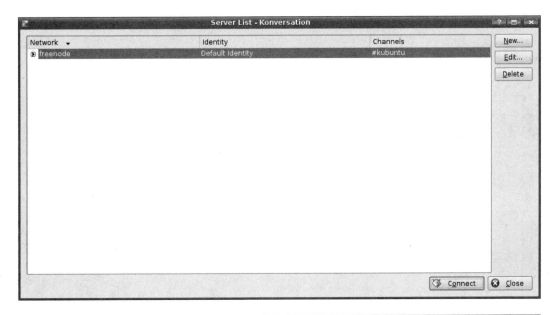

Figure 7-48 Manage identities in Konversation.

Kiosk Mode

Kubuntu allows you to completely configure your desktop, and one of the best examples of this is using Kubuntu in Kiosk mode. Kiosk mode allows an administrator to configure KDE and all aspects of the desktop and prevent the end user from changing the settings.

KDE stores all of its configuration information in text files that are similar to Windows INI files. These files control everything from the default background to whether or not a person can add bookmarks. To see the locations of the configuration files, simply type kde-config-path config from the Konsole. Note that the order applied is the reverse order of what is displayed.

By simply changing one of the files in the highest priority, last listed in kde-config, you can affect what all users see.

To change the background for all users simply edit the Wallpaper section found in kdesktoprc located in /usr/share/kubuntu-default-zettings/kde-profile/default/share/config. See Figure 7-49 for an example of this.

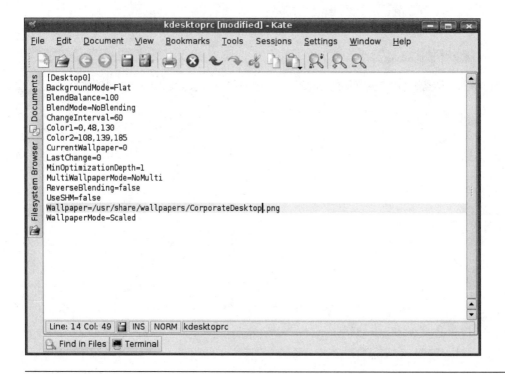

Figure 7-49 Editing the Wallpaper section for Kiosk mode.

As previously discussed, each user can change their desktop to meet his or her own needs. However, an administrator can make it so some things cannot be changed. Simply insert [$i] at the top of the file for each application you would like to make immutable. Figure 7-50 shows the background changed and made immutable.

Along with enabling or setting changes, an administrator can remove user access to certain items by simply editing the kdeglobals file and adding a [KDE Action Restrictions] [$i] section. Figure 7-51 shows the process of removing the capability to start a konsole.

A great tool that can help with setting up Kiosk mode is iosktool.

There are plenty of additional items that can be limited and changed in Kubuntu.

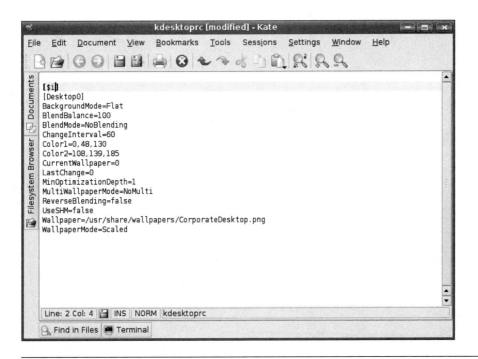

Figure 7-50 A default background made immutable.

```
[KDE Action Restrictions]
[$i]
konsole
```

```
[DesktopIcons]
Animated=true
Size=48
```

```
[General]
font=DejaVu Sans,9,-1,5,50,0,0,0,0,0
fixed=DejaVu Sans Mono,9,-1,5,50,0,0,0,0,0
menuFont=DejaVu Sans,9,-1,5,50,0,0,0,0,0
taskbarFont=DejaVu Sans,9,-1,5,50,0,0,0,0,0
toolBarFont=DejaVu Sans,9,-1,5,50,0,0,0,0,0
widgetStyle=lipstik
selectBackground=74,149,214
selectForeground=255,255,255
buttonBackground=240,240,240
```

```
[PreviewSettings]
BoostSize=true
MaximumSize=5242880
```

```
[KDE]
ShowIconsOnPushButtons=true
ChangeCursor=true
EffectAnimateCombo=true
EffectFadeMenu=false
```

Figure 7-51 Removing access to starting a konsole session.

Exploring the Kubuntu Landscape

Unlike many other OS, Kubuntu includes a large amount of applications right inside the system. These tools have been selected to allow you to install Kubuntu and then just get your work done. Some of the applications installed by default have been covered already. Unfortunately (or fortunately, depending on how you look at it), there are just too many applications to go over due to space restrictions.

To partially solve that problem, here is a quick summary of many programs that are available from the K menu, including how to find them along with a brief description.

- **Kate** K menu > Utilities > Kate

    This simple and powerful text editor is great for editing documents, making quick notes, and programming. There is a vast range of plugins for items such as spellchecking, statistics, and syntax highlighting.

- **Calculator (Speedcrunch)**

  K menu > Utilities > Calculator

  Speedcrunch is an extremely powerful calculator that can help you solve both basic and advanced math problems.

- **Konsole** K menu > Utilities > Konsole

  Beneath the desktop is a very powerful command line core. Konsole allows you access to this powerful command line by putting a nice window frame around it. Konsole is great for the command line junkies, those who prefer to do things with a graphical interface. Konsole can be completely customized to meet your command line needs.

- **Info Center (KinfoCenter)**

  K menu > System > Info Center

  The KinfoCenter provides information about your system, including partitions, network interfaces, and other important features about your system.

- **Performance Monitor (KsysGuard)**

  K menu > System > Performance Monitor

  The Performance Monitor provides information about how your Kubuntu system is functioning. Having problems with an application taking too much memory? How would you know? KsysGuard provides this information.

- **System Logs Viewer (KsystemLog)**K menu > System > System Logs Viewer

  Interested in what is going on with your system? Kubuntu keeps track of files and access logs that can be viewed through this program.

- **CD Player (KsCD)**

  K menu > Multimedia > CD Player

  KsCD is a great little program that will allow you to listen to CDs. KsCD will grab the track information from FreeDB and then display this information as the track is played.

- **Internet Dial-Up Tool (KPPP)**

  K menu > Internet > Internet Dial-Up Tool

Need help connecting to you ISP (Internet Service Provider) through a modem? KPPP will help take care of this. KPPP can help set up your modem and even set up your dial-up connection.

▪ **Remote Desktop Connection (Krdc)**

K menu > Internet > Remote Desktop Connection

KRDC can help you connect to remote systems either through the remote desktop protocol (RDP) or through virtual network connection (VNC). Simply type in the address, and click on connect. The remote desktop connection can save the settings for each computer that you connect to.

▪ **Bluetooth Chat and Bluetooth OBEX Client**

K menu > Internet > Bluetooth Chat

K menu > Internet > Bluetooth OBEX Client

The applications are installed by default and are new to this release of Kubuntu. They both help you connect to various Bluetooth-enabled devices.

▪ **PDF Viewer (KPDF)**

K menu > Graphics > PDF Viewer

KPDF provides you with the ability to open and view files saved in the Adobe PDF format

▪ **Screen Capture Program (KsnapShot)**

K menu > Graphics > Screen Capture Program

KsnapShot is a great application that allows you to take screenshots and save them in different formats. The great thing about KsnapShot is that you specify the exact amount of the screen that will be captured. This program was used to take the screenshots for this chapter.

▪ **Image Viewer (Gwenview)**

K menu > Graphics > Image Viewer

Gwenview is the default application for viewing images in Kubuntu. All different types of images can be opened including .png, .jpeg, and .bmp.

- **Kdevelop**

While not installed by default, Kdevelop is a wonderful Integrated Development Environment (IDE) that can help out with your coding projects. Simply install it using Adept, and you will find it located under the Development menu in the K menu.

Tips and Tricks

The more you use Kubuntu, the more you will learn some tips and tricks to help make your computing experience better and easier. Kubuntu can be configured to do almost anything you would like.

Run Programs Automatically When Kubuntu Starts   Sometimes there are programs you would like to start automatically every time you log in to your system. An example of this is Katapult, which was discussed earlier in the chapter. It starts automatically and runs in the background. There are four easy steps to set this up using the session management feature of KDE. KDE can save everything and then restore those settings for you.

1. Open up System Settings from the K menu and click on the User Account Section.

2. Click the Session Manager button on the left, and make sure that the Restore manually saved session checkbox is enabled.

3. Log out, saving your sessions.

Login Automatically to Kubuntu When the Computer Starts   It is possible to set up Kubuntu so a user is logged in automatically when the computer boots. This change is *not recommended* for must computers as it is insecure and may allow others to access your information.

1. Open up the System Settings from the K menu.

2. Click on Administrator Mode, and entering your password to gain administrator privileges.

3. Select the Convenience tab, and check Enable Autologin.

4. Select the user to autologin from the drop-down menu, and select an appropriate time delay.

Automatically Turn on Num Lock When Kubuntu Starts   If you are sick of always having to turn on your num lock, the change is very simple to make.

1. Open up System Settings from the K menu, and select Keyboard.

2. Under the NumLock on KDE Startup, enable the Turn On checkbox.

3. Click on Apply to save your settings.

Finding Help and Giving Back to the Community

KDE is the best-documented desktop environment around, and Kubuntu strives to match that level. Kubuntu currently ships with three documents: the Release Notes, About Kubuntu, and the Desktop Guide, all of which feature specific Kubuntu material and are maintained by the Ubuntu Documentation Team.

Finding Help

Help is found through the Khelpcenter and is organized around applications and then tasks. Khelpcenter is launched either through the K menu under Help, or is available from the main screen or from the start page of Konquerer. Figure 7-52 shows you Khelpcenter.

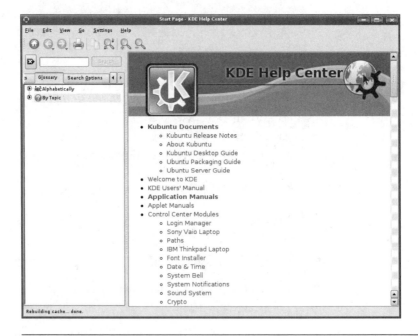

Figure 7-52 The Khelpcenter.

Accessing KDE Help Manuals

Along with the Kubuntu documents, Kubuntu ships with the help documents for all of the major applications that can also be accessed through the KHelpCenter. These manuals can help solve some of your common problems and answer many of your questions.

The default home page for Konqueror lists the help documents that are shipped in Kubuntu. The list includes the following:

- **About Kubuntu**

  This includes information regarding Kubuntu and the Kubuntu project.

- **Release Notes**

  Interested in what is installed by default in Kubuntu? This guide gives a quick overview of what is new and what is supported.

- **Desktop Guide**

  This document is brand new in Kubuntu 6.06 and will guide you through some of the basic needs for operating your Kubuntu system. A lot of information in this chapter can be found in that guide.

- **Packaging Guide**

  Would you like to learn how to package applications to give a hand to the Kubuntu project? This guide will show you what you need to create a package that will be accepted by the maintainers.

- **Server Guide**

  If you are interested in running Kubuntu as a server, this guide will help you get set up. Items that are included are running Kubuntu as a file server and/or a Web server. This is a great resource for more advanced users.

If you still need help after looking in the documentation, Kubuntu provides other means for finding this information. A great place to start is on the IRC channel #Kubuntu, which, as we noted earlier, can be accessed through Konverstation. There are always wonderful and knowledgeable people in this channel who can answer almost any question. If you prefer to use the Web for answers, the Kubuntu wiki, found at wiki.kubuntu.org, has a large amount of information loosely organized with a great search function built in. A third place to find information is the Kubuntu forums at www.kubuntuforums.org. Remember Google is your friend as well. Chances are someone else has come across your problem before and has written a solution to the issue.

Giving Back to the Community

Kubuntu is built around a great community of people who give back what they learn. There are many ways to get involved and share your love of Kubuntu. A great place to find out how you can make a difference is at www.ubuntu.com/community/participate. Not everyone involved has to know how to create packages, understand how their kernel works, or be a great programmer. Kubuntu also has a place for people to write wiki pages or help out with documentation needs.

Summary

Kubuntu is a great part of the Ubuntu project and is quickly maturing. From its start as the idea of a single developer to many people working together, Kubuntu is becoming the KDE distribution of choice. However, there is still room for improvement and additions to the setup. A large community of people discuss every day, either through IRC or e-mail, ways to make these improvements. Bugs and other issues are quickly resolved without the additional cost of new programs.

Kubuntu is going to be around for the long haul, and each new release delivers a better, cleaner, and more polished OS. Help spread the word about the project, and get involved by helping out.

## CHAPTER 8

The Ubuntu Community

- Venues
- Ubuntu Mailing Lists
- IRC Channel List
- Teams, Processes, and Community Governance
- Getting Involved
- Summary

COMMUNITY IS A WORD often used in discussions of Ubuntu. Early articles about Ubuntu bore subtitles asking, "Would you like some community with that?" The earliest press releases and communiqués from the project emphasized a "community-driven approach" to operating system development and distribution. Additionally, the highest level governance board in Ubuntu is called the Community Council. The authors of this book made a very conscious decision to dedicate an entire chapter to describing the Ubuntu community. In fact, the book itself is dedicated to the Ubuntu community!

Still, while the Ubuntu community is important, it is not always easy to succinctly describe it. Ubuntu is, in large part, developed and funded by Canonical Ltd. The community, almost by definition, extends far beyond Canonical Ltd. The Ubuntu project has members and self-declared activists (Ubunteros, formerly Ubuntites) but the Ubuntu community is more than even those with such explicitly declared relationships. The project contains a wide variety of different venues for participation. But while the community is active in each of these areas, its scope is even wider.

The Ubuntu community is the collection of individuals who build, promote, distribute, support, document, translate, and advocate Ubuntu—in myriad ways and in myriad venues. Most people in the Ubuntu community have never met, talked with, or heard of each other. Members of the community are linked together by their contributions, both technical and nontechnical, and by Ubuntu itself. These contributions have built Ubuntu as a distribution, as a social movement, as a set of support infrastructures, and as a project. In short, they have built Ubuntu *as a community*. However, while any active software development project has a number of people making contributions, not every project has a community.

Community is also a term that represents a promise by the Ubuntu project to remain inclusive. Community means that volunteers are not only welcome, but essential. It means that Ubuntu is a "place" where individuals can come together to create something that is greater than the sum of its parts. The word "community" gives a nod to the fact that while much development work is paid for by Canonical Ltd., and while some people contribute more hours, more effort, more code, more translations, more documentation, or more advocacy work to Ubuntu than others, no individual or subgroup can take credit for everything that Ubuntu has become. In Ubuntu, no contribution is expendable. Community also reflects Ubuntu's goal to provide a low barrier for entry for these contributions. Anyone who cares about Ubuntu can contribute to the project and can, in whatever ways are most appropriate, become a participant in the Ubuntu community.

This chapter will provide a bird's-eye view of the venues and processes in which the Ubuntu community is active. First, it takes a tour through the venues through which the Ubuntu community communicates. It continues by looking at the way that the community is organized and the processes by which that organization works. Finally, it walks readers through the ways that *they* can participate in the Ubuntu community and contribute to its success.

Venues

As was described in the introduction, transparent and public communication was an early goal of the Ubuntu project. Technical and community decisions are made publicly and are accessible to all interested parties. When this is impossible (e.g., when there is a face-to-face meeting and it's simply not possible for *everyone* interested to attend), the community attempts to publish summaries and minutes and to provide avenues for feedback. Ubuntu contains no "member only," "developer only," or "decision-maker only" back channels except to preserve individual privacy or security—and the Ubuntu community refuses to create them. All work in Ubuntu occurs in places where *everyone* can view the work and anyone who agrees to engage constructively and respectfully can participate.

Of course, this activity is only public to those who know where to find it. This section tries to document the venues for communication in Ubuntu as completely as possible. It describes the places where discussions of development, support, and advocacy take place. While nobody can engage in communication in *all* of the venues described, knowledge of what exists allows participants to be more informed when they need to choose the right place to ask a question or to make a suggestion.

Mailing Lists

The single most important venue for communication in Ubuntu is the Ubuntu mailing lists. These lists provide the space where all important announcements are made and where more development discussions take place. There are, at the time of this writing, 75 public e-mail lists, although this number is constantly growing. A full list of mailing lists (excluding Local Community teams) is included below.

Ubuntu Mailing Lists

An up-to-date, full page of mailing lists for Ubuntu can be found at http://lists.ubuntu.com/ where users can see a list of available lists, view archived discussions, and can subscribe to lists through a Web interface. Table 8-1 presents the mailing lists organized by topic areas.

Table 8-1 General Ubuntu Lists

List Name	Description
ubuntu-accessibility	Ubuntu accessibility team
ubuntu-announce	Ubuntu announcements
ubuntu-art	Discussion on Ubuntu artwork
ubuntu-backports	Backports discussions
ubuntu-desktop	Desktop team coordination and discussion
ubuntu-devel	Ubuntu developer discussion
ubuntu-devel-announce	Developer-related announcements and information
ubuntu-doc	Documentation team coordination and discussion
ubuntu-doc-commits	Ubuntu documentation team commits
ubuntu-hardened	Ubuntu Linux proactive security deployment and development
kernel-bugs	Kernel bugs tracking
kernel-team	Kernel team discussions
laptop-devel	Laptop-specific development
laptop-testing-team	Ubuntu laptop testing
loco-contacts	Ubuntu local community team (LoCo) contacts
ubuntu-marketing	Discussion on community-based marketing of Ubuntu
ubuntu-marketing	Announcements, feedback, and discussion for Ubuntu mirror maintainers
ubuntu-mirrors	List for those mirroring Ubuntu FTP archives

Table 8-1 General Ubuntu Lists (Continued)

List Name	Description
ubuntu-mono	Packaging Mono for Ubuntu
ubuntu-motu	Mailing list of the Masters of the Universe
ubuntu-news	Interesting news about Ubuntu for users and developers
ubuntu-security-announce	Ubuntu security announcements
sounder	Ubuntu community random chit-chat list
technical-board	Technical board members list
ubuntu-translators	Discussion about translating Ubuntu
ubuntu-users	Ubuntu help and user discussions
ubuntu-women	Ubuntu women

Ubuntu Bugs and Notification Lists (not discussion lists)	
ubuntu-changes-auto	Archive upload notification list, for automated uploads to all Ubuntu releases
ubuntu-bugs	Ubuntu bug tracker changes—HIGH VOLUME
desktop-bugs	Desktop bug tracker changes—HIGH VOLUME
kubuntu-bugs	Kubuntu bug tracker changes
universe-bugs	Universe bug tracker changes—HIGH VOLUME
warty-changes	Warty Warthog archive upload notification list
hoary-changes	Hoary Hedgehog archive upload notification list
breezy-changes	Breezy Badger archive upload notification list
dapper-changes	Dapper Drake archive upload notification list

Subproject Lists	
edubuntu-devel	Edubuntu developer discussion
kubuntu-devel	Kubuntu developer discussion
kubuntu-users	Kubuntu help and user discussions
xubuntu-devel	Xubuntu development discussion

Infrastructure Development and Support Lists	
bazaar	User and development discussion about the Bazaar distributed revision control system
bazaar-announce	Announcements for the Bazaar project
bazaar-commits	Bazaar repository commit notification
bazaar-ng	Bazaar-ng discussion
hct	Discussion about the Hypothetical Changeset tool
launchpad-users	Discussion for Launchpad users
rosetta-users	Rosetta user discussion

Other Lists	
security-review	Discussion about resolving security vulnerabilities

Lists are one of the oldest forms of communication by e-mail. A mailing list provides a single e-mail address that, when mailed to, will then relay the received message to a large number of people. In Ubuntu, lists are topical, and individuals can subscribe to a mailing list if they want to receive information on the list's topic. All mailing lists at Ubuntu are hosted at lists.ubuntu.com. If you would like to send a message to a list, simply e-mail <mailing list name>@lists.ubuntu.com while replacing <mailing list name> with the name of the list you are trying to mail.

With a few exceptions (e.g., the technical board e-mail list), *anybody* can subscribe to any Ubuntu list. In most cases, the capability to send e-mail to lists is restricted to list members (membership in lists is, of course, open to anyone). This means that all e-mail sent to a list from someone who is not a member of that list is put into a queue to be reviewed by a human "moderator" before it is broadcast to list members. This is done as an anti-spam measure. Users can subscribe to lists and then configure the system to never send e-mail. For several e-mail lists, *all* messages are moderated. This is largely to ensure that lists remain "low volume" or "announcement only."

Ubuntu's mailing lists are run by the popular Mailman software, which may be familiar to some users. Mailman makes it simple to subscribe to lists, to unsubscribe, and to configure any number of options about mail delivery. One popular option is to receive a daily "digest" of messages rather than a separate e-mail each time a new message is sent. This is all available through a Web interface at http://lists.ubuntu.com. Users can also subscribe to lists by sending an e-mail with "subscribe" in the subject line to `<mailing list name>-REQUEST@lists.ubuntu.com`.

While each list plays an important role in the Ubuntu community, a few central lists warrant a little more detail and may be a good idea for users to consider subscribing to. These are detailed below.

ubuntu-announce

This fully moderated list relays all important announcements for the Ubuntu project and usually contains less than one e-mail per week. It is *the* first place where new releases are announced and where other important information can be found first. If you use Ubuntu, you may want to consider subscribing to this list. If you only subscribe to one list, this should be it.

ubuntu-devel-announce

This fully moderated list contains announcements related to the development of Ubuntu. It is low volume and contains one to three e-mails per week. If you work with code in Ubuntu, use a development release, or contribute on any technical level, you should be on this list. If you are at all involved in development for Ubuntu, this (in addition to ubuntu-announce) is *the* list you must subscribe to.

ubuntu-users

This is a primarily support-oriented list for questions and answers that Ubuntu users have. It is a *very* high-volume list, but it is an excellent place to ask questions and have them answered. It is a useful general-purpose list for discussion of any issue that pertains primarily to using Ubuntu.

ubuntu-devel

This list is the primary site for general purpose discussion of Ubuntu development. If you are looking to contribute to Ubuntu in any technical way, you should subscribe to this list and begin to follow the discussion. The list is relatively high volume.

sounder

Sounder is the unmoderated community "chitchat" list. Sounder is the collective noun to describe a group of "Warthogs" and was initially the e-mail list that supported the small, invite-only group of users who tested the Ubuntu 4.10 Warty Warthog release before it was announced to the world. The list has been kept for historical reasons under the old name but now provides a venue for the discussion of anything that is "off topic" in the other venues. It frequently hosts discussion of Ubuntu news, events, advocacy, and activism and is an important list for any community member who is participating and contributing to Ubuntu in less technical ways.

Internet Relay Chat (IRC)

While mailing lists provide the primary venue for asynchronous communication (i.e., not at the same time), there is still an important need for synchronous, or real-time, collaboration. Internet relay chat (IRC) fills this niche. While it was designed primarily for group (i.e., many-to-many) communication in "channels," it is also equipped with private messaging capabilities that facilitate one-to-one communication—all instantaneously. It is very similar to instant messaging or chat-room style communication. While time zones and a round globe make it difficult for the global Ubuntu community to meet at the same time, many users and developers take advantage of IRC's capability to let anyone chat about an issue in real time or to ask a question and have it answered immediately.

Like mailing lists, IRC channels provide a venue for a variety of different types of communication in a variety of different subcommunities in Ubuntu. There are many different channels, including channels in a variety of languages. A complete list as of the time of this writing is included below.

IRC Channel List

Table 8-2 presents a list of IRC channels. A complete and up-to-date list can be found at http://wiki.ubuntu.com/InternetRelayChat.

Table 8-2 Ubuntu IRC Channels on Freenode

Support and Talk Channels	
#ubuntu	Ubuntu help channel
#ubuntu+1	Help channel for development versions
#kubuntu	Kubuntu help channel
#edubuntu	Edubuntu channel
#xubuntu	Xubuntu channel
#ubuntu-offtopic	The off-topic channel where everything is on topic
#kubuntu-offtopic	The off-topic channel where everything is on topic
Team Channels	
#kubuntu-devel	Kubuntu development coordination
#ubuntu-accessibility	The Accessibility Team channel
#ubuntu-boot	Boot/Init team
#ubuntu-bugs	Channel for Bugdays
#ubuntu-desktop	The Ubuntu desktop team
#ubuntu-devel	Ubuntu development coordination
#ubuntu-doc	Ubuntu documentation team coordination
#ubuntu-hardened	Discussions on the Ubuntu hardened project
#ubuntu-java	Ubuntu java development coordination
#ubuntu-kernel	Ubuntu kernel team coordination
#ubuntu-laptop	Ubuntu laptop development
#ubuntu-locoteams	Coordination of all local coordination teams
#ubuntu-love	About getting involved with Ubuntu
#ubuntu-meeting	All meetings are held here
#ubuntu-motu	Coordination of the Ubuntu MOTU team
#ubuntu-motu-school	Ubuntu MOTU team schooling channel
#ubuntu-server	Ubuntu server help and discussions
#ubuntu-toolchain	Coordination of the Ubuntu toolchain team
#ubuntu-translators	Coordination and discussions about Ubuntu translations
#ubuntu-women	For Ubuntu women
#ubuntu-xgl	Yes, we all love gooey guis!

Table 8-2 Ubuntu IRC Channels on Freenode (Continued)

Localized Channels	
#ubuntu-au	Australia
#ubuntu-br	Brazil
#ubuntu-ca #ubuntu-qc	Canada
#ubuntu-co	Colombia
#ubuntu-cz	Czech
#ubuntu-de #ubuntu-de-treffpunkt #kubuntu-de #edubuntu-de	Germany
#ubuntu-es #kubuntu-es #edubuntu-es	Spanish speakers —Latin America
#ubuntu-fi	Finland
#ubuntu-fr #kubuntu-fr #ubuntu-fr-meeting	France
#ubuntu-gr	Greece
#ubuntu-hr	Croatia
#ubuntu.hu	Hungary
#ubuntu-il	Israel
#ubuntu-it	Italy
#ubuntu-ko	Korea
#ubuntumexico	Mexico
#ubuntu-nl	The Netherlands
#ubuntu-no	Norway
#ubuntu.pl	Poland
#ubuntu-ph	Philippines
#ubuntu-pt	Portugal
#ubuntu-ru	Russia

Table 8-2 Ubuntu IRC Channels On Freenode (Continued)

Localized Channels	
#ubuntu.se	Sweden
#ubuntu.tr	Turkey
#ubuntu-tw	Taiwan
#ubuntu-uk	United Kingdom
#ubuntu-zh	Chinese
Unofficial Channels	
#ubuntuforums	The Ubuntu forums team

All official Ubuntu IRC channels are located on the Freenode IRC network which also hosts a range of other free and open source software projects. Users can connect to IRC using several pieces of software in Ubuntu including GAIM, XChat, or IRSSI. Like the ubuntu-users e-mail list, #ubuntu is designed for help and support. When joining any channel, users should carefully read the topic as many frequently asked questions are answered in

Figure 8-1 Xchat is an IRC client included in Ubuntu that allows Ubuntu users to connect to the Ubuntu IRC channels.

this topic and moderators of the channel can be annoyed by users who ask questions which they have already taken the time to answer in the channels topic.

Currently the #ubuntu channel is the third biggest channel on the Freenode network and is growing quickly. In the nine months preceding this writing, the population of the channel has almost doubled. Another important channel is #ubuntu-devel, which is reserved for discussion of Ubuntu development. Similarly, Kubuntu developers hang out in #kubuntu. To keep #ubuntu focused on support all general chatter has been moved to #ubuntu-offtopic. Similarly, support for development releases has moved to #ubuntu+1. Maintaining channels with specific foci has allowed the support community to stay focused and help as many people as possible.

Web Forums

The official Ubuntu Forums are other frequently used venues for communication in Ubuntu. For a number of reasons, many users prefer to communicate through a Web-based forum or bulletin board. The Ubuntu forums were created to satisfy this group and have done so with amazing success. Figure 8-2 shows an example of forum use.

Figure 8-2 Example of an open "thread" in the Ubuntu Forums.

The forums are accessible online at www.ubuntuforums.org/ and have shown an impressive amount of utilization. Statistics as of the time of writing show activity of more than 860,000 messages on more than 150,000 topics. The forums also boast more than 80,000 users with more than 1,000 active at a given point. The topics that these groups cover run the gamut. These are roughly broken down into the following categories:

- Support forums for the latest release of Ubuntu that includes:
  - User support for Ubuntu
  - User support for Kubuntu
  - Help with hardware support for Ubuntu
  - Installation and upgrade help
  - A collection of how-to articles, tips, and tricks
  - Information for people attempting to run the latest games on Ubuntu
- A wide variety of other discussion areas provide resources including:
  - Discussion areas outside of the normal support areas (e.g., artwork, server support)
  - Support for third-party Ubuntu projects and products
  - Support for previous releases of Ubuntu
  - Support venues for developers and programmers
- Several other resources that include:
  - A community chat area for general discussion
  - Web-based version of all official announcements that go out on the `ubuntu-announce` and `ubuntu-devel-announce` mailing lists.

Each of the areas mentioned above includes between one and nine different subforums, each of these containing many threads. By covering such ground, the Ubuntu forums provide an impressive support resource. They provide both an excellent venue for asking questions and receiving support as well as for answering questions and making important contributions to the health of the Ubuntu community. If you are interested in either, or both, the forums are a good place to begin.

The only caveat regarding the forums worth mentioning is that they are not frequently used by those developing Ubuntu—although there are exceptions to that rule. If users want to send messages directly to the Ubuntu *developers,* the forums may not provide the most effective tool. If users want to get involved in technical contributions to the project, they will, in all likelihood, have to augment their forums patronage with use of mailing lists. To help mediate this issue, the forums staff has created several forums that act as two-way gateways between the forums and the mailing list. The ubuntu-users mailing list is one such list. This means that users can read and participate in the ubuntu-users mailing list using the Web by simply participating in the associated Web forum—software makes sure that messages go between the two venues. Similarly, there are one-way forums for the ubuntu-announce and ubuntu-devel-announce mailing lists.

The Ubuntu Forums are representative of the Ubuntu community in another notable way: They were created, and for a long period were wholly funded, by the community itself. The forums founder, Ryan Troy, had no association with Canonical Ltd. when he created the forums. He did so without help or suggestion from Canonical Ltd. or others in the Ubuntu community. Canonical Ltd. and others in the Ubuntu project recognized the extremely valuable contribution that the forums were making and the important niche it was filling, so they invited the project to become an "official" part of the Ubuntu community. To this day, the forums are moderated and maintained entirely by volunteers and supported in large part through financial assistance outside of what is provided by Canonical Ltd.

Wikis

Since nearly day one, a large chunk of Ubuntu documentation and support has taken place in the official Ubuntu "wiki" (see Figure 8-3). For those who don't already know, a *wiki*—pronounced "wik-ee"—is a Web site where any viewer can add, remove, or edit content. The first wiki was created by Ward Cunningham in 1995, and wikis have shown themselves to be an extremely effective tool for collaborative writing in recent years. The term is shortened from "wiki wiki"—Hawaiian for "quick." Many wikis have been created. Most famous among these wikis is the online encyclopedia Wikipedia, which now contains more than a million articles in the English version alone.

Figure 8-3 Front page of the Ubuntu wiki.

The primary Ubuntu wiki is at http://wiki.ubuntu.com. It can be edited, added to, or reorganized by anyone in the Ubuntu community. Edits are unrestricted. By requiring registration, each change can be traced to a particular user. The wiki has, over time, grown to include a variety of information useful in support, development, and documentation. Currently, the wiki contains more than 6,000 documents and pages.

Unlike other documentation that ships with Ubuntu, anyone can fix an error, inaccuracy, or out-of-date fact in the wiki. As a result, there is no good way to determine if information in the wiki is correct. It cannot be subjected to the same type of quality assurance workflow that a document such as this book might be. However, it is also *much* more likely to be up-to-date in the quickly changing world of Ubuntu development, where there is a new release every six months. The wiki provides a venue for this level of up-to-date information with a low barrier to entry and, as a result, acts as an invaluable resource for the community.

To use the wiki, one can either search or browse it. Searching is the most commonly used way to get information from the wiki, and users can easily search either titles or the full text of the wiki. To achieve the best results, it is usually best to search titles and then the text to ensure that you look for more relevant information first. For people who prefer to browse, the wiki is explicitly divided into a number of categories that include:

- Documentation
- Community
- Events
- Resources
- Releases
- Non-English Information
- Policies

Most of these categories are relatively self-explanatory. The "policies" section consists primarily of largely technical information that, for the most part, describes the processes by which the Ubuntu archive is divided up. Also worth noting is the section that includes non-English information. While the front page of the Ubuntu wiki is in English, there are also many pages in other languages. The wiki page on language support (http:// wiki.ubuntu.com/LocalSupport) provides both links to pages within the wiki that include documentation and information in languages other than English and links to more than a dozen other wikis that are in another language entirely. Users looking for wiki pages in a language other than English are advised to visit this page.

The Fridge

The Fridge (http://fridge.ubuntu.com/) is the young, quirky, community portal for Ubuntu. In many Western cultures, refrigerators provide a central sort of "bulletin board" in a family's home. Because refrigerators are magnetic, children and parents can use magnets to hang pieces of paper that they want to share with the community of people who come in contact with that fridge. For children, this often includes good grades, news reports, or other information that someone is proud of or wants to share. The Fridge, bearing the tag line, "It's fresh. It's cool. Stick it on The Fridge!" tries to create such a shared resource within the Ubuntu community. The Fridge home page is shown in Figure 8-4.

Figure 8-4 Example of The Fridge home page.

The Fridge is perhaps best described as the community portal for Ubuntu. It is part news site, part grassroots marketing and advocacy site. It hosts developer interviews, news, a picture gallery, a calendar with a list of upcoming events, polls, a list of Ubuntu-in-the-press citations, and much more. The core content on the site is arranged as a Web log. Users frequently set The Fridge as their homepage or subscribe to the site via its RSS feed. The Fridge is unique in the community in that it appeals to a wide variety of different Ubuntu participants—developers, advocates, translators, users—and provides a venue where each group can share information with others. There is a story every two to three days on The Fridge, although this may increase to up to several stories a day with time. Users can comment and discuss each story on The Fridge in an associated forum in the Ubuntu Forums.

Anyone can contribute content to The Fridge. If you would like to contribute, you can do so by sending your suggestion for features, articles, or even a piece of original work (such as an article, photo, or event review) to The Fridge Editors at fridge-devel@lists.ubuntu.com.

Conferences and Sprints

While the vast majority of the work of the Ubuntu community takes place online, Ubuntu developers do, from time to time, meet face to face. Since Ubuntu has released, there have been three public conferences organized and funded by Canonical Ltd.:

▪ The Mataró Sessions in Mataró, Catalonia, Spain, in December 2004

▪ Ubuntu Down Under in Sydney, Australia, in April 2005

▪ Ubuntu Below Zero in Montreal, Canada, in November 2005

With Canonical Ltd., Ubuntu tries to organize these conferences so that they occur once per release, usually toward the very beginning of a release cycle, so that the specifications and goals for the forthcoming release can be discussed, thrashed out, and decided upon. A glance at the previous conferences shows how these conferences move around the globe geographically so that, over a several-year period, a large percentage of the Ubuntu community will be able to attend at least one conference and meet with other developers.

While the format changes slightly each time, these conferences have been between one and two weeks in length. Frequently, a given attendee stays for only one week. At Ubuntu Below Zero, the second week was devoted almost entirely to discussing, implementing, and developing infrastructure related to Launchpad—discussed in detail in Chapter 9. The format of these conferences has changed as the attendees have experimented with different methods for structuring the events and maximizing efficiency of these short periods. One common theme, though, is a process of writing specifications.

At conferences, attendees describe features that they would like to see out in the next Ubuntu release. At an arranged time or in a series of meetings, a small set of interested users and developers work to draft a written specification. This process of drafting involves brainstorming and ends up with a formal, approved "spec" that describes a problem or need and provides a detailed description of how it will be fixed or implemented. While these specifications are often technical in nature, they are also used to describe goals that may pertain to localization, documentation, or community building. For example, both The Fridge and the planning of each conference began as a specification. With time, these specifications are categorized in terms of their priority for the upcoming release. Later, individuals will claim or be assigned some set of these specs. Paid developers at Canonical Ltd. frequently take responsibility for the highest priority technical specs. Each specification is written up and improved on the wiki so that Ubuntu hackers who cannot attend the conference are still able to participate.

These conferences have, so far, occurred in hotels with conference centers and have been attended by up to several hundred people. The conferences have been wholly organized and funded by Canonical Ltd., which ensures that its employees attend and also distributes funds for other active volunteers to travel. This funding tends to be divided up based on the contributions of volunteers over the last release cycle and their geographic proximity to the conference location. This is done to minimize travel expenditure and to ensure that users around the world get a chance to attend a conference when it comes near them.

In addition to the biannual conferences, Canonical Ltd. organizes a number of "sprints" each year. These sprints tend to be one- to three-week long intense collocated work sessions that involve a team or subteam tasked with a well-defined goal. They provide a time where team members can write code, write documentation, make plans, or do whatever else is necessary to fulfill that goal. The sprints attempt to squeeze large amounts of work into a short period of time and have earned a reputation for being exhausting, fulfilling, amazingly productive, fun experiences. These sprints are work sessions and are often limited to a small group of Canonical Ltd. employees. In many situations, they also include volunteer attendees as well.

While conferences act as a site for major technical advances in brainstorming and development, they are also fun and enjoyable experiences. They provide a venue for users to put faces to names, IRC "nicks," and e-mail addresses, and they provide for enjoyable, humorous, and productive interaction. In addition to work, there are frequent card-playing, eating, drinking, and athletic activities. Many Ubuntu users from the local area who've attended because they were curious have gone on to become some of the community's most important contributors. Attending a conference is like taking a drink from an Ubuntu fire hose. It is frequently overwhelming but can ultimately be a useful, productive, and rewarding experience as well.

Planet

It is hardly surprising that most of the Ubuntu community is highly geared toward gathering and distributing information and communication about Ubuntu. Of course, before the Ubuntu community is a group of people working on the project of building, supporting, and spreading a GNU/Linux distribution, it is a first *a group of people.* For the Ubuntu community to really feel like a community, its members should have some idea of what other members are up to—both in their Ubuntu work and in their life that extends beyond Ubuntu.

Planet Ubuntu (http://planet.ubuntu.com) tries to capture this element of the Ubuntu community (see Figure 8-5). Planet is Web log aggregator and can be thought of as a blog of blogs. Planet retrieves the latest journal or Web log entries from Ubuntu members who have chosen to add their content to the system and then publishes a single Web log that includes, in reverse chronological order, all of the latest entries. Much of the content in Planet Ubuntu is about Ubuntu. Sometimes this is because members choose to include only those entries that directly pertain to Ubuntu. Others publish everything from their life, including things that may not directly

Figure 8-5 Example of Planet Ubuntu.

pertain to the project. Often, it also includes information from the personal lives of community members so that the community knows what its members are up to. In this way, Planet provides a good way for participants to put their stamp on the Ubuntu community—both technically and non-technically.

Teams, Processes, and Community Governance

Ubuntu operates under the famous hacker mantra of "rough consensus and running code." The project attempts to forge consensus, to make good technical decisions, and to move forward. It attempts to minimize politicization wherever possible and to distribute power to those who are best at getting good work done. Mark Shuttleworth explains, "This is not a democracy, it's a meritocracy. We try to operate more on consensus than on votes, seeking agreement from the people who will have to do the work."

The project attempts to keep disagreements from spiraling out of control by enforcing mutual respect at all times with its Code of Conduct described in Chapter 1. Disagreements, of course, are inevitable and can be technical or nontechnical in nature. The community needs to be able to deal with these and, toward that end, has created a lightweight governance system that aims to ensure that disagreements are resolved carefully and that the project always has a strong, fair, and responsive direction.

The Ubuntu Web site describes the goals of its community governance system as threefold:

- Ensure that a process is defined that allows people to contribute to decisions regarding the Ubuntu community and distribution

- Ensure that decisions regarding the Ubuntu distribution and community are made in a fair and transparent fashion

- Ensure that necessary decisions are actually made, even when there is no clear consensus amongst the community

With these goals in mind, Ubuntu's system is based on the delegation of decision-making power to small- and medium-sized teams. When disagreements arise, they are handled within a relevant team. When teams cannot resolve their own disagreements or when there are disagreements between teams, issues are forwarded to either the Community Council or the Technical Board—depending on whether the issue is technical in nature. As the financier and the project's progenitor, Mark Shuttleworth sits on both boards and occupies a special position as the self-appointed benevolent dictator for life (SABDFL). Users can participate in the Ubuntu governance structure by serving on teams and by approving members of both the Community Council and the Technical Board as Ubuntu members and maintainers.

Teams

Most work in Ubuntu is delegated to a set of teams that are responsible for a particular area of work in Ubuntu. A sample of important teams (which is by no means complete) might include the marketing, documentation, kernel, server, laptop, and translation teams. Anyone with an interest in a particular aspect of the Ubuntu project can join a team's discussion and contribute to its decisions.

When a group of participants feel that a particular area is underserved, they can go ahead and build a new team by beginning work and writing up a proposal for consideration by the Community Council, which approves the creation of all new teams. Rather than catalyzing work with the creation of a team, the Community Council likes to recognize existing work with official team status. Teams should always involve the participation of several individuals. There are no one-man or one-woman teams in Ubuntu.

Local Community (LoCo) Teams

Local Community Teams, affectionately referred to as LoCo Teams in the community, are a very important type of team. Each LoCo is responsible for promoting, supporting, and representing Ubuntu in a particular locale. These locales are usually geographical and frequently countrywide, although in some situations they may overlap geographically. Ubuntu tries to encourage LoCos to work together whenever it is possible.

LoCos are like Linux User Groups (LUGs) and may often work closely with or be associated with a LUG. LoCos are often involved in localization or translations of Ubuntu into local languages and in advocacy in local schools, public administrations, and communities. The best LoCos meet regularly for social events, talks, and discussion. Often, they meet for "installfests" where team members help new users install Ubuntu onto their computers. Representatives of LoCos are asked to assist with localization matters, to speak on behalf of the Ubuntu project at local conferences and trade shows, and to organize a booth or presence at such events.

Canonical Ltd. provides each team with a mailing list and a domain name (usually in the form of ubuntu-<CC>.org where CC is the country's two-letter country code). Canonical Ltd. also is willing to host LoCo Team's Web pages, wikis, forums, Web logs, download areas, and additional mailing lists. LoCos are open to participation by anyone.

MOTU

Another very special team that deserves an in-depth description in this book is the MOTU. The MOTU are the maintainers of Ubuntu's universe repository and the phrase stands, jokingly (if not slightly embarrassingly), for Masters of the Universe. MOTUs call themselves, "the brave souls who try to keep the universe section of Ubuntu in shape." For more information on universe, please see the description of the different components in Appendix B.

MOTUs are package maintainers. They maintain, as a group, the vast majority of packages in the Ubuntu archive. Several of the packages that have been well maintained by the MOTU have, with time, migrated into the main component and become an official part of the Ubuntu distribution. Because Ubuntu does not make support or quality promises regarding the packages in universe, the MOTU team provides a way for maintainers to sharpen their teeth and (since it's sometimes unavoidable) make mistakes before jumping into the higher responsibility packages in main.

The roles and responsibility of the MOTU are many. Two important ones are:

- Filing and fixing bugs on Ubuntu packages using Malone
- Getting new or updated packages included in Ubuntu's universe

This work is done largely by full-fledged MOTU members who, as team members, can upload directly into Ubuntu. This group is helped by

"MOTU hopefuls," who work closely with the MOTUs and whose work is then "sponsored" into Ubuntu. Many of these hopefuls graduate to full-fledged MOTUs, and many MOTUs eventually are granted full-core developer status. This three-step system is the process by which almost all new maintainers learn to maintain packages in Ubuntu and gain their stripes.

Community Council

The Community Council and the Technical Board are the highest level governance structures within Ubuntu. The Community Council, as it pertains to all Ubuntu members and activities, is arguably the most powerful team within the Ubuntu project. The Community Council is charged with supervising the social structures, venues, and processes of the project.

The Community Council's day-to-day work involves five major areas in Ubuntu. The first, and the most straightforward, is the maintenance of the Ubuntu Code of Conduct. The Community Council is the only body that can approve revisions to the code. Because the Community Council does not ask each member to "re-agree" to the code when it is changed, each of these revisions must be fully within the spirit of the previous drafts.

The second charge of the Community Council is the arbitration of disputes that cannot be handled within a particular team or that arise between teams. Very frequently, these are disputes about the Code of Conduct that may require clarification of a part of the Code of Conduct or a description of whether any of the code was in fact violated by a particular action or behavior. However, the Community Council's purview is not limited to Code of Conduct violations, and the Community Council is available to handle disputes in any nontechnical situation. In most situations, the Community Council does not take action against individuals but, rather, helps groups come to agreement or consensus among themselves. If this fails, the Community Council can ask a maintainer or other member of the community to apologize and refrain from particular behavior or to leave the community. The council promises that nobody will be asked to leave without a substantial review and opportunity to defend themselves.

A third area of council work is the creation and dissolution of teams and the appointment of team leaders. New teams are proposed to the Community

Council in the manner described above in the section on teams, and the Community Council either approves the request or asks the proposer to wait. Defunct or inactive teams can similarly be dissolved by the Community Council. In cases where team leadership is requested, the Community Council can appoint leaders of teams or shift leadership to different team members. In most situations, the appointment of team leaders is an internal team matter but, when requested, the Community Council is available to intervene.

Fourth, the Community Council is responsible for approving and welcoming new members to the project. This will be described in more depth in the subsequent section on membership. Finally, the Community Council is responsible for all community-related structures and processes. New types of teams, requirements for membership, and core philosophical documents should first be approved by the Community Council. Community members who wish to suggest new structures or processes can submit their proposal to the Community Council for discussion and approval.

The Community Council meets every two weeks on IRC. Any community participant can submit an item or proposal for discussion by the Community Council. Meetings are open to the community, but the Council only seeks consensus or votes from Council members—although it consults representatives from the team that submitted the proposal and other community members. If an open meeting becomes too noisy, the Council reserves the right to move to a private channel for the duration of the meeting. To date, this has never happened. In all situations, full transcripts of meetings are published immediately following a Community Council meeting. The Community Council at the time of this writing consists of Benjamin Mako Hill, Mark Shuttleworth, Colin Watson, and James Troup. Appointments to the board are made by Mark Shuttleworth and subject to confirmation by a vote among all members. Appointments are for a period of two years.

Technical Board

The Ubuntu Technical Board is responsible for the Ubuntu project's technical direction. By handling all technical matters the Technical Board complements the Community Council as Ubuntu's highest rung of project governance. In particular, the Technical Board is responsible for three major areas of Ubuntu policy: package policy, release feature goals, and package selection. Additionally, the Technical Board is available to arbitrate any technical disagreements or issues within or between teams in a manner similar to the one described above in relation to the Community Council.

The Technical Board's first responsibility is Ubuntu's Package Policy. The Technical Board maintains the policy document which describe the processes and standards to which all Ubuntu packages are held. Since the policy is constantly evolving, each Ubuntu release is associated with a specific version of the Ubuntu package policy as determined by the Technical Board. Any suggestions or proposals about policy are suggested to and considered by the Technical Board.

Additionally, the Technical Board is responsible for maintaining Ubuntu's feature goals for each release. During each release cycle, there is a date defined as "Feature Freeze" after which no new features are added. The Technical Board is the body that sets these dates and decides when and if the rules can be bent for a particular feature or piece of software.

Finally, the Technical Board is responsible for maintaining the *list* of pieces of software (i.e., packages) in Ubuntu. In this capacity, the Technical Board determines which software is installed in the default desktop installation and which packages qualify for full support as part of the main component of Ubuntu (see Appendix B). Users and developers can propose a particular piece of software for inclusion in main, the base install, or in a desktop install. In all cases, the ultimate decision will be made by the Technical Board.

Like the Community Council, the Technical Board meets at least every two weeks on IRC. Also like the Community Council, any user can submit an item or proposal for discussion by the Technical Board ahead of the meeting. Meetings are open to all interested parties, although decision-making and voting is restricted to Technical Board members. Full transcripts and rules about noise, as they pertain to the Community Council, also apply to the Technical Board. The Technical Board at the time of this writing comprises Matt Zimmerman as board chair, Scott James Remnant, Mark Shuttleworth, and Matthew Garrett. Nominations for the Technical Board are considered at the beginning of each release cycle. Like the Community

Council, appointments are made by Mark Shuttleworth but are subject to confirmation by a vote among the maintainers instead of all members. Appointments are made for a period of one year.

SABDFL

Mark Shuttleworth jokingly refers to himself as Ubuntu's SABDFL—"self-appointed benevolent dictator for life." Mark plays an admittedly undemocratic role as the sponsor of the Ubuntu project and the sole owner of Canonical Ltd. Shuttleworth has the ability, with regard to Canonical Ltd. employees, to ask people to work on specific projects, feature goals, and bugs. He does exactly this.

Mark also maintains a tie-breaking vote on the Technical Board and Community Council but has never used this power and has publicly said that he will not use it lightly. In situations where the boards are split and there is no one "right" answer, the SABDFL will provide a decision instead of more debate. The SABDFL exists to provide clear leadership on difficult issues and to set the pace and direction for the project. In exchange for this power, he has the responsibility to listen to the community and to understand that the use of his SABDFL authority can weaken the project.

Ubunteros and Ubuntu Members

Membership in the Ubuntu project is one official way that the project recognizes sustained and significant contributions. The first level of membership in Ubuntu is as an Ubuntero (formerly, the name was "Ubuntite"). Ubunteros are "Ubuntu activists" and can be any person in the Ubuntu community who has explicitly committed to observe the Ubuntu Code of Conduct. Ubunteros are self-nominated and self-confirmed. Using Launchpad, participants can generate a GPG encryption key and "sign" the Code of Conduct as a way of pledging to uphold it within the Ubuntu community. By doing so, that participant automatically gains status as an Ubuntero.

The next, more significant, step is official membership. Official membership is available to any Ubuntero who has demonstrated a significant and sustained set of contributions to the Ubuntu community. These contributions can be of any kind—technical or nontechnical—but need to be of a form that can be represented to the Community Council, which will consider each application individually. A full list of types of contributions that qualify can be found in the following section on getting involved. The Community Council tries to be flexible in the variety of different types of contributions that it accepts in consideration of membership.

Members are responsible for confirming, by voting, all nominations to the Ubuntu Community Council. They also may be asked by the Community Council to vote on resolutions put to the general membership. In exchange, members gain the right to an e-mail address @ubuntu.com and the right to carry Ubuntu business cards. Membership lasts for two years and is renewable. Members who fail to renew their membership will be marked as inactive but, with renewed activity and a simple procedure that involves approval of the Community Council, can be easily reactivated.

The process to become a member is relatively straightforward and is documented in-depth on the Ubuntu Web site. Most important, it requires that users document their contributions on a wiki page that includes links to code, mailing list messages, documentation, or other relevant material. Additionally, membership applications should also include testimonials on work and involvement in Ubuntu from current Ubuntu members.

Getting Involved

Users can participate in the Ubuntu community on a variety of different levels and in a multitude of ways. The following list of such ways, adapted largely from a page with links to relevant resources online on the Ubuntu Web site (www.ubuntu.com/community/participate), provides a good list of ways in which people can get a running start in the Ubuntu community. The list is broken down into the major ways to get involved.

Advocacy

The easiest way for someone to contribute to the Ubuntu community is simply by telling others about Ubuntu. Advocacy frequently occurs in a variety of ways. One good method involves joining or starting a LoCo Team. LoCos, described above, provide a method through which you can get involved in Ubuntu activities. If users do not have a LoCo and do not have the critical mass of users to start one, they might help build support by giving a talk about Ubuntu to a local Linux User Group or other technical group. Advocates can also order CDs at no cost and can distribute them. Through these and other means, advocacy provides a great way to spread the word about Ubuntu and offers a low-barrier opportunity to make contributions to the community.

Support

One of the most meaningful ways that users can contribute to Ubuntu is by helping others use the software. Users can do this by joining the support-oriented mailing lists, IRC channels, or forums as described in detail earlier in this chapter. By responding to requests for help in each of these venues, users can help other users get up and running on Ubuntu. Even if users are themselves beginners, the knowledge they gain in solving even simple problems enables them to help users who run into the same issues.

Ideas and Feedback

Another way to contribute to Ubuntu is by helping steer the direction of the project by describing a vision or providing ideas. This can be done by participating in discussion and brainstorming sessions at conferences and on the Ubuntu wiki. By monitoring specifications as they are written and creating feedback, especially at early stages, users can make meaningful contributions. However, users contributing ideas should remember that "talk is cheap." Users are wise to work with others to help turn their vision into reality.

Documentation

When a user is stumped by a problem, chances are good that other users will also be frustrated by it. If a user is not in a position to write code to change the situation, they may be able to help others by writing up their experience and documenting the solution. Ubuntu has a vibrant documentation team and community, and writing documentation is a great low-barrier way to make meaningful contributions to the Ubuntu community.

Users aiming to contribute to Ubuntu's documentation would be advised to take notes as they puzzle through problems and to document solutions when they find them. Before writing, users should also check to see if documentation for a particular problem already exists. When it does, users would be wise to choose to improve or augment existing documentation over writing a new document. Similarly, users can also make meaningful contributions by reading through existing documentation and fixing factual, technical, stylistic, spelling, and grammar errors. Users who spend a large amount of time working on documentation may, with time, also want to join the Ubuntu Documentation Team, which can help organize and coordinate this work in terms of Ubuntu documentation goals.

Artwork

For those users who feel that their strengths are primarily artistic, there are many ways to improve the style and feel of the Ubuntu desktop through wholly artistic contributions. For example, Ubuntu is always in need of new ideas for wallpapers, icons, and graphical themes. Inkscape, similar in many respects to Adobe Illustrator, is a great piece of free software in Ubuntu that proves useful for this type of work. As with documentation, there is an Ubuntu Art Team that helps coordinate artistic work within the Ubuntu community.

Translation and Localization

The discussion of LoCo Teams should have already made it clear that translation is a great way that anyone with a firm understanding of English and another language can contribute to the Ubuntu community. Translation through Rosetta (described in more depth in Chapter 9) allows users to translate as little as a single string or as much as an entire application. Through its easy interface and Web-based nature, it provides an easy, low-barrier road to contribution. Serious translators should join a local community team and the ubuntu-translators mailing list so that they can stay in touch with other Ubuntu localizers.

Quality Assurance and Bugs

Quality assurance (QA) is something for which many companies hire special engineers. In Ubuntu, the Development Team relies on itself and the community to test software before it is released to let developers know about problems so that the bugs can be squashed before the vast majority of users ever see it. To test software, users merely need to upgrade to the latest development version of Ubuntu and to upgrade regularly. When users helping out with QA find bugs, they should report them in the Ubuntu bug-tracking system Malone (described in depth in Chapter 9). They can also help by "triaging" bugs, closing or merging duplicates, or verifying bugs and adding information to a bug's description. If you intend to become involved in QA, you should subscribe to the ubuntu-devel-announce mailing list, and you should considering monitoring ubuntu-devel as well.

Programming and Packaging

The final way that users can contribute to the Ubuntu community is through the production of code. Because Ubuntu is free and Open Source software, users can get access to every piece of software that Ubuntu supports. This allows users to package additional software for inclusion in Ubuntu, to fix bugs, and to add features. Developers, like those testing software, should subscribe to the ubuntu-devel-announce mailing list and should consider monitoring ubuntu-devel as well. The best way to begin making contributions is then through the MOTU team as a MOTU hopeful, as described above. Users can also look through a list of specifications to find a project that they find personally interesting. In some situations, there are even "bounties" available—small amounts of money available to those who fulfill a small feature goal that has remained unfilled for some period of time.

Summary

Ubuntu is a vibrant and diverse community that is active around the world and in many languages. Its activities happen primarily online in a variety of virtual venues, including mailing lists, IRC, Web Forums, wikis, and two special Web-based community portals known as The Fridge and Planet Ubuntu. Ubuntu complements this virtual activity with real-life meetings and conferences. The Ubuntu community is broken down into a variety of teams and processes. At the top of this government structure is the Ubuntu Community Council, Technical Board, and SABDFL Mark Shuttleworth. Through a variety of ways, this community is designed to facilitate contributions easily. Ultimately, these contributions are recognized through a process culminating in official project membership and enfranchisement.

## CHAPTER 9

Ubuntu-Related Projects

- Partner Projects
- Derived Distributions
- The Launchpad
- Bazaar
- Summary

UBUNTU IS NOT JUST A COMPLETE OPERATING SYSTEM (OS); it is also the center of a growing ecosystem of GNU/Linux and Solaris-based distributions. Some, referred to as the "partner projects," work closely with and within Ubuntu. Others prefer to work outside the project and are considered full derivatives. Often, these projects are created in order to highlight a specific selection of software or use case such as the nUbuntu project, which focuses on security and networking tools.

Others derive for reasons connected to the international nature of Linux and Open Source. While most Ubuntu development happens in English, there are large developer and user communities in other languages and countries. Thus, a derived distribution, such as Ufficio Zero in Italy, might spring up to satisfy that need. Should you use any of these over Ubuntu? We can't answer that question for you. Some of these projects are fully within and, as a result, not mutually exclusively from Ubuntu. Others might be more appropriate if you are a developer and are most comfortable in a particular language. You can mix, match, and sample these distributions until you find one that works great for you. As we mentioned in the introduction, Ubuntu sees these derivatives as a sign of a healthy and vibrant community. One of the goals of the project is to make it easier for this type of distribution to appear. We can all expect to see more of them in the future.

Partner Projects

Partner projects are those projects that work in close relation with Ubuntu. All partner projects are officially supported by Canonical Ltd. Partner projects also share a common repository of packages and release in sync with Ubuntu.

Kubuntu

Kubuntu is the first and oldest of all the partner projects. First released alongside Ubuntu 5.04 (Hoary Hedgehog), Kubuntu, which means "toward humanity" in Bemba, builds on the strengths of the K desktop environment (KDE) rather than GNOME as Ubuntu does. The project is led by Jonathan Riddell, who now works for Canonical Ltd.

As with Ubuntu, Kubuntu is a complete desktop but one built around KDE and QT. Rather than Ubuntu's brown theme, Kubuntu opts for a more traditional blue and makes a few other visual changes. Rather than the two panels and three menus of Ubuntu with GNOME, Kubuntu uses two menus and a single lower panel, closer in style to that of Microsoft Windows.

Kubuntu also comes with OpenOffice.org, the same Office suite that is included in Ubuntu. Along with this office suite, Kubuntu also includes Krita, a photo manipulation tool, the K3b CD Kreator, and the media player amaroK, all parts of KDE. Kubuntu is explored in much more depth in Chapter 7 so is not given a full treatment here.

TIP   **Kubuntu**
Kubuntu can be found at www.kubuntu.org

Edubuntu

As the name implies, Edubuntu is a version of Ubuntu for use in schools and other educational environments. Edubuntu uses Linux Terminal Server Project's (LTSP) thin client technology as well as a number of programs aimed at the educational market such as Gcompris and the KDE Education suite. Oliver Grawert, a Canonical Ltd. employee, leads the Edubuntu development. Like Ubuntu, Edubuntu uses the GNOME desktop environment. The default desktop is show in Figure 9-1.

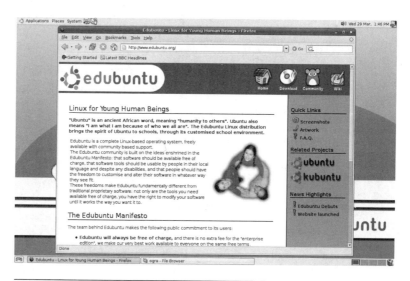

Figure 9-1 Default desktop.

One of Edubuntu's unique features is the inclusion of the LTSP in an easy-to-use, out-of-the-box installer. LTSP uses a different methodology of deploying clients over a network than in traditional computer deployments. Instead of full-blown computers, LTSP uses thin clients, computers that connect to a larger server to do all the processing work. In larger deployments it is often more cost effective to have a few more powerful servers serving applications to less powerful thin clients than to have a collection of medium-speed computers doing their own processing. Since the thin client ends up being a glorified display, LTSP has become a common use for older machines that are typically not powerful enough to run a full OS. It is common for deployments to remove the hard disks from these machines, which can also result in much quieter computers. Since these clients use the standard X11 protocol, many independent vendors also sell thin clients built just for this purpose.

Oliver Grawert has worked with members of the LTSP community with the intention of making the Edubuntu version easy to set up and administer. A teacher with moderate technical skill could easily set up an entire classroom of Edubuntu in under an hour. Additionally, Edubuntu is unlike standard Ubuntu in its inclusion of educational games and activities. For younger children, Gcompris (French Internet slang for "'I understand") offers a large and growing number of games and activities such as learning how to use the mouse and type, reading, geography, and mathematics, (see Figure 9-2).

Edubuntu also includes the KDE Education suite, aimed at a wider age range of 3 to 18. Some notable programs include the planetarium program KStars, the periodic table program Kalzium (see Figure 9-3), and KEduca, a program to create and give tests. There are also a number of programs to help with learning languages and mathematics.

TIP   **Edubuntu**
Edubuntu can be found at www.edubuntu.org

Derived Distributions

Derived distributions usually work outside of the Ubuntu community and usually have their own package repositories. They may not release at the same time as Ubuntu. In the past, several derived distributions have been built upon other distributions such as Arch or Debian. The list of derivative

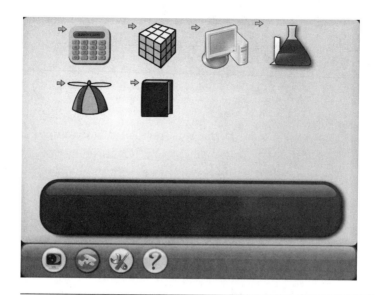

Figure 9-2 Gcompris.

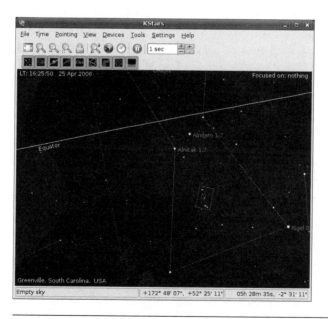

Figure 9-3 KStars.

distributions is quickly growing, and this list will be both incomplete and out-of-date by the time you read it.

Guadalinex

Guadalinex is the GNU/Linux distribution promoted by the regional government of Andalusia, the most populated autonomous community in Spain with almost 8 million inhabitants. It is currently one of the biggest free software implementations worldwide, with more than 200,000 desktops—and increasing. The project is a consequence of the unanimous support of the Andalusian Parliament on the Information Society and Innovation policies approved in 2002 and 2003, urging all the regional institutions to promote and use free software and open licenses. This makes the Guadalinex initiative unique in the world.

Guadalinex was initially released in 2003, and the first two versions were based in Debian. In 2005 the Guadalinex project decided to develop the third version deriving from Ubuntu. Guadalinex V3 was released in January 2006 based on Ubuntu 5.10 (Breezy Badger), and the Andalusian upgrade to this most recent version is being done during the year. The project is part of a government plan to implement free software as the default option in the public schools. At the beginning of 2006 this project involved 500 schools and an approximate total of 200,000 desktops equipped with Guadalinex and free software only. These numbers are increased every year as new courses start every September and new computers are purchased (about 40,000 planned for 2006). This initiative alone puts Guadalinex in the top position as the biggest free software implementation worldwide. Additionally, the software is used in public Internet access centers, senior centers, libraries, women's associations, as well as direct to citizens for use at home.

TIP   **Guadalinex**
Guadalinex can be found at www.guadalinex.org/

Xubuntu

Xubuntu takes Ubuntu and places the Xfce desktop environment on top. The Xfce desktop is primarily designed for older machines because it uses much less memory than its bigger cousins, GNOME and KDE. Unlike the other derived distributions listed here, Xubuntu uses Ubuntu repositories as its base. As a result, the kernel and other underlying pieces are security supported, but the graphical and desktop pieces driven by Xfce are not.

TIP **Xubuntu**
Xubuntu can be found at www.xubuntu.org

Nexenta

Nexenta is unique among the derived distributions in that it does not use the Linux kernel but bases its work on OpenSolaris, a version of Unix, which is developed by Sun Microsystems. The word Nexenta is a contraction of "next" and "cento." The latter is a Roman poetic form meaning "stitched together." Each line of the poem is taken from a different source. In appearance, Nexenta differs little from Ubuntu due to both using GNOME. Nexenta was created by and is supported by Nexenta Systems, based in San Francisco, California.

As Nexenta uses the OpenSolaris kernel over the Ubuntu one, there have been a number of issues that have been raised, both technical and legal. Technically, the Linux and Solaris kernels are quite different with corresponding changes in other layers. This means that programs generally need to be ported to the Solaris kernel.

TIP **Nexenta**
Nexenta can be found at www.gnusolaris.org/

---

nUbuntu

nUbuntu is a collection of security and networking tools that was first released in January 2006. Created by a group of three developers from the United States and the United Kingdom, nUbuntu is aimed at security and networking professionals.

TIP **nUbuntu**
nUbuntu can be found at www.nubuntu.org/

Ufficio Zero

Ufficio Zero is an Italian distribution funded by CreaLabs. It includes only a live CD version. Ufficio Zero only changes the default language (from English to Italian) and the default theme. The idea behind Ufficio Zero is to showcase a Linux desktop for the modern office environment. Until 6.06, Ufficio was based on Arch Linux. Recent versions switched to Ubuntu as the base.

TIP   **Ufficio**
Ufficio can be found at www.ufficiozero.org/

The Open CD

The Open CD is a set of Open Source programs that can be installed on Microsoft Windows, such as The GIMP, OpenOffice.org, Battle for Wesnoth, Firefox, and Thunderbird. The project is led by Henrik Omma, who works for Canonical Ltd. It is actually a modified and rebranded Ubuntu live CD and, thus, can be booted into Ubuntu as well.

TIP   **The Open CD**
The Open CD can be found at www.theopencd.org

Baltix

Baltix is a Lithuanian and Latvian distribution. It also includes support for Estonian, Russian, English, and Norwegian languages. As with Ubuntu, Baltix uses the GNOME desktop environment and many of the same programs.

TIP   **Baltix**
Baltix can be found at baltix.akl.lt

ImpiLinux

ImpiLinux is a South African distribution designed as a commercial derivative of Ubuntu. Charging money allows ImpiLinux to ship software that Ubuntu cannot legally ship, such as MP3 and DVD support. Originally based on Debian for version 1, it was then built from scratch for version 2. The next version, not yet released as of this writing, will be based on Ubuntu after it was announced that in 2005 that Mark Shuttleworth had invested 10M South Africa rand in ImpiLinux (Pty) Inc. ImpiLinux will be available in English, Xhosa, and Afrikaans, and there are plans to add more languages.

TIP   **ImpiLinux**
ImpiLinux can be found at www.impilinux.org/

The Launchpad

As was mentioned in the introduction to the book, a majority of Canonical Ltd.'s technical employees do not work on Ubuntu. Rather, they work on infrastructure. The majority of this infrastructure is a large collection of services which, together, provide the framework through which Ubuntu is built. This superstructure of related applications is, collectively, referred to as the Launchpad. While it has several non-Web-based systems, it is almost wholly accessible over the Web.

While Launchpad is primarily used to develop Ubuntu, the infrastructure was designed to be useful for any free software project. It aims to provide these projects with the code, bug, and translation tracking software necessary to more easily and more powerfully collaborate with others and to develop free and Open Source software. Each of these functions (code, bug, and translation tracking) are highly integrated, making it much more ambitious, and potentially much more powerful, than traditional Web-based solutions with similar goals. The Launchpad Web page describes the project as:

> A collection of services for projects in the Open Source universe. You can register your project, and then collaborate with the Open Source community on translations, bug tracking, and code.

In addition to code, bug, and translation tracking, Launchpad also provides the ability to deal with code not just on a per-package or per-project level but on the distribution level as well. If a bug has been reported against a piece of software in Ubuntu, it is visible to both the "upstream" and "downstream" projects. The project can track how its software evolves over time and see, at a glance, whether bugs apply or not. Developers can track translations in a similar way.

A source of controversy in the free and Open Source software world is the fact that the source code to Launchpad is not distributed. This has led to fear by some about the risk of enclosure or dependence that comes from using a tool which developers cannot change, update, or copy. Additionally, while all code and history can be fully copied, some information (such as bug information and metadata) stays within the Launchpad system. Some developers have felt insecure about providing this data to Canonical Ltd. in such a way that they cannot copy or replicate it. Mark Shuttleworth has replied to these fears saying that the goals of Launchpad required that he build a community before the code allowing forking is distributed but that with time, the code to all of Launchpad will be distributed.

The best way to understand Launchpad is to see it in action and to look at the specifics. This section will walk through the individual pieces of Launchpad in more depth. Much of the Ubuntu infrastructure is highly integrated into Launchpad. If you have created an account for the wiki or to order CDs at http://shipit.ubuntu.com, you already have a Launchpad account.

TIP   **Launchpad**
Launchpad can be found at www.launchpad.net/

Soyuz

Soyuz is the distribution and archive management software that is integrated into Launchpad. It handles all of the automatic building of software in Ubuntu on each of the architectures and the integration of successfully built software into the archive. Soyuz means "union" in Russian and is the name of the spacecraft that Mark Shuttleworth traveled in during his voyage to space.

Soyuz works almost entirely behind the scenes. It was first activated in early February of 2006 but had no initial effect on the way that software was uploaded or downloaded in Ubuntu. What Soyuz does is to integrate the process by which software is built and inserted into different parts of the Ubuntu archive. The building of software cannot be tracked using the Launchpad Web infrastructure.

TIP **Recent Builds**
The status of recent builds in Ubuntu can be found at https://launchpad.net/distros/ubuntu/+builds

---

Rosetta

Rosetta is a Web-based translation system integrated into Launchpad. It was the first piece of Launchpad to be publicly released. It was named after the Rosetta Stone, the famous piece of dark gray granite with the same text in three scripts that led to the deciphering of Egyptian hieroglyphics.

Rosetta is a Web-based version of a "PO" file editor. In other words, it provides a simple mechanism by which translators can view a list of untranslated phrases or "strings" and then translate each of them into their language. At the moment, the system only works with translations *from* English. Rosetta's non-Web-based predecessors including Kbabel and Gtranslate—both of which can be downloaded and installed on Ubuntu. By putting this functionality on the Web and integrating it into the archive management scripts, Rosetta lowers the barrier of entry for translation and lowers the chance that a translation will not make it into the distribution.

Rosetta includes each of the translatable strings contained in every application in Ubuntu. When new software is uploaded into Ubuntu, Rosetta will check to see if any strings have changed or been added. Changes to a string that has previously been translated will result in the translation being marked as "fuzzy" until a translator can check the translation and the new string, make any necessary changes, and then mark the translation as no longer fuzzy. By tracking new strings, Rosetta can easily prompt translators with new strings to translate as they appear as well as provide statistics on the percentage of strings within a particular application or within all of Ubuntu that have been translated into a particular language.

As users translate strings, they build up positive "karma" within the system. Users are also able to work together in localization teams (called "l10n teams" because the word "localization" has ten letters between its first and last letters). Rosetta provides a great way for Ubuntu users to get involved in the distribution. Anybody who knows English and another language can begin contributing. Because the system is integrated into Launchpad, users do not need to "submit" their translation to have it included in Ubuntu— the project already has them. Several days later, new translations are pushed out to Ubuntu users who use Ubuntu in the translator's language.

TIP   **Rosetta**
Rosetta can be found at www.launchpad.net/rosetta

Malone

Malone is a Web-based bug system like the Mozilla project "Bugzilla," which might be familiar to some users. It provides a location for users to file bugs that they find in their Ubuntu software using easily accessible pieces of software such as Bug Buddy and the command-line `reportbug` or over the Web. Malone's name is a reference to the gangster movie musical *Bugsy Malone.*

Malone's first role is to provide a location where users can submit bugs. Malone's role is not just in collecting complaints though. Rather, its job is to track and record a bug through its full life cycle from report to close. Bugs can be assigned to a particular developer or reassigned. If the bug is, in fact, with another application, the bug can be reassigned to another package. Bugs can be rated according to severity or "tagged" and categorized in any number of useful manners. Information, files, and "patches" that fix a bug can be uploaded into Malone. When the bug has been resolved, it can be closed. The Malone bug report provides a single venue in which to collect information from the bug submitter, the bug fixer, the upstream maintainer if necessary, and any other involved party.

All of this, of course, is exactly what you would expect from any usable modern bug tracker. Where Malone aims to distinguish itself from its competitors is through its integration in Launchpad. First and foremost, this means that users of Malone can track the status of a bug as it relates to a particular patch or a particular piece of code. Because Ubuntu supports *every* release for 18 months and some releases, such as Ubuntu 6.06, for much longer, it's important that Ubuntu be able to track which bugs show up in which releases. As derivative works of Ubuntu are created in Launchpad, Malone also allows these derivatives to use Malone to see if bugs submitted against Ubuntu or other distributions apply to their code and, if so, to quickly grab a fix. A bug in cfengine has been confirmed in Ubuntu generally, fixed in the Breezy or 5.10 release of Ubuntu, and not yet confirmed by the actual developers of cfengine itself.

As with Rosetta, Launchpad "karma" can be built up by fixing, reporting, and interacting with bugs over time. Bug "triage" that involves closing irreproducible bugs and merging duplicate bugs is one way that users can build up their karma. Of course, simply running developer versions and submitting new bugs is another great way to build good karma.

TIP   **Malone**
Malone can be found at www.launchpad.net/malone

Other Functionality

In addition to Malone and Rosetta, the two visible flagship products within Launchpad and Soyuz (the hidden but diligent workhorse that allows Ubuntu to work), Launchpad has several other important uses. We've already alluded to the fact that Launchpad handles all the authentication for all the Ubuntu Web sites. If you want to edit or create a Web page in the Ubuntu wiki or even order a CD, you must first create an account in Launchpad. In addition to just creating a username and password, it can contain rich information about each individual including their GNU Privacy Guard encryption key, wiki pages, contact information, and more. More important, it also contains representations of every team and group within Ubuntu and handles permission within the entire Ubuntu world. For example, the only people who are allowed to upload core packages to Ubuntu are people who are part of the Ubuntu Core Developers team in Launchpad.

NOTE   The system is also playing an increasingly important role in coordinating sprints, tracking events in a calendar, and tracking the status of specifications that describe work in Ubuntu that were detailed in the section on conferences above. With time, Launchpad's functionality is only likely to grow and its help in supporting the new type of development with it.

Bazaar

Bazaar is a distributed revision control system. What does that really mean? A revision control system is a program that tracks how the source code of a program changes. It tracks what the specific change was, such as addition of a new piece of code, as well as who made the change. It also allows a developer to roll back to a previous version or create a branch to try out a new idea.

The second key piece about Bazaar is that it is distributed. Traditional revision control systems have a single place that the code is stored. Only certain people can access this place and change the code there. A distributed revision control system is different in that there is no single place that code is stored. Each branch that a developer is working on is equal, and they all take code from each other. This system is much like a number of equal merchants at a bazaar, hence the name.

Bazaar started out as a fork of the Arch distributed revision control system. A fork means that the developers disagree on where to take the program and break into different groups to work toward each group's different goals. However, Bazaar 2 was completely rewritten, as it was found that the current code did not work in the long term.

TIP   **Bazaar**
Bazaar can be found at www.bazaar-ng.org/

Summary

In addition to building a great OS that many use, Ubuntu has grown into an OS that those building other OS use as a basis to build from. This has come in the form of both internal partner projects and external derivative distributions. Together, these span languages, continents, and markets. Additionally, Ubuntu is tightly linked to Canonical Ltd.'s other projects, Launchpad and Bazaar. While Bazaar provides a compelling version control system, the Launchpad provides a one-stop show for bugs, translations, and much more.

Welcome to the Command Line

One of the most powerful parts of any Ubuntu system is the command line. It can also be one of the most daunting to dive into. There is often little help, and commands are not easy to find. But if you are willing to learn, the power of the command line will speed up your work and can be a great education.

While the command line is a nice addition to a desktop user's life, it is completely invaluable if you run a server. The Ubuntu server installs without any graphical user interface, so the tools explained in this chapter and other books will be absolutely critical to success. And hey, remember to have fun!

Starting Up the Terminal

The terminal can be found under Accessories > Terminal. When it first launches, you will see something similar to that shown in Figure A-1.

You will see a blinking cursor immediately preceded by a string ending in a $. The first word in that string is your user name, followed by the @ symbol. After the @ the hostname of your computer is listed followed by the name of the folder you are currently in (currently your home folder), which is represented by a ~ symbol.

There are many dozens of commands. Here are a few, broken down by category.

Moving around the Filesystem

Commands for moving around the file system include the following:

- **pwd:** The pwd command will allow you to know the directory in which you're located (pwd stands for "print working directory").

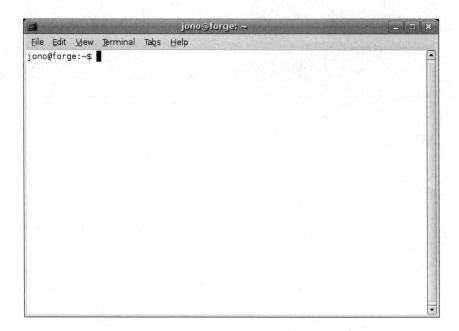

Figure A-1 The terminal window.

For example, pwd in the desktop directory will show ~/Desktop. Note that the GNOME Terminal also displays this information in the title bar of its window. See the example presented in Figure A-1.

▪ **cd:** The cd command will allow you to change directories. When you open a terminal you will be in your home directory. To move around the file system you will use cd. For example, cd ~/Desktop will move you to your desktop directory.

  ▪ To navigate into the root directory, use cd /

  ▪ To navigate to your home directory, use cd~

  ▪ To navigate up one directory level, use cd ..

  ▪ To navigate to the previous directory (or back), use cd -

  ▪ To navigate through multiple levels of directory at once, use cd /var/www for example, which will take you directly to the /www subdirectory of /var/.

Manipulating Files and Folders

You can manipulate files and folders using the following commands:

- **cp:** The cp command will make a copy of a file for you. For example, cp file foo will make an exact copy of file and name it "foo," but the file "file" will still be there. When you use mv, that file would no longer exist, but when you use cp the file stays and a new copy is made.

- **mv:** The mv command will move a file to a different location or will rename a file. Examples are as follows: mv file foo will rename the file "file" to "foo." mv foo ~/Desktop will move the file "foo" to your desktop directory but will not rename it. You must specify a new file name to rename a file.

- To save on typing, you can substitute ~ in place of the home directory.

NOTE   If you are using mv with sudo you will not be able to use the ~ shortcut. Instead, you will have to use the full pathnames to your files.

- **rm :** Use this command to remove or delete a file in your directory. It will not work on directories in which there are files.

- **ls:** The ls command will show you the files in your current directory. Used with certain options, you can see file sizes, when files were created, and file permissions. For example, ls ~ will show you the files that are in your home directory.

- **mkdir:** The mkdir command will allow you to create directories. For example, mkdir music will create a music directory.

- **chmod:** The chmod command will change the permissions on the files listed.

Permissions are based on a fairly simple model. You can set permissions for user, group, and world, and you can set whether each can read, write, and execute the file. For an example, if a file had permission to allow everybody to read but only the user could write, the permissions would read rwxr-r-. To add or remove a permission, you append a + or a – in front of the specific permission. For example, to add the capability for the group to edit in the previous example, you could type chmod g+x file.

- **chown:** The chown command allows the user to change the user and group ownerships of a file. For example, chown jim file would change the ownership of the file to "Jim."

System Information Commands

System information commands include the following:

- **df:** The df command displays filesystem disk space usage for all partitions. The command df-h is probably the most useful. It uses megabytes (M) and gigabytes (G) instead of blocks to report. (-h means "human-readable.")

- **free:** The free command displays the amount of free and used memory in the system. For example, free -m will give the information using megabytes, which is probably most useful for current computers.

- **top:** The top command displays information on your Linux system, running processes, and system resources, including the CPU, RAM, swap usage, and total number of tasks being run. To exit top, press Q.

- **uname -a:** The uname command with the -a option prints all system information, including machine name, kernel name, version, and a few other details. Most useful for checking which kernel you're using.

- **lsb_release -a:** The lsb_release command with the -a option prints version information for the Linux release you're running. For example:

```
user@computer:~$ lsb_release -a
LSB Version:    n/a
Distributor ID: Ubuntu
Description:    Ubuntu (The Breezy Badger Release)
Release:
Codename:       breezy
```

- **ifconfig:** This reports on your system's network interfaces.

- **iwconfig:** The command iwconfig will show you any wireless network adapters and the wireless specific information from them, such as speed and network connected.

- **ps:** The command ps allows you to view all the processes running on the machine.

The following commands list the hardware on your computer, either a specific type or with a specific method. They are most useful for debugging when a piece of hardware does not function correctly.

- **lspci:** The command lspci lists all PCI buses and devices connected to them. This commonly includes network cards and sound cards.

- **lsusb:** The command lsusb lists all USB buses and any connected USB devices, such as printers and thumb drives.

- **lshal:** The command lshal lists all devices the hardware abstraction layer (HAL) knows about, which should be most hardware on your system.

- **lshw:** The command lshw lists hardware on your system, including maker, type, and where it is connected.

Searching and Editing Text Files

Search and edit text files using the following commands:

- **grep:** The command grep allows you to search inside a number of files for a particular search pattern and then print matching lines. For example, grep blah file will search for the text "blah" in the file and then print any matching lines.

- **sed:** The sed (or Stream EDitor) command allows search and replace of a particular string in a file. For example, if you wanted to find the string "cat" and replace it with "dog" in a file named pets, you would type sed s/cat/dog/g.

Both grep and sed are extremely powerful programs. There are many excellent tutorials available on using them, but here are a few good Web sites to get you started:

- http://pegasus.rutgers.edu/~elflord/unix/grep.html
- http://pegasus.rutgers.edu/~elflord/unix/sed.html
- www.itworld.com/Comp/2378/swol-1199-unix101/

Three other commands that are useful for dealing with text include:

- **cat:** The cat command, short for concatenate, is useful for viewing and adding to text files. The simple cat FILENAME will display the contents of the file. Using cat filename file adds the contents of the first file to the second.

- **nano:** Nano is a simple text editor for the command line. To open a file, use nano filename. Commands listed at the bottom of the screen are accessed via ctrl+letter name.

- **less:** The less command is used for viewing text files as well as standard output. A common usage is to pipe another command through less to be able to see all the output, such as ls | less.

Dealing with Users and Groups

You can use the following commands to administer users and groups:

- **adduser:** The adduser command will create a new user. To simply create a new user, type sudo adduser $loginname. This will create the user's home directory and default group. It will prompt for a user password and then further details about the user.

- **passwd:** The passwd command will change the user's password. If simply run by a regular user, it will change his password. If run using sudo, it can change any user's password. For example, sudo passwd joe will change Joe's password.

- **who:** The who command will tell you who is currently logged into the machine.

- **addgroup:** The addgroup command will add a new group. To create a new group, type sudo addgroup $groupname.

- **deluser:** The deluser command will remove a user from the system. To remove their files and home directory, you need to add the -remove-home option

- **delgroup:** The delgroup command will remove a group from the system. You cannot remove a group that is the primary group of any users.

Getting Help on the Command Line

This section will provide you with some tips on getting help on the command line. The commands –help and man are the two most important tools at the command line.

Virtually all commands understand the -h (or –help) option which will produce a short usage description of the command and its options, then exit back to the command prompt. Try man -h or man –help to see this in action.

Every command and nearly every application in Linux will have a man (manual) file, so finding them is as simple as typing man *command* to bring up a longer manual entry for the specified command. For example, man mv will bring up the mv (Move) manual.

Some helpful tips for using the man command include:

- **arrow keys:** Move up and down the man file using the arrow keys.

- **q:** Quit back to the command prompt by typing q.

- **man man:** man man will bring up the manual entry for the man command, which is a good place to start!

- **man intro:** man intro is especially useful. It displays the Introduction to User Commands, which is a well-written, fairly brief introduction to the Linux command line.

There are also info pages, which are generally more in-depth than man pages. Try info info for the introduction to info pages.

Searching for Man Files

If you aren't sure which command or application you need to use, you can try searching the man files.

- **man -k foo:** This will search the man files for "foo." Try man -k nautilus to see how this works.

NOTE   man -k foo is the same as the apropos command.

▪ **man -f foo:** This searches only the titles of your system's man files. Try man -f gnome, for example.

man -f foo is the same as the whatis command.

Using Wildcards

Sometimes you need to look at or use multiple files at the same time. For instance, you might want to delete all .rar files or move all .odt files to another directory. Thankfully, there are series of wildcards you can use to acomplish this.

▪ * will match any number of characters. For example, *.rar will match any file with the ending of .rar

▪ * ? will match any single character. For example, ?.rar will match a.rar but not ab.rar

▪ * [characters] will match any of the character within the brackets. For example, [ab].rar will match a.rar and b.rar but not c.rar

▪ * [! characters] will match any characters that are not listed. For example, [!ab].rar will match c.rar but not a.rar or b.rar.

Executing Multiple Commands

Often you may want to execute several commands together, either one after another or by passing output from one to another.

Run Sequentially

If you need to execute multiple commands in sequence, but don't need to pass output between them, you can run them using ; between each command. Each command will be executed, and the following command will be run. If you want to make the running of the second command conditional on the successful completion of the first command, separate the commands with &&.

If you need to execute multiple commands in sequence, but don't need to pass output between them, there are two options based on whether or not you want the subsequent commands to run only if the previous commands succeed or not. If you want the commands to run one after the other regardless of whether or not preceding commands succeed, place a ; between the commands. For example, if you want to get information about your hardware, you could run `lspci ; lsusb`, which would output information on your PCI buses and USB devices in sequence.

However, if you need to conditionally run the commands based on whether the previous command has succeeded, insert && between commands. An example of this is building a program from source, which is traditionally done with `./configure`, `make`, and `make install`. The commands `make` and `make install` require that the previous commands have completed successfully, so you would use `./configure && make && make install`.

Passing Output

If you need to pass the output of one command so that it goes to the input of the next, you need something called *piping* after the character used between the commands, |, which looks like a vertical bar or pipe.

To use the pipe, insert the | between each command. For example, using the | in the command `ls | less` allows you to view the contents of the ls more easily.

Moving on to More Advanced Uses of the Command Line

There are a great number of good books out there for working the command line. In addition, because most of the command line has not changed in a great many years, there is a large body of information available on the Internet. If you need help with something, often simply searching for the command will turn up what you need.

To get you started, here are some recommendations:

Books and Web Sites

- *A Practical Guide to Linux® Commands, Editors, and Shell Programming* by Mark G. Sobell and published by Prentice Hall in 2005.

- **Linux Command.org**, found at http://linuxcommand.org/, is an excellent Web site designed to help people new to using the command line.

- **The Linux Documentation Project**, found at www.tdlp.org/ is an excellent and free resource for many things Linux.

Ubuntu Foundation Documents

This appendix contains the foundation documents for the Ubuntu project. The Canonical Ltd. location for each of these documents is the Ubuntu Web site, and any updated versions can be found there. These documents are presented verbatim except where wording or presentation assumed a Web-based reading. The appendix contains the following documents:

- Code of Conduct
- Ubuntu Philosophy
- Description of Ubuntu Components
- Ubuntu License Policy

Code of Conduct

Ubuntu is an African concept of "humanity toward others." It's "the belief in a universal bond of sharing that connects all humanity." The same ideas are central to the way the Ubuntu community collaborates. Members of the Ubuntu community need to work together effectively, and this Code of Conduct lays down the "ground rules" for our cooperation.

NOTE The latest version of the Code of Conduct can be found at: www.ubuntu.com/community/conduct

Introduction

Desmond Tutu described Ubuntu in the following way:

> A person with Ubuntu is open and available to others, affirming of others, does not feel threatened that others are able and good, for he or

she has a proper self-assurance that comes from knowing that he or she belongs in a greater whole.

–Archbishop Desmond Tutu, in *No Future Without Forgiveness*

We chose the name Ubuntu for this distribution because we think it captures perfectly the spirit of sharing and cooperation that is at the heart of the Open Source movement. In the free software world, we collaborate freely on a volunteer basis to build software for everyone's benefit. We improve on the work of others, which we have been given freely, and then share our improvements on the same basis.

That collaboration depends on good relationships between developers. To this end, we've agreed on the following Code of Conduct to help define the ways that we think collaboration and cooperation should work.

Ubuntu Code of Conduct

This Code of Conduct covers your behavior as a member of the Ubuntu Community, in any forum, mailing list, wiki, Web site, IRC channel, install-fest, public meeting, or private correspondence. The Ubuntu Community Council will arbitrate in any dispute over the conduct of a member of the community.

> **Be considerate.** Your work will be used by other people, and you in turn will depend on the work of others. Any decision you make will affect users and colleagues, and we expect you to take those consequences into account when making decisions. For example, when we are in a feature freeze, please don't upload dramatically new versions of critical system software, as other people will be testing the frozen system and not be expecting big changes.
>
> **Be respectful.** The Ubuntu community and its members treat one another with respect. Everyone can make a valuable contribution to Ubuntu. We may not always agree, but disagreement is no excuse for poor behavior and poor manners. We might all experience some frustration now and then, but we cannot allow that frustration to turn into a personal attack. It's important to remember that a community where people feel uncomfortable or threatened is not a productive one. We expect members of the Ubuntu community to be respectful when dealing with other contributors as well as with people outside the Ubuntu project, and with users of Ubuntu.
>
> **Be collaborative.** Ubuntu and free software are about collaboration and working together. Collaboration reduces redundancy of work done in the

free software world, and improves the quality of the software produced. You should aim to collaborate with other Ubuntu maintainers, as well as with the upstream community that is interested in the work you do. Your work should be done transparently, and patches from Ubuntu should be given back to the community when they are made, not just when the distribution releases. If you wish to work on new code for existing upstream projects, at least keep those projects informed of your ideas and progress. It may not be possible to get consensus from upstream or even from your colleagues about the correct implementation of an idea, so don't feel obliged to have that agreement before you begin, but at least keep the outside world informed of your work, and publish your work in a way that allows outsiders to test, discuss, and contribute to your efforts.

When you disagree, consult others. Disagreements, both political and technical, happen all the time, and the Ubuntu community is no exception. The important goal is not to avoid disagreements or differing views but to resolve them constructively. You should turn to the community and to the community process to seek advice and to resolve disagreements. We have the Technical Board and the Community Council, both of which will help to decide the right course for Ubuntu. There are also several Project Teams and Team Leaders who may be able to help you figure out which direction will be most acceptable. If you really want to go a different way, then we encourage you to make a derivative distribution or alternative set of packages available using the Ubuntu Package Management framework, so that the community can try out your changes and ideas for itself and contribute to the discussion.

When you are unsure, ask for help. Nobody knows everything, and nobody is expected to be perfect in the Ubuntu community (except of course the SABDFL). Asking questions avoids many problems down the road, and so questions are encouraged. Those who are asked should be responsive and helpful. However, when asking a question, care must be taken to do so in an appropriate forum. Off-topic questions, such as requests for help on a development mailing list, detract from productive discussion.

Step down considerately. Developers on every project come and go and Ubuntu is no different. When you leave or disengage from the project, in whole or in part, we ask that you do so in a way that minimizes disruption to the project. This means you should tell people you are leaving and take the proper steps to ensure that others can pick up where you leave off.

Mailing Lists and Web Forums

Mailing lists and Web forums are an important part of the Ubuntu community platform. This Code of Conduct applies very much to your behavior in those forums too. Please follow these guidelines in addition to the general Code of Conduct:

1. Please use a valid e-mail address to which direct responses can be made.

2. Please avoid flame wars, trolling, personal attacks, and repetitive arguments. On technical matters the Technical Review Board can make a final decision. On matters of community governance, the Community Council can make a final decision.

Ubuntu Philosophy

Our work on Ubuntu is driven by a philosophy of software freedom that we hope will spread and bring the benefits of software technology to all parts of the globe.

NOTE   The latest version of the Ubuntu Philosophy can be found at: www.ubuntu.com/ubuntu/philosophy

Free and Open Source Software

Ubuntu is a community-driven project to create an operating system and a full set of applications using free and Open Source software. At the core of the Ubuntu Philosophy of Software Freedom are these core philosophical ideals:

1. Every computer user should have the freedom to run, copy, distribute, study, share, change, and improve their software for any purpose without paying licensing fees.

2. Every computer user should be able to use their software in the language of their choice.

3. Every computer user should be given every opportunity to use software, even if they work under a disability.

Our philosophy is reflected in the software we produce and included in our distribution. As a result, the licensing terms of the software we distribute are measured against our philosophy using the Ubuntu License Policy.

When you install Ubuntu almost all of the software installed already meets these ideals, and we are working to ensure that every single piece of software you need is available under a license that gives you those freedoms. Currently, we make a specific exception for some "drivers" which are only available in binary form, without which many computers will not complete the Ubuntu installation. We place these in a restricted section of your system which makes them trivial to remove if you do not need them.

For more information on the components of Ubuntu, please see the components section below.

Free Software

For Ubuntu, the "free" in "free software" is used primarily in reference to freedom and not to price—although we are committed to not charging for Ubuntu. The most important thing about Ubuntu is not that it is available free of charge, but that it confers rights of software freedom on the people who install and use it. It is those freedoms that enable the Ubuntu community to grow, sharing its collective experience and expertise to improve Ubuntu and make it suitable for use in new countries and new industries.

Quoting the Free Software Foundation's "What is Free Software," the freedoms at the core of free software are defined as:

- The freedom to run the program for any purpose.
- The freedom to study how the program works and adapt it to your needs.
- The freedom to redistribute copies so you can help others.
- The freedom to improve the program and release your improvements to the public, so that everyone benefits.

Free software has been a coherent social movement for more than two decades. This movement has produced millions of lines of code, documentation, and a vibrant community of which Ubuntu is proud to be a part.

Open Source

Open Source is a term coined in 1998 to remove the ambiguity in the English word "free." The Open Source Initiative described Open Source software in the Open Source Definition. Open source continues to enjoy growing success and wide recognition.

Ubuntu is happy to call itself Open Source. While some refer to free and Open Source software as competing movements with different ends, we do not see free and Open Source software as either distinct or incompatible. Ubuntu proudly includes members who identify with both the free software and Open Source camps and many who identify with both.

Components

The Ubuntu software repository contains thousands of software packages organized into four "components" on the basis of the level of support we can offer them and whether or not they comply with our Free Software Philosophy. The components are called "main," "restricted," "universe," and "multiverse."

NOTE   The latest version of Components can be found at: www.ubuntu.com/ubuntu/components

The Ubuntu software repository is divided into four components, main, restricted, universe and multiverse on the basis of our ability to support that software, and whether or not it meets the goals laid out in our Free Software Philosophy.

The standard Ubuntu installation is a subset of software available from the main and restricted components. You can install additional software using the Synaptic Package Manager or Aptitude. Other components are added by editing the /etc/apt/sources.list file. See `man sources.list` for more information on editing the sources.list file.

"Main" Component

The main distribution component contains applications that are free software, can freely be redistributed, and are fully supported by the Ubuntu team. This includes the most popular and most reliable Open Source applications available, much of which is installed by default when you install Ubuntu.

Software in main includes a hand-selected list of applications that the Ubuntu developers, community, and users feel are important and that the Ubuntu security and distribution teams are willing to support. When you install software from the main component you are assured that the software will come with security updates and technical support.

We believe that the software in main includes everything most people will need for a fully functional desktop or Internet server running only Open Source software.

The licenses for software applications in main must be free, but main may also may contain binary firmware and selected fonts that cannot be modified without permission from their authors. In all cases redistribution is unencumbered.

"Restricted" Component

The restricted component is reserved for software that is very commonly used, and which is supported by the Ubuntu team even though it is not available under a completely free license. Please note that it may not be possible to provide complete support for this software since we are unable to fix the software ourselves but can only forward problem reports to the actual authors.

Some software from restricted will be installed on Ubuntu CDs but is clearly separated to ensure that it is easy to remove. We include this software because it is essential in order for Ubuntu to run on certain machines. Typical examples are the binary drivers that some video card vendors publish, which are the only way for Ubuntu to run on those machines. By default, we will only use Open Source software unless there is simply no other way to install Ubuntu. The Ubuntu team works with such vendors to accelerate the open-sourcing of their software to ensure that as much software as possible is available under a free license.

"Universe" Component

The universe component is a snapshot of the free, Open Source, and Linux world. In universe you can find almost every piece of Open Source software and software available under a variety of less open licenses, all built automatically from a variety of public sources. All of this software is compiled against the libraries and using the tools that form part of main, so it should install and work well with the software in main, but it comes with *no guarantee of security fixes and support.* The universe component includes thousands of pieces of software. Through universe, users are able to have the diversity and flexibility offered by the vast Open Source world on top of a stable Ubuntu core.

> **NOTE** Universe is not enabled by default when you install Ubuntu. You need to turn it on yourself. Canonical Ltd. does not provide a guarantee of regular security updates for software found in universe but will provide these where they are made available by the community. Users should understand the risk inherent in using packages from the universe component.
>
> You can enable the universe component by editing the file /etc/apt/sources.list after installing Ubuntu.

Popular or well-supported pieces of software will move from universe into main if they are backed by maintainers willing to meet the standards set for main by the Ubuntu team.

"Multiverse" Component

The "multiverse" component contains software that is "not free," which means the licensing requirements of this software do not meet the Ubuntu main Component License Policy.

The onus is on you to verify your rights to use this software and comply with the licensing terms of the copyright holder.

This software is not supported and usually cannot be fixed or updated. Use it at your own risk.

License Policy

Ubuntu is a collection of many computer programs and documents created by thousands of individuals, teams, and companies. Each of these works might come under a different license. Our License Policy describes the process that we follow in determining which software we will ship and by default include on the Ubuntu Install CD.

NOTE   The latest version of the License Policy can be found at: www.ubuntu.com/ubuntu/licensing

The Ubuntu team is committed to free and Open Source software. The exact details of what that means can lead people into a very long debate indeed, often ending up with both sides in violent agreement. The short answer is that it is our absolute conviction that the world is a better (more efficient, more supportable, safer, more interesting, more compassionate, fairer—there are lots of ways to define it) place if you have the source code to all the software on your computer and the right to *use* that source code in constructive ways.

We believe that this is important *even if you are not a software developer,* because someone else in your family who uses your computer might find that they have that interest and talent, and because you could hire someone to exercise those rights on your behalf. We really do believe that this is the central idea that will drive innovation and development in the software industry for the next 20 years—right up until the computers take over, and who knows, maybe they will feel the same way. And we hope to be one of many teams that sticks around sustainably, making a living working in that new world. We would invite you to read more about our Free Software Philosophy and help to shape this policy further.

The Ubuntu Free Software Philosophy really only addresses the software that you will find in main and restricted. Those components contain software that is fully supported by the Ubuntu team and must comply with this policy. In the universe component you will find just about every other piece of software you can imagine, under a huge variety of licenses—really the full software universe. If you install software from universe please take the time to check the license for yourself.

There are many definitions of free and free software so we have included our own set of guidelines listed below.

To comply with the Ubuntu Main Component License Policy, all application software included in the Ubuntu main component:

- **Must include source code.** The main component has a strict and nonnegotiable requirement that application software included in it must come with full source code.

- **Must allow modification and distribution of modified copies under the same license.** Just having the source code does not convey the same freedom as having the right to change it. Without the ability to modify software, the Ubuntu community cannot support software, fix bugs, translate it, or improve it.

Ubuntu "Main" and "Restricted" Component License Policy

All application software in both main and restricted must:

- **Allow redistribution.** Your right to sell or give away the software alone or as part of an aggregate software distribution is important because:

  - You, the user, must be able to pass on any software you have received from Ubuntu in either source code or compiled form.

  - While Ubuntu will not charge license fees for this distribution, you might well want to charge to print Ubuntu CD's, or create your own customized versions of Ubuntu which you sell, and you should have the freedom to do so.

- **Not require royalty payments or any other fee for redistribution or modification.** It's important that you can exercise your rights to this software without having to pay for the privilege and that you can pass these rights on to other people on exactly the same basis.

- **Allow these rights to be passed on along with the software.** You should be able to have exactly the same rights to the software as we do.

- **Not discriminate against persons, groups, or against fields of endeavor.** The license of software included in Ubuntu cannot discriminate against anyone or any group of users and cannot restrict users from using the software for a particular field of endeavor—a business for example. Thus we will not distribute software that is licensed "freely for noncommercial use."

- **Not be distributed under a license specific to Ubuntu.** The rights attached to the software must not depend on the program's being part of Ubuntu system. So we will not distribute software for which Ubuntu has a "special" exemption or right, and we will not put our own software into Ubuntu and then refuse you the right to pass it on.

- **Not contaminate other software licenses.** The license must not place restrictions on other software that is distributed along with it. For example, the license must not insist that all other programs distributed on the same medium be free software.

- **Require source modifications to be distributed as patches if necessary.** In some cases, software authors are happy for us to distribute their software and modifications to their software as long as the two are distributed separately so that people always have a copy of their pristine code. We are happy to respect this preference. However, the license must explicitly permit distribution of software built from modified source code.

Documentation, Firmware, and Drivers

Ubuntu contains licensed and copyrighted works that are not application software. For example, the default Ubuntu installation includes documentation, images, sounds, video clips, and firmware. The Ubuntu community will make decisions on the inclusion of these works on a case-by-case basis, ensuring that these works do not restrict our ability to make Ubuntu available free of charge, and that Ubuntu remains redistributable by you.

The Ubuntu team recognizes that many users have vital hardware in their computer that requires drivers that are currently only available in binary format. We urge all hardware vendors to insist that their suppliers provide Open Source drivers for their components, but we recognize that in some cases binary drivers are the only way to make your hardware work. As a result, Ubuntu includes several of these drivers on the CD and in the repository, clearly separated from the rest of the software by being placed in the restricted component.

Binary drivers are a poor choice, if you have a choice. Without source code, Ubuntu cannot support this software. We only provide it for users who require it to be able to run the free software we provide in main. Also, we cannot make binary drivers available on other architectures (such as Mac or IPAQ) if we don't have the ability to port the software source code ourselves. If your hardware is fully supported with Open Source drivers you can simply remove the restricted component, and we would encourage you to do so.

Software Installed by Default

When you install Ubuntu, you will typically install a complete desktop environment. It is also possible to install a minimal set of software (just enough to boot your machine) and then manually select the precise software applications to install. Such a "custom" install is usually favored by server administrators, who prefer to keep only the software they absolutely need on the server.

All of the application software installed by default is free software. In addition, we install some hardware drivers that are available only in binary format, but such packages are clearly marked in the restricted component.

Creative Commons Attribution-ShareAlike 2.0 Open Publication License

Attribution-ShareAlike 2.0

Creative Commons Corporation is not a law firm and does not provide legal services. Distribution of this license does not create an attorney-client relationship. Creative Commons provides this information on an "as-is" basis. Creative Commons makes no warranties regarding the information provided, and disclaims liability for damages resulting from its use.

License

The work (as defined below) is provided under the terms of this Creative Commons public license ("CCPL" or "license"). The work is protected by copyright and/or other applicable law. Any use of the work other than as authorized under this license or copyright law is prohibited.

By exercising any rights to the work provided here, you accept and agree to be bound by the terms of this license. The licensor grants you the rights contained here in consideration of your acceptance of such terms and conditions.

1. **Definitions**

   a. **"Collective Work"** means a work, such as a periodical issue, anthology or encyclopedia, in which the Work in its entirety in unmodified form, along with a number of other contributions, constituting separate and independent works in themselves, are assembled into a collective whole. A work that constitutes a

Collective Work will not be considered a Derivative Work (as defined below) for the purposes of this License.

b. **"Derivative Work"** means a work based upon the Work or upon the Work and other pre-existing works, such as a translation, musical arrangement, dramatization, fictionalization, motion picture version, sound recording, art reproduction, abridgment, condensation, or any other form in which the Work may be recast, transformed, or adapted, except that a work that constitutes a Collective Work will not be considered a Derivative Work for the purpose of this License. For the avoidance of doubt, where the Work is a musical composition or sound recording, the synchronization of the Work in timed-relation with a moving image ("synching") will be considered a Derivative Work for the purpose of this License.

c. **"Licensor"** means the individual or entity that offers the Work under the terms of this License.

d. **"Original Author"** means the individual or entity who created the Work.

e. **"Work"** means the copyrightable work of authorship offered under the terms of this License.

f. **"You"** means an individual or entity exercising rights under this License who has not previously violated the terms of this License with respect to the Work, or who has received express permission from the Licensor to exercise rights under this License despite a previous violation.

g. **"License Elements"** means the following high-level license attributes as selected by Licensor and indicated in the title of this License: Attribution, ShareAlike.

2. **Fair Use Rights.** Nothing in this license is intended to reduce, limit, or restrict any rights arising from fair use, first sale or other limitations on the exclusive rights of the copyright owner under copyright law or other applicable laws.

3. **License Grant.** Subject to the terms and conditions of this License, Licensor hereby grants You a worldwide, royalty-free, non-exclusive,

perpetual (for the duration of the applicable copyright) license to exercise the rights in the Work as stated below:

a. to reproduce the Work, to incorporate the Work into one or more Collective Works, and to reproduce the Work as incorporated in the Collective Works;

b. to create and reproduce Derivative Works;

c. to distribute copies or phonorecords of, display publicly, perform publicly, and perform publicly by means of a digital audio transmission the Work including as incorporated in Collective Works;

d. to distribute copies or phonorecords of, display publicly, perform publicly, and perform publicly by means of a digital audio transmission Derivative Works.

e. For the avoidance of doubt, where the work is a musical composition:

    i. **Performance Royalties Under Blanket Licenses.** Licensor waives the exclusive right to collect, whether individually or via a performance rights society (e.g., ASCAP, BMI, SESAC), royalties for the public performance or public digital performance (e.g., webcast) of the Work.

    ii. **Mechanical Rights and Statutory Royalties.** Licensor waives the exclusive right to collect, whether individually or via a music rights society or designated agent (e.g., Harry Fox Agency), royalties for any phonorecord You create from the Work ("cover version") and distribute, subject to the compulsory license created by 17 USC Section 115 of the US Copyright Act (or the equivalent in other jurisdictions).

f. **Webcasting Rights and Statutory Royalties.** For the avoidance of doubt, where the Work is a sound recording, Licensor waives the exclusive right to collect, whether individually or via a performance-rights society (e.g., SoundExchange), royalties for the public digital performance (e.g., webcast) of the Work, subject to the compulsory license created by 17 USC Section 114 of the US Copyright Act (or the equivalent in other jurisdictions).

The above rights may be exercised in all media and formats whether now known or hereafter devised. The above rights include the right to make such modifications as are technically necessary to exercise the rights in other media and formats. All rights not expressly granted by Licensor are hereby reserved.

4. **Restrictions.** The license granted in Section 3 above is expressly made subject to and limited by the following restrictions:

   a. You may distribute, publicly display, publicly perform, or publicly digitally perform the Work only under the terms of this License, and You must include a copy of, or the Uniform Resource Identifier for, this License with every copy or phonorecord of the Work You distribute, publicly display, publicly perform, or publicly digitally perform. You may not offer or impose any terms on the Work that alter or restrict the terms of this License or the recipients' exercise of the rights granted hereunder. You may not sublicense the Work. You must keep intact all notices that refer to this License and to the disclaimer of warranties. You may not distribute, publicly display, publicly perform, or publicly digitally perform the Work with any technological measures that control access or use of the Work in a manner inconsistent with the terms of this License Agreement. The above applies to the Work as incorporated in a Collective Work, but this does not require the Collective Work apart from the Work itself to be made subject to the terms of this License. If You create a Collective Work, upon notice from any Licensor You must, to the extent practicable, remove from the Collective Work any reference to such Licensor or the Original Author, as requested. If You create a Derivative Work, upon notice from any Licensor You must, to the extent practicable, remove from the Derivative Work any reference to such Licensor or the Original Author, as requested.

   b. You may distribute, publicly display, publicly perform, or publicly digitally perform a Derivative Work only under the terms of this License, a later version of this License with the same License Elements as this License, or a Creative Commons iCommons license that contains the same License Elements as this License (e.g., Attribution-ShareAlike 2.0 Japan). You must include a copy of, or the Uniform Resource Identifier for, this License or other license specified in the previous sentence with every copy or phonorecord of each Derivative Work You distribute, publicly display, publicly perform, or publicly digitally perform. You may not offer or impose any terms on the Derivative Works that alter or restrict the terms of this License or the recipients' exercise of the rights granted hereunder, and You must keep intact all notices that refer to this License and to the disclaimer of warranties. You may not distribute, publicly display, publicly perform, or publicly digitally perform the Derivative Work with any technological measures that control access or use of the Work in a manner inconsistent with the terms of this License Agreement. The above applies to the Derivative Work as incorporated in a Collective Work, but this does not require the Collective Work apart from the Derivative Work itself to be made subject to the terms of this License.

c. If you distribute, publicly display, publicly perform, or publicly digitally perform the Work or any Derivative Works or Collective Works, You must keep intact all copyright notices for the Work and give the Original Author credit reasonable to the medium or means You are utilizing by conveying the name (or pseudonym if applicable) of the Original Author if supplied; the title of the Work if supplied; to the extent reasonably practicable, the Uniform Resource Identifier, if any, that Licensor specifies to be associated with the Work, unless such URI does not refer to the copyright notice or licensing information for the Work; and in the case of a Derivative Work, a credit identifying the use of the Work in the Derivative Work (e.g., "French translation of the Work by Original Author," or "Screenplay based on original Work by Original Author"). Such credit may be implemented in any reasonable manner; provided, however, that in the case of a Derivative Work or Collective Work, at a minimum such credit will appear where any other comparable authorship credit appears and in a manner at least as prominent as such other comparable authorship credit.

5. **Representations, Warranties, and Disclaimer**

Unless otherwise agreed to by the parties in writing, Licensor offers the work as-is and makes no representations or warranties of any kind concerning the material, express, implied, statutory or otherwise, including, without limitation, warranties of title, merchantibility, fitness for a particular purpose, noninfringement, or the absence of latent or other defects, accuracy, or the presence of absence of errors, whether or not discoverable. Some jurisdictions do not allow the exclusion of implied warranties, so such exclusion may not apply to you.

6. **Limitation on Liability.** Except to the extent required by applicable law, in no event will licensor be liable to you on any legal theory for any special, incidental, consequential, punitive or exemplary damages arising out of this license or the use of the work, even if licensor has been advised of the possibility of such damages.

7. **Termination**

   a. This License and the rights granted hereunder will terminate automatically upon any breach by You of the terms of this License. Individuals or entities who have received Derivative Works or Collective Works from You under this License, however, will not have their licenses terminated provided such individuals or entities remain in full compliance with those licenses. Sections 1, 2, 5, 6, 7, and 8 will survive any termination of this License.

   b. Subject to the above terms and conditions, the license granted here is perpetual (for the duration of the applicable copyright in the Work). Notwithstanding the above, Licensor reserves the right to release the Work under different license terms or to stop distributing the Work at any time; provided, however that any such election will not serve to withdraw this License (or any other license that has been, or is required to be, granted under the terms of this License), and this License will continue in full force and effect unless terminated as stated above.

8. **Miscellaneous**

   a. Each time You distribute or publicly digitally perform the Work or a Collective Work, the Licensor offers to the recipient a license to the Work on the same terms and conditions as the license granted to You under this License.

   b. Each time You distribute or publicly digitally perform a Derivative Work, Licensor offers to the recipient a license to the original Work on the same terms and conditions as the license granted to You under this License.

c. If any provision of this License is invalid or unenforceable under applicable law, it shall not affect the validity or enforceability of the remainder of the terms of this License, and without further action by the parties to this agreement, such provision shall be reformed to the minimum extent necessary to make such provision valid and enforceable.

d. No term or provision of this License shall be deemed waived and no breach consented to unless such waiver or consent shall be in writing and signed by the party to be charged with such waiver or consent.

e. This License constitutes the entire agreement between the parties with respect to the Work licensed here. There are no understandings, agreements, or representations with respect to the Work not specified here. Licensor shall not be bound by any additional provisions that may appear in any communication from You. This License may not be modified without the mutual written agreement of the Licensor and You.

Creative Commons is not a party to this License, and makes no warranty whatsoever in connection with the Work. Creative Commons will not be liable to You or any party on any legal theory for any damages whatsoever, including without limitation any general, special, incidental or consequential damages arising in connection to this license. Notwithstanding the foregoing two (2) sentences, if Creative Commons has expressly identified itself as the Licensor hereunder, it shall have all rights and obligations of Licensor.

Except for the limited purpose of indicating to the public that the Work is licensed under the CCPL, neither party will use the trademark "Creative Commons" or any related trademark or logo of Creative Commons without the prior written consent of Creative Commons. Any permitted use will be in compliance with Creative Commons' then-current trademark usage guidelines, as may be published on its website or otherwise made available upon request from time to time.

Creative Commons may be contacted at http://creativecommons.org/.

Ubuntu Equivalents to Windows Programs

For those of you who are moving to Ubuntu from Windows, often simply knowing which application to use is half the battle. Here is a table showing common Windows applications and their Ubuntu counterparts. Your Windows-using friends shouldn't be completely shut out, so there are some applications for them to use also.

On the Ubuntu Desktop

Listed below are common Windows applications that already have an equivalent installed on the Ubuntu desktop. There are also some common alternatives listed.

Word Processing

- **Windows:** Word

- **Ubuntu:** OpenOffice.org Writer

- **Alternatives:** Abiword

Spreadsheet

- **Windows:** Excel

- **Ubuntu:** OpenOffice.org Calc

- **Alternatives:** Gnumeric

Presentation

- **Windows:** PowerPoint

- **Ubuntu:** OpenOffice.org Impress

Database

- **Windows:** Access
- **Ubuntu:** OpenOffice.org Base
- **Alternatives:** Glom

Web Browser

- **Windows:** Internet Explorer or Mozilla Firefox
- **Ubuntu:** Mozilla Firefox
- **Alternatives:** Epiphany, Mozilla

NOTE Mozilla Firefox runs on Windows as well as Linux, allowing you to have the same browsing experience.

E-Mail

- **Windows:** Outlook Express, Outlook, or Mozilla Thunderbird
- **Ubuntu:** Evolution
- **Alternatives:** Mozilla Thunderbird

Media Players

- **Windows:** Windows Media Player, iTunes, Winamp
- **Ubuntu:** Rhythmbox, Totem Movie Player
- **Alternatives:** Banshee, Muine, Beep Media Player

NOTE Due to patent restrictions, Ubuntu cannot install the codecs for some media codecs. Please see Chapter 3 for information on how to do this.

Photo Editor

- Windows: Adobe Photoshop or the GIMP
- Ubuntu: The GIMP

Instant Messaging

- Windows: AIM, Yahoo, ICQ, or Gaim

- Ubuntu: Gaim

NOTE Gaim can connect to AIM, Yahoo, ICQ, and Google Talk networks.

Voice Over IP

- Windows: Skype or GizmoProject

- Ubuntu: Ekiga Softphone or Skype

NOTE Skype uses a proprietary protocol that only Skype can understand. Ekiga uses an open protocol, called SIP, so if you are just starting out with voice over IP, use Ekiga to avoid being tied to one program. Ekiga can also talk H.323, so you can connect with Windows NetMeeting clients as well.

Additional Applications

The Ubuntu desktop does not cater to everybody, so there are some classes of applications that, by default, are not installed. Some of the common ones are listed this section.

Office and Finance
Personal Accounting

- **Windows:** Quicken, Microsoft Money

- **Ubuntu alternatives:** Grisbi, Gnucash

Accounting

- **Windows:** Intuit Quickbooks

- **Ubuntu alternative:** TurboCASH

Desktop Publishing

- **Windows:** Microsoft Publisher
- **Ubuntu alternative:** Scribus

Project Management

- **Windows:** Microsoft Project
- **Ubuntu alternative:** Planner

Drawing and Modeling

Vector Drawing

- **Windows:** Adobe Illustrator, Inkscape
- **Ubuntu alternative:** Inkscape

3D Modeler

- **Windows:** Alias Maya, Blender
- **Ubuntu alternative:** Blender

Diagram Editing

- **Windows:** Microsoft Visio
- **Ubuntu alternative:** Dia

Games and Edutainment

Planetarium

- **Windows:** Starry Night, Voyager III
- **Ubuntu alternative:** Stellarium

Space Simulator

- **Windows:** Orbiter
- **Ubuntu alternative:** Celestia

Flight Simulator

- **Windows:** Microsoft Flight Simulator, FlightGear
- **Ubuntu alternative:** FlightGear

Typing Tutor

- **Windows:** Mavis Beacon Teaches Typing
- **Ubuntu alternatives:** Tux Typing, KTouch

Index

Note: Italicized page locators indicate a figure; tables are denoted with a *t*.

Abiword, 232

About Kubuntu document, 308, 309

Accounting, Ubuntu equivalents to Windows programs for, 389

Accounts dialog box, in Gaim, 81

Account settings, editing, in Evolution, 74

ACID2 test, 279

Add Applications
    installing and using, 118, 119, 121
    main screen, 119
    search bar with results, 120
    sequence involved in installing a universe
        application, 120

Add a Printer wizard, 135

addgroup command, 362

Add/Remove Programs (Adept), installing applications
        with, 265, 266

Address book icon, Ekiga window, 90

adduser command, 240, 362

Adept, 256
    Add/Remove Programs in, 266
    editing repositories in, 269
    installing mysql-server with, 272
    keeping system up-to-date with, 273–274
    package installation with, 269–272
    parts within, 265
    previewing changes in, 272
    repositories with universe enabled in, 270
    repository management with, 268–269
    search bar in, for finding packages, 271
    search feature with, 267
    starting, 265

Adept Manager, 268

Adept Updater, 273

Adept-Updater-Notifier, 273

Administration submenu, 61

Adobe Photoshop, GIMP vs., 76

Advanced Linux Sound Architecture, 86, 87

Advanced Package Tool, 121, 265
    sources and repositories, 163–164

Advanced tab, in printer properties window, 139

Advocacy, 338–339

AIM, Kopete and, 293

Akregator, 290, 296, 297
    using RSS icon to add a feed to, 297

Alias box, in Gaim, 81

ALSA. *See* Advanced Linux Sound
        Architecture

Alternative CD installation, 45–54
    changing artwork, 52
    configuring login screen, 52
    configuring user, 51–52
    creating partitions, 48–51
    enabling automatic logins, 52
    enabling remote graphical logins, 53
    finishing up, 52
    location, 46
    networking, 47–48
    post-installation, 52–53
    printer set up, 53–54

Alternative CD menu, 45

amaroK, 281, 284, 345
    choosing default look of, 286
    music management with, 284–287

AMD K7 computer, slow speed with
        Ubuntu on, 239

AMD64/EM64T, Ubuntu support for, 170

AMD64 Ubuntu version, 32

Andalusian Parliament on the Information Society and
        Innovation policies, 348

Apache project, 7

Apache Webserver, 236

Applets, 61–62
    customizing in Kubuntu, 262–263

Applications, 199
    another way of running, 66
    compiling, 194–195
    hanging, 200
    replacing with autopackages, 193

Applications *continued*
  starting, 58
  using, 65–66
Applications area, Ubuntu desktop taskbar, 63
Apply button, 65
Appointments
  adding to calendar, 74
  setting up in Kontact, 296–297
APT. *See* Advanced Package Tool
apt-cache, 167
apt-get tool, 165, 166–167
  aptitude and, 172
  running distribution upgrades and, 169–170
aptitude, 172
Arch Linux, 346, 350, 356
Arguments, 21
Arrow keys, man command and, 365
Artificial Intelligence Laboratory (MIT), 4
Art manager, 208, 209
Arts sound server, 206
Art web sites, 208
Artwork
  changing with alternate install CD, 52
  contributions of, to Ubuntu
    community, 342
Attribute-ShareAlike 2.0
  fair use rights, 380
  license definitions, 379–380
  license grant, 380–381
  limitation on liability, 384
  mechanical rights and statutory royalties, 381
  miscellaneous, 384–385
  performance royalties under blanket
    licenses, 381
  representations, warranties, and disclaimer,
    383–384
  restrictions, 382–383
  termination, 384
attr package, 167–168, 171
Audacity, 207
Audio, configuring with Ekiga, 86, 87
Audio applications, problems with, 206
Audio CD creator, 93
Audio CDs
  creating, 131
  ripping with Konqueror, 281–282
Audio files, listening to, with Ubuntu,
    110–112
Authentication, wireless, 213–214
Automatic logins, 197
  enabling with alternate install CD, 52
Autopackages, running, 193–194

Backgrounds
  changing in Kiosk mode, 302, 303
  changing in Ubuntu, 101
  finding and installing, 208–209
  in Kubuntu, 261
Backing up data
  creating partitions and, 41
  before doing distribution upgrade, 199
  RAID setup and, 156
Backports repository, in Ubuntu package archive,
    163, 164
Baltix, 350
Baobab, 198
Battery monitor, 62
Battle for Wesnoth, 350
Bazaar, 26, 29, 356
Bazaar-NG, 26
Beagle, 95, 96
  installing, 202
Big Iron kernel, 151
BIOS problems
  Desktop CD install and, 36
  root partition and, 50
BitKeeper, 26
Blanket licenses, performance royalties
    under, 381
Blender, 94
Bluefish, 97, 98
Bluetooth
  copying photos from mobile phone to Ubuntu
    computer with, 222
Bluetooth Chat, 306
Bluetooth OBEX Client, 306
Bookmarking favorite sites, with
    Firefox, 68
Bookmarks, file chooser and, 99–100
Books, on command line, 367
Bootloader, broken, 185
Boot sector, 185
  backing up and restoring, 185–186
Bread, Ubuntu, 243–245
Breezy Badger, 169, 273, 348
Bug # 1
  closing, 30
  text of, 23–24
Bug Buddy, 354
Bug fixes, distribution and, 15
Bug reports, filing, 241–243
Bugs, 246, 310
  fixing, released distributions and, 22
  quality assurance and, 342–343
Bugs and Notification Lists, 315*t*

Bug tracking
  another way into system, 242
  with Malone, 27
Bugzilla, 356
Bulletin boards, 322
Burn from Disc Image function, 36
Burning CDs, 34, 131–132
  from an image, 131–132
  creating audio CDs, 131
Business cards, Ubuntu, 338

C, Eclipse support for, 98
C++, Eclipse support for, 98
Calc program, within OpenOffice.org, 288
Calculator, 91
Calculator (Speedcrunch), 305
Calendar(s)
  managing in Evolution, 74–75
  multiple, 75
Canonical, creating, 11–12
Canonical Ltd., 17, 29, 30, 163, 250, 265, 312, 324, 350
  Bazaar-NG and, 26
  conferences organized and funded by, 330, 331
  founding of, 24
  incorporation of, 25
  Launchpad and, 26, 27, 351, 352
  LoCo Team's Web pages, wikis, forums, Web logs, etc. hosted by, 335
  Mark Shuttleworth's sole ownership of, 339
  partner projects supported by, 346
  service and support through, 25–26
  sprints organized by, 331
Cardbus adapter, difficulties with, 219
cat command, 364
CCMP, 216
CD burning application, 34–36
  in Linux with GNOME, 35
  with Mac OS X, 36
  in Windows with ISO Recorder, 35
  in Windows with Nero Burning ROM, 35
cd command, 143, 358
CD creation, in Kubuntu, 290–292
CDDB. See Compact Disk Database
CD images, 34
CD Player (KsCD) menu, 305
CD ripper, 93
CD-ROM, problems with, 221
CDs
  burning, in Ubuntu, 131–132
  playing and ripping, 112
  playing with Kaffiene, 299–301

CD writers, 131
Certificate authorities, 8
Certificates, 215
cfengine, 357
chmod command, 175, 359
chown command, 175
CJK (Chinese, Japanese, and Korean Language) support, with Kubuntu, 252
Clock, 63
Close Window icon, hanging application and, 200
CoC. See Code of Conduct
Code, contributing to community through production of, 343
Codecs, 205
  installing, 109–110
  support for, 110t
Code of Conduct, 20–21, 331, 337
  approving revisions to, 334
  mailing lists and Web forums, 369–370
  Ubuntu, 367–370
Collaboration, 21
  Ubuntu Code of Conduct and, 368–369
Collective work, definition of, 379–380
Colorspace box, in GIMP, 77
Command box, 60
Command line, 141
  advanced uses of, 365–366
  dealing with users and groups, 362
  executing multiple commands, 364
  getting help on, 363
  manipulating files and folders, 359–360
  moving around filesystem, 357–358
  searching and editing text files, 361–362
  searching for man files, 363–364
  starting up terminal, 357
  system information command, 360–361
  using wildcards, 364
Commands
  finding different options for, 236
  multiple, executing, 364
Comment box, 60
Common Unix Print System, 275
Communication, with Gaim, 81–83
Community, giving back to, 308–309. See also Ubuntu community
Community Council, 17, 21, 28, 312, 332, 334–335, 336, 341
  arbitration of disputes by, 334
  community related structures, processes and, 335
  new project members welcomed by, 335

Community Council   *continued*
 teams proposed by; team leaders appointed by,
  334–335
 Ubuntu Code of Conduct maintained by, 334
Community governance system, goals of, 331
Compact Disk Database, 293
Components, within Ubuntu software repository, 372–374
Computer, shutting down, 64–65
Computer item, in Places menu, 60
Computer speed, performance problems with, 236
Conduct goals and Code of Conduct, Ubuntu project,
 20–21
Conferences, 328–329
Configuration files, in Linux, 104
Configuring system, 61
Connection protocols, specifying, for remote
 printing, 137
Connection speed, configuring in Ekiga, 84, 86
Connection tab, in printer properties window, 139
Connect to Server, 60
Connect to Server, in Places menu, 60
Consideration, Ubuntu Code of Conduct and, 368–369
cp command, 359
CreaLabs, 350
Creative Commons Attribution-ShareAlike 2.0 Open
 Publication License, 379–385
Creative Commons Corporation, 379
cron daemon, 228
cron job layout, 228–229
cron system, scheduling things to happen with, 228
crontab, 228
 command options, 229–230
crontab files, editing, 230
Crontab sections, 228
Cropping images, in GIMP, 81
CUPS. *See* Common Unix Print System
CUPS Manager, printer configuration
 with, 133
CVE number, for security vulnerability, 126–127
CVS, 26

Dapper Drake (Ubuntu 6.06), 22, 152, 169, 170, 174, 252
 changing from Breezy Badger to, 273
 release of, 3
Dash (-), command lines tools and, 143
Database applications, Ubuntu equivalents to Windows
 programs, 388
DB2 database, 25
.deb filename extension, 165
Debian Project, 2, 7, 9, 13, 14, 28, 164, 346, 351
 and free software universe, 15–16
 package files ("debs"), 165
Deleted items, restoring, in file manager, 195

delgroup command, 362
deluser command, 362
Dependencies, 134, 206
"Dependency hell," preventing, 272
Derivation, as highest form of compliment, 29
Derivatives, 15
Derivative work, definition of, 380
Derived distributions, 344, 346–351
 Baltix, 350
 Guadalinex, 348
 ImpiLinux, 350–351
 Nexenta, 349
 nUbuntu, 349
 Open Cd, 350
 Ufficio Zero, 350
 Xubuntu, 348–349
Deskbar package, 202
Desktop
 accessing remote server's files graphically on,
  140–141
 adding TrueType fonts to, 191–192
 hanging, 196
Desktop CD, for Kubuntu, 255
Desktop CD installation, 36–44
 disk space, 41–44
 finishing up, 44
 identification, 39–40
 keyboard configuration, 38
 language, 37
 location, 38
Desktop folder, in Places menu, 60
Desktop Guide, for Kubuntu, 306, 308
Desktop publishing, Ubuntu equivalents to Windows
 programs for, 390
Desktops, desktop CD for Ubuntu, 32
Desktop search, installing, 202
Desktop themes, finding and installing,
 208–209
Development Team, quality assurance and, 340
Device icons, 58
devscripts package, 171
df command, 198, 360
DHCP. *See* Dynamic Host Control Protocol
Diagram editing, Ubuntu equivalents to Windows
 programs for, 390
Dictionaries, 100
Dictionary, 91
Digital cameras, using in Ubuntu, 132
Digital photography, Ubuntu and, 132
Directories, in Konqueror, 281
Disagreements
 resolving, 331
 Ubuntu Code of Conduct and, 369

Disk partitioning, in Kubuntu, 258, 259
Disks
    fixing, after power failures, 234–235
    formatting, 224–225
Disk space, 41–44
    deciding on your partitions, 41–42
    freeing up, 197–198
    manually partitioning, 42–44
    using entire disk, 42
Disputes, arbitration of, 334
Distributions ("distros")
    bug fixes and, 15
    description of, 12–13
    ecosystem of, 14–15
Distribution upgrades, running, 169–172
Distrowatch, 14
dist-upgrade, 169
DMA mode, turning on, 205
DNS. *See* Domain Name Service
DNS server, 212
Documentation, Ubuntu, 339–340
Documents
    creating, with OpenOffice.org, 69–71
    saving, in Writer program (OpenOffice.org), 288
Dollar sign ($), as standard Unix shell symbol, 166
Domain Name Service, in Kubuntu, 278
Double ampersands (&&), between multiple
    commands, 364, 365
Downloading, extensions, 69
dpkg (Debian package manager), 165
dpkg-deb utility, 165
dpkg-dev package, 171
Drawings, editing and creating in Krita, 298
Draw program, within OpenOffice.org, 288
DRIVER option, 215
Drivers, 377, 378
    for Linux Infra Red Control, 227
    for wireless cards, 214
Driver selection, for printer configuration, 136, 136
Driver tab, in printer properties window, 139
Dual-booting, 41
du command, 198
DVD drive, ejection problems with, 221
DVD playback, 205
    jittery and jumpy problem with, 205–206
DVDs, unencrypted, Ubuntu support for, 115
DVD support package, 209
Dynamic Host Control Protocol, 265

Eclipse, 97, 98
Editing
    repositories in Adept, 269, 269
    text files, commands for, 361–362

Wallpaper section for Kiosk mode, 302
Edit Menus, 59
Edubuntu, 151, 345–346
    default desktop, 345
    distribution, 33
Edubuntu project, 3, 29
Effect filter, adding in GIMP, 78–79
802.1x, 214
Ejection problems, with DVD drive, 221
Ekiga, 92
    audio configured with, 86, 87
    making a call with, 89–90
    NAT settings detection and, 86
    setting up, 83, 84
    video configured with, 88, 89
    voice over IP with, 83–90
    Web camera configured with, 88–89
Ekiga.net, free SIP service with, 83, 85
e-mail
    account setup, 71–74
    managing with Evolution, 71–74
    running in Evolution, 203–204
    setting up with Kontact, 296
    working with, in Evolution, 74
e-mail applications, Ubuntu equivalents to Windows
    programs for, 388
e-mail lists, subscribing to, 316
Emblems, in Nautilus, 108–109
Employees, in Ubuntu community, 17
Empty the Wastebasket, 64, 199
ENABLED option, 215
Encryption, 216
Encyclopedia "Wikipedia," 324
Errors
    memory, 222
    system upgrade, 197
esd sound server, 206
Ubiquity
    Kubuntu installation process with,
        256–260
    welcome screen, 257
Ethernet cards, 211
Ettrich, Matthias, 250, 251
Evolution, 63
    calendar management with, 74–75
    e-mail not working in, 203–204
    indexing e-mails in, 202
    loading, 72, 72
    main interface, 73
    managing e-mail with, 71–74
    multiple calendars in, 75
    Webmail and, 72
Excel, 288

ext3, 223, 224, 225
    using for Ubuntu partitions, 43
Extensions
    downloading, 69
    plug-in, with Firefox, 68

Fair use rights, 380
FAT16, 223, 224
FAT32, 223, 224
    creating partition shared between Ubuntu and
        Windows with, 43
fdisk command, 238
Feature Freeze, 336
Feedback, 339
File chooser, in Ubuntu, 99, 99
File management, with Kubuntu, 279–288
File manager
    finally deleting files in, 199
    not seeing hidden dot files and folders in, 195
    restoring deleted items in, 195
Files
    copying from one computer to another, 230
    copying to hard disk, 131
    copying to or from USB stick, 220–221
    finding, 60
    listing those owned by a package, 172–173
    managing in Ubuntu, 103
    manipulating in command line, 359
    owner packages and, 173
    package providers and, 173
    selecting, copying, and moving in Nautilus,
        107–108
    storage and organization of, in Linux, 103–105,
        104
    transferring with Secure SHell, 212–213
Filesystem, fun with, 223–224
Filesystem combo box, 43
Filesystem security, 175–176
    noatime option, 176
    nodev option, 175–176
    noexec option, 176
    nosuid option, 176
Fill combo box, in GIMP, 77
Filters, package listings in Adept and, 270
Fingers, pain or numbness in, 246
Firefox, 189, 232, 289, 350
    bookmarking favorite sites with, 68
    browsing the Web with, 66–69, 290
    loading, 84
    Macromedia flash plug-in for, 201–202
    opening, 66

    plug-in extensions, 68–69
    saving time with live bookmarks, 68
    tabbed browsing with, 67
Firewalls, 86
Firmware, 377–378
First-Run Wizard
    in amaroK, 285, 286
    choosing database to store music collection in
        with, 287
    selecting location of your catalog with, 286
Flight Simulator, Ubuntu equivalents to Windows
        programs for, 391
Floppy disks, 130
    using in Ubuntu, 132
Folders
    finding, 60
    finding with Konqueror, 282
    Linux, 105*t*
    manipulating in command line, 359
    in Nautilus, 106–107
    selecting, copying, and moving in Nautilus,
        107–108
Folder structure, in Linux, 104
Fonts
    in OpenOffice.org, 70
    problems with, 188–189
    with Ubuntu, 78
Forgetting system password, 237–238
Formatting disks, 224–225
FreeCell Patience, 92
free command, 360
Freenode IRC network, 321
    Ubuntu IRC channels on, 319–321*t*
Free software, 3–5
    community and, 16–17
    freedoms at core of, 371
    Ubuntu philosophy on, 370, 371–372
Free Software Foundation, 371
Free software movement, Open Source movements
        and, 6
FREE SPACE, 49, 50, 51, 157, 161
Free space on disk, 197–198
Fridge, The, 326–327, 328, 341
    contributing to, 327
    home page, 327
fsck program, 234–235
F-Spot, 95, 96

Gaim
    communicating with, 81–83
    different types of accounts supported in, 81, 82

indexing instant messaging
    conversations in, 202
    instant messaging used in, 82–83
    setting up accounts in, 81–82
    support for IRC channels in, 83
Galeon, 232
Garrett, Matthew, 336
Gcompris, 345, 346
General tab, in printer properties
    window, 139
Gentoo project, 13, 14
Get Hot New Stuff, 262
    framework at work, 263, 263
GFS. *See* Global File System
GHNS. *See* Get Hot New Stuff
Gigabytes (GB), partition size indicated in, 50
GIMP, 350
    filters added with, 78–79, 79
    graphics created with, 75–81
    starting, 76
    templates in, 77
Global File System, 152
GNOME, 56, 231, 251, 256
    Art Web site, 208
    backgrounds, 209
    Baker application, 132
GNOME-Bluetooth package, 222
GNOME CUPS Manager, printer configuration with,
    133–134
GNOME desktop, 186–187
GNOME desktop environment, 345
GNOME Meeting, 83, 92
GNOME-obex-server, 222
GNOME Printers dialog box, 134
GNOME project, 2
GNOME Terminal, 232
    window, 358
GNOME tools, using, 134
Gnometris, 91
GNU, 8, 15, 16
    early days of, 12
GNU Arch project, 2
Gnu General Public License, 251
GNU Image Manipulation Package. *See* GIMP
GNU/Linux, 3, 5, 9
    distributions and, 12–13
Gnumeric, 232
GNU Privacy Guard encryption keys, 355
Google, 67, 227, 310
    Konqueror and, 289, 289
    searching for wireless card on, 214

Governance
    Community Council, 334–335, 336
    Technical Board, 334, 335–337
GPG encryption keys, 337
GPL. *See* Gnu General Public License
Grammar checkers, 100
Graphical applications, remote usage
    with ssh, 213
Graphical interface, getting text instead of, when starting
    computer, 186–87
Graphical system display, in Kubuntu, 275–276
Graphics, creating with GIMP, 75–81
Grawert, Oliver, 345, 346
grep command, 144, 361
Groups, administering, commands for, 362
GRUB bootloader, 185
gstreamer sound server, 206
gstreamer-10-ugly-multiverse package, installing, 113
Gtalk, 293
GTK, 216
Gtranslate, 353
Guadalinex, 29, 348
GUI, optimizing, 231
Gwenview, 306
gzip, 177

HAL. *See* Hardware abstraction layer
Hard disks, 216
    copying files to, 131
Hardware
    knowing compatibility with Ubuntu, before
        purchasing, 227
    solving problems with, 216–227
Hardware abstraction layer, 361
Hardware devices, problems with, in Ubuntu,
    221–222
Hardware platforms, Ubuntu support
    for, 170
Hardware section, within System Settings in Kubuntu,
    275
Harmony, 251
Harvard Computer Society, 177
HBD, 8
Help
    on command line, 363
    finding, 145, 308
    Ubuntu Code of Conduct and asking for, 369
-help command, 363
-help options, 236
Hibernate option, 64, 65
Hidden files, cautionary note on, 195

Hide/Show Desktop button, 63
Hill, Benjamin Mako, 335
Hoary Hedgehog (Ubuntu 5.04), 150, 252, 344
Home folder
 in Places menu, 60
  looking files in, 142
-h option, 198
Hostname
 adding during alternate
  install CD, 47
 fun themes, 40
HP laptops, Ubuntu installed on, in Europe, 25–26

IBM, 25
ICEWM, 231
Icons, shortcut, 61
ICQ, Kopete and, 294
Ideas and feedback, 339
ifconfig command, 360
ifplugd, 216
ifup, 216
Images
 burning CDs from, 131–132
 creating in Krita, 298
 cropping, in GIMP, 81
Image Viewer (Gwenview), 306
ImpiLinux, 350–351
Impress program, within OpenOffice.org, 288
Index updating, with desktop search, 202
Info Center (KinfoCenter), 305
info info command, 363
Infrastrucutre Development and Support Lists, Ubuntu,
 316t
Inkscape, 94, 95
Install CD, 32
"Installfests," 333
INSTALL file, 194
Install Missing Plug-ins button, 201
Instant messaging
 with Kopete, 293–295
 Ubuntu equivalents to Windows programs for, 389
 using in Gaim, 82–83
Integrated Development Environment, 307
Intel Centrino, 214
Intel x86
 Ubuntu support for, 170
INTERFACE option, 215
International Space Station, 8
Internet, navigating around, with
 Konqueror, 289
Internet and Network section, within System Settings in
 Kubuntu, 276–278

Internet Dial-Up Tool (KPPP), 305
Internet Explorer, 67, 289
Internet phone, 92
 with Ekiga, 83–86, 89
Internet Relay Chat, 92, 301, 318, 341
Internet Service Provider, 295
IP address, changing, 211
iPods, KaudioCreator and converting music from CDs
  into format for, 293
iptables command, 179
IRC. *See* Internet Relay Chat
IRC channel list, 318, 319–321*t*
IRC channels, 339
 Gaim and support for, 83
Isle of Man, 25, 28
iso, verifying, 193
ISO files, testing working of, 192–193
ISO Recorder, burning image with use of, 35
ISP. *See* Internet Service Provider
-i switch, in sudo, 237
iwconfig command, 360

Jabber protocol, 293
Jack sound server, 206
Java, Eclipse support for, 98
Java libraries, installing, 202

Kaffiene, 299–301
Kalach (Ukranian egg bread), 243–245
Kalzium, 346
Karma, good, building, 353, 355
Katapult, 252, 253, 288, 293
 KaudioCreator launched through, 293
 Kcontrol in, 274
 Krita launched through, 297
Kat K menu, 304
KaudioCreator, 283, 292–293
Kbabel, 353
Kcontrol, 274
K Control Center, replacement of, with System Settings
 application, 274
kdeglobals file, editing, 303
KDE (K Desktop Environment), 256, 307, 344, 345
 Education suite, 345, 346
 help manuals, accessing, 309–310
 history of, 250
 Menu editor, 264
 system, 56
Kdesktop, 261
 customizing, 261–262
Kdevelop, 306–307
KEduca, 346

Kernel, 185
    devices supported by, 222
Keyboard
    dealing with incorrect settings for, 225–226
    Desktop CD install and configuration of, 38
    selecting layout in Kubuntu, 258
Khelpcenter, 308
Kicker, customizing in Kubuntu, 263–264
KinfoCenter, 305
Kiosk mode, 302–303
    editing Wallpaper section for, 303
kioslaves, 281, 282
Kmail, 295
K menu
    applications available through, 288
    customizing, in Kubuntu, 260, 264–265
    in Kubuntu, 252, 253
    programs available from, 304–306
    shutting computer down, 254
    system updates and, 273
Konqi mascot, for KDE, 251
Konqueror, 282
    accessing USB drives in, 283–284
    file management with, 279
    finding files and folders with, 281
    ripping audio CDs with, 281–282
    shortcut, 253
    using locate: to find files in, 282
    Web browsing with, 288–290
    Windows partitions accessed in, 283
Konsole, 283
    with commands, 283
Konsole K menu, 305
Konsole session, removing access to starting of, 304
Kontact, 295–297
    e-mail account setup with, 295
    opening up, 294
    shortcut, 253
    using Korganize, 296–297
Konversation, 301
    #Kubuntu accessed through, 309
    managing identities in, 301
Kopete
    instant messaging with, 293–295
    launching, 294
    welcome screen, 293
Korganize, using, 296
KPDF, 306
KPPP, 305
KRDC, 306
Krdc, 306
Kreator, 292

Krita, 297–301, 345
    creating new images with, 297
    custom document in, 298
    main window in, 299
    manipulating existing document in, 298
    pasting into new image in, 300
    selecting area in, 300
KsCD, 305
KsnapShot, 306
Kstars, 347
KsysGuard, 305
KsystemLog, 306
K3b, 291, 290
K3b CD Kreator, 345
Kubuntu, 28, 29, 151, 344–345
    adding users through system settings in, 279
    automatically turn on numlock, with start
        of, 308
    backgrounds in, 261
    burning CDs-audio and data, 290–292
    choosing your language, 257
    clean desktop in, 254
    configuring computer name and username, 259
    customizing, 260–265
    disk partitioning in, 258, 259
    distribution, 33
    file management with, 279–288
    finding, 255–256
    finishing installation in, 260
    giving back to the community, 310
    graphical interface in, 265
    guided installation, 256
    history of, 251–252
    installing, 255–260
    installing from desktop CD, 256–258
    installing new packages in, 265–268
    Kicker customized in, 263–264
    in Kiosk mode, 302–303
    K menu customized in, 264–265
    login automatically to, when computer starts, 307
    main goal of, 250
    navigating in, 252–254
    OpenOffice.org application in, 288–289, 345
    overview of, 249
    running programs automatically with start of, 307
    shutting computer down and logging out, 254
    switching to, even if Ubuntu already installed, 256
    systems administration in, 265–280
    System Settings application in, 274–280
    tips and tricks with, 307–308
    universal viewer with, 281
    upgrading, 273

Kubuntu 6.06, Desktop Guide shipped
with, 309
#kubuntu channel, 324
Kubuntu forums, 310
Kubuntu Main Component License
Policy, 268
Kubuntu project, 3
Kubuntu wiki, 310
Kynaptic, 265

Lame, 292
LAMP (Linux, Apache, MySQL, PHP)
stack, 152
LAN. *See* Local area network
Languages
choosing with Kubuntu, 257
Desktop CD install and, 37
Ubuntu support for, 100
Ubuntu wiki pages and, 326
Laptops
desktop CD for, 32
network-manager for, 213–214
Launchpad, the, 29, 337, 351–355, 356
bug reports handled on, 241, 242
Malone, 354–355
other functionality with, 355
Rosetta, 353–354
Soyuz, 352–353
Launchpad project, 25, 26, 27
Layers, 79
Layers window, in GIMP, 79, 80
less command, 144, 362
output fed into, 198
Lexmark Z33 printer, 134, 135
printers window showing addition
of, 138
libxine-extraodecs, 285
License elements, definition of, 380
License grant, 380–381
License policy, 374–377
Licensing, Ubuntu philosophy on, 370
Licensor, definition of, 380
Linspire, 13
Linux, 5, 8, 15, 16, 176
early days of, 12
file storage and organization in, 103–105
folders, 105*t*
popularity of, 56, 227
printer configuration and, 132–133
scalability with, across different computers,
231
Linux Command.org, 366

Linux Documentation Project, The, 366
Linux Infra Red Control (LIRC) package, installing for
remote control, 226–227
Linux kernel, 216
optimizing for specific processors, 239
Linux Terminal Server Project, 29
with Edubuntu, 346
thin client technology, 345
Linux User Groups, 332, 339
Linux Virtual Server, 152
Linux with GNOME, burning image with use
of, 35
lirc package, 209
Live bookmarks, saving time with, 68
Live CD, 32
Local area network
access problems with, 211
hostname for identification on, 47
Localization, Ubuntu community and, 340
Localization teams, Rosetta and, 353
Local printers, Ubuntu support for, 53
locate: kioslave, finding files with, 282
Location
alternate install CD install and, 46
Desktop CD install and, 38, 39
Lock Screen option, 64, 65
Lock Screen When Screensaver Is Active checkbox,
103
LoCo (Local Community) teams, 332–333
advocacy and, 338
Logging out, 64–65
Logical Volume Management, 48, 49
Logical Volume Manager, 158
overview of, 158–159
redundancy and, 161
setting up, 160–161
theory and jargon, 159–160
Login, automatic, without having to enter details about,
197
Login screens, 209
configuring with alternate install CD, 52
Log Out option, 64, 65
Logs and spools, separating, 153
Log toolbox, 178
Long Term Support, by version number, 163
lsb_release -a command, 360
ls command, 360
lshal command, 361
lshw command, 361
lsusb command, 361
LTS. *See* Long Term Support
LTSP. *See* Linux Terminal Server Project

LUGs. *See* Linux User Groups
LVM. *See* Logical Volume Management
LVM array, managing, 162

Mac OS X, burning images with use of, 36
Mac OS X Tiger, 202
Mahjongg, Ubuntu application, 92
Mailing lists
    Code of Conduct and, 369–370
    general, 314–315*t*
    Ubuntu, 314–318, 341
Mailman software, 317
Main distribution component, within Ubuntu software
        repository, 372–373
Main repository
    in Adept, 267
    in Ubuntu package archive, 163
Malone, 27, 354–355
    bug-tracking system in, 341
    first bug in, 23
man command, 363
Mandriva, 14
man -f foo command, 364
Man files, searching for, 363–364
man intro command, 363
man -k foo command, 363
man man command, 363
man page, 236
Manual (or man) pages, 145
Many-to-many communication, with Internet relay
        chat, 318
Mark All Upgrades, in Synaptic, 127
Mark for Installation
    pop-up on, 123
    in Synaptic, 122
Mark for removal, 123
    in Synaptic, 122
Master boot record, 186, 232, 233
Masters of the Universe, 268
Mataró Sessions, 328
Math program, within OpenOffice.org, 288
Mauelshagen, Heinz, 159
MBR. *See* Master boot record
McNealy, Scott, 180
Media files
    accessing with Konqueror, 281
    problems with playing, 205
Media players, Ubuntu equivalents to Windows
        programs for, 388
Meetings
    adding to calendar, 74, 75
    setting up in Kontact, 296

Megabytes (M), partition size indicated in, 50
Memory errors, 222
memtest option, 222
Menu editor, 59, 59
    KDE, 264, 264
Menu layout, changing, 59–60
Micropauses, 246
Microphone, solving problems with, 206–207
Microsoft Office, 288, 289
Mini-pager, 263
MIT, Artificial Intelligence Laboratory at, 4
mkdir command, 359
mkfs command, 225
Mobile phone, transferring photo files
        to Ubuntu computer with
        Bluetooth, 222
MOTU. *See* Masters of the Universe
MOTU (Masters of the Universe) teams, 341
    roles and responsibilities of, 333–334
Mounting
    disks, 238
    USB sticks, 219–220
Mount points, 146, 238
Mouse scroll wheel, enabling, 226
Movie Player, 92
Movies, watching with Kaffiene, 299, 301
Mozilla Firefox, 189
MP3, 109, 205
.mp3 files, installing libxine-extraodecs
        and, 285
mp3 player, KaudioCreator and converting music from
        CDs into format for, 293
MP3s, ripping songs as, 113
MSN Messenger, Kopete and, 293
MSN Webcams, Kopete and, 293, 294
msttcorefonts, installing, 188–189
Multimedia
    common problems with Ubuntu desktop and,
        204–210
    Ubuntu and, 109–115
Multiple commands
    executing, 364
    passing output, 365
    running sequentially, 364–365
Multiverse component, within Ubuntu software
        repository, 374
Multiverse repository, 190
    in Adept, 267, 268
    in Ubuntu package archive, 163
Mount Point combo box, 44, 44
Music, ripping with KaudioCreator, 292
Music file management, with amaroK, 282, 284–288

mv command, 359

MySQL, storing music in, 285, 287

mysql-server, installing with Adept, 272

MythTV, front-end and back-end parts of, 210

MythTV box, turning Ubuntu computer into, 209–210

Nameserver problems, 212

nano command, 362

NAT settings. *See* Network Address Translation settings

Nautilus, 103

creating folders in, 106–107

emblems in, 108–109

extending with scripts, 200–201

selecting, copying, and moving files/folders in, 107–108

sidebar in, 108, 108*t*

speeding up, 191

starting, 105–106

Nautilus-actions package, 201

Nautilus script, sample, 201

Nautilus window, parts of, 106

nUbuntu project, 344

Nero Burning ROM, burning images with use of, 35

Netscape, 67, 289

Network, secure SHell used for transferring files across, 212–213

Network Address Translation settings, 86

Network blocks, 215

Network cards, 216

Network configurations, common, 215

Networking

alternate install CD install and, 47–48

problems with, 210–216

Network interface, configuring in Kubuntu, 278

Network-manager, for laptops, 213–214

Network printer, installing, 136

Network Printer radio button, 136, 137

Network protocol, choosing, 136–137

Network section, within System Settings in Kubuntu, 276–278

Network security administration, 178–179

Network servers option, in Places menu, 60

Network Ubuntu, 29

New Calendar, 75

New Folder, bookmarking and, 68

Nexenta, 349

Nexenta Systems, 349

Nibbles, 91

noatime option, filesystem security, 176

nodev option, filesystem security, 175

noexec option, filesystem security, 176

Normal user account, 144

Notification area, 62

Novell, 251

Novell's SuSE, 13, 14

NTFS system, 223

nUbuntu (Network Ubuntu), 29, 349

NUMA, 151

Numlock, automatically turning on, when Kubuntu starts, 308

NVU, 97

OCFS2 file system (Oracle), 152

Office and finance applications, Ubuntu equivalents to Windows programs for, 389–390

Oggs, ripping songs at, 113

Ogg Theora Codec, 109, 110, 205

Ogg Vorbis Codec, 109, 110, 205

Older computers

faster desktops and, 231–232

Ubuntu taking up too much disk space on, 235–236

Omma, Henrik, 350

1s command, 141, 143

One-to-one communication, with Internet relay chat, 318

Open CD, 350

OpenOffice.org, 69, 231, 288–289, 345, 350

document creation with, 69–71

OpenSolaris, 350

Open Source, 5–7

community and, 16

popularity of, 56

Open Source Definition, 372

Open Source Initiative, 6, 372

Open Source movement

free software movement and, 6

Ubuntu and, 368

Open Source software, 8

Ubuntu philosophy on, 370, 372

Opera, 67, 289

Operating system, another, running in Ubuntu, 240–241

Original author, definition of, 380

Package cache, cleaning out, 198

Package maintainers, 333–334

Package manager, 121

Package Policy, Ubuntu, 336

Packages

building from source, 170–172

finding with Synaptic, 124–125

installing, 189–190

installing in Kubuntu, 265–268
installing with Adept, 269–272
installing with Synaptic, 122
listing files owned by, 172–173
locating in Synaptic, 231
manual installation of, 165–166
removing with Synaptic, 122
in Ubuntu, 121
Package selection, Technical Board and, 336
Packaging Guide, with Kubuntu, 309
Paper tab, in printer properties window, 139
Partitioning
    disks, 48
    main view, 42
    Ubuntu Server, 153–154
Partitions
    configuring, 43
    creating with alternate install CD, 48–51
    deciding on, 41–42
    options for, with alternate install CD, 49, 50
    Windows, accessing, 238–239
Partner projects, 345–347
    Edubuntu, 346–347
    Kubuntu, 345–346
passwd command, 362
Password box, in Gaim, 81
Passwords, 57, 61
    creating in Kubuntu, 258
    entering with alternate install CD, 52
    storing in desktop key ring, 140
    system, forgetting, 237–238
    system administration section within Kubuntu
        and, 279
    WEP, 47
Patience, 189
PCs, PC version of Ubuntu for, 32
PDF Viewer (KPDF), 306
Pentium class computers, installing
    Linux-686 kernel on, 239
Perens, Bruce, 6
Performance Monitor (KsysGuard), 305
Performance royalties, under blanket
    licenses, 381
Perl, 177
    Eclipse support for, 98
Permissions
    adding/removing, 359
    writing to USB storage device, 223
Personal accounting, Ubuntu equivalents to Windows
    programs for, 389
Personal Information Manager, in Kubuntu, 254,
    294

Personal section, within System Settings in Kubuntu,
    275
PEs. *See* Physical extents
Philosophical goals, of Ubuntu project, 18–20
Photo editor, Ubuntu equivalents to Windows programs
    for, 388
Photos
    copying from mobile phone to Ubuntu computer
        with Bluetooth, 222
    editing and creating in Krita, 297
PHP, Eclipse support for, 98
Physical extents, 159, 160
Physical volumes, 159, 160
PIM. *See* Personal Information Manager
ping command, 204
Pipelines, 141
    building, 143–144
Pipe symbol, 143
Piping, 365
Places menu, 60
Planetarium, Ubuntu equivalents to Windows programs
    for, 390
Planet Ubuntu, 68, 330–331, 341
    example of, 330
Plug-ins, with Firefox, 68, 290
Podcasts, listening to, 112
Ports, USB, 134
POSIX model, 175
PostgreSQL, storing music in, 285, 287
Power failures, fixing disk after, 234–235
PowerPC, Ubuntu support for, 170
PowerPC Ubuntu version, 33
PowerPoint, 288
Practical Guide to Linux® Commands,
    Editors, and Shell Programming (Sobell), *365*
Preferences submenu, 61
Presentation applications, Ubuntu equivalents to
    Windows programs for, 387
Printer configuration
    driver selection, 136
    gathering information, 134–135
    with Gnome CUPS Manager, 133–134
    in Kubuntu, 275
    launching the wizard, 135–137
    remote printing, 136–137
    step 1 for adding printer in Ubuntu, 135
    in Ubuntu, 132–140
Printers, setting up, 53–54
Printers window, 138
Project management applications, Ubuntu equivalents
    to Windows programs for, 390
Protocol box, in Gaim, 81

ps ax command, 144
ps command, 361
PVs. *See* Physical volumes
pwd command, 357–358
Python, 23, 177
     Eclipse support for, 98

QA. *See* Quality assurance
QEMU Project, 240
QPL. *See* Q Public License
q prompt, 363
Q Public License, 251
QT, 345
QT Toolkit, 251
Quality assurance, bugs and, 340–341
Quick Launcher Applet, 263
QuickTime, 109, 205

RAID
     array failure and spare devices, 158
     other modes of, 156
     setting up, 156–158
     story of, 154–155
RAID array, managing, 162
RAID 5, 155
RAID level, choosing, 156
RAID 1, 155
RAID 0 ("striped set"), 155
Raymond, Eric S., 6
README file, 194
Really Simple Syndication, 296
Realmedia, 109
Recent documents submenu, in
     Places menu, 60
Recovery mode kernel, 185
Red Hat, 13, 14
Red Hat Cluster Suite, 152
Redundant array of inexpensive disks.
     See RAID
Refresh rates, choosing in Kubuntu, 262
Release cycles, 22
Release Notes, with Kubuntu, 308, 310
Releases
     KDE, 251
     Kubuntu, 252, 272
     next, moving to, 128–129
     Technical Board and feature goals
       for, 336
     Ubuntu's support cycles for, 163, 354–355
Reload button, in Synaptic, 127
Remnant, Scott James, 336
Remote control, making it work, 226–227

Remote Desktop Connection (Krdc), 306
Remote files, graphically accessing, 139–140
Remote graphical logins, enabling with alternate
     install CD, 53
Remote printers, Ubuntu support for, 53
Remote printing, 137
     entering printer location and
       description, 147
Repetitive Strain Injury, preventing, 246
reportbug, 354
Repositories
     in Adept, 267–268
     enabling, 235
     management of, in Adept, 269–270
Repositories dialog box, 191
Repository or software channel, 121
Repository run-down, 190–191
Resource limit, example, 177
Respect, 21
     Ubuntu Code of Conduct and, 368
Restart option, 65
Rest breaks, importance of, 246
Restricted component, within Ubuntu software
     repository, 373
Restricted repository
     in Adept, 267, 268
     in Ubuntu package archive, 163
Revision control systems, 356
Rhythmbox, 110, 111
     using, 111–112
Riddell, Jonathan, 250, 251, 252, 344
rm command, 359
Root, automatically logging in, 197
Root account, enabling/disabling, 236–237
Root partition, 50
Rosetta, 27, 353–354
     translation through, 340
Rosetta Stone, 27
RSI. *See* Repetitive Strain Injury
RSS (Really Simple Syndication) feed, 290
Ruby, Eclipse support for, 98
Russian Soyuz TM-34 mission,
     Shuttleworth's voyage as civilian cosmonaut
       on, 8, 352

SABDFL (self-appointed benevolent dictator for life),
     Mark Shuttleworth as, 332, 337, 341
Safari, 67
Samba, 137
Scalable Vector Graphics, 94
Schwartz, Jonathan, 180
scp command, 230

Screen Capture Program (KsnapShot), 306
Screen Name box, in Gaim, 81
Screen resolution, wrong, 196
Screensavers
    changing in Kubuntu, 262
    configuring in Ubuntu, 102–103
Screen sizes, choosing in Kubuntu, 261
Scripts
    installing, 200–201
    Nautilus, sample, 201
    Nautilus extended with, 200
Search for files, in Places menu, 60
Searching
    for man files, 363–364
    text files, commands for, 361–362
    Ubuntu wiki, 325–326
Security, 179
    automatic logins and, 52
    partition, 153
    server, 173–174
    Ubuntu Server, 173–179
    updates, 125–128
Security update icon, 126
Security vulnerability list, 316t
sed command, 361
sed tool, 169
Select File Type expander, 81
Serial mouse, malfunctioning, 226
Serpentine, creating audio CDs with, 131
Server Guide, with Kubuntu, 309
Servers
    alternate install CD for, 32
    installing, 45
Server security, 173–174
Services, configuring, in Kubuntu, 279, 281, 280
setgid bit, 176
setuid, 176
Shell examples, 166
Shortcut icons, 61
Show Notifications option, deselecting, 200
Shut down option, 65
Shutting computer down, 64–65
Shuttleworth, Mark, 2, 7–8, 9, 10, 11, 17, 21, 23,
    27, 180, 331
    Canonical Ltd. founded by, 24
    Community Council board
        appointments made by, 335
    investments in ImpiLinux by, 351
    Launchpad and, 352
    as SABDFL, 332, 337, 341
    Technical Board appointments made
        by, 336–337

    voyage taken by, as civilian cosmonaut, on Russian
        Soyuz TM-34 mission, 8, 352
Shuttleworth Foundation, 8
Sidebar, in Nautilus, 108, 108t
Single System Image, 180
SIP, free service, with Ekiga, 83, 85
Slackware, 14
Sleep option, 65
slocate database, 230
SLS. See Softlanding Linux System
Smart updates, with Synaptic, 128
SMP, 151
Sobell, Mark G., 365
Softlanding Linux System, 14
Software
    inaccuracies, bugs, and usability problems
        with, 246
    optimizing, 231
    steps in compiling of, 194
Software channel, 121
Songs
    ripping as MP3s, 113
    ripping at Oggs, 113
sort, 198
Sound cards, 216
    list of devices and relevant kernel module,
        217–218
    old, Ubuntu detection of, 216–218
sounder list, 318
Sound Recorder, 93
Sound servers, 206
South Africa, post-apartheid, Ubuntu and, 10
Soyuz, 27, 352–353, 355
Space Simulator, Ubuntu equivalents to Windows
    programs for, 390
Spci command, 361
Specifications, writing, at Ubuntu
    conferences, 328
Speedcrunch, 305
Spillner, Josef, 262
Splash screens, 209
    problems with, 186
Spools and logs, separating, 153
Spreadsheets, Ubuntu equivalents to Windows
    programs for, 387
Sprints, 329
SQLIte, storing music in, 285, 287
ssh (Secure SHell)
    file transfer across network with, 212–213
    using graphical application remotely with, 213
SSI. See Single System Image
Stallman, Richard M., 3, 4, 5, 6

Statutory royalties
    mechanical rights and, 381
    webcasting rights and, 381–382
Stream EDitor (sed), 361
Subproject lists, Ubuntu, 315*t*
Subversion, 26, 98
sudo, using, 259
sudo command, 144, 236, 237
sudo mechanism, Ubuntu Server and system
    administration with, 173–174
Sun Microsystems, 349
Superuser account, 144
Support, 339
SUSE Linux, 251
SuSE (Novell), 13, 14
Suspend, 64
SVG. *See* Scalable Vector Graphics
Switch User option, 64, 65
Synaptic, 189, 193, 256
    checking for updates with, 127–128
    finding, 121
    finding packages with, 124–125
    installing and using, 121
    installing application not in, 190
    installing QEMU with, 240
    Java libraries installation and, 202
    locating package in, 231
    main window, 122
    meaning of name, 121
    packages installed with, 122
    pop-up on mark for installation, 122, 123
    preferences, 128
    removing packages with, 122
    searching for required tools with, 194
    updating your system with, 122
Syntax, for crontab commands, 230
sysadmin, 171
System administration, solving problems with, 227–240
System administration section, within System Settings in
    Kubuntu, 279–280
System administrator account, 144
System administrator terminal, 93
System configuration, 61
System information commands, 360–361
System log files, 177–178
System Logs Viewer (KsystemLog)
    K menu, 206
System menu, 61
System menu icon, on Kubuntu task bar, 253
System monitor, 93
System resource limits, 176–177
Systems administration, in Kubuntu, 265–280

System Settings application, in Kubuntu,
    274, 274–280
System upgrade, getting error with, 197

Tabbed browsing, with Firefox, 67
Taskbar, 63–64
Teams, 331, 332–333
Technical Board, 17, 332, 334, 335–337, 341
    package selection and, 336
    release feature goals and, 336
    Ubuntu Package Policy and, 336
Technical goals, of Ubuntu project, 21–23
Template combo box, in GIMP, 77
Templates, in GIMP, 77
Terminal, 91, 141–145
    command line and starting up, 367
    getting started with, 142–143
Terminal server client, 92
Test Settings, 89
Tetris, 91
Text chat icon, in Ekiga window, 89
Text Editor, 91
Text editor, crontab loaded into, 228
Thawte, 8
Theme
    changing in Ubuntu, 101–102
    new, installing in Ubuntu, 102
This command, 215
3D modeler, Ubuntu equivalents to Windows programs
    for, 390
Thunderbird, 350
Tilde, for home directory, 142
Time zone, selecting in Kubuntu, 257
Tip of the Day window, 76
TKIP, 216
top command, 236, 360
Torvalds, Linus, 5
Totem media player, 114
Translations, Ubuntu community and, 340
Translations box, 100
"Triaging" bugs, 341, 355
Trolltech, 251
Troup, James, 335
Troy, Ryan, 324
TrueType fonts, adding to desktop quickly,
    191–192
TurboLinux, 13
Tutu, Desmond, ubuntu described by, 10, 367–368
Tux Paint, 190
Type-ahead, 124, 125
Typing Tutor, Ubuntu equivalents to Windows
    programs for, 391

Ubiquity
    Kubuntu installation process with, 256–260
welcome screen, 257
Ubunteros (formerly Ubuntites), 20, 312, 337
Ubuntu
    adding/removing programs and packages,
        118, 122
    brief history of, 7–10
    Bugs and Notification Lists, 315*t*
    burning CDs in, 131–132
    choosing version of, 32–33
    CUPS Manager, 133
    customizing, 101–103
    digital cameras used with, 132
    digital photography and, 132
    disk space taken up by, on old computer, 235–236
    distributions and, 12–13
    file chooser and bookmarks in, 99–100
    file management in, 103
    finding a package in, 124
    floppy disks used with, 132
    fonts with, 78
    getting, 34–36
    graphically accessing remote files in, 140–141
    growth in distribution of, 2–3
    infrastructure development and support lists, 316*t*
    installing/using Add Applications in, 118–121
    keeping computer updated, 125–128
    meaning of, 10–11
    moving to next release of, 128–129
    multimedia and, 109–115
    partitions for, 41–42
    printer configuration in, 132–140
    printer set up with, 53–54
    problems with starting, after reinstalling
        Windows, 232–234
    running another operating system in, 240–241
    running distribution upgrade in, 169–172
    security vulnerability list, 316*t*
    selecting printing application from Administra-
        tion menu in, 133
    starting problems with, 185–186
    subproject lists in, 315*t*
    subprojects, derivatives, and spin-offs, 28–30
    symbiotic relationship between Debian and, 16
    terminal, 141–145
    terminology, 121
    updating your system with, 122
    upgrading to new version of, 199
    USB key rings used with, 130
    USB storage devices in, 130
    Web site, 116
    working with Windows, 145–147
    WPA with wireless cards used in, 215
    in your language, 100
ubuntu-announce list, 317, 324
Ubuntu archive, 150, 151
Ubuntu-audio, 189
Ubuntu Below Zero conference, 328
Ubuntu bread, recipe for, 243–245
#ubuntu channel, 322
#ubuntu+1 channel, 322
Ubuntu community, 16–17, 312–341
    advocacy, 338–339
    artwork, 340
    Community Council, 334–335
    conferences and sprints, 328–329
    documentation, 339–340
    The Fridge, 326–327
    ideas and feedback, 339
    Internet relay chat, 318
    IRC channel list, 318–322
    mailing lists, 313–318
    MOTU, 333–334
    overview of, 312–313
    participating in, 338–341
    Planet, 330–331
    programming and packaging, 341
    quality assurance and bugs, 340–341
    SABDFL, 337
    summary about, 341
    support, 339
    teams, processes, and community governance,
        331–333
    Technical Board, 335–337
    translation and localization, 340
    Ubunteros and Ubuntu members, 337–338
    venues, 313
    Web forums, 322–324
    wikis, 324–326
Ubuntu Community Council. *See*
    Community Council
Ubuntu desktop, 57, 187
    desktop part of screen, 58
    panel in, 57
    taskbar, 58
    usuability and, 64
ubuntu-devel-announce list, 317, 324, 341
#ubuntu-devel channel, 322
ubuntu-devel list, 317–318
Ubuntu developers, sending messages
    to, 324
Ubuntu Documentation Team, 308
Ubuntu Down Under conference, 328

Ubuntu equivalents to Windows programs, 387–391
    accounting, 389
    database, 388
    desktop publishing, 390
    diagram editing, 390
    e-mail, 388
    Flight Simulator, 391
    instant messaging, 389
    media players, 388
    personal accounting, 389
    photo editor, 388
    Planetarium, 390
    presentation, 387
    project management, 390
    Space Simulator, 390
    spreadsheet, 387
    3D modeler, 390
    Typing Tutor, 391
    vector drawing, 390
    voice over IP, 389
    Web browser, 388
    word processing, 387
Ubuntu 5.04 (Hoary Hedgehog), 344
Ubuntu 5.10 (Breezy Badger), 348
Ubuntu Forums, 184, 243, 247, 322–324
    example of open "thread" in, 322
    searching for wireless card on, 214
    topic categories, 323
Ubuntu forums wiki, 222
Ubuntu Foundation, 27–28, 30
Ubuntu Foundation documents
    Code of Conduct, 367–370
    components, 372–374
    documentation, firmware, and drivers, 377–378
    license policy, 374–377
    software installed by default, 378
    Ubuntu philosophy, 370–372
Ubuntu 4.10 (Warty Warthog), 150, 318
Ubuntu Free Software Philosophy, 375
Ubuntu installation CD, 32
Ubuntu License Policy, 370
Ubuntu logo, odd appearance of, 186
Ubuntu "Main" and "Restricted" Component License Policy, 376–377
Ubuntu Member, becoming, 20
#ubuntu-offtopic channel, 322
Ubuntu package management, 162–173
    apt-get and apt-cache, 166–168
    APT sources and repositories, 163–164
    dpkg manager, 165
    finding which package owns a file, 173
    finding which package provides a file, 173

    installing a package, 168
    listing files owned by a package, 172–173
    manual package installation, 165–166
    performing system updates, 168–169
    removing a package, 168
    running a distribution upgrade, 169–172
    Ubuntu archive, 162–163
Ubuntu philosophy, on free and open source software, 370–372
Ubuntu Philosophy of Software Freedom, 18, 370
Ubuntu Project, 2
    Canonical's supporting role with, 26
    membership in, 337–338
    transparent and public communication and, 313
Ubuntu promises and goals, 18–24
    bug # 1, 23–24
    conduct goals and Code of Conduct, 20–21
    philosophical goals, 18–20
    technical goals, 21–23
Ubuntu-related projects, 344–356
    Bazaar, 356
    derived distributions, 346–351
    Launchpad, 351–355
    partner projects, 344–346
Ubuntu releases, longer support cycles for, 163
Ubuntu Security Team, 173
Ubuntu Server, 150–152
    communicating about, 181
    description of, 150–152
    installing, 152–154
    partitioning, 153–154
    security, 173–179
Ubuntu Server 6.06, 152
Ubuntu Server Team, 150
Ubuntu 6.06 (Dapper Drake), 22, 128–129
    release of, 3
Ubuntu 6.10, 129
Ubuntu software repository, components within, 372–374
Ubuntu suite of applications
    Audio CD Creator, 93
    Beagle, 95, 96
    Blender, 94, 94
    Bluefish, 97, 98
    Calculator, 91
    CD Ripper, 93
    Dictionary, 91
    Eclipse, 97, 98
    exploring, 90–98
    FreeCell Patience, 92

F-Spot, 95, 96
Gnometris, 91
Inkscape, 94, 95
Internet Phone, 92
Internet Relay Chat, 92
Mahjongg, 92
Movie Player, 92–93
Nibbles, 91
NVU, 97, 97
Sound Recorder, 93
System Administrator Terminal, 93
System Monitor, 93
Terminal, 91
Terminal Server Client, 92
Text Editor, 91
Ubuntu system, 184–185
ubuntu-translators mailing list, 340
ubuntu-users mailing list, 317, 324
Ubuntu wiki, 339
restricted formats page, 115
Ufficio Zero, 344, 350
uname command, 360
unbutu-devel list, 343
Universal viewer, with Kubuntu, 281
universe, enabling, 164
Universe application, sequence involved in installation
of, 120
Universe component, within Ubuntu software
repository, 374
Universe repository, 190
in Adept, 267, 268
enabling in Adept, 269
in Ubuntu package archive, 163
UNIX, 5, 141, 349
Unmounting devices, problems with, 130
updateb, running, crontab setup for, 230
Updates
checking for, with Synaptic, 127–128
installing, 126
learning about, 126–127
system, with Synaptic, 122, 124
Update window, 127
Upgrade button, 199
Upgrade notification bubble, switching off, 200
Upgrades, executing, 129
USB, forms of, 131
USB connections, attaching printer to, 134
USB drives, accessing with Konqueror, 283
USB key rings, using, 130
USB stick
copying files to or from, 220–221
problems with, 219–220

USB storage device
problems with writing to, 222–223
using, 220
US Copyright Act, 381
User access, removing, in Kiosk mode, 303
User accounts, 57
administration of, 174–175
creating, 39–40
useradd command, 174
User configuration, with alternate install CD,
51–52
Usernames, creating in Kubuntu, 258
Users
adding, 239–240
administering, commands for, 362
Usuability, Ubuntu desktop and, 64

Vector drawing, Ubuntu equivalents to Windows
programs for, 390
Vendor lock-in, 71
Venues, Ubuntu, 313
Verisign, 8
Versions
KDE, 251
Kubuntu, 252
new, upgrading to, 199
VFAT, 224
V4L, Ubuntu support for, 88
VGs. *See* Volume groups
Video, configuring with Ekiga, 88, 89
Video cards, 216
Videos, watching in Ubuntu, 114–115
Video streams, Totem support for, 114
View mode icon, in Ekiga window, 89
View Webcam icon, in Ekiga window, 90
Virtual desktops, moving applications between, 63–64
Virtualization technology, 240
Virtual network connection, 306
Visual theme, changing, 207–208
VNC. *See* Virtual network connection
Voice over IP
with Ekiga, 83–90, 92
Ubuntu equivalents to Windows programs
for, 389
Volkerding, Patrick, 14
Volume groups, 159, 160, 161

Wallpapers
finding and installing, 208
new, in Kubuntu, 263
Wallpaper section, editing, for Kiosk mode, 302
Warthogs, 2, 8–10

Warty Warthog (Ubuntu 4.10), 2, 16–17, 150, 318
Wastebasket, 64, 195
    file removal and, 199
Watson, Colin, 335
wc tool, 144
Weather, monitoring, 243
Weather applets, 243
Web browser applications, Ubuntu equivalents to
    Windows programs for, 388
Web browsing
    with Firefox, 66–69, 290–291
    with Konqueror, 288–290
Web cameras, 216
    configuring with Ekiga, 88–89
Webcasting rights, statutory royalties and, 381–382
Web Forums, 341
    Code of Conduct and, 369–370
    Ubuntu, 322–324
Webmail, Evolution and, 72
Web sites, on command line, 365–366
WEP, 214
    passwords, 47
who command, 362
Wikis, 341
    front page of, 325, 326
    Ubuntu, 324–326, 339
Wildcards, using, 364
Windows. *See also* Ubuntu equivalents to Windows
    programs
    problems starting Ubuntu, after reinstall of,
        232–234
    working with, 145–147
Windows applications, running, 146
Windows files, using on another partition, 146–147
Windows fonts, 188–189
Windows Media, 205
Windows Media Format, 109
Windows NT, 223
Windows partitions
    accessing, 238–239
    accessing in Konqueror, 283
Windows Vista, WinFS in, 202
winecfg tool, 145
Wine project, 145

WinFS, 202
Wireless authentication, 214
Wireless cards, solving problems with, 213–215
Wireless networks, network-manager for connecting
    Ubuntu system to, 213–214
Word processing, Ubuntu equivalents to Windows
    programs for, 387
Workrave, 246
Workspaces, 63
WPA, 214
    using, 215
wpa_cli, 215, 216
wpasupplicant package, 215
WPA Supplicant Web site, 215
Writer program, within
    OpenOffice.org, 288
Writing, to USB storage device, 222–223
Writing Aids box, 100
WYSIWYG, 97

Xchat, connecting to IRC with, 321, 321
Xfce desktop environment, 348
Xfce environment, 56
Xfce4, with Xubuntu distribution, 232
xfce session, 231, 232
X icon, 200
xkill, 200
xmltv package, 209
X server, 186
xterm, 232
Xubuntu, 29, 56, 151, 348–349
Xubuntu distribution, 33
    Xfce4 in, 232
X Window System, 13
    remote graphical logins and, 53

Yahoo Messenger, Kopete and, 293

zcat file, 178
Zerconf Discovery, 252, 276
zgrep files, 178
Zimmerman, Matt, 336
zless file, 178

THIS BOOK IS SAFARI ENABLED

INCLUDES FREE 45-DAY ACCESS TO THE ONLINE EDITION

The Safari® Enabled icon on the cover of your favorite technology book means the book is available through Safari Bookshelf. When you buy this book, you get free access to the online edition for 45 days.

Safari Bookshelf is an electronic reference library that lets you easily search thousands of technical books, find code samples, download chapters, and access technical information whenever and wherever you need it.

TO GAIN 45-DAY SAFARI ENABLED ACCESS TO THIS BOOK:

- Go to **http://www.prenhallprofessional.com/safarienabled**
- Complete the brief registration form
- Enter the coupon code found in the front of this book on the "Copyright" page

If you have difficulty registering on Safari Bookshelf or accessing the online edition, please e-mail customer-service@safaribooksonline.com.

PRENTICE
HALL

DVD Warranty

Prentice Hall PTR warrants the enclosed DVD to be free of defects in materials and faulty workmanship under normal use for a period of ninety days after purchase (when purchased new). If a defect is discovered in the DVD during this warranty period, a replacement DVD can be obtained at no charge by sending the defective DVD, postage prepaid, with proof of purchase to:

Disc Exchange
Prentice Hall PTR
Pearson Technology Group
75 Arlington Street, Suite 300
Boston, MA 02116
Email: AWPro@aw.com

Prentice Hall PTR makes no warranty or representation, either expressed or implied, with respect to this software, its quality, performance, merchantability, or fitness for a particular purpose. In no event will Prentice Hall PTR, its distributors, or dealers be liable for direct, indirect, special, incidental, or consequential damages arising out of the use or inability to use the software. The exclusion of implied warranties is not permitted in some states. Therefore, the above exclusion may not apply to you. This warranty provides you with specific legal rights. There may be other rights that you may have that vary from state to state.

More information and updates are available at: http://www.phptr.com/